AQA Geography A
New Edition

Judith Canavan

Alison Rae
Simon Ross

Editor

Simon Ross

OXFORD
UNIVERSITY PRESS

OXFORD

UNIVERSITY PRESS

Great Clarendon Street, Oxford, OX2 6DP, United Kingdom

Oxford University Press is a department of the University of Oxford.
It furthers the University's objective of excellence in research, scholarship,
and education by publishing worldwide. Oxford is a registered trade mark of
Oxford University Press in the UK and in certain other countries

First published by Nelson Thornes Ltd in 2011
This edition published by Oxford University Press in 2014

British Library Cataloguing in Publication Data
Data available

978-1-4085-1708-6

10 9 8 7 6 5

Printed by Vivar Printing Sdn Bhd., Malaysia

Acknowledgements

Cover: thinair28/iStockphoto
Illustrations: David Russell Illustration, Tim Jay,
Peters & Zabransky and GreenGate Publishing
Page make-up: GreenGate Publishing, Tonbridge, Kent

Although we have made every effort to trace and contact all
copyright holders before publication this has not been possible in all
cases. If notified, the publisher will rectify any errors or omissions at
the earliest opportunity.

Links to third party websites are provided by Oxford in good faith
and for information only. Oxford disclaims any responsibility for
the materials contained in any third party website referenced in
this work.

Contents

4 Contents

About these resources

Oxford University Press has worked hard to make sure that this book and the accompanying online resources offer you excellent support for your GCSE course.

You can be sure that they provide you with useful support throughout your course.

These print and online resources together **unlock blended learning**; this means that the activities in the book and the activities online blend together to maximise your understanding of a topic and help you achieve your potential.

These online resources are available on Kerboodle which can be accessed via the internet at **www.kerboodle.com/** anytime, anywhere. If your school or college subscribes to Kerboodle you will be provided with your own personal login details. Once logged in, access your course and locate the required activity.

For more information and help on how to use Kerboodle visit **www.kerboodle.com**.

How to use this book

In this section you will learn

This is a checklist of what the section covers.

Study tip

Don't forget to read the **Study tips** throughout the book as well as answering the **Practice questions**.

This specification focuses on the physical and human processes and factors that have shaped the environment in which we live. You will learn about the interdependence of physical environments and how human activity affects the environment, and vice versa. You will also gain an understanding of the need for sustainable management of both physical and human environments. You will learn to appreciate the differences and similarities between people, places and cultures and improve your understanding of societies and economies.

Your GCSE geography course has three units (Unit 1: Physical Geography; Unit 2: Human Geography, and Unit 3: Local Fieldwork Investigation, which will be based on a topic covered in the first two units). Units 1 and 2 each have two sections, A and B, and the chapters of this book take their titles from the topic titles in these sections.

■ Unit 1 Physical Geography

In the exam, you must answer three questions. One question should be taken from Section A, one from Section B and the third question from either section.

Section A

- The Restless Earth
- Rocks, Resources and Scenery
- Challenge of Weather and Climate
- Living World

Section B

- Water on the Land
- Ice on the Land
- The Coastal Zone

These topics are intended to provide you with a solid foundation in physical geography to enable you to fully appreciate the physical world in which you live.

A great deal of emphasis has been placed on topicality, using up-to-date case studies and examples to explore themes and concepts, such as the 2011 Japanese tsunami and recent floods in Boscastle and Cockermouth.

All of the physical geography topics have a link to human activities. For example, in *The Restless Earth* you will study the impact of tectonic hazards on people's lives. The impacts of climate change are also discussed in *Challenge of Weather and Climate*.

Sustainable development is a key concept in all topics. For example, in *The Coastal Zone*, strategies for coastal defence and coastal zone management are underpinned by the need for a sustainable approach. In *Living World*, sustainability is at the heart of ecosystem management, whether it is hot deserts or tropical rainforest.

■ Unit 2 Human Geography

In the exam, you must answer three questions. One question should be taken from Section A, one from Section B and the third question from either section.

Section A

- Population Change
- Changing Urban Environments
- Changing Rural Environments

Section B

- The Development Gap
- Globalisation
- Tourism

These topics have been chosen to reflect current thinking and interests in geography in the 21st century. They all involve the study of recent issues and extensive use is made of up-to-date case studies and examples. For example, in *Population Change*, detailed consideration is made of the implications of China's controversial 'one child policy'. The current (and future) issue of ageing populations in Europe is also considered.

Sustainable development is a significant consideration in human geography. For example, in *Tourism*, you will discuss the issues surrounding mass tourism as well as examining recent trends such as ecotourism and adventure tourism. In *Globalisation*, topics such as renewable energy and pollution control are also tackled.

As you study human geography there will be many opportunities for you to discuss and debate real world issues, such as Fairtrade in *The Development Gap* and organic farming in *Changing Rural Environments*. You will be able to formulate and share your own opinions and, hopefully, you will be able to make a positive difference to the world around you.

1.1   Why is the earth's crust unstable?

The structure of the earth

The **crust** – the outer layer of the earth – is relatively thin (diagram **A**). The crust is not one single piece of skin, like that of an apple. Instead, it is split into **plates** of varying size and at **plate margins** it is liable to move. This is because the slabs of crust float on the semi-molten upper **mantle**. **Convection currents** within the mantle determine the direction of plate movement. Therefore, in some cases the plates are moving together and sometimes they are moving apart. There are two types of crust: oceanic and continental (diagram **B**). The location of the plates, plate boundaries and direction of movement of the plates is shown in map **C**.

In this section you will learn

about the structure of the earth and the difference between oceanic and continental crust

how and why destructive, constructive and conservative plate margins are different

how the earth's crust is unstable, especially at plate margins.

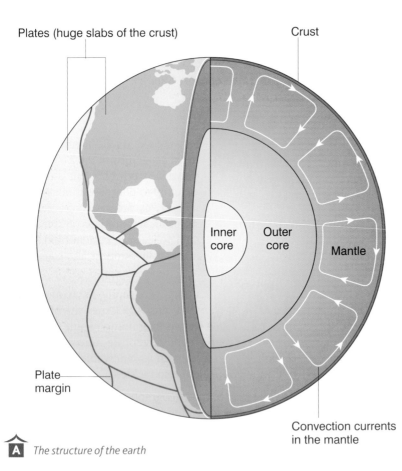

Plates (huge slabs of the crust)

Crust

Inner core

Outer core

Mantle

Plate margin

Convection currents in the mantle

A *The structure of the earth*

Key terms

Crust: the outer layer of the earth.

Plate: a section of the earth's crust.

Plate margin: the boundary where two plates meet.

Mantle: the dense, mostly solid layer of the earth between the outer core and the crust.

Convection currents: the circular currents of heat in the mantle.

Did you know ???????

The earth's crust is divided into 14 major plates and 38 minor plates, making a total of 52 jigsaw pieces altogether.

OCEANIC CRUST
- Newer – most less than 200 million years old
- Denser
- Can sink
- Can be renewed and destroyed

CONTINENTAL CRUST
- Older – most over 1500 million years old
- Less dense
- Cannot sink
- Cannot be renewed or destroyed

Continental crust

Oceanic crust

Convection currents in the mantle

B *Contrasts between oceanic and continental crust*

Eurasian Plate

North American Plate

Juan de Fuca Plate

Pacific Plate

Caribbean Plate

Iranian

Arabian

Philippines Plate

Cocos Plate

African Plate

Indo-Australian Plate

Nazca Plate

South American Plate

Antarctic Plate

C *World tectonic plates and margins*

Map key

➡ Direction of plate movement

Destructive margin – one plate sinks under another (subduction)

Destructive (collision) margin – two continental plates move together

Constructive margin – two plates move away from each other

Conservative margin – two plates slide alongside each other

Uncertain plate boundary

Activities

1   Study diagram **A**.
a   Draw a cross-section through the earth and label it to show the four layers.
b   On your diagram, add a definition of each term you have labelled.

2   Study diagram **B**.
a   Draw a simple labelled diagram to describe the differences between the two types of crust.
b   Explain what the convection currents are in the mantle and how they cause plate movement.

3   Study map **C**. Copy and complete the table below.

Plate margin	Direction of plate movement	Example of plate margin
Destructive – subduction		
Destructive – collision		
Constructive		
Conservative		

Types of plate margin

Destructive plate margins

Convection currents in the mantle cause the plates to move together. If one plate is made from oceanic crust and the other from continental crust, the denser oceanic crust sinks under the lighter continental crust in a process known as **subduction**. Great pressure is exerted and the oceanic crust is destroyed as it melts to form magma.

If two **continental plates** meet each other, they collide rather than one sinking beneath the other. This **collision** boundary is a different type of destructive margin.

Key terms

Destructive plate margin: a plate margin where two plates are moving towards each other resulting in one plate sinking beneath the other.

Constructive plate margin: a plate margin where two plates are moving apart.

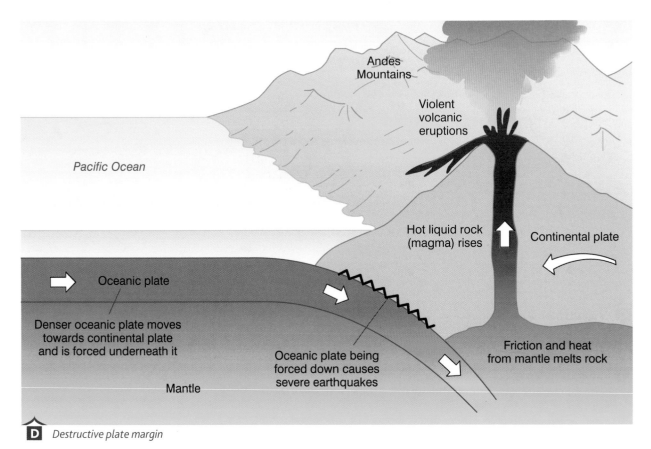

D Destructive plate margin

Constructive plate margins

When plates move apart, a constructive plate boundary results. This usually happens under the oceans, as shown in map **C**. As these **oceanic plates** pull away from each other, cracks and fractures form between the plates where there is no solid crust. Magma forces its way into the cracks and makes its way to the surface to form **volcanoes**. In this way new land is formed as the plates gradually pull apart.

Key terms

Continental plate: a tectonic plate made of low density continental rock that will not sink under another plate.

Oceanic plate: a tectonic plate made of dense iron-rich rock that forms the ocean floor.

Subduction: when oceanic crust sinks under continental crust at a destructive margin.

Collision: when two plates of continental crust meet 'head on' and buckle.

Volcano: an opening in the earth's crust through which molten lava, ash and gases are ejected.

E *Constructive plate margin*

Key terms

Conservative plate margin: a plate margin where two plates are sliding alongside each other.

Earthquake: a sudden and often violent shift in the rocks forming the earth's crust, which is felt at the surface.

Conservative plate margins

At conservative plate margins, the plates are sliding past each other. They are moving in a similar (though not the same) direction, at slightly different angles and speeds. As one plate is moving faster than the other and in a slightly different direction, they tend to get stuck. Eventually, the build-up of pressure causes them to be released. This sudden release of pressure causes an **earthquake**. At a conservative margin, crust is being neither destroyed nor made. With no source of magma, volcanoes are absent.

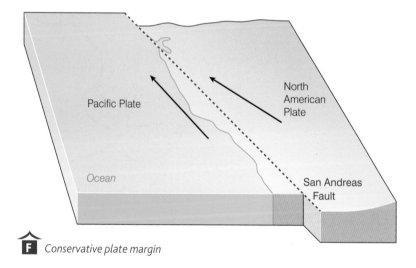

F *Conservative plate margin*

Study tip

Drawing and labelling a diagram of an oceanic plate being subducted beneath a continental plate is a good way of remembering the important features.

Activity

4   Study diagrams **D**, **E** and **F**.
a   Read the task you have to complete in **b** below. Before starting the task, discuss with a partner what information the diagrams ought to have on them, and how they might be drawn and presented to ensure the information is clear.

b   For each plate margin, draw a labelled cross-section to describe the characteristics of the boundary and the processes that are occurring there.

⊂⊃links

You can find out more about plates and the different types of crust at **http://en.wikipedia.org/wiki/List_of_tectonic_plates**.

1.2 What landforms are found at different plate boundaries?

Fold mountains and ocean trenches

Young **fold mountains** (those that have been formed in the last 65 million years) are the highest areas in the world. All peaks over 7,000 m are in central Asia, including Mt Everest at 8,850 m. This dwarfs the highest mountain in England – Scafell Pike at 978 m. Young fold mountains include ranges such as the Himalayas, the Rockies, the Andes and the Alps. Older ranges of fold mountains that are less high due to erosion include the Cambrian mountains and the Cumbrian mountains in the UK. **Ocean trenches** form some of the deepest parts of the ocean. The distribution of young fold mountains and ocean trenches is shown in map **A**. Look back at map **C** on page 9 to see the link between these landforms and plate margins.

> **In this section you will learn**
>
> why fold mountains and ocean trenches form at destructive plate margins
>
> the differences between composite volcanoes, which are associated with destructive plate margins, and shield volcanoes, which are associated with constructive plate margins.

A Young fold mountains and ocean trenches

Key
▲ Young fold mountains
— Ocean trenches

0   2000 km

Both fold mountains and ocean trenches result from plates moving together. If both landforms occur in the same area, they are found in association with subduction. If fold mountains occur by themselves, they are in areas where collision is taking place. Either way, the sequence relating to their formation is similar, as shown in diagram **B**.

> **Study tip**
>
> Make sure you know the correct sequence of formation of fold mountains.

B *The formation of fold mountains (e.g. the Alps)*

◯◯links

Investigate further facts and figures about landforms resulting from plate movements at **www.geology. com** and **www.extremescience.com**.

■ Composite and shield volcanoes

There are two types of volcano: **composite volcanoes**, which occur at destructive plate margins, and **shield volcanoes**, which occur at constructive plate margins (diagrams **C** and **D**).

C *Composite volcano*

D *Shield volcano*

Activities

1   Study map **C** on page 9 and map **A** opposite. You will need a world map outline showing the plates and plate boundaries.

a   On your map, add the young fold mountains shown in map **A** and name them.

b   Add the ocean trenches.

c   At what type of plate boundary do fold mountains and ocean trenches form?

2   Study diagram **B**.

a   Make a copy of each part of the diagram.

b   Use the key terms on the right to help you label each diagram to explain the formation of fold mountains.

c   Draw another diagram to explain the formation of ocean trenches (see diagram **D** on page 10).

3   Study diagrams **C** and **D**.

a   On your own, write five questions you would ask to find out about the contrasts between a composite volcano and a shield volcano.

b   Swap questions with a partner and answer their questions.

c   What were the good points about the questions you have just answered? How might they be improved?

d   Use an internet search engine to find images of composite and shield volcanoes. Draw a sketch of each image and label them to show the characteristics of each type of volcano.

e   Summarise how and why composite and shield volcanoes are different.

Key terms

Fold mountains: large mountain ranges where rock layers have been crumpled as they have been forced together.

Ocean trenches: deep sections of the ocean, usually where an oceanic plate is sinking below a continental plate.

Composite volcano: a steep-sided volcano that is made up of a variety of materials, such as lava and ash.

Shield volcano: a broad volcano that is mostly made up of lava.

1.3 How do people use an area of fold mountains?

The Andes and its people

The Andes is a range of young fold mountains formed some 65 million years ago (map **A**, page 12). It is the longest range of fold mountains in the world at 7,000 km and extends the length of South America. The Andes are about 300 km in width and have an average height of 4,000 m.

Farming

Despite the high altitude of the Andes, the mountain slopes are used for farming. In Bolivia, many **subsistence** farmers grow a variety of crops on the steep slopes, including potatoes which are a main source of food. The use of **terraces** (photo **A**) creates areas of flat land on the slopes. Terracing offers other advantages in trying to farm in this harsh environment. The flat areas retain water in an area that receives little. They also limit the downward movement of the soil in areas where the soils are thin in the first place. Most crops are grown in the lower valleys (photo **B**) and a patchwork of fields can be seen indicating the range of crops grown. Some cash crops are produced such as soybeans, rice and cotton.

Llamas are synonymous with the Andes. For hundreds of years they have been pack animals, carrying materials for **irrigation** and buildings into inhospitable and inaccessible areas. The ancient settlement of Machu Picchu (photo **C**) relied on llamas to transport materials and goods due to its remote location. These surefooted animals can carry over 25 per cent of their body weight (125–200 kg). The mining industry often relied on them as a form of transport. Today, this use still exists – largely of male llamas. The females are used for meat and milk, and their wool is used in clothes as well as rugs.

In this section you will learn

how people use areas of fold mountains

how people adapt to the difficult conditions within them.

Key terms

Subsistence: farming to provide food and other resources for the farmer's own family.

Terraces: steps cut into hillsides to create areas of flat land.

Irrigation: artificial watering of the land.

Hydroelectric power: the use of flowing water to turn turbines to generate electricity.

Study tip

With reference to a specific range of fold mountains, ensure that you can list and explain the uses that people make of this environment.

A *Farming in the Andes*

B *The lower valleys*

Mining

The Andes has a range of important minerals and the Andean countries rank in the top 10 for tin (Peru and Bolivia), nickel (Colombia), silver (Peru and Chile) and gold (Peru). More than half of Peru's exports are from mining. The Yanacocha gold mine (map **D** and photo **E**) is the largest gold mine in the world. It is a joint venture between a Peruvian mining company and a US-based one that has a 51 per cent share. It is an open pit and the gold-bearing rock is loosened by daily dynamite blasts. The rock is then sprayed with cyanide and the gold extracted from the resulting solution. This can lead to contamination of water supplies.

C   *Machu Picchu*

The nearby town of Cajamarca has grown from 30,000 inhabitants (when the mine began) to about 300,000 in 2010. This brings with it alternative sources of jobs. However, this growth also brings many problems, including a lack of services and an increased crime rate.

Hydroelectric power

The steep slopes and narrow valleys that limit farming are an advantage for **hydroelectric power** (HEP). They can be more easily dammed than wider valleys and the relief encourages the rapid fall (flow) of water needed to ensure the generation of electricity. The melting snow in spring increases the supply of water, but the variation throughout the year is a disadvantage rather than an advantage. In 2009 the El Platanal HEP power plant began to generate electricity. Involving a huge dam across the Cânete River, the $US200 million project is the second largest in Peru (map **D**).

D   *The location of Yanacocha gold mine and the El Platanal HEP project*

Tourism

There are many natural attractions in the Andes such as mountain peaks, volcanoes, glaciers and lakes. Some tourist attractions show how people settled in these inhospitable areas, such as the remains of early settlements built by the Incas like Machu Picchu (photo **C**). The Inca Trail combines both (extract **F**).

E   *Yanacocha gold mine*

The Inca Trail is South America's best-known trek

The Inca Trail is South America's best-known trek. It combines a stunning mix of Inca ruins, mountain scenery, lush forest and tropical jungle. Over 250 species of orchid exist in the Machu Picchu historic sanctuary, as well as numerous species of birds. The sanctuary is an important natural and archaeological reserve – it is only one of 23 UNESCO world heritage sites to be classified as important both culturally and naturally.

The Inca Trail is a hike that finishes at Machu Picchu, the sacred mysterious 'Lost City of the Incas'. The 45 km trek is usually covered in four days, arriving at Machu Picchu at daybreak on the final day before returning to Cusco by train in the afternoon. The trek is best undertaken from April to October, when the weather is drier. Any fit person should be able to cover the route. It is fairly challenging and altitudes of 4,200 m are reached, so it is important to be well acclimatised.

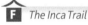

F *The Inca Trail*

∞ links

Investigate further facts and discussion about gold mining by searching on **www.google.co.uk**.

For more on the Inca Trail, go to **www.incatrailperu.com**.

Activities

1. Study map **C** on page 9 and an atlas map of South America. Locate the Andes on the map of South America. Using these resources, produce a fact file about the Andes to provide the following information:

   - location
   - countries
   - plates responsible for mountains
   - direction of plate movement
   - type of plate margin
   - dimensions
   - highest peak and its location.

2. Study photos **A** and **B**.

   a. Describe how the mountains are used for crops.

   b. Outline the role of the llama in the life of Andean residents.

   c. Explain how difficulties of steep relief and poor soils are overcome.

3. Study map **D**.

   a. Work in pairs to produce a short presentation to include:

   - a map showing the location of the Yanacocha gold mine
   - the advantages of the area for the mine and for Peru as a whole
   - the disadvantages of the area for the mine and for Peru as a whole.

   b. Show your presentation to another group.

4. Research HEP and specifically that produced in the Andes. On one side of A4 paper, define HEP, explain why the Andes is suitable for the development of HEP and give details of one HEP project. Include at least one map and one photo to illustrate your information.

5. Read extract **F**. Imagine you have visited Peru and part of your holiday included the Inca Trail. Write a postcard to send home, which includes the following:

   - a map showing the trail
   - a description of how you got to the trail
   - a description of the attractions (natural and human) that you saw. Explain why these were so awesome and different to what you had seen previously.

1.4   How do volcanoes affect people?

▉ The distribution of volcanoes

Volcanoes are an example of a **natural hazard**. Their spread relates closely to plate margins (map **A** and map **C**, page 9). The area around the Pacific Ocean is especially prone to volcanoes and is known as 'the Pacific Ring of Fire'. Occasionally, active volcanoes are found away from plate margins. We are going to study two recent volcanic eruptions that have had significant impacts on people's lives.

Key
▲ Well-known volcanoes
🔺 Volcanic activity
☐ Supervolcanoes

NORTH AMERICA
Heimaey
EUROPE
Vesuvius
Etna
Mount St Helens
Atlantic Ocean
ASIA
Fuji
AFRICA
Popocatepetl
Montserrat
Pinatubo
Mauna Loa
Paricutin
Nevada del Ruiz
Mayon
Equator
Cotopaxi
Pacific Ocean
SOUTH AMERICA
Indian Ocean
AUSTRALIA
Aconcagua

A *The distribution of active volcanoes and supervolcanoes*

In this section you will learn

where volcanoes are found

how the primary and secondary effects of volcanoes can be positive as well as negative

about immediate and long-term responses to eruptions, including monitoring and prediction.

Did you know ??????

Harry Truman, aged 83, who lived at Mt St Helens Lodge at Spirit Lake with his 16 cats, believed that 'this old mountain ain't never going to erupt'. He refused to leave and was one of the victims of the 1980 eruption of Mt St Helens. The lodge was buried under 50 m of debris. His body was never found.

Key terms

Natural hazard: an event over which people have little control, which threatens people's lives and possessions. This is different from a natural event as volcanoes can erupt without being a hazard.

Primary effects: the immediate effects of the eruption, caused directly by it.

Secondary effects: the after-effects that occur as an indirect effect of the eruption on a longer timescale.

Aid: money, food, training and technology given by richer countries to poorer ones, either to help with an emergency or for long-term development.

Case study

The eruption of Nyiragongo, Africa (2002)

On 17 January 2002, Nyiragongo volcano in the Democratic Republic of Congo was disturbed by the movement of plates along the East African rift valley. This led to lava spilling southwards in three streams. The speed of the lava reached 60 kph, which is especially fast. The lava flowed across the runway at Goma airport (photo **C**) and through the town, splitting it in half (map **B**). The lava destroyed many homes as well as roads and water pipes, set off explosions in fuel stores and power plants, and killed 45 people. These were the **primary effects**. In addition, there were many **secondary effects**. Half a million people fled from Goma into neighbouring Rwanda to escape the lava. They spent the night sleeping on the streets of Gisenyi. Here, there was no shelter, electricity or clean water as the area could not cope with the influx. Diseases such as cholera were a real risk. People were frightened of going back. However, looting was a problem in Goma and many residents returned within a week in the hope of receiving **aid**. In the aftermath of the eruption, water had to be supplied in tankers. Aid agencies, including Christian Aid and Oxfam, were involved in the distribution of food, medicine and blankets.

C *Lava on the runway at Goma airport*

B *The location of Nyiragongo volcano*

Case study

The eruption of Eyjafjallajökull, Iceland 2010

Iceland lies on the Mid-Atlantic Ridge, a constructive plate margin separating the Eurasian plate from the North American plate (map **C** p9). As the plates move apart magma rises to the surface to form several active volcanoes located in a belt running roughly SW–NE through the centre of Iceland (map **D**). Eyjafjallajökull (1,666 m high) is located beneath an ice cap in southern Iceland 125 km south east of the capital Reykjavik.

D *The plate margin in Iceland and main volcanoes*

The eruption

In March 2010, magma broke through the crust beneath Eyjafjallajökull glacier. This was the start of two months of dramatic and powerful eruptions that would have an impact on people across the globe. The eruptions in March were mostly lava eruptions. Whilst they were spectacular and fiery they represented little threat to local communities.

However, on 14 April a new phase began which was much more explosive. Over a period of several days in mid-April violent eruptions belched huge quantities of ash into the atmosphere (photo **E**).

Local impacts and responses

The heavier particles of ash (such as black gritty sand) fell to the ground close to the volcano, forcing hundreds of people to be evacuated (an **immediate response**) from their farms and villages. As day turned to night, rescuers wore face masks to prevent them choking on the dense cloud of ash. These ash falls, which coated agricultural land with a thick layer of ash, were the main primary effects of the eruption (photo **E**).

E *The ash cloud and subsequent ash falls had a huge impact on farming*

One of the most damaging secondary effects of the eruption was flooding. As the eruption occurred beneath a glacier, a huge amount of meltwater was produced. Vast torrents of water flowed out from under the ice. Sections of embankment that supported the main highway in southern Iceland were deliberately breached by the authorities to allow the floodwaters to pass through to the sea. This action successfully prevented expensive bridges being destroyed. After the eruption, bulldozers were quickly able to rebuild the embankments and within a few weeks the highway was reconstructed.

International impacts and responses

The eruption of Eyjafjallajökull became an international event in mid-April 2010 as the cloud of fine ash spread south-eastwards towards the rest of Europe (map **F**). Concerned about the possible harmful effects of ash on aeroplane jet engines, large sections of European airspace closed down. Passenger and freight traffic throughout much of Europe ground to a halt.

F Map showing the spread of the ash cloud over Europe

The knock-on effects were extensive and were felt across the world (table **G**). Business people and tourists were stranded, unable to travel in to or out of Western Europe. Industrial production was affected as raw materials could not be flown in and products could not be exported by air. As far away as Kenya, farm workers lost their jobs or suffered pay cuts as fresh produce such as flowers and beans perished, unable to be flown to European supermarkets. The airline companies and airport operators lost huge amounts of money.

Some people felt that the closures were an over-reaction and that aeroplanes could fly safely through low concentrations of ash. However, a scientific review conducted after the eruption concluded that under the circumstances it had been right to close the airspace. Further research will be carried out as a **long-term response** to find better ways of monitoring ash concentrations and improving forecast models.

Not all bad news!

There can be positive impacts of volcanic activity. Eyjafjallajökull has become a new Icelandic tourist attraction with its own visitor centre. The Icelandic Tourist Board now encourages people to visit the 'land of ice and fire' bringing benefits to local people and industries.

Lava and ash are rich in nutrients making the soils in volcanic areas very fertile and good for agricultural use. The rocks themselves can be used for building. The valuable source of geothermal energy just below the surface of the earth is usually relatively easily to access. This can be used to produce electricity and provide hot water for industrial processes, heating swimming pools and even melting snow on pavements.

Small quantities of valuable minerals such as copper, gold, silver, lead, and zinc are often found in volcanic regions. Deposits of sulphur can be mined from volcanic craters and used to bleach sugar and make matches and fertiliser.

G Impacts of the eruption

Local	National	International
• Some 800 local people living close to the volcano had to be evacuated. • Homes and roads were damaged and services (electricity, water, etc) disrupted. • Local flood defences had to be reconstructed. • Crops (particularly grass used for hay) were damaged by heavy falls of ash. • Local water supplies were contaminated with fluoride.	• Tourism was affected with the number of international tourists dropping during the summer 2010. This affected the Icelandic economy as well as local people's jobs and incomes. • Road transport was disrupted as roads were washed away by floods. • Agricultural production was affected as crops were smothered by a thick layer of ash. • Reconstruction of roads and services was expensive.	• Over a period of 8 days, some 100,000 flights were cancelled accounting for 48 per cent of total air traffic. Ten million passengers were affected. The Airport Operators' Association estimated the total loses to be £80 million. • Industries were affected by a lack of imported raw materials, e.g. Honda announced a partial halt to production. • Fresh food could not be imported, affecting supermarkets and producers across the world. • In sport, a number of international events were affected by the flight ban including the Japanese Motorcycle Grand Prix, French rugby league teams competing in the Challenge Cup and the Boston Marathon on 19 April.

Monitoring and predicting volcanoes

Unlike earthquakes, volcanoes usually provide warning signs of an impending eruption. Active volcanoes across the world are monitored by scientists using high technology equipment and warnings are issued if a volcano seems likely to erupt.

- An increase in earthquake activity is an indication that magma is rising beneath a volcano, causing rocks to crack and fracture. Map **H** shows the concentration of earthquakes just before the eruption of Eyjafjallajökull in 2010. Earthquakes are recorded using instruments called seismometers that are placed in the ground.

- Tiltmeters can be placed on the ground to measure slight changes in the tilt of the ground caused by rising magma (diagram **I**). Just before Mt St Helens erupted in 1980 the north face of the volcano bulged as magma rose within the volcano. Global positioning systems (GPS) use satellite technology to measure very slight changes of as little as 1 mm (photo **K**). Laser beams can also be used to measure changes in distance between two fixed points on a volcano. If the volcano swells, the distance between two places will increase.

- Digital cameras (photo **J**) can be placed on the rim of craters to record small eruptions or landslides that might indicate rising magma (e.g. White Island, New Zealand). Controlled from a distance, this is a safe way to monitor crater activity.

- Gases emitted from a volcano, such as sulphur dioxide, can change in concentration prior to an eruption. Continuous gas monitoring stations are used by scientists to monitor activity at Kilauea volcano on Hawaii.

Historic information from previous eruptions, such as evidence of ash falls, lava flows and **lahars**, can be used to construct **hazard maps**. These identify zones at risk from particular hazards. They can be used in deciding which areas are safe for developments such as housing and also in making plans for evacuations.

H Earthquakes recorded over 48 hrs prior to 3 March 2010 indicating that an eruption is likely at Eyjafjallajökull

Key terms

Lahar: mudflows resulting from ash mixing with melting ice or water – a secondary effect of a volcano.

Hazard maps: a map that shows areas that are at risk from hazards such as earthquakes, volcanoes, landslides, floods and tsunamis.

I Tiltmeters detect a change in slope caused by shifting magma beneath the surface

 Time-lapse cameras in the crater allow geologists to make safe observations

K   *GPS use satellites to detect minute movement*

∞ links

Further information with many superb links about the eruption of Eyjafjallajökull can be found at **www. geographyinthenews.rgs.org** search for Eyjafjallajökull.

Activities

1   Study map **A** on page 17.

a   Describe the distribution of the world's active volcanoes.

b   Compare the distribution with map **C** on page 9. Provide evidence to support the statement that 'volcanoes usually occur at plate boundaries'.

c   Explain the cause of the Nyiragongo eruption.

2   Study map **B** and photo **C** on page 18.

a   Draw a sketch map based on the map to show the location of the volcano, the countries and the main towns. Use an arrow to show the flow of the lava towards Goma.

b   Label your sketch map to show the primary and secondary effects of the eruption at Nyiragongo.

3   Study photo **E**. Produce a front-page newspaper report for 15 April 2010 detailing the eruption of Eyjafjallajökull. Your article should be illustrated with a map showing the location and at least one labelled photo. The text should describe the nature of the eruption and its cause. Refer to the tectonic details and suggest the likely impacts of the eruption.

4   Study the text and Table **G**.

a   How were local farmers and their families affected by the eruption of Eyjafjallajökull?

b   Describe the impact of the eruption on tourism.

c   How did the closure of European airspace affect

■ European businesses and industries

■ supermarkets

■ farming in Kenya

■ sporting events?

5   Read the text.

a   Describe and compare the immediate responses to the eruptions at Nyiragongo and Eyjafjallajökull.

b   Describe the long-term responses at Eyjafjallajökull.

6   Tourism is one positive effect of volcanoes. Use the internet to research answers to the following questions.

a   How has Eyjafjallajökull become a tourist attraction?

b   Research two other positive effects of volcanic activity in Iceland. Present your information to describe each positive effect and provide an example of where this occurs.

7   Study the text together with map **H**, diagram **I**, photos **J** and **K**.

a   Make a list of the different means of monitoring and predicting volcanoes.

b   Describe in detail two methods of monitoring volcanoes. Explain the reasons for each form of monitoring and how it indicates that an eruption is likely.

c   How successful do you think these methods are in predicting volcanoes?

1.5   What is a supervolcano?

A **supervolcano** is a huge volcano with the potential to erupt catastrophically and with enormous power. Look back to map **A** on page 17 to locate the world's supervolcanoes.

Characteristics of a supervolcano

Supervolcanoes are on a much bigger scale than volcanoes. They emit at least 1,000 km³ of material – compare this with an eruption on the magnitude of Mt St Helens in 1980, which emitted some 1 km³. Supervolcanoes do not look like a volcano with its characteristic cones. Instead, they are large depressions called **calderas**, often marked by a rim of higher land around the edges (diagram **A**).

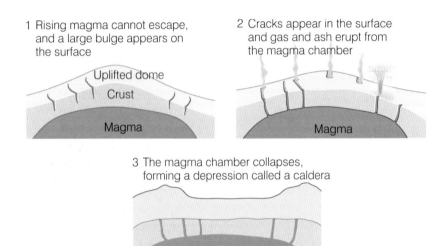

1 Rising magma cannot escape, and a large bulge appears on the surface

2 Cracks appear in the surface and gas and ash erupt from the magma chamber

3 The magma chamber collapses, forming a depression called a caldera

A   The formation of a supervolcano

The Yellowstone supervolcano

Many visitors stand in awe looking at Old Faithful and the **geothermal** features of the Norris **Geyser** basin without realising the vulnerability of where they are standing. The very forces that created such a unique area could be responsible for its destruction and threaten the existence of people – at the very least in North America, if not globally. Map **B** shows the area of Yellowstone and some of its attractions.

There is evidence that the magma beneath Yellowstone is shifting. The caldera is bulging up beneath Lake Yellowstone. There are signs of increasing activity at Norris and the ground has risen 70 cm in places. Is this just part of a natural cycle? The magma chamber beneath Yellowstone is believed to be 80 km long, 40 km wide and 8 km deep. It is not known whether the magma is on top of other materials, which would be necessary for an eruption.

Eruptions have occurred at this **hot spot** 2 million years ago, 1.3 million years ago and 630,000 years ago. An eruption today would have a catastrophic effect. It is potentially five times the minimum size for a supervolcanic eruption by the size of the magma chamber.

In this section you will learn

what a supervolcano is and how it differs from a volcano

the potential impact of a supervolcano eruption in contrast to a volcano eruption.

Key terms

Supervolcano: a mega colossal volcano that erupts at least 1,000 km³ of material.

Caldera: the depression of the supervolcano marking the collapsed magma chamber.

Geothermal: water that is heated beneath the ground, which comes to the surface in a variety of ways.

Geyser: a geothermal feature in which water erupts into the air under pressure.

Hot spot: a section of the earth's crust where plumes of magma rise, weakening the crust. These are away from plate boundaries.

Did you know ??????

The last supervolcano eruption occurred on Sumatra when Toba erupted 74,000 years ago. It is thought world temperatures fell by between 3 and 5°C. Toba exuded 3,000 km³ of magma and covered India in a layer of ash 15 cm deep.

Study tip

Make notes to reinforce your understanding of the differences between a volcano and a supervolcano.

B   *The location of the Yellowstone caldera*

1   Study map **A** on page 17.

a   Describe the distribution of supervolcanoes.

b   How is the distribution of supervolcanoes different from that of volcanoes?

2   Study diagram **A**.

a   Draw simple diagrams of a volcano and a supervolcano.

b   Label your diagrams to show the characteristics and contrasts between them.

3   Study map **B**.

a   Measure the size of the caldera at its widest point north to south and west to east.

b   Describe the attractions in the area.

4   Produce a front-page report for a newspaper published in the UK describing the local, national, international and global impacts as 'Yellowstone supervolcano erupts'.

An eruption is likely to destroy 10,000 km² of land, kill 87,000 people, 15 cm of ash would cover buildings within 1,000 km and 1 in 3 people affected would die. The ash would affect transport, electricity, water and farming. Lahars (mud flows) are a probability. The UK would await the arrival of the ash some five days later. Global climates would change, crops would fail and many people would die.

C   *Cascade Geyser at Yellowstone National Park*

∞links

Investigate the Yellowstone supervolcano further at **www.discovery.com** and **www.bbc.co.uk**. Enter Yellowstone supervolcano into the search box in both websites.

1.6 What are earthquakes and where do they occur?

Characteristics of earthquakes

The place where earthquakes begin, deep within the earth's crust, is called the **focus** (diagram **A**). Deep-focus earthquakes cause less damage and are felt less than shallow-focus ones. This is why the earthquake at Market Rasen in Lincolnshire on 27 February 2008, measuring 5.2 on the **Richter scale**, was felt so widely but not severely. The focus was 18.6 km below the surface. The point on the ground surface immediately above the focus is called the **epicentre**. Radiating out from this point are **shock waves**. These shock waves (seismic waves) cause the ground shaking that is responsible for much of the destruction caused by earthquakes.

Measuring earthquakes

When earthquakes occur, seismographs record the extent of the shaking by a pen identifying the trace of the movement on a rotating drum. The line graph produced is called a seismogram (graph **B**).

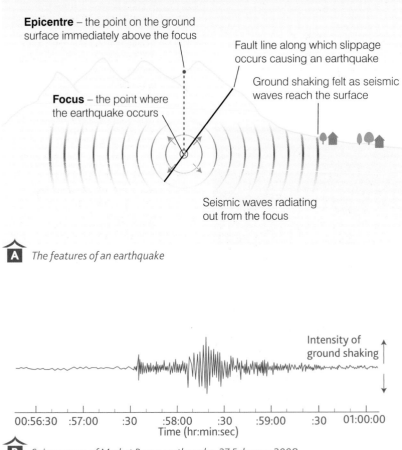

A *The features of an earthquake*

Epicentre – the point on the ground surface immediately above the focus

Focus – the point where the earthquake occurs

Fault line along which slippage occurs causing an earthquake

Ground shaking felt as seismic waves reach the surface

Seismic waves radiating out from the focus

Intensity of ground shaking

| 00:56:30 | :57:00 | :30 | :58:00 | :30 | :59:00 | :30 | 01:00:00 |

Time (hr:min:sec)

B *Seismogram of Market Rasen earthquake, 27 February 2008*

In this section you will learn

the features of an earthquake and how they are measured

where volcanoes occur and why they are found at constructive, destructive and conservative plate margins.

Key terms

Focus: the point in the earth's crust where the earthquake begins.

Richter scale: a scale ranging from 0 to 10 used for measuring earthquakes, based on scientific recordings of the amount of movement.

Epicentre: the point at the earth's surface directly above the focus.

Shock waves: seismic waves generated by an earthquake that pass through the earth's crust.

Mercalli scale: a means of measuring earthquakes by describing and comparing the damage done, on a scale of I to XII.

Did you know ??????

The most powerful earthquake ever recorded hit Valdivia in Chile in 1960 and measured 9.5 on the Richter scale. The two quakes that caused the most deaths occurred in China, with 830,000 people dying in Shensi in 1556 (over 8.0 on the Richter scale) and 255,000 (official figure) or 655,000 (unofficial figure) dying in Tangshan in 1976. The most powerful earthquake in the UK was 6.0 at Dogger Bank in 1931.

The Richter scale

The strength of earthquakes is generally given according to the Richter scale. There is no upper limit to this scale. The logarithmic nature of the scale means that there is a 10-fold increase every time the scale increases by 1. So a scale 2 earthquake on the Richter scale is 10 times more powerful than a scale 1; a scale 3 earthquake is 10 times more powerful than a scale 2 and 100 times more powerful than a scale 1.

The Mercalli scale

The Mercalli scale measures the effects of earthquakes using a scale from I to XII. It uses subjective descriptions of the resulting damage (table **C**).

Where and why do earthquakes occur?

Map **E** shows the location of areas prone to earthquakes. Look back at map **C** on page 9, and you will see a close link between plate margins and where earthquakes occur. The friction and pressures that build up where the plates meet are the causes of earthquakes.

- **Destructive margins** – the pressure resulting from the sinking of the subducting plate and its subsequent melting can trigger strong earthquakes as this pressure is periodically released.

- **Constructive margins** – here earthquakes tend to be less severe than those at destructive or conservative plate margins. The friction and pressure caused by the plates moving apart is less intense than at destructive plate margins.

- **Conservative margins** – here, where the plates slide past each other, the plates tend to stick for periods of time. This causes stresses and pressure to build. The release of the pressure occurs in a sudden, quick release of the plates and often results in powerful earthquakes.

C	*The Mercalli scale*
I	Barely felt
II	Felt by a few sensitive people; some suspended objects may swing
III	Slightly felt indoors as though a large truck were passing
IV	Felt indoors by many people; most suspended objects swing; windows and dishes rattle; standing cars rock
V	Felt by almost everyone; sleeping people are awakened; dishes and windows break
VI	Felt by everyone; some are frightened and run outside; some chimneys break; some furniture moves; slight damage
VII	Considerable damage in poorly built structures; felt by people driving; most are frightened and run outside
VIII	Slight damage to well-built structures; poorly built structures are heavily damaged; walls, chimneys and monuments fall
IX	Underground pipes break; foundations of buildings are damaged and buildings shift off foundations; considerable damage to well-built structures
X	Few structures survive; most foundations destroyed; water moved out of banks of rivers and lakes; avalanches and rockslides; railroads are bent
XI	Few structures remain standing; total panic; large cracks in the ground
XII	Total destruction; objects thrown into the air; the land appears to be liquid and is visibly rolling like waves

D   *Buildings damaged by the Christchurch earthquake. What is the level of damage according to the Mercalli scale (Table C)?*

Study tip

Ensure that you can describe
and explain the distribution of
earthquakes – where they occur
and why.

E *The location of earthquake zones*

⚭**links**

There are many facts and figures
available at **http://earthquake.
usgs.gov** and **www.earthquakes.
bgs.ac.uk.**

Activities

1 Study diagram **A**.

a Draw your own diagram to illustrate:
  ■ the focus
  ■ the epicentre
  ■ the spread of the seismic (shock) waves.

b Include a definition of the terms next to your diagram.

2 a Make a bulleted list of the main points about the Richter scale.

b Illustrate the logarithmic scale by drawing a bar graph for 1 to 4 on a simple diagram of the scale.

c How many times more powerful is an earthquake measuring 7 than an earthquake measuring 5 on the Richter scale?

d How many times more powerful is an earthquake measuring 9 than an earthquake measuring 5 on the Richter scale?

3 Describe the seismogram for the Market Rasen earthquake (graph **B**).

4 Study table **C**.

a Select two scores on the Mercalli scale that are at least four apart and draw simple diagrams to illustrate the damage.

b What are the advantages and the disadvantages of the two methods of measuring earthquakes?

5 Study map **E**, above, and map **C** on page 9.

a On an outline map of the world, shade in the areas that experience earthquakes.

b Label your map to describe the distribution of earthquakes. Use an atlas to help you with place names.

c Add the locations of the following recent earthquakes to your map:
  ■ Christchurch, New Zealand (2011)
  ■ Port-au-Prince, Haiti (2010)
  ■ Sichuan, China (2008)
  ■ Kashmir, Pakistan (2005)
  ■ Bam, Iran (2003)
  ■ Kobe, Japan (1995).

Add any additional recent earthquakes.

d Provide evidence to support the hypothesis that earthquakes mostly occur at plate boundaries.

6 Study diagrams **D**, **E** and **F** on pages 10 and 11, and the text on these pages.

a Draw simple, cross-sectional diagrams of each type of plate margin.

b Label your diagrams to explain where and why earthquakes occur at each plate margin.

c Give an example of an earthquake that has happened at each plate margin and name the plates responsible for it.

1.7 How do the effects of earthquakes differ in countries at different stages of development?

Case study

The Kobe earthquake, Japan

At 5.46am on 17 January 1995, the Philippines Plate shifted uneasily beneath the Eurasian Plate along the Nojima fault line that runs beneath Kobe (diagram **A**). This collision of plates led to an earthquake measuring 7.2 on the Richter scale, with tremors lasting 20 seconds.

In this section you will learn

case studies of earthquakes in countries at different stages of development – their causes, effects and responses

how and why the effects and responses are different in these two areas

the ways of trying to reduce the impact of earthquakes: the three Ps.

❶ Philippines Plate moves towards Eurasian Plate.

❷ Philippines Plate is forced down as it is oceanic crust.

❸ Plates jam together and pressure builds up.

❹ Pressure is suddenly released and plate jerks forward.

❺ Earthquake shockwaves travel outwards.

A Timeline of the Kobe earthquake

The effects of the Kobe earthquake

In this short time, the earthquake claimed the lives of 6,434 people and seriously injured over 40,000. Some 300,000 were made homeless. Gas mains were ruptured, water pipes fractured, sections of elevated roads collapsed (photo **B**) and railway lines buckled. Two million homes were without electricity and one million people had to cope without water for 10 days.

Fires engulfed parts of the city, especially to the west of the port, devouring the wooden structures (photo **C**). Damage to roads and water supply made attempts to extinguish them impossible. People huddled in blankets on the streets and in tented shelters in parks in fear of returning to buildings damaged by the earthquake. The damage caused was in excess of $220 billion and the economy suffered. Companies such as Panasonic had to close temporarily.

B The Great Hanshin Expressway

Responses to the Kobe earthquake

Friends and neighbours searched through the rubble for survivors, joined by the emergency services when access was possible. Hospitals struggled to cope with the injured, treating people and operating in corridors. Major retailers such as 7-Eleven helped to provide essentials and Motorola maintained telephone connections free of charge. The railways were 80 per cent operational within a month. It took longer to restore the road network – most was operational by July, although it was not until September 1996 that the Hanshin Expressway was fully open again. A year later, the port was 80 per cent operational, but much of the container shipping business had been lost.

Buildings and structures that had survived the earthquake had been built to a 1981 code, whereas those that had complied with earlier 1960s practices had collapsed. This led to changes. New buildings were built further apart, to prevent the domino effect. High-rise buildings had to have flexible steel frames; others were built of concrete frames reinforced with steel instead of wood. Rubber blocks were put under bridges to absorb shocks.

C   *Fire in the area west of Kobe port*

Did you know ??????

The Japanese practise an earthquake drill every year to prepare them for an event such as that at Kobe. Over 800,000 people took part in a drill in August 2006.

The Haiti earthquake 2010

Case study

At 16:53 on 12 January 2010 the Caribbean island of Haiti was struck by a powerful 7.0 magnitude earthquake. The epicentre of the earthquake was just 15 km SW of the capital Port-au-Prince. The earthquake was caused by stress building up along the conservative plate margin marking the boundary between the North American plate and the Caribbean plate (map **D**). The stress was released by a sudden slippage along a fault (crack in the earth's crust) running parallel to the plate boundary just south of Port-au-Prince. Following the main earthquake there were several minor tremors measuring up to 5.0 on the Richter scale.

The effects of the Haiti earthquake

The earthquake devastated large parts of the capital Port-au-Prince and resulted in a massive loss of life making it one of the most destructive earthquakes of all time.

- Approximately 230,000 people were killed.
- Over 2 million people were affected by the earthquake and 1.5 m were made homeless.
- About 180,000 homes were destroyed by ground shaking – this is an example of a primary effect (photo **E**).
- The homeless were accommodated in over 1,100 squalid camps with limited services such as water and sanitation. Many remained in these camps for well over a year (photo **F**).

D   *Haiti earthquake 2010 – the tectonic setting*

- Cholera claimed the lives of several hundred people, mainly children in the aftermath of the earthquake. This is a good example of a secondary effect. Storms and flooding caused further hardship in the camps.

- The earthquake created some 19 million cubic metres of rubble and debris in Port-au-Prince – enough to fill a line of shipping containers stretching end to end from London to Beirut.

- Approximately 5,000 schools were damaged or destroyed.

- Services such as electricity, water, sanitation and communications were badly disrupted or destroyed.

- The total cost of repairing the damage done by the earthquake is $US11.5 bn over a period of 5–10 years.

E   *The impacts of the earthquake*

Why did Haiti suffer so much?

Later in 2010, Christchurch in New Zealand was affected by an earthquake of exactly the same magnitude as the one that struck Haiti, 7.0 on the Richter scale. Yet, no one was killed. So why did Haiti suffer so much?

There are several reasons why Haiti suffered so much death and destruction:

- Haiti is an incredibly poor country. It was unprepared for an earthquake and could not cope adequately after the event. Before the earthquake most people survived on just $US2 a day.

- Over 80 per cent of the people in Port-au-Prince lived in poorly constructed, high density concrete buildings that simply fell apart when the earthquake struck.

- The earthquake was very close to the capital city Port-au-Prince and had a shallow focus. This meant that the city experienced very severe ground shaking.

- The port was largely destroyed and the airport badly damaged making it hard to bring in emergency supplies.

- The lack of a stable government resulted in limited and, at times, chaotic search and rescue efforts and recovery was very slow.

- There was a lack of doctors, hospitals (most were destroyed) and medical supplies. Many people died from their injuries or from diseases.

Responses to the Haiti earthquake

The main **short-term response** involved search and rescue. Teams of specially trained medics with sniffer dogs and high tech heat-sensitive equipment were flown into the country to assist local people in rescuing those trapped by the collapsed buildings. Aid in the form of food, water, medical supplies and temporary shelter was brought in to the country from the USA and neighbouring Dominican Republic. The United Nations and USA provided security to maintain law and order and ensure a fair distribution of aid. The UK's Disasters Emergency Committee (DEC) raised over £100m. This money was used to support over 1.2 million people by providing emergency shelter, medical consultations, clean drinking water and sanitation.

In the weeks and months that followed there were several longer-term responses:

- Three-quarters of the damaged buildings were inspected and repaired.

- Some 200,000 people have received cash or food for public work, such as clearing the many tonnes of rubble.

- Several thousand people have decided to move away from Port-au-Prince to stay with family; some have even emigrated to other countries.

- The World Bank pledged $US100m to support reconstruction and recovery programmes in Haiti.

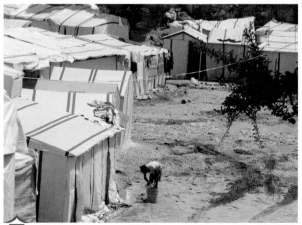

F   *Temporary camp set up to house the homeless in Port-au-Prince*

Prediction, protection and preparation

The three Ps provide the key to trying to reduce the impact of earthquakes. **Prediction** involves trying to forecast when an earthquake will happen. Japan tries to monitor earth tremors with a belief that warning can be given, but this did not happen at Kobe. Foreshocks do occur, but not on a timescale useful to evacuation. Experts know *where* earthquakes are likely to happen, but struggle to establish *when*. Even looking at the time between earthquakes in a particular area does not seem to work. Similarly, experts struggle to pinpoint exactly where along a plate margin they will occur. Animal behaviour has been used in the east, but it is viewed sceptically in the USA. China evacuated the city of Haicheng (population 1 million) in 1975, partly due to the strange, unexplained behaviour of animals. Days later an earthquake struck, measuring 7.3 on the Richter scale. There were relatively few deaths, but it is estimated that 150,000 would have died without the evacuation.

Building to an appropriate standard and using designs to withstand movement is the main way of ensuring **protection** (photo **G** and diagram **H**). **Preparation** involves hospitals, emergency services and inhabitants practising for major disasters, including having drills in public buildings and a code of practice so that people know what to do to reduce the impact and increase their chance of survival.

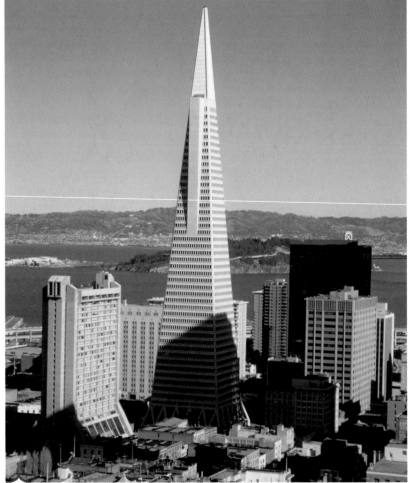

G *The Transamerica Pyramid, San Francisco*

Computer-controlled weights on roof to reduce movement

'Birdcage' interlocking steel frame

Steel frames that can sway during earth movements

Outer panels flexibly attached to steel structure

Fire-resistant building materials

Automatic window shutters to prevent falling glass

Roads to provide quick access for emergency services

Open areas where people can assemble if evacuated

Foundations sunk into bedrock, avoiding clay

Rubber shock-absorbers to absorb earth tremors

H *Earthquake-proofed building*

∞ links

To research Kobe, go to **www.seismo.unr.edu**; for Haiti go to **http://earthquake.usgs.gov**.

For information on earthquake preparation and drills, visit **www.bbc.co.uk** and **www.sfgate.com**. Enter 'earthquake drill' into the search box.

Activities

1 Study diagram **A** and photos **B** and **C**.

a   Produce a fact file to summarise the main points about the Kobe earthquake such as the date, time, focus and epicentre.

b   Imagine you are the science editor on a newspaper. Explain the specific causes of the Kobe earthquake.

c   Imagine you are a resident of Kobe. Describe the effects of the earthquake, distinguishing between primary and secondary effects in your account. Make sure what you write relates specifically to Kobe.

d   Summarise the immediate and long-term responses to the earthquake in Kobe. Do this as a piece of writing, a table or a list of bullet points.

2 Copy the table below to summarise key facts about the two earthquakes.

Feature	Kobe earthquake	Haiti earthquake
Cause		
Primary effects		
Secondary effects		
Immediate responses		
Long-term responses		

3 Describe how and explain why the effects of an earthquake differ in countries at different stages of development.

4 For each of prediction, protection and preparation, answer the following questions.

a   Explain the meaning of the term.

b   Give an example of the method for reducing the impact of earthquakes from either Kobe or Haiti.

c   Give one advantage and one disadvantage of the method.

d   Which of the three Ps do you think is the most useful in reducing the impact of earthquakes? Justify your choice.

5 Draw an illustrated earthquake code for a school in an earthquake-prone area.

1.8 Why is a tsunami hazardous?

How tsunamis form

Tsunamis are usually triggered by earthquakes. The crust shifting is the primary effect; a knock-on (secondary) effect of this is the displacement of water above the moving crust. This is the start of a tsunami.

A normal, wind-driven wave may have a length of 100 m from crest to crest, but a tsunami may be 200 km in length. The heights also greatly differ: 2 m for a normal wave versus 1 m for a tsunami out at sea. Tsunamis move at speeds of around 800 kph, rapidly approaching the coast almost unnoticed. As they near land they slow, reduce in length and gain in height (diagram **A**).

a Tsunami — Crest only 1 m high · Crests 200 km apart · Water travelling at 800 kph · Height increases · Wavelength shortens · 30 m · Slip on fault line causes water above to move upwards

b Normal wave — Wind speed 32 kph · Crests 100 m apart · Wave height 2 m · Breaking wave

A *Comparing wind-driven waves and tsunamis*

Case study

The Tohoku tsunami, Japan 2011

In the space of just a few years powerful tsunami have caused widespread destruction and huge loss of life. On 26 December 2004 a massive earthquake in the Indian Ocean measuring 9.3 on the Richter scale triggered a tsunami up to 25 m high that swept onshore killing an estimated 220,000 people in Indonesia, India and Sri Lanka.

On 11 March 2011, another very powerful earthquake measuring 9.0 on the Richter scale occurred about 100 km east of Sendai on Honshu, Japan. In just 30 minutes a wall of water up to 40 m high hit the coast of north western Japan. It was followed in places by up to 9 additional 'waves' of up to 10 m in height. Some 3,000 km of coastline were affected by the waves, which tore through coastal defences and inundated the coastal plains.

B *Aerial view of the impact of the Japanese tsunami*

Causes

The earthquake that triggered the tsunami occurred at the destructive plate margin where the Pacific plate is being subducted beneath the North American plate. Scientists believe that a segment of rock, some 200 km in length slipped suddenly resulting in an upwards 'flick' of the earth's crust by between 5 –10 m. It was this sudden uplift that triggered the tsunami.

Effects

There were a number of effects of the tsunami:

- Over 20,000 people were killed as the waves swept up to 10 km onshore. The high death toll was due to the power of the surge of water which overtopped tsunami defences and flooded areas thought to be safe from tsunami.

- Some 500 km² of coastal plains were inundated, destroying farmland, settlements and communications. The port city of Sendai (population 100,000) was virtually destroyed. A total of 200,000 buildings were damaged or destroyed by the earthquake and tsunami.
- Ruptured gas pipes led to fires that raged for several days.
- Explosions occurred at the Fukushima nuclear power plant as seawater over-topped the flood defences. There were considerable concerns about nuclear contamination and the possibility of a meltdown as the cooling systems failed to operate.
- Electricity was cut off in almost six million homes and over one million people were left without running water.
- Heavy snow, roads blocked by debris and landslides and over 1,000 aftershocks hampered relief efforts. In some areas, stocks of food, water and medical supplies ran low.

- Stock markets around the world fell over concerns about Japan's rising debts in the face of billions of US$ worth of damage

Responses

- Over 100,000 Japanese soldiers were deployed in search and rescue. They distributed blankets, water and food to the people affected by the disaster.
- Specialist search and rescue teams were flown in to the area from overseas.
- An exclusion zone was set up around the Fukushima nuclear plant and people were evacuated from the area.
- In the longer-term, a huge re-building and reconstruction programme is planned involving houses, infrastructure and communications systems (roads, railways, etc.). Port facilities will need to be re-built. The system of tsunami defences will need to be reconsidered and may well be extended in height beyond the standard 12 m that is currently the accepted level.

C   The cause of the Tohoku tsunami

1 One tectonic plate is dragged beneath the other causing the edges of the plates to flex and deform causing pressure to build over time.
   A Plate subducts beneath the other
   B Pressure builds up gradually causing distortion

2 The massive stresses eventually cause the plate to snap back displacing a vertical column of water which causes a tsunami.
   C Fracture causes water displacement

3 At the fault line the tsunami is merely a ripple but as it approaches land it gains height as the water becomes shallower slowing the wave.
   D Column of water splits into two; one travels out to sea, the other towards land
   E Wave height increases as it reaches shallower water

Activity

Working in small groups of three or four, produce a report or presentation on the Japanese tsunami to include the following:

a   A definition of 'tsunami', supported by a labelled diagram.

b   The cause of the tsunami from a science editor's viewpoint, supported by a labelled diagram.

c   The effects of the tsunami from a resident's or tourist's point of view. Include a labelled photograph showing the impact and a map showing the areas affected.

d   The immediate responses to the tsunami – a resident's, doctor's or Red Cross volunteer's eyewitness account. Try to capture the feelings of the person involved.

e   The long-term responses to the tsunami – the views of a resident as rebuilding continues, or of a government or aid agency worker.

f   A summary of 10 important facts about the tsunami.

It must be clear that you are writing about the Japanese tsunami. You should try to convey the scale of the disaster and the human suffering.

2.1   How were rocks formed?

What is the geological timescale?

Although we measure time in minutes and hours, geologists are seldom interested in anything less than hundreds of thousands of years! Scientists believe that the earth is about 4,600 million years old. For much of that time the earth was cooling and forming a basic atmosphere. Life on earth only became abundant some 542 million years ago. It is from this time that geologists have divided time into eras and periods to form the **geological timescale** (diagram **A**). The boundaries between the different periods represent critical stages in the earth's history, such as periods of mountain building or widespread sea-level change.

Era	Millions of years ago	Period	Major UK events
Cenozoic	23	Quaternary* / Neogene	Ice Age
Cenozoic		Palaeogene	Formation of Alps caused folding of rocks in UK
Cenozoic	65		
Mesozoic		Cretaceous	Much of England covered by sea
Mesozoic	145		
Mesozoic		Jurassic	Limestone deposited that now forms the Cotswold Hills
Mesozoic	199		
Mesozoic		Triassic	Much of the UK would have been desert
Mesozoic	251		
Palaeozoic (Late)		Permian	
Palaeozoic (Late)	299		
Palaeozoic (Late)		Carboniferous	Tropical conditions affected the UK. Coal formed
Palaeozoic (Late)	359		
Palaeozoic (Late)		Devonian	
Palaeozoic (Early)	416		
Palaeozoic (Early)	443	Silurian	
Palaeozoic (Early)		Ordovician	Volcanoes active in Wales. Great Glen Fault formed in Scotland
Palaeozoic (Early)	488		
Palaeozoic (Early)		Cambrian	* The Quaternary period is divided into the PLEISTOCENE (ICE AGE) and the most recent period (from 10,000 years ago until the present day) called the HOLOCENE
Palaeozoic (Early)	542		
		Pre-Cambrian	

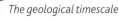

A The geological timescale

Key terms

Geological timescale: the period of time since life became abundant 542 million years ago, which geologists have divided into eras and periods.

Igneous rocks: rocks formed from the cooling of molten magma.

Sedimentary rocks: most commonly, rocks formed from the building up of sediment on the sea floor.

Metamorphic rocks: rocks formed when the chemistry and texture have been changed because of heating and/or pressure.

Study tip

When studying rocks and landscapes, it is important to appreciate that processes have been operating for an extremely long period of time, often measured in millions of years.

Did you know ???????

If the whole of geological time were to be represented by a single calendar year, humans started to walk on the earth at 1 minute to midnight on 31 December.

As methods of dating have improved in recent years, the boundary dates on the geological timescale have changed slightly. The geological timescale in diagram **A** was published in 2004.

In this chapter we will be focusing on four rocks that are abundant in the UK. They were formed at different times on the geological timescale:

- granite – formed about 280 million years ago
- Carboniferous limestone – formed some 340 million years ago
- chalk – formed during the Cretaceous period
- clay – formed on many occasions throughout geological time but especially during the Jurassic, Cretaceous and Tertiary periods. We will look at landscapes formed on clay deposited during the Cretaceous period.

Rock types

The earth's crust is the thin outer layer of the earth, surrounding the mantle and the core. Look at diagram **A** on page 8 to see the structure of the earth and plate margins.

Three types of rock make up the earth's crust: **igneous**, **sedimentary** and **metamorphic**. Table **B** summarises the formation and characteristics of these three rock groups.

Activity

Study diagram **A**.

a Use a ruler to draw the geological timescale to scale – a scale of 4 cm = 100 million years will work well. Note that the youngest periods are at the top and oldest at the bottom.

b Write the names of the eras and periods. Write the dates alongside the boundary lines.

c Use arrows to locate the times when granite, Carboniferous limestone, chalk and clay were formed.

d Select a few 'Major UK events' to add to your diagram.

∞ links

The British Geological Survey has a good website at **www.bgs.ac.uk**.

B   *Formation and characteristics of igneous, sedimentary and metamorphic rocks*

Rock type	Formation	Characteristics	Examples	Photo
Igneous	Formed by the cooling of molten magma either underground (intrusive) or on the ground (extrusive) by volcanic activity.	Igneous rocks are composed of interlocking crystals (they are said to be crystalline). They are generally tough rocks and are resistant to erosion.	Basalt, andesite and rhyolite are examples of extrusive lavas. Granite, gabbro and dolerite are intrusive rocks.	
Sedimentary	Formed by the compaction and cementation of sediments; usually deposited in the sea. Also includes organic material (e.g. coal) and rocks precipitated from solutions (e.g. limestone).	Sedimentary rocks usually form layers called beds. They often contain fossils. Although some rocks can be tough (e.g. limestone), most are weaker than igneous and metamorphic rocks.	Common sedimentary rocks include sandstone, limestone, shale, clay and mudstone. The rock chalk is a form of limestone.	
Metamorphic	Formed by the alteration of pre-existing igneous, sedimentary or metamorphic rocks by heat and/or pressure.	Metamorphic rocks are also crystalline. They often exhibit layering (not beds) called cleavage (as with the rock slate) and banding. Metamorphic rocks tend to be very tough and resistant to erosion.	Slate is one of the most common metamorphic rocks. Other examples include gneiss (pronounced 'nice') and schist.	

2.2   The rock cycle

Rocks are constantly being recycled. For example, igneous rocks are broken down by weathering and transported to the sea as sediment. On the sea bed the sediment is turned into sedimentary rock. When uplifted to form a new mountain range, the sedimentary rock is put under enormous pressure. Some of it is transformed into metamorphic rock. Some might be completely melted to form magma and, on cooling, brand-new igneous rock.

The connections between the main rock groups can be described as the **rock cycle** (diagram **A**).

In this section you will learn

the three types of rock which can be linked by the rock cycle.

Key term

Rock cycle: connections between the three rock types shown in the form of a diagram.

Did you know ??????

What is thought to be the oldest rock on earth was discovered encased in gneiss (metamorphic rock) in Canada. It is over 4,000 million years old.

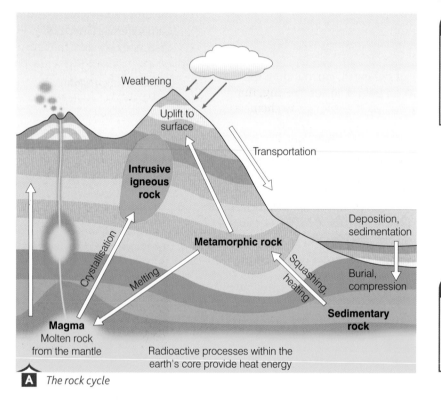

A   *The rock cycle*

Study tip

Ensure that you learn the three definitions of rock types and practise labelling the various parts of the rock cycle.

Activity

Study diagram **A**.

a   Make a large copy of the rock cycle diagram.

b   Draw lava coming out of the volcano and add the label 'extrusive igneous rock'.

c   What is the difference between extrusive and intrusive igneous rock?

d   Where does magma come from?

e   What provides the heat to melt rocks deep within the earth?

f   How do metamorphic rocks become exposed on the ground surface?

g   In what environment do most sedimentary rocks form?

h   Describe in your own words how a metamorphic rock may become a sedimentary rock.

2.3   What is weathering and how does it operate?

What is weathering?

Weathering is the disintegration or decay of rocks in their original place at or close to the ground surface. As the name suggests, it is largely caused by elements of the weather such as rainfall and changes in temperature.

Weathering affects natural outcrops of rock as well as manmade structures such as churches, bridges and schools. Close inspection of a wall often reveals small pits, flaking of the outer surface or discolouration. This is weathering.

Types of weathering

There are three types of weathering:

1 **Mechanical weathering** – also known as physical weathering, this involves the disintegration (breakup) of rocks without any chemical changes taking place. It often results in piles of angular rock fragments called **scree** found at the foot of bare rocky outcrops.
2 **Chemical weathering** – here, a chemical change occurs when weathering takes place. Rainwater, being slightly acidic, can slowly dissolve certain rocks and minerals. Those minerals or particles unaffected by chemical weathering are usually left behind to form a fine clay deposit.
3 **Biological weathering** – this involves the actions of flora and fauna. Plant roots are effective at growing and expanding in cracks in the rocks (photo **A**). Rabbits can be effective in burrowing into weak rocks such as sands.

Mechanical weathering

Freeze–thaw weathering

Freeze–thaw weathering, or frost shattering as it is sometimes known, involves the action of water as it freezes and thaws in a crack or hole in the rock. It is a common process and operates wherever there is plenty of water and where temperatures fluctuate repeatedly above and below freezing point.

Look at diagram **B**. The process of freeze–thaw starts with liquid water collecting in cracks or holes (**pores**) in a rock. At night, this water freezes and expands by approximately nine per cent. If the water is in a confined space, the expansion creates stresses within the rock, widening any cracks that already exist. When the temperature rises and the ice thaws, the water seeps deeper into the rock along newly formed cracks. After repeated cycles of freezing and thawing, fragments of rock may become detached and fall to the foot of the slope to collect as scree.

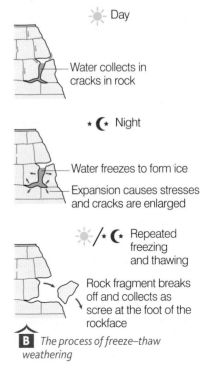

A   *Biological weathering involving the expansion of tree roots*

Day

Water collects in cracks in rock

Night

Water freezes to form ice

Expansion causes stresses and cracks are enlarged

Repeated freezing and thawing

Rock fragment breaks off and collects as scree at the foot of the rockface

B   *The process of freeze–thaw weathering*

Exfoliation

Look at photo **C**, which shows an outcrop of rock that has been affected by **exfoliation** over time. Note how the outer 'skin' of the rock appears to be flaking away from the rest of the rock. You can see why exfoliation is sometimes known as onion-skin weathering.

C   *Exfoliation in rocks exposed in Antrim, Northern Ireland*

Exfoliation is most commonly associated with large fluctuations in temperature, which occur particularly in hot deserts. Rock is a poor conductor of heat. This means that only the outer part of a rock warms and cools in response to changes in temperature. As it warms during the day it expands and as it cools at night it contracts. Repeated cycles of expansion (heating) and contraction (cooling) can ultimately lead to the outer skin peeling away from the rest of the rock. The presence of water is important for exfoliation to take place as it weakens the rock, making it more vulnerable to flaking.

▊ Chemical weathering

Solution

In the same way that sugar dissolves in tea, some minerals and rocks dissolve in rainwater. This dissolving process is called **solution**. Rock salt is a sedimentary rock that formed under desert conditions from the accumulation of salt crystals on a dried-up lakebed. Deposits of rock salt are found in Cheshire and it is extracted and used as a de-icer on roads and pavements in winter. Just like table salt, rock salt dissolves in water and is therefore vulnerable to the weathering process of solution.

Key terms

Weathering: the breakup or decay of rocks in their original place at or close to the earth's surface.

Mechanical weathering: a process where physical forces break down or reduce rock into smaller fragments.

Scree: deposits of rock fragments found at the foot of rock outcrops.

Chemical weathering: the process where chemical reactions change or destroy minerals when rock comes into contact with water and/or air.

Biological weathering: weathering caused by living things such as tree roots or burrowing animals.

Freeze–thaw weathering: weathering involving repeated cycles of freezing and thawing.

Pores: holes in rock.

Exfoliation: flaking of the outer surface of rocks mainly caused by repeated cycles of hot and cold.

Solution: dissolving of rocks or minerals by rainwater. This is a means of transportation as well as an erosion process.

Carbonation: weathering of limestone and chalk by acidic rainwater.

Carbonation

Carbonation is similar to solution in that it involves dissolving. It affects rocks that are made up of calcium carbonate ($CaCO_3$) such as limestone and chalk. Look at diagram **D** to see how the process of carbonation works. Carbonation is responsible for forming some of the landforms associated with limestone landscapes.

Rainwater picks up carbon dioxide (CO_2) from the air

Rainwater becomes a weak carbonic acid

Acidic rainwater reacts with calcium carbonate ($CaCo_3$) to form calcium bicarbonate, which then dissolves

LIMESTONE or CHALK ($CaCo_3$)

D The process of carbonation

Study tip

Learn the definition of weathering and of the various processes. Using diagrams to describe weathering processes is effective and makes them easier to learn.

Activities

1 Study photo **A**.
  a What is the meaning of the term 'weathering'?
  b How is the tree root breaking up the rock?
  c Apart from tree roots and rabbits, can you think of any other forms of biological weathering?
  d How does chemical weathering differ from biological weathering?

2 Study diagram **B**. Draw your own series of diagrams to describe the process of freeze–thaw.

3 Make a sketch of photo **C**. Add annotations or a written commentary to explain how the process of exfoliation operates.

4 Work in pairs to produce a PowerPoint presentation to describe one of the processes of weathering. Freeze–thaw, exfoliation and carbonation lend themselves particularly well to this. Use labelled photos and diagrams to describe your chosen process. Do not use more than six slides.

links

Further information and links can be found at **www.geographypages.co.uk/weathering.htm**.

2.4   What are the characteristics of granite landscapes?

The formation and distribution of granite

Granite is an intrusive igneous rock that was formed deep underground. Following uplift and the erosion of the overlying rocks, the granite has become exposed on the surface.

In south-west England the apparently isolated exposures of granite (map **A**) are actually all part of the same enormous igneous rock mass called a **batholith**. The irregular upper surface is gradually being exposed by erosion. One day, south-west England will appear to be almost completely granite.

The distribution of granite in the UK is patchy (map **A**). Apart from the exposures in south-west England, granite is only found in parts of north-west England, Scotland and Ireland.

A   *Distribution of granite in the UK*

The characteristics of granite

Granite is a tough rock resistant to the processes of weathering and erosion. This explains why it forms upland areas such as Dartmoor and Bodmin in south-west England. Granite consists of three main minerals: grey-coloured quartz, black mica and pink feldspar. Feldspar is a mineral that is vulnerable to chemical weathering and will decay to form white clay called china clay or kaolin.

Granite contains cracks or **joints**. Vertical joints formed when the granite cooled and contracted. Horizontal joints in granite resulted from pressure release as the overlying rocks were removed by erosion. The rock expanded as the pressure was released, causing the joints to form roughly parallel to the ground surface. The presence of these joints makes granite vulnerable to freeze–thaw weathering and, in some places, exfoliation.

Key terms

Batholith: a huge irregular-shaped mass of igneous rock that only reaches the surface when the overlying rocks are removed.

Joints: cracks that may run vertically or horizontally through rock.

Impermeable rock: a rock that does not allow water to pass through it.

Tor: an isolated outcrop of rock on a hilltop, usually in granite landscapes.

Mass movement: the downhill movement of material under the influence of gravity.

Did you know ??????

Hard, durable and criss-crossed with joints, granite is a popular rock with climbers. Several popular peaks in the Mont Blanc range in France are made of granite.

Study tip

Tors are one of the main features of a granite landscape and you should be able to describe their features. A labelled diagram can often be the best way to learn and also to explain these features.

Despite the presence of the joints, granite is an **impermeable rock** – it does not allow water to pass through it. Therefore, granite landscapes are often wet and marshy with plenty of rivers. As photo **B** shows, granite moorlands tend to be bleak, wet and windswept. As upland areas, they experience heavy rainfall and snow in winter. Low grasses with a few stunted trees mostly cover the moors, which are deeply dissected by rivers.

Granite landforms

The most distinctive granite landform is an isolated outcrop of rock called a **tor** (photo **C**). Tors are found on the tops of hills and initially look like a pile of rocks dumped on the ground. They are, however, part of the solid geology.

There are several theories about the formation of these desolate rocky outcrops. The most widely accepted theory was suggested by Linton in 1955 (diagram **D**).

B *Granite landscape (with Hound Tor in the distance)*

Horizontal joints formed by pressure release when the overlying rocks were removed

Rounded edges caused by chemical weathering

Vertical joints formed when the granite cooled

Broken rocks at the foot of the tor resulting from freeze–thaw weathering

Enlarged joints caused by freeze–thaw weathering

C *Haytor, one of Dartmoor's most impressive tors*

Linton suggested that the spacing of the vertical joints in granite varied across an area and that this influenced the effectiveness of weathering.

While underground and in a previously warmer and wetter climate, the closely spaced joints were weathered rapidly compared with the zone of more widely spaced joints.

As the granite became exposed on the surface during the Ice Age, erosion and **mass movement** (slumping) removed the broken-up granite, leaving behind the largely unweathered jointed granite to form a tor. Under current conditions, the tor has continued to be weathered by physical and chemical processes.

a Horizontal cracks caused by pressure release

Soil

Zone of widely spaced joints

Vertical joints caused by cooling

Zone of closely spaced joints

b Deep chemical weathering under warm and wet conditions

Weathered granite

Zone of widely spaced joints is weathered less rapidly than where the joints are closely spaced

c Weathered granite removed by surface processes to leave the tor exposed

Tor

D *Formation of tors*

Activities

1 Study map **A**.

a On a blank outline map of the UK, draw the areas of granite shown on the map.

b Using an atlas, locate and name the moors of south-west England.

c Add locational labels to other outcrops of granite on your map.

d Write a few sentences describing the distribution of granite in the UK.

2 Study photo **C**.

a Draw a sketch of Haytor from the photo.

b Use arrows to locate the features listed in the photo.

c Describe the main features of the tor.

d Is there evidence that the tor is being weathered under present-day climatic conditions?

3 Study diagram **D**. Draw a series of annotated diagrams to show the formation of tors as suggested by Linton in 1955.

⚭ links

Further information about granite and Dartmoor can be found at **www.dartmoor-npa.gov.uk**. Enter 'geology and landforms' into the search box.

2.5 What are the characteristics of chalk and clay landscapes?

Chalk and clay are two examples of sedimentary rocks. They were both formed under the sea and then uplifted by **tectonic activity** to form land. Although they are similar in terms of their formation, they are rocks with very different characteristics.

Map **A** shows the distribution of chalk in the UK. It is found in the south and east of England, and tends to form bands rather than the isolated outcrops that we saw with granite (map **A**, page 40). This is because, being a sedimentary rock, chalk forms beds (layers) that cover large areas. When exposed at the surface, these beds appear as bands. Clay is such a common rock, formed throughout geological time, that it is not really feasible to plot every outcrop on a map.

In this section you will learn

the formation and characteristics of chalk and clay

the distinctive landforms associated with chalk and clay.

Key terms

Tectonic activity: activity (such as volcanic eruptions and earthquakes) caused by the movement of tectonic plates.

Permeable rock: a rock that allows water to pass through it.

Water table: the upper surface of underground water.

Spring: water re-emerging from the rock onto the ground surface. Springs often occur as a line of springs (spring line) at the base of a scarp slope.

Vale: in the landscape, a flat plain typically formed on clay.

Key
■ Chalk

N

0   200 km

A *Distribution of chalk in the UK*

Characteristics of chalk and clay

Chalk, familiar to most people as forming the 'white cliffs of Dover', is physically a tough rock although it is not as strong as granite. It does form upland areas such as the Chilterns, Yorkshire Wolds and the South Downs, but this is partly because chalk is a **permeable rock**. This means that it does not readily support rivers, and a lack of rivers means a lack of erosion.

Chalk is permeable because it is heavily jointed and porous (it contains holes or pores). Rainwater soaks through the joints and pores until it reaches the **water table** (diagram **B**). This is the upper surface of underground water. Water stored within the chalk is a valuable resource, as you will discover later. Where the water table reaches the ground surface, **springs** are formed.

Did you know ??????

Classroom chalk is not the same as rock chalk. It is made of a much softer mineral called gypsum, which is the same as the substance used to make plaster boards in buildings and the plaster used to mend broken bones.

Escarpment/Cuesta

Dry valley: formed by a river either when the chalk was frozen during the Ice Age or when the water table was much higher than it is today

Chalk dips in this direction

Spring line

Dip slope

Scarp slope

Clay

Water table

Chalk

Clay

Spring: where water re-emerges onto the ground surface

B *Landscape features associated with chalk and clay*

Chalk is a pure form of limestone and rich in calcium carbonate ($CaCO_3$). This means that it is vulnerable to the chemical weathering process of carbonation (page 39). As it contains many joints and pores, chalk is also vulnerable to freeze–thaw weathering, which has been held responsible for some notable recent cliff collapses (photo **A**, page 160).

In contrast, clay is a weak and impermeable rock. Rivers easily erode clay, which explains why it mainly forms low, flat ground called **vales**.

Chalk and clay landscapes

Look at diagram **B**, which describes the main landscape features associated with chalk and clay. The key thing to note is that the rocks are exposed at the ground at a slight angle rather than being horizontal. This is due to the rocks being folded by tectonic activity centred at the Alps in southern Europe. As you can see, this has had a profound effect on the landscape features.

> ### Remember
>
> **Permeability** is the ability of a rock to allow water to pass through it.
>
> **Permeable** means water can pass through a rock (via joints and/or pores).
>
> **Impermeable** means water cannot pass through a rock.
>
> **Porosity** is a description of the relative amount (percentage) of pore spaces (holes) in a rock.
>
> **Porous** means there is high proportion of pores.
>
> **Non-porous** means there is a low proportion of pores.
>
> **Granite** is impermeable and non-porous.
>
> **Chalk** is permeable and porous.
>
> **Clay** is impermeable and can be porous, but the pores are so tiny that it tends to become waterlogged.
>
> **Carboniferous limestone** is permeable but non-porous (water passes through joints in the rock).

C *1 : 50,000 OS map extract of the Chiltern Hills near Chinnor, part of map sheet 165*

Activities

1 Study map **A**.

a On a blank outline map of the UK, draw the areas of chalk shown on the map.

b Using an atlas, locate and name the upland areas formed by chalk.

c Write a few sentences describing the distribution of chalk in the UK.

d Explain why chalk tends to form bands of rock when exposed at the surface, whereas granite tends to form 'blobs'.

2 Study map **C**, which is a 1:50,000 OS map extract of part of the Chiltern Hills. The chalk **escarpment/cuesta** is the hilly area to the south-east of the map extract. The steeper scarp slope is at the north-western edge of the chalk. The clay vale is the flatter area to the north-west of the map extract.

a What is the highest point and what is its six-figure grid reference?

b What is the lowest point on the clay and what is its six-figure grid reference?

c Give an example of a springline settlement.

d At roughly what height do you think the junction between the chalk and the clay lies? Support your answer with evidence from the map.

e In which grid square is the scarp slope clearly evident? With the aid of a simple sketch map, describe how the scarp slope can be recognised on the map.

f Locate grid square 7799. In the centre of the square, a **dry valley** can be seen clearly by the shape of the contours. Draw a simple sketch (include a scale) to show the shape of these contours and label the dry valley.

g Compare the land uses between the chalk and the clay. Refer to place names and grid references in your answer.

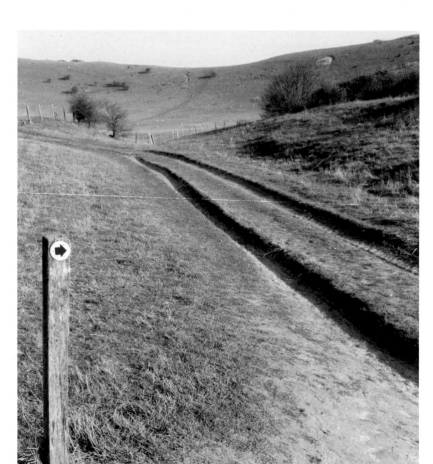

D *The Chilterns*

Key terms

Escarpment/cuesta: an outcrop of chalk made up of a steep scarp slope and a more gentle dip slope.

Dry valley: a valley formed by a river during a wetter period in the past but now without a river.

∞ links

Further information about the Chiltern Hills can be found at **www.chilternsaonb.org**.

The White Cliffs Countryside Partnership has information on chalk at **www.whitecliffscountryside.org.uk**. Click on the 'Chalk' link.

2.6 What are the characteristics of Carboniferous limestone landscapes?

Carboniferous limestone is a sedimentary rock so named because it was formed during the Carboniferous geological period about 340 million years ago. It was formed by the accumulation of calcium carbonate ($CaCO_3$) in warm tropical seas, rather like the present-day Caribbean. The corals and shellfish that were present in these ancient seas are often preserved in the limestone as fossils.

Map **A** shows the distribution of Carboniferous limestone. Like chalk (map **A**, page 42), limestone forms bands across the UK. One of the main exposures of Carboniferous limestone runs down the spine of England to form the Pennine Hills.

The characteristics of carboniferous limestone

Carboniferous limestone is a tough and resistant rock. It forms upland areas in the UK such as the Pennine Hills and the Mendips. When exposed at the coast, as it is in parts of south Wales, it forms dramatic towering cliffs.

Despite being physically strong, it is chemically weak. As it is composed of calcium carbonate, it is vulnerable to the slow dissolving action associated with carbonation. It is well jointed, with horizontal joints called bedding planes between the layers (beds) of limestone and regularly spaced vertical joints. These joints promote freeze–thaw weathering. They also account for limestone being a permeable rock.

Carboniferous limestone landscapes

Carboniferous limestone tends to form high ground, often with exposures of bare rock and steep-sided valleys or **gorges** (photo **B**). Weathering produces thin soils that support grass, used for grazing by sheep, and just a few isolated trees.

> **In this section you will learn**
>
> about the formation and characteristics of Carboniferous limestone
>
> about the distinctive landforms associated with Carboniferous limestone.

> **Study tip**
>
> Draw a large labelled diagram to help you learn and recognise the main limestone features.

> ∞ **links**
>
> Find out more at **www.bbc.co.uk**. Enter 'upland limestone' into the search box.

> **Key terms**
>
> **Gorge:** a narrow, steep-sided valley.

Hard, grey, full of fossils (e.g. coral), well jointed and permeable

A Distribution of Carboniferous limestone in the UK

B Limestone landscape near Malham, Yorkshire

There are several distinctive features associated with Carboniferous limestone landscapes (diagram **C**). Some features are found on the surface whereas others are underground.

C Features associated with Carboniferous limestone landscape

Surface features

Bare rocky surfaces called **limestone pavements** are common features. The pattern of jointing results in a blocky appearance, with blocks called clints separated by enlarged joints called grikes. Chemical weathering causes the surface of the limestone pavement to be relatively smooth. Water flowing over adjacent impermeable rocks disappears down holes in the limestone called **swallow holes**. These are found at the intersection of the joints and are enlarged by weathering processes and river erosion.

Dry valleys are common features in limestone areas. They are formed in much the same way as the dry valleys in chalk (page 44). Most were probably formed by meltwater at the end of the last ice advance, when some of the limestone was still frozen and impermeable and water tables were much higher than today. Occasionally very narrow gorges can be found. These may result from the collapse of roofs of underground **caverns**. Springs or **resurgences** occur where water flowing underground emerges onto the ground surface, often from a small cave.

Underground features

Unlike granite, chalk or clay, limestone exhibits a number of underground features. As water flows through the joints in the limestone, weathering and erosion enlarge the joints to create tunnels and caverns. When water, rich in dissolved calcium carbonate, drips from the roofs of caverns it leaves a minute deposit of calcite as it evaporates. Over hundreds and thousands of years an icicle-like **stalactite** forms hanging down from the roof. The drips on the floor of the cavern also deposit calcite but, due to the splatter effect, the resultant **stalagmite** is shorter and stubbier. In rare cases, the two features join together to form a **pillar**. Calcite can be deposited over a wider surface where water flows over a rock face or drips occur in many places along a crack in a wall. This can result in the formation of a sheet-like **curtain** rather than an individual stalactite.

2.7 What are the uses of rocks?

Rocks have many uses to people. They can be extracted to provide raw materials for industry or used as building stone or for **cement**. They provide opportunities for water supply, either by storing water underground in cracks and pores or, if impermeable, by enabling surface reservoirs to be constructed. Soils that develop from rocks enable farming to take place. Rocks also create distinctive landscapes and scenery, providing a tremendous breadth of opportunity for leisure and recreation.

Table **A** outlines some of the main uses for the four types of rock that you have been studying in this chapter.

In this section you will learn

the opportunities for human use of granite, chalk, clay and Carboniferous limestone.

Key terms

Cement: mortar used in building, made from crushed limestone and shale.

A *Uses of granite, chalk, clay and Carboniferous limestone*

Rock type	Resource for extraction	Farming	Water supply	Scenery
Granite	Building stone used throughout Cornwall. Aberdeen is known as the 'city of granite'.\n\nCommonly used for kitchen surfaces.\n\nIn the past, granite contained valuable veins of tin and other metals. Kaolin (china clay) – used in industry as a whitener – originated as granite.	Mainly extensive sheep farming on poor pastures and in harsh environmental conditions.\n\nThis is because granite forms upland areas.	Impermeable rock. Several reservoirs have been constructed in steep valleys, such as the Burrator Reservoir which supplies Plymouth.	Bleak and windswept, granite forms wild and attractive moorland scenery.\n\nAttractive for outdoor activities especially walking, bird watching, mountain biking and climbing.\n\nWater sports (fishing, sailing) on the reservoirs.
Chalk	Quarried to be manufactured into cement.\n\nSource of lime for industry and farming, to neutralise acidic soils.	Reasonably fertile land used for sheep farming and some arable crops such as wheat and barley.	Important store of underground water (aquifers). Supplies large parts of the south-east of England including London.	Characterised by rolling hills. Popular with naturalists due to rich wildlife, particularly flowers and birds. Opportunities for walking and horse riding.
Clay	Used in making bricks and for pottery.	Fertile soils but with a tendency to become waterlogged. Mostly used as pasture for sheep and dairy cattle.	Impermeable rock. Some reservoirs have been constructed but flat land is not ideal.	Featureless landscape is not especially attractive.
Carboniferous limestone	Quarried to be manufactured into cement.\n\nSource of lime for industry and farming, to neutralise acidic soils.\n\nUsed as a building stone and in dry-stone walls as field boundaries.\n\nPopular stone for gardens, which has led to some destruction of limestone pavements.	Generally thin, upland soils (most of the limestone dissolves when weathered) so mostly used for sheep.	Spring water flowing out of the limestone can be a source of water.	Attractive upland scenery is popular with tourists. A number of National Parks and Areas of Outstanding Natural Beauty are on limestone areas, e.g. Peak District and Yorkshire Dales.\n\nMany opportunities for walking, mountain biking, climbing and potholing.

Farming on Dartmoor

Over the last 5,000 years farming has been the main land use on Dartmoor. Over 90 per cent of the land within the National Park today is farmed; half of this is open moorland, which is used for grazing livestock, and the rest is made up of fringe farmland and improved grassland.

The whole of Dartmoor is now designated as an Environmentally Sensitive Area and farmers enter into management agreements, for payment, to carry out agricultural practices that conserve the upland landscape and wildlife habitats. This may include reducing the numbers of livestock grazing sensitive areas, but they must also restrict the use of fertilisers and pesticides. Farmers are paid to maintain stone walls and hedgerows, to develop hay meadows and to adopt agricultural practices that help to protect the area's archaeological and historic interest.

B *A sheep farm on Dartmoor*

The London Basin chalk aquifer

The rocks underneath London form a basin called a **syncline** (diagram **C**). Water soaks into the chalk where it is exposed on either side of London and then percolates through the chalk to form a giant underground reservoir called an **aquifer**. For hundreds of years this water has supplied London with its water. The aquifer is carefully managed by the Environment Agency to ensure that its use is sustainable. In the 1960s, industrial use caused the water table to drop to 88 m below sea level, which resulted in some seawater contamination. Following careful management and reduced demand from industry since the 1990s, the water table has risen by as much as 3 m a year.

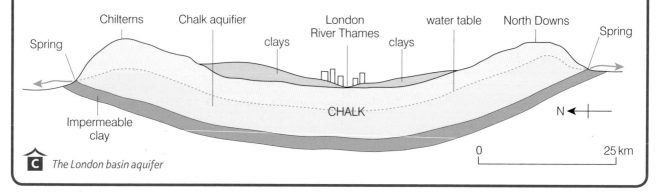

C *The London basin aquifer*

Limestone scenery: recreation in the Yorkshire Dales

The Yorkshire Dales is a National Park largely made up of Carboniferous limestone. The landscape is spectacular, with steep valleys, cliffs and extensive grassy plateaux (photo **B**, page 45).

The Yorkshire Dales offers many opportunities for leisure and recreation. The area is criss-crossed with footpaths including the long-distance footpath known as the Pennine Way. There are opportunities for nature tourism (birds and wild flowers), as well as more adventurous outdoor pursuits such as climbing (limestone is an excellent rock for climbing with its many joints), mountain biking and caving. The area around Malham (map **D**) is a particular focus for tourism. For this reason it is referred to as a honeypot site (think bees and honeypot!).

Tourism brings both benefits and costs to the Yorkshire Dales. Tourists bring money into the area, which they spend in shops, cafés and hotels. Many local people benefit from employment opportunities, working in restaurants and hotels or acting as guides. Local craft industries and farms also benefit from the visitors. However, there are costs associated with tourism. Traffic jams form in the narrow roads and cause additional pollution. People leave litter, which spoils the area and can be harmful to wildlife. Farm gates may be left open and animals worried by dogs. Shop prices may be higher than elsewhere as people cash in on the tourists, which is bad news for local residents. House prices may also be higher than elsewhere due to a demand for holiday homes. Thoughtful and sustainable management is vital if the area is to retain its special beauty in the future.

∞ links

The Yorkshire Dales National Park website is a useful source of information at **www.yorkshiredales.org.uk**.

A number of excellent farm case studies are available at the Farming and Countryside Education (FACE) site at **www.face-online.org.uk**.

Further information about Malham can be found at **www.malhamdale.com**.

D 1 : 50,000 OS map extract of Malham, part of map sheet 98

Key terms

Syncline: the lower arc of the fold in fold mountains.

Aquifer: an underground reservoir of water stored in pores and/or joints in a rock, e.g. chalk.

Activities

1 Study map **D**.

a Using grid references or place names, suggest some activities available for visitors in this area.

b What amenities have been provided for tourists?

c The Field Studies Council runs a popular Field Centre at Malham Tarn. In which grid square is the Field Centre located?

d Why do you think the Field Studies Council decided to run a centre in this area?

e Look closely at the roads. What challenges does the landscape create for travelling in the area?

f Malham is popular with visitors and it gets extremely busy at peak times. When do you think the 'peak times' are and why?

g Suggest some problems that might occur in the area resulting from the high number of visitors.

h Suggest some benefits that tourism might bring to the area.

2 Use the internet to find out more about recreational activities available in the Yorkshire Dales. A good starting point is the Yorkshire Dales National Park website at **www.yorkshiredales.org.uk**. Present your information in the form of a single-page advertisement encouraging people to visit the Yorkshire Dales. You might like to focus on just one or two activities, such as climbing and caving.

2.8 What are the issues associated with quarrying?

Limestone quarrying in the Peak District

As early as Roman times, limestone was quarried in the Peak District. It has many uses including building stone, cement, lime for use in farming, and as **aggregate** (crushed stone) for road building and the construction industry. In 2008 there were 13 active quarries in the Peak District. The amount of limestone extracted from the area has increased from 1.5m tonnes in 1951 to 7.9m tonnes in 2008. This mainly reflects increasing demand for aggregate.

In this section you will learn

the advantages and disadvantages of a quarry.

Key terms

Aggregate: crushed stone made from tough rocks such as limestone, used in the construction industry and in road building.

Case study

Hope Quarry, Castleton

Hope Quarry is one of the largest limestone quarries in the Peak District. It is located on the outskirts of Castleton in the Peak District National Park (map **A**). It supplies 2 m tonnes of limestone a year to the nearby Hope Cement Works, which produces 1.3 m tonnes of cement a year. The cement works was opened in 1929 to exploit the nearby reserves of limestone and shale, both of which are required to make cement.

The quarry and cement works, now owned by the Lafarge Group, employs about 200 local people, many of whom live in nearby Hope. The local economy enjoys huge benefits, as the locally employed people support nearby shops and services. This is called the multiplier effect.

The quarry is estimated to have reserves for another 30 to 35 years and is working to a planned programme of extraction and restoration.

Quarrying and the environment

In 1951 the Peak District National Park was designated. It is the responsibility of the Park Authority to strike a balance between the conservational needs of the environment and the economic and social needs of the area.

Key
- • Caves open to public
- ⌗ Caravan site
- ▲ Camp site
- ≈ Minor road
- ⋈⋈ Railway
- — Contour (heights in metres)

A Location map of Hope Quarry

Hope Quarry is a huge hole in the ground (photo **B**) and it has a massive visual impact on the landscape. Several initiatives have been undertaken to minimise the effects of the quarry and the cement works on the environment:

Did you know ??????

In 2003 Hope Cement Works started to use chipped tyres as a fuel to preserve fossil fuels and recycle materials.

- Landscaping and tree planting have reduced the visual impact of the quarry.
- Efforts have been made to reduce dust.
- Some £20m has been spent to improve transport. Rail is used rather than road to reduce the impact of heavy traffic. A single train is equivalent to 57 lorries.
- Hope Cement Works produces 1m tonnes of carbon dioxide a year but, in 2003 in an attempt to offset some of this, 7,000 trees were planted.
- One old quarry area is now managed as a wetland reserve.
- In 2010 Lafarge were granted permission to burn processed sewage pellets (PSP) as a sustainable fuel in the cement works. This will reduce **carbon emissions**.

B   *Hope Quarry*

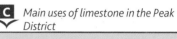

C   *Main uses of limestone in the Peak District*

Use	%
Aggregate	56
Cement	23
Chemicals	17
Iron and steel	4

Study tip

Be aware of the various advantages and disadvantages of quarrying. Facts and figures from case studies help to reinforce your argument.

Key terms

Carbon emissions: release of carbon (usually in the form of carbon dioxide) often by burning fossil fuels.

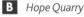

Activities

1   Study table **C**.
  a   Draw a pie graph to present the information in the table.
  b   What is aggregate and what is it used for?
  c   Why has the demand for aggregate increased in recent years?
  d   Why is limestone extracted from Hope Quarry?
  e   What factors will determine how long limestone continues to be extracted from the quarry?

2   Work in pairs or small groups for this activity.
  a   Draw a table with two columns. At the top of one column write the heading 'Benefits of quarrying' and at the top of the other 'Problems caused by quarrying'.
  b   With reference to Hope Quarry and the cement works, complete the table using the text and the resources in this section. Consider the economic (money), social (people) and environmental impacts of quarrying.
  c   On balance, do you think quarrying should be allowed to continue at Hope Quarry or should it be stopped? Give reasons for your answer.

links

The Virtual Quarry site offers a great deal of related information at **www.virtualquarry.co.uk/text/textlimestonelandscapes.htm**.

The Peak District National Park has a quarrying factsheet available at **www.peakdistrict.gov.uk**. Search for 'education factsheets'.

2.9   How can quarries be restored?

Quarrying has the potential to create tremendous environmental damage. Apart from the visual impact, quarrying can cause pollution of rivers and underground aquifers and can destroy habitats when trees and vegetation are removed.

There are now strict environmental controls on quarrying, both during the operation phase and after the resource is exhausted. Quarrying companies are expected to restore or improve on the original environmental qualities of the area. This is called **quarry restoration**.

Quarry restoration can begin while work is still in progress. Parts of a quarry that have been exhausted can be restored while other parts continue to be worked. However, most of the environmental repair work takes place when quarrying operations have ceased completely.

There are many uses for exhausted quarries. They can be restored to farmland by having the topsoil replaced. They can create interesting undulating courses for motocross or mountain bikes. Waste tips can be used as dry ski slopes. Often quarries contain lakes and these are ideal for wildlife reserves, fishing or water sports.

In this section you will learn

the options for quarry restoration during extraction and after the resource has been exhausted.

Key terms

Quarry restoration: restoring or improving the environment of a quarry, either during its operation or afterwards.

Did you know ??????

The National Watersports Centre near Nottingham is the site of an old quarry.

Case study

Restoration during extraction

Drayton Sand and Gravel Quarries are located near Chichester in West Sussex. There are two quarries: Drayton North and Drayton South. Drayton North has been worked for some time and the site is now being extended to incorporate Drayton South.

A *Quarry restoration at Drayton Quarries, Chichester*

Even before extraction started on the new site, restoration had begun. This involved planting hedgerows and creating an avenue of oak trees in between the two quarries. Much of the site is waterlogged and it will be worked wet to retain and deepen the existing lake.

When quarrying has been completed, an extensive lake covering some 15 ha will have been created. It will have reed beds, deep and shallow areas to provide a range of habitats and small islands. The edges of the lake will be grassland and woods (photo **A**). Nesting boxes will be sited to encourage birds into the area. The operators expect to have increased biodiversity in an area that was previously species-poor intensive farmland.

Restoration after extraction

Hollow Banks Quarry is a 20 ha quarry near Catterick, North Yorkshire where sand and gravel were extracted between 1999 and 2003. Soon after the quarry closed in 2003, the owners Tarmac Ltd began restoration (photo **B**):

- The site was contoured to create a gently undulating landscape with small ponds bordered by grass and woodland.
- After soil had been added, it was loosened and had stones removed. It was then divided into separate parcels of land, some of which were sown with grasses for pasture (farming) and others established as woodland. By planting a variety of plants and trees, a number of different habitats were created for animals and birds.
- Woodland areas have been fenced to prevent trees being damaged by browsing farm animals.
- Over 20,000 trees and shrubs raised locally were planted during 2004 and 2005.
- Aquatic plants have been planted at the margins of the ponds.
- Footpaths have been established to provide public access to the woods and ponds.

links

The British Cement Association has some good case studies at **www.cementindustry.co.uk**. Look under Sustainability, Our sustainability agenda, Quarry restoration.

Further information on Drayton Quarries is at the West Sussex County Council website at **www.westsussex.gov.uk**. Type 'Drayton quarries' into the search box.

For more information on Tarmac Ltd, go to **www.tarmac.co.uk**.

Study tip

Be prepared to debate various options for quarry restoration.

B   *Restoration of Hollow Banks Quarry, Catterick*

Activities

1 Study photo **B**.

a What is meant by 'quarry restoration'?

b What is the evidence that restoration has taken place here?

c Describe the different habitats that will exist in a few years' time.

d Do you think it is important to provide public access to this site? Explain your answer.

e For what reasons do you think people might wish to visit this site in the future?

f Can you suggest any other improvements that could be made?

2 Study photo **B** on page 51. Suggest how Hope Quarry could be restored over the remaining 30 to 35 years of its productive life. Consider options that will restore the environment and provide amenity land for local people and visitors. Include a plan or simple sketch to illustrate your proposed restoration.

The **climate** of the UK is largely influenced by its global position (diagram **A**). It lies in an atmospheric battleground between warm tropical air and cold polar air. As the two distinctly different types of air battle one another for control over the mid-latitudes, the UK experiences contrasting and changeable **weather** conditions as a result.

The global position of the UK also affects the relative position of the sun in the sky and the impact of the seasons. Unlike places nearer to the Equator, we experience significant differences in the relative position of the sun during the year. During the summer, the sun is high in the sky bringing long periods of potential warm sunshine. Occasionally the high temperatures can trigger **convectional rainfall**, resulting in thunderstorms. During the winter, our global position results in a much lower-angled sun. This is less powerful and accounts for much lower winter temperatures.

A number of other factors control our climate:

- Ocean currents – a warm ocean current called the North Atlantic Drift is a major driving force, particularly in the winter when it results in much milder conditions than would otherwise be expected for our **latitude**.

- **Prevailing winds** – the North Atlantic Drift coincides with the south-westerly prevailing winds in the UK. This accounts for our relatively mild but damp climate, with winds mostly approaching the UK from a warm ocean.

- **Maritime influence** – the sea has a significant effect on the climate of the UK. Being an island, the air over the UK tends to be humid. This explains the relatively high amounts of rainfall together with the predominantly cloudy weather we tend to experience.

- **Continentality** – inland areas away from the influence of the sea tend to be drier than the coast. In summer, energy from the sun (insolation) heats up the land more rapidly than the sea. This explains the higher summer temperatures inland. In winter, the land loses heat more rapidly and this accounts for colder winters inland.

- **Altitude** – upland areas tend to record higher amounts of **precipitation**, as air is forced to rise up and over them (diagram **B**). Temperatures decrease with altitude, which is why it is often colder in upland areas.

In this section you will learn

the difference between weather and climate

the characteristics and factors affecting the climate of the UK.

A Factors affecting the climate of the UK

Key terms

Climate: the average weather conditions recorded over a period of at least 30 years.

Weather: the day-to-day conditions of the atmosphere involving, for example, temperature, cloud cover and wind direction.

Convectional rainfall: intense rainfall often in the form of thunderstorms resulting from very high temperatures and rapidly rising and cooling air.

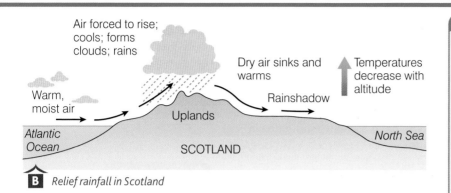

Air forced to rise; cools; forms clouds; rains

Dry air sinks and warms

Temperatures decrease with altitude

Warm, moist air

Rainshadow

Uplands

Atlantic Ocean

North Sea

SCOTLAND

B *Relief rainfall in Scotland*

Characteristics

The maps in **C** show some of the characteristics of the climate of the UK. Take time to study the key for each of the maps and look closely at the overall patterns and some of the anomalies (exceptions to the general rule). Note the features listed overleaf.

Key terms

Latitude: determines the geographic north-south position of a point on the earth. 0° is at the Equator and 90° are at the poles.

Prevailing winds: the dominant wind direction.

Maritime influence: the influence of the sea on climate.

Continentality: the influence of the sea on climate. Inland areas well away from the coast have a continental climate.

Altitude: height above sea level, usually given in metres.

Precipitation: the transfer of water from the atmosphere to the ground, for example rain and snow.

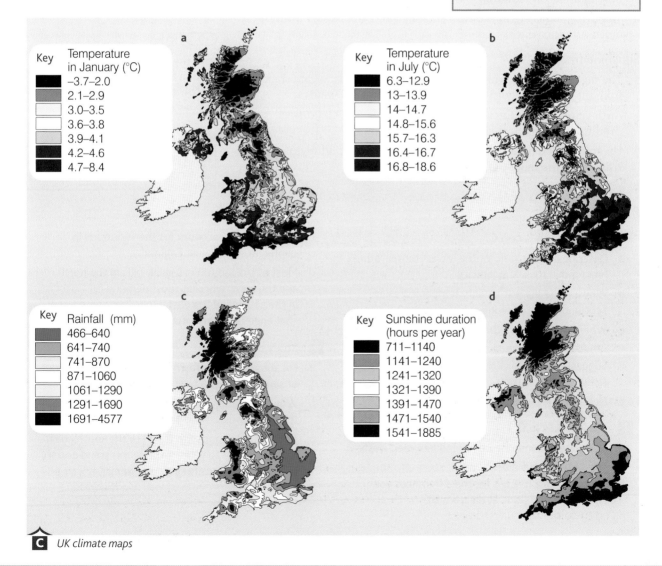

a

Key	Temperature in January (°C)
	−3.7–2.0
	2.1–2.9
	3.0–3.5
	3.6–3.8
	3.9–4.1
	4.2–4.6
	4.7–8.4

b

Key	Temperature in July (°C)
	6.3–12.9
	13–13.9
	14–14.7
	14.8–15.6
	15.7–16.3
	16.4–16.7
	16.8–18.6

c

Key	Rainfall (mm)
	466–640
	641–740
	741–870
	871–1060
	1061–1290
	1291–1690
	1691–4577

d

Key	Sunshine duration (hours per year)
	711–1140
	1141–1240
	1241–1320
	1321–1390
	1391–1470
	1471–1540
	1541–1885

C *UK climate maps*

Temperature in January (map a):

- In winter, the warmest parts of the UK are to the west and the south where the North Atlantic Drift has a big influence.
- The coldest areas are in the north where the sun is at a lower angle in the sky. It is particularly cold over the mountains due to the effect of altitude.
- Cold polar air moving south is likely to have a greater influence in the north of the UK than in the south.
- The sea warms up the coastal fringe of the UK.

Temperature in July (map b):

- In summer, the warmest places are in the south. Here the sun is more powerful than in the north.
- Warm air from southern Europe often nudges into the south of the UK during the summer.

Precipitation, or rainfall (map c):

- The prevailing south-westerly winds explain the relatively high precipitation values in western areas. Note also the effect of the upland areas on rainfall.
- The driest areas are in the east, sheltered by the uplands from the moist Atlantic winds.

Sunshine (map d):

- The highest sunshine values are in the south and east, again sheltered from the relatively moist and cloudy south-westerly winds.
- **Anticyclones** from the south that bring stable and cloud-free conditions often affect coastal areas in the south.
- Upland areas tend to have less sunshine than lowland regions as air rising over the mountains cools to form clouds.

Study tip

Take time to study the patterns on the climate maps. It will extend your knowledge if you are able to describe and explain these patterns on similar maps.

Did you know ??????

The highest temperature ever recorded in the UK was 38.5°C at Faversham in Kent on 10 August 2003 during the European heatwave. The lowest recorded temperature was −27.2°C, which was recorded at Altnaharra in the Scottish highlands on 30 December 1995.

links

Visit the Met Office education section on UK climate at **www.metoffice.gov.uk/education/teens**.

Key term

Anticyclone: an area of high atmospheric pressure.

Activities

1 Study maps **a** & **b** in **C**.

a Describe and account for the lowest temperatures recorded in the UK in January.

b Why are the highest January temperatures in Scotland recorded along the west coast?

c Where in the UK are the highest January temperatures recorded?

d Suggest reasons for the location of the highest January temperatures.

e Describe the pattern of UK temperatures in July.

2 Study map **c** in **C**.

a Compare the amounts of rainfall between western and eastern Scotland.

b Try to suggest reasons for the differences you have described (look at diagram **B**).

c Using an atlas, account for the variations in rainfall in south-west England.

d Most of the rainfall in the UK falls in the north and the west, whereas most demand for water is in the south and the east. How does this present challenges for water management in the UK?

3 Study map **d** in **C**.

a Locate your home town or city. How many hours of sunshine do you receive on average each year?

b Why do upland areas tend to receive less sunshine than lowlands?

c Many people choose to travel to the south coast for holidays or to retire. Explain this trend and try to suggest reasons for your answer.

3.2   What causes the weather in the UK?

The formation and development of depressions

A **depression** is an area of low atmospheric **pressure**. In a depression, air is rising and this leads to the formation of cloud and rain. In the UK most of our weather is associated with the passage of depressions which, having formed over the Atlantic, pass across the UK from west to east driven by the prevailing winds. Winds in a depression in the northern hemisphere circulate in an anticlockwise direction.

Depressions are isolated storms that form at the boundary of cold polar air moving south and warm tropical air moving north. This boundary is called the polar **front** (diagram **A**). Once formed, the depression intensifies and starts to rotate, with air spiralling upwards to form cloud and rain.

In this section you will learn

the formation and development of a depression
the sequence of weather associated with a depression
the characteristics of an anticyclone and the contrasting weather conditions between winter and summer.

Key terms

Depression: an area of low atmospheric pressure.

Pressure (atmospheric): pressure exerted on the Earth's surface by the mass of the overlying atmosphere.

Front: a boundary between warm and cold air.

Warm front: a boundary with cold air ahead of warm air.

Cold front: a boundary with warm air ahead of cold air.

Occluded front: a front formed when the cold front catches up with the warm front.

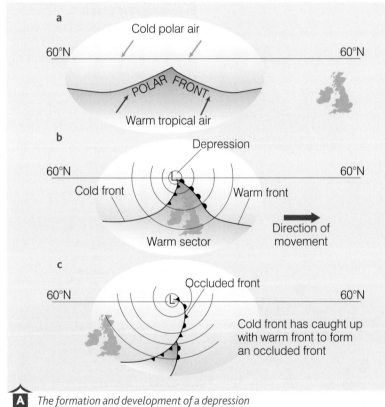

A *The formation and development of a depression*

The boundaries between the warm and the cold air are called fronts (diagram **A**). The **warm front** marks the front of warmer air and the **cold front** represents the front of colder air. At these fronts air is forced to rise, often forming distinct bands of cloud and rain. Over time the cold front catches up with the warm front to form a single boundary called an **occluded front**. Eventually the depression fizzles out and dies.

Look at satellite photo **B**. It shows a satellite image of an intense depression over the UK in 1998. Look closely at the labels to see the main features of the depression.

B *Satellite image of a depression, 26 December 1998*

■ Weather associated with depressions

When a depression passes over the UK it brings a sequence of weather conditions. Look at satellite photo **C**. There is a depression centred off Northern Ireland to the west coast of Scotland. The warm front stretches through the North Sea and the cold front runs through the centre of England. Note on chart **D** that weather symbols have been used to describe the weather at a number of locations. The symbols are explained in the key (**E**).

Ahead of the warm front, conditions slowly become cloudier before a prolonged period of steady rain sets in (diagram **F** and table **G**). Behind the warm front the temperature increases in the **warm sector**. It remains cloudy with patchy rain and drizzle. The cold front brings a short period of heavy rain, often accompanied by strong and gusty winds. Behind the cold front the temperature drops sharply. The rain stops but heavy showers may occur. A frontal system similar to the one in diagram **D** would usually take between 12 and 18 hours to cross the UK.

> **Key terms**
>
> **Warm sector:** an area of warm air between a warm front and a cold front.

> **Did you know** ??????
>
> On 29 January 2008 a cold front caused temperatures to drop from +6°C to −23°C in a few hours at La Crosse in Minnesota, USA.

C Satellite image, 1800 hours, 4 January 2008

D Depression off Northern Ireland: 1800 hours, 4 January 2008

1000 Isobars – lines of equal pressure (values in millibars)
The closer the isobars, the stronger the wind

X — Y Cross-section through the frontal system

Wind direction

Indicates a north-westerly wind direction

Fronts

●●● Warm front
▲▲▲ Cold front
▲●▲● Occluded front

Station model

Temperature
4 — Cloud cover
● Precipitation
Wind speed and direction

Pressure

1000 Isobars are drawn at intervals of 4 mb

Temperature

4   Given in °C

Cloud symbols

○ Clear sky
◔ Sky ⅛ covered
◑ Sky ⅔ covered
◑ Sky ⅜ covered
◐ Sky ¼ covered
◕ Sky ⅝ covered
◑ Sky ⅚ covered
◕ Sky ⅞ covered
● Sky ⅞ covered
⊗ Sky obscured

Wind speed

Symbol	Wind speed (knots)	Force
◎	Calm	0
⟋○	1–2	1
⟋○	3–7	2
⟍○	8–12	3
⟍○	13–17	4

For each additional half feather, add 5 knots or an extra force

Weather symbols

⌇ Thunderstorm
● Rain
❜ Drizzle
✳ Snow
✲ Rain and snow
△ Hail
▽ Shower
═ Fog
≡ Mist

E Weather symbols

F *Cross section through a depression*

G *Weather associated with the passage of a depression*

	Cold sector	Passage of the cold front	Warm sector	Passage of the warm front	Ahead of the warm front
Pressure	Continues to rise	Starts to rise	Steadies	Continues to fall	Starts to fall steadily
Temperature	Remains cold	Sudden drop	Quite mild	Continues to rise	Quite cold, starts to rise
Cloud cover	Clouds thin with some cumulus	Clouds thicken (sometimes with large cumulonimbus)	Cloud may thin and break	Cloud base is low and thick (nimbostratus)	Cloud base drops and thickens (cirrus and altostratus)
Wind speed and direction	Winds are squally	Speeds increase, sometimes to gale force, sharp change in wind direction	Remain steady	Wind changes direction and becomes blustery with strong gusts	Speeds increase
Precipitation	Showers	Heavy rain, sometimes hail, thunder or sleet	Rain turns to drizzle or stops	Continues, and sometimes heavy rainfall	None at first, rain closer to front, sometimes snow on leading edge

Activities

1 Study diagram **D**.

a Describe the weather experienced at weather station **A**.

b Why is it raining at **A**?

c Describe the weather experienced at **B**.

d Why is it much colder at **B** than at **A**?

e What is the weather like in the warm sector?

2 Draw simple sketches to show what the following weather features would look like on a satellite image (photo **C**):

- a front
- the centre of a depression
- showers.

3 Place the following statements in their correct order to describe the weather associated with the passage of a depression (diagram **F**):

- short period of heavy rain and gusty winds
- cloud gradually thickens and sun becomes hazy
- cold and showery
- warm and cloudy with light patchy rain
- prolonged period of steady rain.

Study tip

You should learn the cross section and the sequence of weather associated with the passage of a depression. Make sure you can recognise features on a weather chart or satellite image.

∞ links

The Met Office has regular updated weather charts and satellite images at **www.metoffice.gov.uk**.

■ The characteristics of anticyclones

An anticyclone is an area of high atmospheric pressure caused by air sinking towards the ground surface. The sinking air stops pockets of air from rising. Rainfall is unlikely and for much of the time the conditions are clear and sunny. Winds in an anticyclone in the northern hemisphere circulate in a clockwise direction.

In the winter the clear, cloudless conditions result in sunny and crisp days (photo **H**). At night, heat from the ground is lost rapidly due to the absence of a blanket of cloud. This can lead to **frosty** nights. Surrounded by sea, the air over the UK is often moist. Under cold conditions this moist air readily condenses to form low cloud and **fog**. Sometimes these overcast and rather depressing conditions (known as 'anticyclonic gloom') can last for several days at a time.

In the summer, the sun is more powerful and it is able to burn off any low cloud and fog. This often leads to warm and sunny days, typical of summer (photo **I**).

> ### Key terms
>
> **Frost:** the result of water vapour condensing and freezing when the temperature of the ground or of the air drops below 0°C.
>
> **Fog:** water that has condensed close to the ground to form a dense low cloud with poor visibility.

H *Typical winter's day under the influence of an anticyclone*

I *Warm sunny day during a summer anticyclone*

Case study

Winter anticyclone, 2 February 2006

At the end of January and into the start of February 2006, a large anticyclone became established over the UK (chart **K**). It contained a great deal of moisture and, with the low winter temperatures and little wind (see how the isobars are far apart), it resulted in dull and overcast conditions with mist and fog (satellite photo **J**). If the air had been drier continental air, conditions would have been different with cold, crisp and sunny days and frosty nights.

J *Foggy weather associated with anticyclone*

K *Synoptic chart of winter anticyclone, 2 February 2006*

Summer anticyclone, 24 July 2008

In mid-July 2008 an anticyclone settled to the east of the UK (satellite photo **L**). With air circulating around the anticyclone in a clockwise direction, this introduced warm easterly winds to much of the UK. Map **M** shows the weather experienced in the UK on 24 July 2008. Note the following points:

- There is very little cloud in the centre of the anticyclone. This is because air is sinking, suppressing cloud formation.

- There is more cloud at the edge of the anticyclone where conditions are slightly less settled. This accounts for the cloudier weather in south-west England and Wales.

- The lack of cloud in the summer accounts for the high temperatures in much of the UK.

- Although the easterly winds have brought warm and dry air to much of southern England, note that it is cooler and cloudier over parts of the north-east coast. This is because the wind has travelled over the cooler (and wetter) North Sea.

L   *Satellite image of summer anticyclone, 24 July 2008*

M   *Weather chart of summer anticyclone, 24 July 2008*

Activities

4   Study chart **K** and satellite photo **J**.

a   What was the pressure at the centre of the anticyclone and where in the UK was it recorded?

b   What is the evidence on the synoptic chart that explains why the winds were light across the UK?

c   Which parts of the UK were most affected by low cloud and foggy conditions?

d   Where would you have travelled to see some sunshine?

e   Describe some of the typical weather experienced by a winter anticyclone in the UK.

5   Study satellite photo **L** and map **M**.

a   Using an atlas, suggest the location of the centre of the anticyclone.

b   Why is there so little cloud in the centre of the anticyclone?

c   Describe and explain the weather experienced in south-east England.

d   Why did the coast of north-east England experience different weather from that in the south-east?

e   How does the weather around the edge of the anticyclone contrast with the weather experienced at the centre?

6   Use the information in this section, together with internet research, to find out about the effects of anticyclonic weather on agriculture (consider frost, drought, sunshine, excessive heat), health (consider the effects of extreme heat and cold) and transport (consider ice, fog and snow). Try to refer to both positive and negative impacts.

3.3 Is the weather in the UK becoming more extreme?

Extreme weather events

In recent years there have been a number of **extreme weather** events in the UK:

- 2003 – Europe suffered from an intense heatwave (photo **A**) and the UK recorded its highest ever temperature of 38.5°C in Kent.

- 2007 – several people were killed and many thousands left homeless following floods that inundated towns and river valleys across the UK. In the north, Hull and Sheffield were badly hit. The village of Toll Bar near Doncaster was particularly badly affected, with some people being unable to return to their homes for over a year. In the south of the UK, several rivers burst their banks. Flooding was particularly serious along the River Severn, affecting Tewkesbury and parts of Gloucester. Vast areas of farmland were flooded, destroying crops and drowning livestock, and several major roads including the A38 were impassable.

- 2008 – during a very wet summer there were several flooding incidents caused by torrential rain landing on already saturated ground. In May parts of Somerset were flooded and in September rivers burst their banks in south Wales, Worcestershire and Northumberland, flooding hundreds of properties. The town of Morpeth in north-east England was particularly badly affected.

- 2009 – there were heavy February snowfalls affecting most of Great Britain and Ireland with the Bristol Channel and the South West being the most severely affected. Over 55cm of snow fell on Okehampton in Devon. Around 20cm settled in parts of London which is unusual for the capital. Widespread disruption was caused to public transport including the temporary closure of Heathrow Airport. In November, extreme flooding in the Lake District resulted from prolonged and heavy rainfall (see Cockermouth case study on p114).

- 2010 – severe winter weather in two waves hit the UK unusually early in December. The exceptionally low temperatures and considerable snowfall caused widespread disruption. Northern Ireland hit a record low temperature of −18.7 °C at Castlederg on 23 December.

Key terms

Extreme weather: a weather event such as a flash flood or severe snowstorm that is significantly different from the average.

Global warming: an increase in world temperatures as a result of the increase in greenhouse gases (carbon dioxide, methane, CFCs and nitrous oxide) in the atmosphere brought about by the burning of fossil fuels, for example.

Climate change: long-term changes in the climate, such as cooling leading to an Ice Age or the current trend of global warming.

A *A forest fire caused by the 2003 European heatwave*

■ Links to global warming and climate change

Some people, particularly in the media, have linked these recent extreme weather events (particularly the European heatwave of 2003) to **global warming**. Although extreme weather events may become more frequent as the atmosphere warms up, no individual event can be blamed on global warming. Evidence would have to be drawn from a much longer period of time – hundreds of years – before any reliable links can be made.

> *'You can say that due to the Earth getting warmer there will be on average more extreme events,' said Malcolm Haylock of the University of East Anglia's Climate Research Unit, UK, 'but you can't attribute any specific event to climate change.'*
>
> *Source: BBC*

Did you know ??????

An estimated 1,422m litres of water flowed through Boscastle in just two hours during the flood of 2004. This is equal to 21 petrol tanker loads of water every second.

The Boscastle flash flood, 2004

During the afternoon of Monday 16 August, the small picturesque Cornish village of Boscastle (map **B**) was hit by a tremendous thunderstorm. About 200 mm of rain fell in 24 hours, most of it in just five hours. The average rainfall in Boscastle for the whole of August is 75 mm.

This incredible quantity of rainfall poured down the steep-sided valley slopes and swelled the normally small River Valency flowing towards the harbour, causing it to burst its banks. The floodwaters quickly spread across the car park before surging down the narrow streets towards the harbour (photo **C**). Many cars were picked up and carried by the floodwaters. Together with tree trunks and large branches, the cars acted like battering rams smashing into bridges and buildings.

Luckily, no one was killed, but a number of people had to be airlifted to safety.

Case study

N

Key
■ Land over 200 m
■ Land over 100 m

Exmoor
● Barnstaple

DEVON

● **BOSCASTLE**
Bodmin Moor

Dartmoor

● Exeter

CORNWALL

● Plymouth

● Torbay

● Penzance

0   50 km

B *Location of Boscastle*

C The flood in Boscastle

Effects

Although nobody was killed, the flood caused significant short-term and longer-term effects on the village and the local community:

- A total of 58 buildings were flooded, some of which had to be demolished (photo **D**).
- Some 25 business properties were destroyed by the flood.
- A total of 84 wrecked cars were recovered from the harbour and a further 32 were lost, presumably washed out to sea.
- The cost of the damage to Boscastle and the surrounding area where several roads and bridges were damaged is estimated to have been at least £15m.
- Many people – both locals and tourists – were traumatised by the event and suffered increased levels of stress.

In the months that followed the event, buildings were dried out using dehumidifiers and fans and a great deal of rebuilding took place. However, during this time local businesses lost much of their income. By the summer of 2005 several shops and businesses had reopened and tourists had returned.

Planning for the future

Warnings were issued of possible thunderstorms in the Boscastle area. Storms like the one that hit Boscastle are localised and can develop quickly, making them difficult to predict with any degree of accuracy. Once a storm has formed, satellite and radar can be used to monitor and track its development, and warnings can be issued to the public and to the emergency services.

The Met Office has a three-tier system of warnings:

1 Advisory of severe or extreme weather. These advisories are issued well in advance of a potential period of severe or extreme weather. A traffic light system is used (yellow: 'be aware'; amber: 'be prepared'; red: 'take action') to warn people living in areas of the UK deemed to be at risk.

2 Early warnings of severe or extreme weather are issued when there is a 60 per cent or greater confidence that severe weather will occur.

3 A flash warning of severe or extreme weather is issued when there is an 80 per cent or greater confidence that an extreme event will occur in the next few hours.

At each level, the Met Office identifies the areas at risk, the level of risk and the likely duration of the risk.

The Environment Agency is the UK government's body with responsibility for flood management. A dedicated telephone Floodline offers warnings, help and advice to people. It is possible to use the Environment Agency's website to identify 'at-risk' areas based on individual postcodes.

The Boscastle flood event was a 1-in-400-year event. This means that it has a reocurrence rate of once every 400 years.

For an event of such rarity it is simply not cost effective to build expensive flood defences. However, some limited modification to the stream channel and the bridges has been made. People have been allowed to rebuild their homes and their lives with the knowledge that an event of similar magnitude is unlikely to occur again for hundreds of years.

This is the site of a historic building, which was completely destroyed

Youth hostel badly damaged

Fire brigade searching for possible fatalities

Gifts flushed out from nearby shops and deposited here

D *The immediate effects of the Boscastle flood*

∞ links

There are several extreme weather events that would make excellent research projects. The Met Office has a dedicated website at **www. metoffice.gov.uk/education/teens**. Look for relevant headings or enter 'Boscastle' or 'extreme weather' into the search box to find out some useful information.

The Environment Agency flood pages are at **www.environment-agency.gov.uk/homeandleisure/floods**.

Activities

1 Read the case study about Boscastle. Use additional information from the internet if you wish.

a Why was the term 'flash flood' used to describe the weather event in Boscastle?

b Boscastle is situated at the confluence of two rivers, both of which flow through steep valleys. Suggest how these physical factors contributed to the flood event.

c Despite being full of summer visitors, nobody was killed by the flood. Why do you think this was?

2 Study photo **C**. Describe what is happening in the photo.

3 Use photo **D** to help you describe some of the effects of the flood.

4 Write a few sentences outlining the long-term impacts of the flood on the people of Boscastle.

5 The Boscastle flood has a recurrence rate of 1 in 400 years. Do you think it is right that people have been allowed to rebuild their homes and re-establish their businesses or should the area have been completely cleared to prevent similar flood damage occurring in the future?

3.4 What is the evidence for global warming?

The global climate has been changing since the beginning of time and will do so in the future. There have been periods in the geological past when the poles were completely ice-free and other times when ice coverage was much more extensive than it is now. During the **Pleistocene period** (the so-called Ice Age), fluctuating temperatures resulted in cold periods called glacials and warm periods called interglacials (page 124). At the end of the last glacial period about 10,000 years ago, the climate began to warm up. We are living in this post-glacial warm period.

Throughout the last few hundred years, temperatures have continued to fluctuate (graph **A**). During the medieval period, the climate displayed a warming trend. From about 1550 to 1750, there was a period of lower temperatures that became known as the 'Little Ice Age'. These changes took place before there were cars or power stations and can be considered to be completely 'natural'.

Since about 1950, there is evidence of a very steep increase in temperatures. It is this recent dramatic increase in global temperatures that is known as global warming.

In this section you will learn

the principles of climate change and global warming

the debate surrounding the evidence for global warming

the greenhouse effect and its connection with global warming.

Key terms

Pleistocene period: a geological time period lasting from about 2 million years ago until 10,000 years ago. Sometimes this period is called the Ice Age.

A *Global temperature changes, 700–2000*

Assessing the evidence for global warming

Evidence for global warming comes from the direct measurement of temperatures using thermometers (mostly post-1850 as indicated on graph **A**), together with data derived from other sources such as historical records, ice cores and sea-floor sediment samples.

Instrument readings

Measurements recorded directly using thermometers suggest a clear warming trend in the last few decades (graph **B**). Average global temperatures have risen by 0.74°C during the last 100 years and by 0.5°C since 1980. Although scientists have little doubt about the overall trend, there are some factors that might be responsible for causing minor inaccuracies in the data. Site characteristics may change over time, such as the growth of vegetation. This may make comparisons of historical records unreliable.

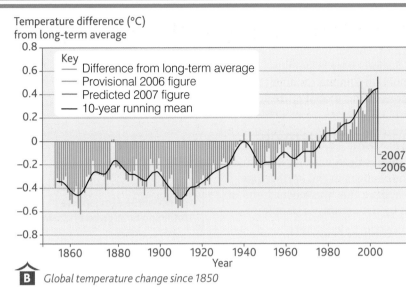

Temperature difference (°C) from long-term average

Key
— Difference from long-term average
— Provisional 2006 figure
— Predicted 2007 figure
— 10-year running mean

2007
2006

Year

B *Global temperature change since 1850*

Glacial retreat

There is strong photographic evidence that many of the world's glaciers have been retreating over the last 50 to 100 years (photo **C**, page 127). In 2001 the World Glacier Monitoring Service reported a significant retreat of glaciers since 1980. It estimates that up to 25 per cent of global mountain glacier ice could disappear by 2050.

Retreat could, however, be caused as much by a reduction in snowfall as by an increase in melting. Some models of global warming even suggest an increase in snowfall, which would be evidenced by glaciers advancing rather than the retreating.

Key terms

Glacial retreat: melting of the ice causes a glacier to retreat up-valley.

Arctic ice cover

Over the last 30 years, the Arctic ice has thinned to almost half its earlier thickness. Permanent ice cover is contracting at a rate of nine per cent each decade and the Arctic could be completely ice-free by the end of the century. As the ice continues to thin, less solar radiation will be reflected back to space. Instead, the darker sea will absorb more radiation, increasing temperatures further.

Ice cores

Some of the most compelling evidence for global warming has been the scientific study of deep ice cores extracted from Greenland and Antarctica (photo **C**). When snow falls year on year, it builds up a record going back thousands of years, just like rings in a tree. Water molecules and trapped air can be analysed to detect subtle changes in temperatures and atmospheric gas concentrations at the time when each layer of snow fell. Scientists from the Antarctic Survey in Cambridge have found clear evidence of a rapid increase in temperature in recent decades.

Early spring

In the last 30 years, there have been many signs of seasonal shifts, with spring in particular seeming to arrive earlier than in the past. Birds are nesting earlier and bulbs such as crocuses and daffodils are flowering earlier. Winters also appear to be less severe, with fewer frosts and days of snow cover.

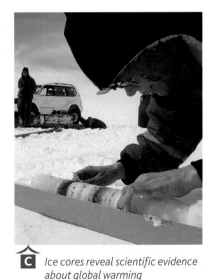

C *Ice cores reveal scientific evidence about global warming*

The directly recorded data, scientific research of stored data and direct observations all point to the same conclusion – that we are currently witnessing an increase in global temperatures. Global warming does appear to be taking place. This is the conclusion overwhelmingly accepted by the UN Intergovernmental Panel on Climate Change (IPCC), now working towards international solutions to this global problem.

Causes of climate change and global warming

Natural climate change is thought to be the result of various shifts and cycles associated, for example, with slight changes in the earth's axis or orbit around the sun. Many scientists believe that the recent trend of global warming is to some extent caused by the actions of people.

One important natural function of the atmosphere is to retain some of the heat lost from the earth. This is known as the **greenhouse effect** (diagram **D**). Without this 'blanketing' effect it would be far too cold for life to exist on earth.

Just like a greenhouse, the atmosphere allows most of the heat from the sun (short-wave radiation) to pass straight through it to warm up the earth's surface. However, when the earth gives off heat in the form of long-wave radiation, some gases such as carbon dioxide and methane are able to absorb it. These gases are called **greenhouse gases** (table **E**). In the same way that panes of glass keep heat inside a greenhouse, the greenhouse effect keeps the earth warm.

Key terms

Greenhouse effect: the blanketing effect of the atmosphere in retaining heat given off from the earth's surface.

Greenhouse gases: gases such as carbon dioxide and methane, which are effective at absorbing heat given off from the earth.

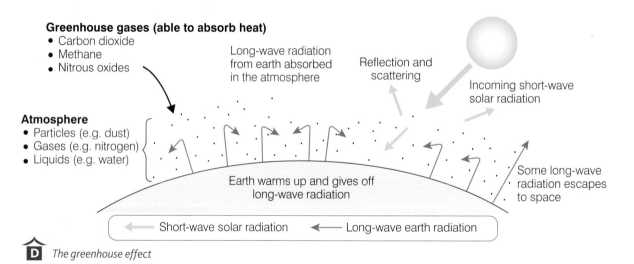

D The greenhouse effect

E Greenhouse gases

Greenhouse gas	Sources
Carbon dioxide: accounts for an estimated 60 per cent of the 'enhanced' greenhouse effect. Global concentration of carbon dioxide has increased by 30 per cent since 1850	Burning fossil fuels (e.g. oil, gas, coal) in industry and power stations to produce electricity, car exhausts, deforestation and burning wood
Methane: very effective in absorbing heat. Accounts for 20 per cent of the 'enhanced' greenhouse effect	Decaying organic matter in landfill sites and compost tips, rice farming, farm livestock, burning biomass for energy
Nitrous oxides: very small concentrates in the atmosphere are up to 300 times more effective in capturing heat than carbon dioxide	Car exhausts, power stations producing electricity, agricultural fertilisers, sewage treatment

Human activities and global warming

In recent years, the levels of greenhouse gases (principally carbon dioxide and methane) have increased (graph **F**) and many scientists believe that this is the result of human activities such as the burning of fossil fuels in power stations, the dumping of waste in landfill sites and burning trees during deforestation.

It is the increased effectiveness of the greenhouse effect that scientists believe is causing global warming. For the first time in history, human activities appear to be affecting the atmosphere with potentially dramatic effects on the world's climate. In 2007 the IPCC stated that global climate change is 'very likely' to have a human cause. It made a prediction that by the end of the 21st century temperatures would rise by between 1.8°C and 4°C and that this would lead to a sea-level rise of 18–59 cm.

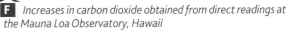

F *Increases in carbon dioxide obtained from direct readings at the Mauna Loa Observatory, Hawaii*

Activities

1 Study graph **B**.

a Describe the changes in temperature from 1850 to 2007, as shown by the 10-year running mean line.

b With reference to graph **A**, suggest why data obtained before 1850 are of limited use in studying climate change.

c Are data obtained directly from thermometers totally reliable?

d How does ice-core analysis provide information about past global temperatures?

e What additional observations support the recent trend of global warming?

f Do you think there is sufficient evidence to support global warming? Justify your answer.

2 Study diagram **D**.

a Make a large copy of the diagram.

b Use table **E** to add the main sources of greenhouse gases to your diagram. Use simple sketches if you prefer.

c Why is the greenhouse effect vital in supporting life on earth?

d Why has the greenhouse effect become more effective in recent years?

3 Study graph **F**.

a Describe the trend of carbon dioxide concentration in the atmosphere.

b Suggest why carbon dioxide in the atmosphere increases in the winter but decreases in the summer. (Hint: think about plants.)

c Does the graph support the suggestion that human activities may be contributing to global warming? Explain your answer.

Study tip

Think about the validity of the evidence for global warming. Connections between observations and global warming may appear obvious but they are not absolutely certain. Learn the diagram showing the greenhouse effect.

∞ links

An excellent summary of global warming can be found on the Met Office's website at **www.metoffice. gov.uk/climate-change**.

The Met Office Hadley Centre for Climate Change is at **www. metoffice.gov.uk/climate-change/ resources/hadley**.

Search for 'climate change' at **www.bbc.co.uk**.

3.5 What are the possible effects of global warming?

In this section you will learn

the possible impacts of global warming in the UK and the world.

Arctic plants in Scotland may face extinction

Droughts and floods will become more likely as extreme weather events become more frequent

Scottish ski resorts could be threatened with closure as snow becomes less common

Windier weather may provide additional power for wind farms

Winter heating costs will go down

Intensive agriculture will be able to spread further north into Scotland

Low-lying Norfolk Broads, worth £5m as a tourist destination, may become flooded

Conifer trees will thrive in Wales and Scotland

Coastal erosion on soft-rock coastlines, such as north Norfolk, will increase

Heat-induced deaths may increase, particularly among the elderly

Sea levels could rise by 26–86 cm by 2080 in the south-east, threatening low-lying coastal areas and cities such as London with flooding

Broad-leaved trees could suffer in drought conditions, especially in Wales

Accidents and disruption to transport will be less likely to occur in the winter, with less snow and ice on the roads

Recently introduced crops such as vines (grapes) and olives may prosper in southern England

Coastal habitats such as salt marshes will become squeezed between the sea and coastal defences as sea levels rise

New crops such as oranges and peaches may be able to be grown in southern Britain

Warm climate diseases such as malaria may spread to the UK

Increased length of growing season promotes farming and increases food supply

Increased demand for water in hotter summers will put added pressure on water supplies

N

Key

Areas less than 5 m above present-day mean sea level, liable to flooding

Gains   Losses

0   200 km

A *Possible impacts of global warming in the UK*

Impacts of global warming in the UK

The Department for Environment, Food and Rural Affairs (Defra) estimates that annual average temperatures in the UK may rise by between 2°C and 3.5°C by 2080. This could have significant effects on the geography of the UK. Temperatures are expected to rise most in the south and east. High summer temperatures will become more common and cold winters are expected to be increasingly rare. Computer models suggest that winters will become wetter and summers drier. The amount of snow is expected to decline.

Map **A** describes some of the possible impacts of global warming on the UK.

Impacts of global warming in the world

Table **B** lists some of the advantages and disadvantages that global warming may have. It is important to remember that these impacts are highly speculative and based on computer models, which may turn out to be inaccurate. Always consider these impacts to be 'possible' rather than 'probable'. Nonetheless, take note that global warming could have very severe impacts indeed.

links

More about global warming can be found at www.defra.gov.uk/environment/climate.

B

Advantages of global warming	Disadvantages of global warming	
■ Frozen regions of the world such as Siberia and northern Canada may be able to grow crops in a milder climate	■ Higher sea levels may flood low-lying areas such as Bangladesh, Myanmar and the Netherlands, threatening the lives of 80 million people	■ Tropical storms affecting the Caribbean and the USA may increase in magnitude
■ Canada's North-west Passage may become ice-free and can be used by shipping	■ Islands such as the Maldives and Tuvalu may completely disappear as sea levels rise	■ Loss of glaciers (fresh water) in the Himalayas may threaten agriculture and water supply in India, Nepal and China
■ Energy consumption may go down as temperatures increase in densely populated parts of the world such as north-west Europe	■ Parts of Africa may become drier and more prone to droughts, leading to starvation and civil war	■ Hazards such as landslides, floods and avalanches may become more common in mountainous areas such as the Alps
■ Fewer deaths or injuries due to cold weather	■ Cereal yields are expected to decrease in Africa, the Middle East and India	■ Arctic ice may melt completely
■ Longer growing season in rich agricultural areas such as Europe and North America will increase food production	■ An additional 220–400 million people may be at risk from malaria, particularly in China and central Asia	■ Some species, whose habitat changes, may become extinct – there is considerable concern about polar bears in the Arctic
		■ Alpine ski resorts may be forced to close due to lack of snow

Activity

Study table **B**.

a Present the information in the table as labels on a blank outline map of the world, in a similar style to map **A**.

b Conduct an internet search to see if you can find some more advantages of global warming. As you can see, there are not very many in table **B**.

c What do you consider to be the three disadvantages that could have the greatest impact on the geography of the world? Explain your answer.

d Which advantage do you think will bring the greatest benefits to the world? Explain why you think this.

3.6 What are the responses to global warming?

Individual and local responses

Faced with the issue of global warming, individuals often feel helpless. How can the actions of one person possibly help to solve a global crisis? Individuals are, however, important as they set the trends for others to follow. They start campaigns and invent new technology. Individual actions include:

- Conserving energy at home by using low-energy light bulbs, switching off electrical appliances, insulating lofts and wearing an extra sweater rather than turning up the heating.
- Walking or cycling to work or school rather than using cars.
- Reducing waste by reusing materials or **recycling** (page 211).
- Buying organic food to reduce the use of chemical fertilisers.
- Paying a carbon offset when making a journey, particularly a flight. Air passengers can pay a voluntary amount to a recognised organisation to offset the carbon emitted by the plane. Most commonly this money is used to plant trees, which absorb carbon dioxide from the atmosphere.

Local authorities are active in trying to reduce carbon emissions:

- They promote public transport by using park-and-ride schemes in towns and cities.
- Grants are available for people to insulate their homes.
- People are encouraged to recycle waste materials at domestic refuse sites and there are separate waste collections for garden waste and recyclables.
- In some cities, such as London and Edinburgh, **congestion charging** has been introduced to discourage cars from entering the city centre (photo **A**). Bus lanes and car-sharing lanes encourage people to save energy by leaving the car at home.

National responses

The UK government has introduced tougher MOT tests on vehicle exhausts and it has set higher road taxes for 'gas-guzzling' vehicles. It supports transport initiatives such as bus lanes and cycleways, and it encourages recycling and waste reduction initiatives. Power stations in the UK have been fitted with filters to reduce emissions.

The government is committed to reducing carbon dioxide emissions by 34 per cent by 2020 and 80 per cent by 2050 (against 1990 levels). In order to meet this aim, it has set a target of producing 30 per cent of electricity using renewable sources by 2020 (in 2005 it was four per cent). To meet these targets, the government is encouraging energy conservation in the home as well as seeking to develop new sources of energy such as wind and wave power.

Key terms

Recycling: using materials, such as aluminium or glass, time and again.

Congestion charging: charging vehicles to enter cities, with the aim of reducing the use of vehicles.

Kyoto Protocol: an international agreement to try to reduce carbon emissions from industrialised countries.

Carbon credits: a means of trading carbon between organisations or countries in order to meet an overall target.

A *Congestion charging in London*

Did you know ??????

In London, most vehicles are charged £10 per day to enter the centre of the city. All of the money raised is used to improve London's transport system.

International responses

On 16 February 2005, after seven years of debate between world leaders, politicians and scientists, the **Kyoto Protocol** became international law. It states that:

- The 37 industrialised countries that have signed the treaty are legally bound to reduce their carbon emissions by an average of 5.2 per cent below their 1990 levels by 2012.

- Of the major greenhouse gas emitters, only the USA and Australia have refused to sign the treaty. Those that have signed it – including Russia – account for over 60 per cent of carbon dioxide emissions. 191 countries had signed the agreement by August 2011.

- The USA has refused to sign on the grounds that the costs of reducing carbon emissions would harm its economy. It is also unhappy that the binding agreement only applies to industrialised countries.

Carbon credits can be used nationally or internationally to trade carbon between organisations or countries. Organisations that have not used up their carbon quota, which are set by national governments, can trade their credit on the open market. Organisations that have exceeded their quota may choose to buy carbon credits (photo **B**) rather than installing expensive equipment. The same principle applies to countries. Overall a balance is achieved and the target can be met.

B   *Tree planting buys carbon credits*

Study tip

Be clear about the different levels of responses to global warming.

C   *Individual, national and international responses to global warming*

Gas	Sources	Individual responses	National responses	International responses
Carbon dioxide				
Methane				
Nitrous oxides				

Did you know ???????

The Durban conference in 2011 agreed to a legally binding deal comprising all countries, including USA, China and India, which will take effect in 2020. There was also progress regarding the creation of a Green Climate Fund distributing US$100 billion per year to help poor countries adapt to climate impacts.

Activity

For this activity you should work in pairs or small groups.

a   Make a large copy of table **C**.

b   Look back at table **E** on page 68 to remind yourself of the sources of the three main greenhouse gases. Write these in your table.

c   Discuss the individual, national and international responses that would lead to reductions in the emissions of each of the gases.

d   Complete your table with your suggestions.

∞ **links**

An excellent summary of the Kyoto Protocol can be found at **www.bbc.co.uk/climate/policies/kyoto.shtml**.

3.7 What is the hurricane hazard?

How are hurricanes formed?

A **hurricane** or tropical cyclone is a deep area of low pressure formed in the Tropics (satellite photo **A**). In other parts of the world it is known as a cyclone (south-east Asia) or a typhoon (Japan and the Philippines). Hurricanes are immensely powerful storms capable of devastating large areas and causing considerable damage to property and loss of life.

Although scientists are not certain what actually triggers a hurricane, they tend to form:

- over warm water (over 26.5°C), which explains why they are found in the Tropics
- in summer and autumn when sea temperatures are at their highest
- at a latitude greater than 5°N or S – any closer to the Equator there is not sufficient 'spin' resulting from the rotation of the earth
- in tropical regions of severe air instability where air is converging on the surface and rising rapidly.

As air rises over a warm ocean, a huge quantity of water is evaporated quickly. As it rises it cools and condenses to form cloud. The cloud condenses and releases latent heat, which serves to power the hurricane. More and more water is drawn up from the ocean, so the clouds continue to grow and the storm intensifies. Several smaller thunderstorms may coalesce (join together) to form one large storm. The rotation of the earth sets up a spinning motion and the storm assumes its characteristic Catherine-wheel shape (satellite photo **A**). When surface winds reach an average of 120 kph (75 mph), the storm officially becomes a hurricane.

In the centre of the growing storm cooler, denser air sinks down towards the ground. This is the '**eye**' of the hurricane (diagram **C**). Here, conditions are deceptively calm and clear. On either side of the eye is a towering bank of cloud called the **eye wall**. It is here that the winds are usually at their strongest and where the heaviest rainfall occurs. Once formed, the hurricane is carried across the ocean by the prevailing winds (map **B**), generally from east to west. As it moves it continues to pick up moisture from the sea, becoming ever more powerful. On reaching land the supply of water – the hurricane's fuel – is cut off and the storm begins to weaken.

In this section you will learn

how hurricanes are formed

the effects of hurricanes, with particular reference to a rich country and a poor country

how to reduce the hurricane hazard.

Key terms

Hurricane: a powerful tropical storm with sustained winds of over 120 kph (75 mph). Also known as a tropical cyclone, a cyclone or a typhoon.

Eye: the centre of a hurricane where sinking air creates clear conditions.

Eye wall: a high bank of cloud either side of the eye where wind speeds are high and heavy rain falls.

Track: the path or course of a hurricane.

A *The distinctive shape of a hurricane in the Caribbean*

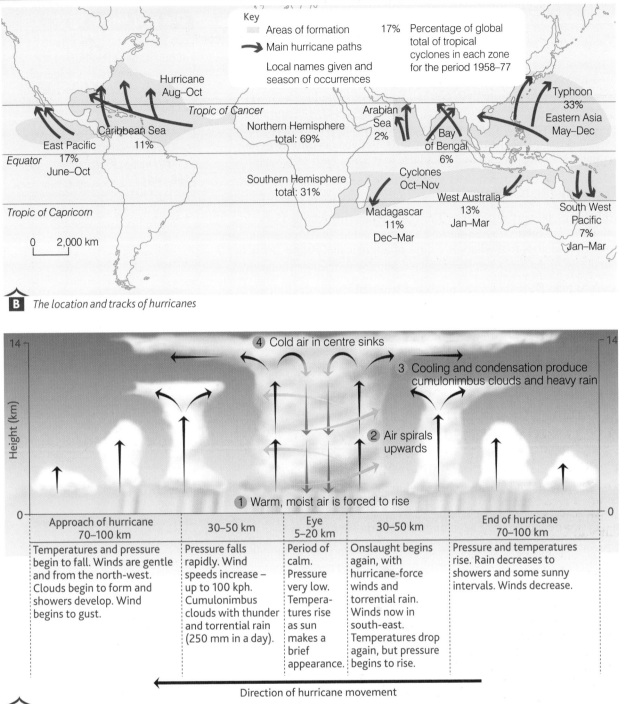

B   *The location and tracks of hurricanes*

C   *The structure of a hurricane (in the northern hemisphere)*

The effects of hurricanes

Hurricanes are capable of causing great destruction. The main causes of destruction are:

- Strong winds – with sustained wind speeds in excess of 120 kph (75 mph) and gusts in excess of 200 kph (125 mph), hurricanes can cause a great deal of damage. Roofs are blown off houses, power lines are torn down. Flimsy houses will be totally destroyed. The damage to crops could have long-lasting economic consequences.

Study tip

Take time to compare and contrast the effects of and responses to hurricanes in rich and poor countries.

- Heavy rainfall – there is the potential for huge amounts of rain to fall, often in excess of 200 mm. This causes widespread flooding as rivers burst their banks. Landslides may be triggered in upland regions.
- Storm surge – a hurricane is an area of intense low pressure. As it moves over the sea, the level of the sea rises as it is under less atmospheric pressure than normal. Driven onshore by the strong winds these high seas, often 3 to 5 m in height, surge inland over low-lying areas and up river valleys. Storm surges are the biggest killers during hurricanes. A storm surge flattens everything in its path. It destroys crops and inundates vast areas with salty water.

Reducing the hurricane hazard

Hurricanes are very distinctive. They can be clearly identified by satellites and their progress tracked and monitored. Previous data enable computer models to predict the course of a hurricane. People living in hurricane-prone areas can be instructed on how to prepare themselves.

Look at map **D**. It shows the predicted **track** of Hurricane Katrina in August 2005. Locate the current position of the hurricane and see how a 'forecast cone' has been drawn ahead of it. Note the two levels of advisory: hurricane watch and the more serious hurricane warning.

Hurricanes tend to be more destructive in poorer parts of the world where communications are less effective. Emergency services are often unable to cope with the aftermath of a hurricane.

Following terrible disasters in Bangladesh (up to 500,000 were killed in 1970 and in 1991 a further 138,000 were killed) several initiatives have been introduced:

- Hurricanes are carefully monitored by the Bangladesh Meteorology Department and warnings are broadcast over the radio.
- Trained wardens help to spread the word in remote villages.
- Cyclone shelters have been built to provide shelter.

In 2007 Cyclone Sidr caused the deaths of 3,000 people in Bangladesh, which, however tragic, is significantly lower than previous death tolls.

Did you know

The impact and after-effects of hurricanes are different for countries at different stages of development. Two hurricanes demonstrate this:

- Hurricane Katrina, 2005 (USA)
- Cyclone Nargis, 2008 (Myanmar (Burma))

See table **E**.

Did you know

The deadliest cyclone was the 1970 Bhola Cyclone, which killed an estimated 500,000 people in Bangladesh.

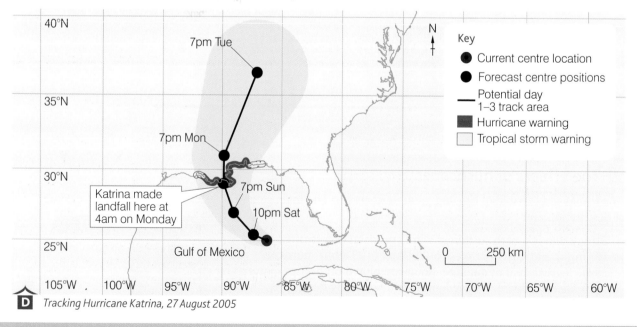

D Tracking Hurricane Katrina, 27 August 2005

E *Comparing Hurricane Katrina and Cyclone Nargis*

Impact	Hurricane Katrina, 2005 (USA)	Cyclone Nargis, 2008 (Myanmar)
Event details	• Sixth most powerful North American hurricane ever recorded. Formed over the Bahamas and then passed over Florida. It intensified in the Gulf of Mexico and made landfall close to New Orleans, Louisiana. Strongest winds recorded were 280 kph. Over 200 mm of rain fell. The system of levees (waterway embankments) failed, resulting in widespread flooding.	• Cyclone developed in the Bay of Bengal in April and made landfall in the south-west of Myanmar on 2 May 2008. • Winds of up to 215 kph battered the coastline. • The Irrawaddy delta region was particularly badly affected by a storm surge.
Deaths	• 1,836 confirmed dead.	• 138,000 confirmed dead.
Homeless	• Hundreds of thousands displaced from their homes; many evacuated.	• Hundreds of thousands were made homeless. • In the Irrawaddy delta region an estimated 95 per cent of all homes destroyed.
Number affected	• 3 million people left without electricity. 80 per cent of New Orleans flooded.	• 2.4 million.
Economic losses	• $89bn (the costliest US hurricane ever).	• Approximately $4bn. 42 per cent of food stocks were destroyed and 200,000 farm animals were killed.
Time for help to arrive	• A few hours.	• The government refused to admit foreign aid and relief workers for several weeks.
Services damaged	• All services (electricity, water, sanitation) severely affected in New Orleans.	• Almost total destruction of services (electricity, telephones, water).
Short-term responses	• Rescuing people from floodwaters; treating injured; providing food, water and shelter for those left in New Orleans.	• Identification and burial of the dead. • Treating the injured. • Providing safe water, food and medicines.
Long-term responses	• Massive rebuilding of New Orleans. • Some evacuees have still not returned. • Strengthening of levees.	• Rebuilding homes and workplaces. • Reclaiming farmland from salty water. • Rebuilding services and transport networks.
Environmental effects	• Floodwaters became severely polluted. • Physical changes to the Mississippi delta. • Some coastal habitats lost or damaged.	• Salt water inundation of farmland and water sources. • Burst sewage pipes caused pollution.
Warnings	• Katrina had been monitored and predictions were accurate. • 80 per cent evacuated. • Public transport closed down ahead of the storm.	• Most people had no idea that the cyclone was approaching.

Activities

1 Study map **B**.

a On a blank map of the world, make a copy of the areas of hurricane formation and the main hurricane paths.

b Use an atlas to label some of the countries most at risk from hurricanes.

c What percentage of hurricanes form in the northern hemisphere?

d Which area of the world spawns the greatest percentage of hurricanes?

e What time of year are hurricanes most likely to affect the Caribbean?

f Why do hurricanes form in the Tropics over oceans?

g Why are there no hurricanes at the Equator?

2 Conduct a research project comparing the impacts of hurricanes in rich and poor countries. You could compare Hurricane Katrina and Cyclone Nargis (table **E**) or choose other examples using the internet. Describe the events and the impacts using maps and photos. Compare the social, economic and environmental impacts of your chosen hurricanes.

An **ecosystem** is a natural system that comprises plants (flora) and animals (fauna) and the natural environment in which they live. There are often complex relationships between the living and non-living components in an ecosystem. Non-living components include the climate (primarily temperature and rainfall), soil, water and light.

Ecosystems can be identified at different scales. A local ecosystem can be a pond (diagram **A**) or a hedge. Larger ecosystems can be lakes or woodlands. It is possible to identify ecosystems on a global scale, such as tropical rainforests or deciduous woodland. These global ecosystems are called **biomes**.

In this section you will learn

the concept of an ecosystem and its key components, such as producers, consumers and food chains

how change can have a considerable effect in an ecosystem.

Case study

The freshwater pond ecosystem

Freshwater ponds provide a variety of habitats for plants and animals (diagram **A**). Note that there are considerable variations in the amount of light, water and oxygen available in different parts of a pond. Animals living at the bottom in deep water need different **adaptations** to those living on the margins of the pond. Certain plants such as water lilies tolerate total immersion by sending their flowering stems to the surface of the water. Reeds and other similar plants are better adapted to being right on the edges as they can tolerate drier conditions.

There are a number of important ecological concepts that you need to understand:

- **Producers** and **consumers** – organisms can be either producers or consumers. Producers convert energy from the environment (typically sunlight) into sugars (glucose). The most obvious producers are plants, which convert energy from the sun by the process of photosynthesis. Consumers obtain their energy from the sugars made by the producers. The grasses at the margins of the pond in diagram **A** are good examples of producers. A pond snail is a good example of a consumer because it eats the plants.

- **Food chain** – this shows the links (hence the term 'chain') between producers and consumers. Diagram **B** shows a food chain that might exist in a typical pond. Note that it is a simple linear series of connections.

- **Food web** – this shows the connections between producers and consumers in a rather more detailed way, hence the term 'web' rather than 'chain' (diagram **C**).

- **Scavengers** and **decomposers** – when living elements (plants and animals) of an ecosystem die, scavengers and decomposers break them down and effectively recycle their nutrients. Scavengers eat dead animals and plants. A rat-tailed maggot is a good example of a freshwater pond scavenger. Flies and earthworms are examples of scavengers found on land. Decomposers are usually bacteria and fungi. They break down the remaining plant and animal material, often returning the nutrients to the soil.

Key terms

Ecosystem: the living and non-living parts of an environment and the interrelationships that exist between them.

Biomes: global-scale ecosystems.

Adaptations: the ways that plants evolve to cope with environmental conditions such as lots of rainfall.

Producers: organisms that get their energy from a primary source such as the sun.

Consumer: organisms that get their energy by eating other organisms.

Food chain: a line of linkages between producers and consumers.

Food web: a diagram that shows all the linkages between producers and consumers in an ecosystem.

Scavengers: organisms that consume dead animals or plants.

Decomposers: organisms such as bacteria that break down plant and animal material.

Nutrient cycling: the recycling of nutrients between living organisms and the environment.

- **Nutrient cycle** – nutrients are foods that are used by plants or animals to grow, such as nitrogen, potash and potassium. There are two main sources of nutrients: rainwater washes chemicals out of the atmosphere and weathered rock releases nutrients into the soil. When plants or animals die, the scavengers and decomposers recycle the nutrients, making them available once again for the growth of plants or animals.

A *Freshwater pond ecosystem*

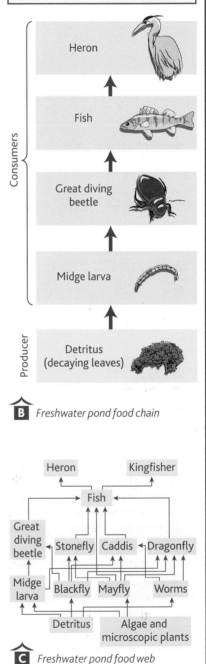

B *Freshwater pond food chain*

The impact of change on the freshwater pond ecosystem

The diversity and relative numbers of the components in an ecosystem can change over time. This can be caused by natural factors such as environmental change (e.g. flood, fire, drought) or human-induced change (e.g. drainage, reclamation, fish stocking). Once a change has occurred it is rarely isolated and often has an impact on other parts of the ecosystem.

If predatory fish are introduced into the pond in diagram **A** they will eat more of the smaller fish and small animals such as frogs. This will affect the numbers of those creatures, which will in turn reduce the amount of food available to creatures further up the food chain. At the same time, with fewer frogs in the pond, numbers of those creatures below frogs in the food chain such as slugs will increase.

C *Freshwater pond food web*

D *Freshwater pond species and energy sources*

Species	Energy source (sunlight or food)
Algae	Sunlight
Dragonfly	Other adult insects
Dragonfly nymph	Tadpoles, young fish, water fleas, beetles
Duck	Water plants, insects, tadpoles, small fish, pond snails
Frog	Insects, water worms, snails
Great diving beetle	Water fleas, midge larvae, pond snails, nymphs, tadpoles, water boatmen
Heron	Fish, frogs and tadpoles, larger insects
Kingfisher	Small fish, tadpoles, small frogs, great diving beetle
Marsh marigold	Sunlight
Midge larvae	Microscopic plants, small particles of dead plants
Perch	Small fish, beetles, water fleas
Pond snail	Large water plants, algae
Rat-tailed maggot	Decaying plants
Reed mace	Sunlight
Sticklebacks	Tadpoles, young fish, water fleas, beetles
Tadpole	Microscopic plants, algae, midge larvae
Water boatmen	Tadpoles, water worms, midge larvae, water fleas
Water flea	Microscopic plants, small particles of dead plants
Water lily	Sunshine
Water worm	Small particles of dead animals

Study tip

It is important that you learn the terminology of ecosystems and understand the principles of change in an ecosystem.

links

Excellent ecosystems links can be found at **www.geography.pwp.blueyonder.co.uk**.

Activities

1 Study diagram **A** and table **D**.

a Identify some producers that live in a freshwater pond.

b From where do these producers obtain their energy?

c Bacteria and fungi are decomposers in a pond ecosystem. Can you name some scavengers?

d Which pond species are at the top level in the food chain, i.e. they are not eaten by any other species in the ecosystem?

e Select one of the species listed in **D** and draw a food chain diagram with your chosen species at the top. Include sunlight in your diagram and add sketches to make it look more interesting.

2 Study diagram **A** and table **D**.

a In pairs, draw a food web for the species shown in diagram **A** and listed in table **D**.

b Identify the producers in your food web.

c Add some simple sketches or photos using the internet if you wish.

3 Study diagram **A** and table **D**.

a Imagine that the landowner cuts down all the vegetation at the side of the pond to create a wooden deck for fishing. How would this affect the ecosystem in the short term and the long term?

b Imagine that disease wipes out all the frogs. How would this affect the ecosystem in the short term and the long term?

c Suggest another change that could happen to this ecosystem and describe the effects that this change might have on the species living in the pond.

4.2 What are the characteristics of global ecosystems?

The distribution of global ecosystems

Global ecosystems are known as biomes. The dominant type of vegetation cover usually defines a biome. Map **A** shows the global distribution of the major world biomes.

The biome in the UK is **temperate deciduous forest**. This is the natural vegetation that would occur in much of the UK in response to climates and soils. It does not mean that the entire country is covered by woodland. However, if no land management took place at all in the UK for 100 years or so, then the landscape would start to revert back to natural deciduous woodland.

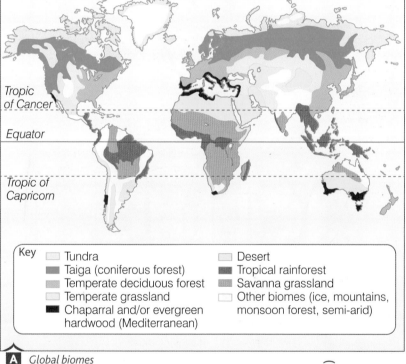

Key
- Tundra
- Taiga (coniferous forest)
- Temperate deciduous forest
- Temperate grassland
- Chaparral and/or evergreen hardwood (Mediterranean)
- Desert
- Tropical rainforest
- Savanna grassland
- Other biomes (ice, mountains, monsoon forest, semi-arid)

A Global biomes

Key term

Temperate deciduous forest: forests made up of broad-leaved trees such as oak that drop their leaves in the autumn.

Temperate deciduous forests

Temperate deciduous forests are found across much of north-west Europe, eastern North America and parts of East Asia. They occur in these regions because they are well suited to the moderate climate (graph **B**). Rainfall is distributed evenly throughout the year, summers are warm but not too dry, winters are cool but not too cold. There is a long growing season lasting up to seven months.

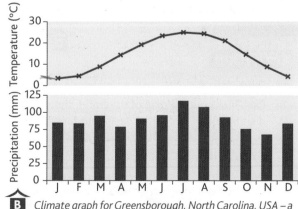

B Climate graph for Greensborough, North Carolina, USA – a temperate deciduous forest biome

Soils that develop under these climatic conditions tend to be rich and fertile. Weathering is active, providing plenty of nutrients, and the annual leaf fall provides organic matter to enrich the soil further. The common soil found in this biome is a brown soil.

Look at photo **C**, which shows oak woodland in southern England. This is typical temperate deciduous woodland. The main feature of the trees in this biome (e.g. oak, beech, birch, ash) is that they shed their leaves in autumn. This is what the term 'deciduous' means. They drop their leaves in response to reductions in light and heat, which enables them to conserve water. Deciduous trees are typically broad-leaved, which means there is a great deal of potential for water loss through the holes (stomata) on the underside of their leaves. Leaf fall comes early in some years if there has been a shortage of water in late spring and summer.

Deciduous woodlands are rich in their diversity of vegetation and they provide a great range of habitats for the many plants and animals that live there (diagram **D**). One typical characteristic of deciduous woodland is the layering or **stratification** of the vegetation:

- The top of the fully grown trees provides a canopy, which acts like an umbrella. The main trees forming this layer are oak and ash.
- Beneath this is a sub-canopy of saplings and smaller trees, such as hazel.
- Below this is a herb layer of brambles, bracken, bluebells, wild garlic and ivy.
- Finally there is a ground layer close to the soil surface. Here, it is damp and dark – ideal conditions for moss to grow.

For much of the year it is quite dark in deciduous woodland, which is not ideal for flowering plants. This helps to explain why bluebells, for example, commonly flower in the early spring before the canopy has fully developed.

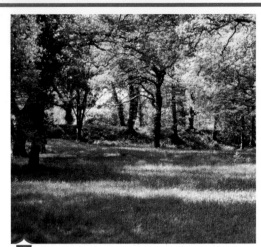

C *A typical oak woodland in southern England*

D *A temperate deciduous forest ecosystem*

Rainfall – carries nutrients

Sunlight

Height (m)

Dominant oak   Ash sapling in gap   Dominant oak

Bramble   Hazel

Hazel

Ivy

Height (m)

0.1 1.0 10 100
Percentage of full sunlight (log scale)

Roots occupy different soil layers

Moss-litter, with herbs in less dense shade

Bare (leaves)

Bracken, bluebells

Herbs

Bedrock: weathered to release nutrients (red arrows) into the soil

Activity

3 Study diagram **D**.

a What is the evidence from the diagram that the temperate deciduous forest supports a great diversity of wildlife?

b What is meant by stratification and how is this exhibited in a deciduous forest? Draw a diagram to support your answer.

c Why do you think stratification exists?

d How have flowers like bluebells adapted to living in a deciduous forest?

Did you know ??????

The tallest tree in the world is a coast redwood found in Redwood National Park, California, which measures an extraordinary 115.55 m. In 2008 scientists claimed to have discovered the oldest tree in the world in Sweden, a Norway spruce said to be 9,550 years old.

■ Tropical rainforests

Tropical rainforests are found in a broad belt through the tropics (map **A**), from Central and South America, through central parts of Africa, in South-east Asia and into the northern part of Australia. This biome is characterised by a plentiful supply of rainfall (over 2,000 mm a year) and high temperatures (averaging 27°C) throughout the year. This climate (graph **E**) provides ideal conditions for plant growth.

Tropical rainforests have extremely lush and dense vegetation. If you were to enter a rainforest, you would need a torch and good shoes as it is dark and damp. The trees in a tropical rainforest grow to be extremely tall, often up to 45 m in height. There is a great variety of species, typically up to 100 in a single hectare. This explains why the wood is such a valuable resource.

As with deciduous woodlands, a tropical rainforest has a clear stratification (diagram **F**). It is interesting to note that, unlike deciduous forests where most plants and animals live close to the forest floor, in a tropical rainforest the majority are found in the canopy where there is maximum light. Some tree leaves are specially adapted to twist and turn to face the sun as it arcs across the sky. In contrast, rainforest floors are often too dark to support many plants.

Tropical rainforests support the largest number of plant and animal species of any biome. The constant environmental conditions of its climate promote plant growth and result in a great variety of food sources and natural habitats. Many birds live in the canopy. Some mammals, such as monkeys, are well adapted to living in the trees. Animals such as deer live on the forest floor eating seeds and berries.

Tropical rainforest soils are surprisingly infertile considering the lush growth of the vegetation. Most of the nutrients are found at the surface where dead leaves decompose rapidly in the hot and humid conditions. Many of the trees and plants have shallow roots to absorb these nutrients and fungi growing on the roots transfer nutrients straight from the air. The heavy rainfall quickly dissolves and carries away nutrients. This is called **leaching**. It leaves behind an infertile red-coloured soil called latosol, which is rich in iron (hence the colour) and very acidic (photo **G**).

Key terms

Stratification: layering of forests, seen particularly in temperate deciduous forests and tropical rainforests.

Tropical rainforests: the natural vegetation found in the tropics, well suited to the high temperatures and heavy rainfall of these latitudes.

Leaching: the dissolving and removal of nutrients from the soil, often in tropical rainforests because of the heavy rainfall.

Arid: dry conditions typically associated with deserts.

Hot deserts: deserts have a rainfall of less than 250 mm per year. Hot deserts are generally found between 30°N and 30°S.

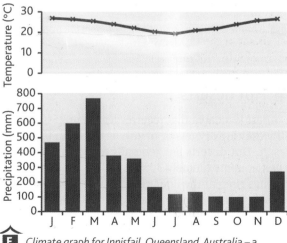

E *Climate graph for Innisfail, Queensland, Australia – a tropical rainforest*

Fast-growing trees such as capoc out-compete other trees to reach sunlight – such trees are called emergents

Many leaves have flexible bases so that they can turn to face the sun

Many leaves have a 'drip tip' to allow the heavy rain to drip off the leaf

Water drips off leaves

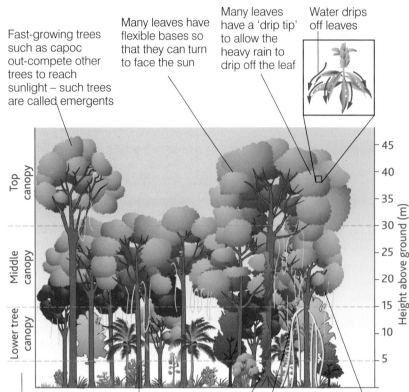

Shrub layer and ground layer

Thin, smooth bark on trees to allow water to flow down easily

Buttresses – massive ridges help support the base of the tall trees and help transport water. May also help oxygen/carbon dioxide exchange by increasing the surface area

Lianas – woody creepers rooted to the ground but carried by trees into the canopy where they have their leaves and flowers

Plants called epiphytes can live on branches high in the canopy to seek sunlight – they obtain nutrients from water and air rather than soil

F *Stratification and vegetation adaptations in a tropical rainforest*

G *Latosol: a typical soil found in the tropical rainforest biome*

⬭⬭ **links**

For more information on plant adaptations in arid environments, go to www.cwnp.org/adaptations.html.

◼ Hot deserts

A desert is an area that receives less than 250 mm of rainfall per year. The resulting dryness or **aridity** is the main factor controlling life in the desert. **Hot deserts** are generally found in dry continental interiors in a belt at approximately 30°N and 30°S. It is at these latitudes where air that has risen at the Equator descends, forming a persistent belt of high pressure (anticyclone). This explains the lack of cloud and rain and high daytime temperatures. It also explains why, with the lack of cloud cover, temperatures can plummet to below freezing at night during the winter.

Desert soils tend to be sandy or stony, with little organic matter due to the general lack of dense vegetation. Soils are dry but can soak up water rapidly after rainfall. Evaporation draws salts to the surface, often leaving a white residue on the ground. Desert soils are not particularly fertile.

Activities

4 Study graph **E**.

a How does the climate of a tropical rainforest compare with that of a temperate deciduous forest?

b How is the climate ideal for the growth of plants?

c How does the climate provide opportunities as well as problems for the plants and animals living in this environment?

5 Study diagram **F**.

a What name is given to the tall trees that break through the canopy?

b How high can the tallest trees grow?

c On the ground in a tropical rainforest, in which layer of the forest would you be in?

d How have the leaves of the tallest trees adapted to gain maximum sunlight?

e Describe how leaves are designed to shed water quickly during torrential downpours.

f What are lianas and how have they adapted to live successfully in tropical rainforests?

g What is a buttress and what are the possible reasons why some trees have them?

h Select and write about one other plant adaptation in a tropical rainforest.

6 Study photo **G**.

a What name is given to a tropical rainforest soil?

b Describe the characteristics of the soil in the photo.

c Why are most of the nutrients found near the surface of the soil?

d How have plants adapted to this?

e What is leaching and why is it a problem?

7 In the past, some people cut down rainforest trees and replaced them with commercial crops expecting a wonderful harvest. Instead, the new plants grew poorly. From what you have learned, explain why this happened.

8 Use the information in fact file **H**, together with your own internet research and the text here, to complete a short research project on desert ecosystems. You should include the following information:

■ Draw a map to show the main areas of hot desert. Use an atlas to name the deserts.

■ Using a climate graph, describe the climatic conditions experienced in hot deserts. Why are hot deserts hostile environments?

■ With the aid of labelled photos or sketches, describe the adaptations of plants and animals to hot desert conditions. A good website to get you started is www.cwnp.org/adaptations.html.

Death Valley, California

	J	F	M	A	M	J	J	A	S	O	N	D
Average temperature (°C)	11	15	19	24	29	35	38	37	32	25	17	10
Average precipitation (mm)	0.8	1.2	0.8	0.4	0.2	0.1	0.3	0.2	0.4	0.3	0.6	0.4

Plant adaptations

1 Desert yellow daisy – small linear leaves that are hairy and slightly succulent.

2 Great basin sagebrush – tap roots up to 25 m long and small needle-like leaves to reduce water loss.

3 Giant saguaro cactus – roots very close to the surface so that it can soak up water before it evaporates. Outside skin is pleated so that it can expand when water is soaked up. Grows very slowly.

4 Joshua tree – needle-like leaves coated with a waxy resin.

 1

 2

 3

4

H *Desert ecosystem fact file*

4.3 What are temperate deciduous woodlands used for?

Epping Forest, Essex

Epping Forest is an ancient deciduous forest that runs north-east of London on a high gravel ridge. It covers an area of about 2,500 ha and is about 19 km long and 4 km wide. It is the largest area of public open space near London.

Although 70 per cent of Epping Forest is deciduous woodland (mostly beech), there are a number of other natural environments including grasslands and marshes. It is home to a rich variety of wildlife including all three native species of woodpeckers and wood-boring stag beetles. Fallow deer still roam the forest.

Early uses and management

Since Norman times, kings and queens of England have used Epping Forest for hunting deer. Local people ('commoners') were able to use the forest to graze their animals and to collect wood for firewood and building.

For many years the practice of **pollarding** was used to manage the woodland. This involves cutting the trees at about shoulder height, above the level of browsing by animals such as deer (photo **A**). Pollarded trees reshoot at this height, thereby producing new wood for future cutting. This is a good example of **sustainable management** as it ensures a supply of wood for future generations. It also accounts for the presence of some ancient trees because, rather than being felled for timber, they were pollarded.

As royal use declined in the 19th century, local landowners made attempts to buy parts of the forest. In response to this threat, in 1878 the Epping Forest Act of Parliament was passed in which it was stated that 'the Conservators shall at all times keep Epping Forest unenclosed and unbuilt on as an open space for the recreation and enjoyment of the people'.

Since 1878 the Forest has been managed by the City of London Corporation.

Recent management

Epping Forest is an excellent example of a natural deciduous forest that is being managed sustainably for the future. Over 1,600 ha of the forest has been designated a Site of Special Scientific Interest and a European Special Area of Conservation. This offers protection under law to its large number of ancient trees, which support a vast variety of flora and fauna.

A *An ancient pollarded tree, Epping Forest*

The overall planning responsibility of Epping Forest lies with the City of London Corporation, which produces management plans to ensure that the forest continues to provide open space for the public while conserving the natural environment. Planning measures adopted include the following:

- managing recreation by providing appropriate car parks, toilets and refreshment facilities and by maintaining footpaths (photo **B**)

In this section you will learn

the various uses of a temperate deciduous forest

how deciduous forests can be managed sustainably.

Key terms

Pollarding: cutting off trees at about shoulder height to encourage new growth.

Sustainable management: a form of management that ensures that developments are long lasting and non-harmful to the environment.

⚭ links

Further information about Epping Forest can be found at **www.bbc.co.uk**. Type 'Epping forest' into the search box.

The Epping Forest Information Centre can be found at High Beach, Loughton, Essex IG10 4AF.

Did you know ?????

Epping Forest is a renowned location for the rare stag beetle due to the presence of dead and decaying wood. The stag beetle is one of several species of wildlife that are considered to be rare or endangered.

Study tip

Take time to learn the various measures of sustainable management that have been adopted, both past and present.

- providing three easy-access parks to allow access for people with disabilities
- allowing old trees to die and collapse naturally unless they are dangerous
- controlling some forms of recreation, such as riding and mountain biking, which may damage or affect other forms of recreation
- preserving ancient trees by re-pollarding them to enable new shoots to grow – since 1981, over 1,000 ancient trees have been re-pollarded
- encouraging grazing to maintain the grassland and the flora and fauna associated with it
- preserving ancient earthworks and buildings
- maintaining ponds to prevent them silting up
- preserving the herd of fallow deer.

B *Recreation in Epping Forest*

Key
- Non-coniferous trees
- P Car park
- 0 — 500 m

C *1 : 25,000 OS map extract of Epping Forest, part of map sheet 174.*

Activities

1 Study photo **A**.

a What is meant by pollarding? Draw a sketch of the tree in the photo to illustrate your answer.

b Why are trees pollarded?

c Why is pollarding an example of sustainable management?

d How does pollarding lead to the survival of ancient trees?

e Suggest why trees are being re-pollarded today.

2 Study map extract **C**.

a Identify the different types of natural environment.

b What are the attractions and opportunities for recreation?

c Suggest any conflicts that might arise between people visiting Epping Forest.

d Why do you think it is important to have properly designated car parking?

e You may have noticed that there is a field study centre. Why is this a good location for an education centre?

3 Do you think the Forest is being managed sustainably? Explain your answer.

4.4 Deforestation in Malaysia

■ Malaysia's tropical rainforests

Malaysia is a country in south-east Asia. It is made up of Peninsular Malaysia and Eastern Malaysia, which is part of the island of Borneo (maps in **A**). Along with neighbouring countries, the natural vegetation in Malaysia is tropical rainforest. Nearly 60 per cent of Malaysia is forested and commercial tree crops, primarily rubber and oil palm, occupy a further 13 per cent. Trees and forest cover an area equivalent to the whole of the UK.

a World location map

b Regional location map

A Location of Malaysia

In the past most of the country was covered by **primary (virgin) rainforest**. In Peninsular Malaysia most of this has now gone and little is left on Borneo. Today an estimated 18 per cent of Malaysia's forest is virgin forest.

Malaysian rainforests support over 5,500 species of flowering plants (the UK has 1,350), 2,600 species of tree (UK 35) and over 1,000 species of butterflies (UK 43). Of the 203 species of mammals, 78 per cent live only in forests. Malaysia's rainforests are clearly special places.

In this section you will learn

the causes of deforestation in tropical rainforests

the effects of deforestation in tropical rainforests.

Key terms

Primary (virgin) rainforest: rainforest that represents the natural vegetation in the region unaffected by the actions of people.

Deforestation: the cutting down and removal of forest.

Clear felling: absolute clearance of all trees from an area.

Selective logging: the cutting down of selected trees, leaving most of the trees intact.

Did you know ??????

The rainforests of South-east Asia are the heartland for the giant dipterocarp trees, of which there are 515 species. These tall, straight trees dominate the tropical timber trade. They are only found in virgin forests and form vital vertical structures in the forests by supporting many species of wildlife.

Threats to Malaysia's rainforests

Recent statistics from the United Nations (UN) suggest that the rate of **deforestation** in Malaysia is increasing faster than in any other tropical country in the world, increasing 85 per cent between the periods 1990 to 2000 and 2000 to 2005. Since 2000, some 140,200 ha of forest have been lost on average every year. There are several threats to the rainforests in Malaysia.

Logging

During the 1980s, rampant logging on Borneo led to Malaysia becoming the world's largest exporter of tropical wood. **Clear felling**, where all trees are felled in an area, was common and this led to the total destruction of forest habitats. In recent years the main logging practice has been **selective logging**. Theoretically only fully grown trees are felled and those with important ecological qualities are left unharmed. Although selective logging is far less damaging, it reduces biodiversity. All forms of logging require road construction to bring in machinery and take away the timber (photo **B**).

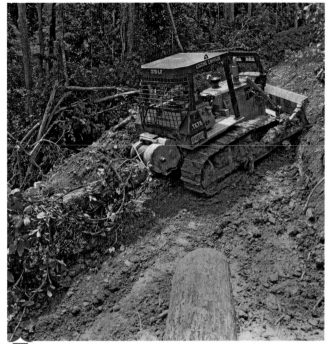

B   *Road construction and logging in Sarawak, East Malaysia*

Malaysia has one of the best rainforest protection policies in the region, but environmental groups claim to have found evidence of illegal logging in Borneo. Here, increasingly marginal slopes have been logged, leading to problems of soil erosion and mudslides.

Not only has logging reduced biodiversity, it has also threatened indigenous tribes. In 2003 a local Penan community in the village of Long Lunyim in Sarawak state protested against the encroachment by a logging company. Some members of the community were imprisoned for their protests, and the company pushed on to the community's forest reserve to exploit the timber.

Energy

The $2bn Bakun Dam project in Sarawak, due for completion in 2012, will result in the flooding of thousands of hectares of forest in order to supply hydroelectric power mainly for industrialised Peninsular Malaysia. An estimated 230 km^2 of virgin rainforest will have to be cut down for the project. Some 10,000 indigenous people have been forced to move from the flooded area. They are traditional subsistence farmers with little money, yet they are being asked to pay to be rehoused. Many now suffer from depression and alcoholism is rife.

Mining

Mining has been widespread in Peninsular Malaysia, with tin mining and smelting dominating. Areas of rainforest have been cleared to make way for mining operations and the construction of roads. In some places, the mining activities have led to pollution of the land and rivers. Drilling for oil and gas has started on Borneo.

Did you know ??????

The orang-utan is a great ape found only in south-east Asia. Able to reason and think, it is one of our closest relatives, sharing 97 per cent of our DNA. It is the largest tree-living mammal in the world.

Commercial plantations

Malaysia is a major producer of oil palm and rubber. In the early 20th century, forest was cleared to make way for the rubber plantations. In recent decades, however, synthetic rubber has led to a steep decline in rubber exports and many plantations have either been abandoned or converted to oil palm (photo **C**).

Today, Malaysia is the largest exporter of palm oil in the world. During the 1970s, large areas of land were converted to palm oil plantations. With plantation owners receiving a 10-year tax break, increasing amounts of land have been converted to plantations. Deforestation for palm oil is taking place on Borneo and threatening the survival of many species of wildlife including the orang-utan.

Resettlement

In the past, poor urban dwellers were encouraged to move into the countryside to relieve pressure on cities. This policy is called **transmigration**. Between 1956 and the 1980s, an estimated 15,000 ha of rainforest was felled to accommodate the new settlers, many of whom set up plantations.

Fires

Fires are common on Borneo. Some are natural, resulting from lightning strikes, whereas others result from forest clearance or arson. Occasionally, 'slash and burn' agriculture – where local people clear small areas of land in order to grow food crops – results in wildfires.

C *Oil palm plantation in Malaysia*

Key terms

Transmigration: a population policy that aims to move people from densely populated areas to sparsely populated areas and provide them with opportunities to improve the quality of their lives.

Slash and burn: a form of subsistence farming in tropical rainforests where some trees are felled and land is cleared by burning before being replanted.

Activities

1   Study this section on the threats to Malaysia's rainforest.

a   Briefly outline the main causes of deforestation in Malaysia.

b   To what extent do you think deforestation in Malaysia has been driven by economic gain (i.e. making money)?

c   What have been the environmental effects of deforestation?

d   What have been the social effects (i.e. on the people) of deforestation?

e   Despite government policies to preserve Malaysia's rainforests, why do you think deforestation continues to be an issue in Malaysia?

2   Complete a large revision diagram to summarise the threats to Malaysia's rainforests, using an A3 sheet of paper if possible. Include some internet research information if you can.

a   At the centre of your diagram, place a photo or sketch to show the features of Malaysia's rainforest. You could include a map too.

b   Around the central feature, create a series of illustrated text boxes describing the main threats to the rainforest. Use arrows to link these boxes to the central image. Use plenty of colour and think carefully about your design to ensure that the final outcome supports your revision.

Study tip

Be sure to identify the difference between 'threats', 'causes' and 'effects' of deforestation and make sure that you use each term correctly.

∞ links

For further information on Malaysia's rainforests, go to **http://rainforests.mongabay. com/20malaysia.htm**.

For information on deforestation in Brazil, go to **www.mongabay.com/ brazil.html**.

4.5   Sustainable rainforest management in Malaysia

■ National Forest Policy

Widespread logging in Malaysia started after the Second World War due to improvements in technology (e.g. chainsaws, trucks). The government responded by passing the National Forestry Act in 1977. The Act paved the way for sustainable management of Malaysia's rainforests and had the following aims:

- Develop timber processing to increase the profitability of the exported wood and reduce demand for raw timber. The export of low-value raw logs is now banned in most of Malaysia.
- Encourage alternative timber sources (e.g. from rubber trees).
- Increase public awareness of forests.
- Increase research into forestry.
- Involve local communities in forest projects.

One of the main initiatives of the 1977 Act was to introduce a new approach to forest management known as the **Selective Management System** (diagram **A**). This is recognised as one of the most sustainable approaches to tropical forestry management in the world.

In this section you will learn

the concept of sustainable management of tropical rainforests

the range of national and international options for sustainable management.

Key terms

Selective Management System: a form of sustainable forestry management adopted in Malaysia.

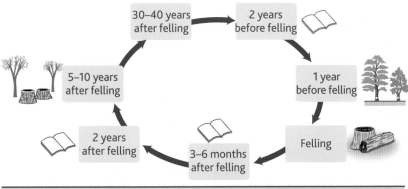

Stage	Actions
2 years before felling	Pre-felling study to identify what is there.
1 year before felling	Commercially viable trees marked for felling. Arrows painted on trees to indicate direction of felling to avoid damaging other valuable trees.
Felling	Felling carried out by licence holders.
3–6 months after felling	Survey to check what has been felled. Prosecution may result from illegal felling.
2 years after felling	Treatment plan drawn up to restore forest.
5–10 years after felling	Remedial and regeneration work carried out by state forestry officials. Replacement trees planted.
30–40 years after felling	Cycle begins again.

A *Malaysia's Selective Management System*

Unfortunately, a lack of trained officials to enforce and monitor the system across the country has led to the continuation of abuses and illegal activities. Remedial measures, such as replanting, have not always been carried out satisfactorily. Deforestation is still taking place in Borneo where land is being converted to oil palm plantations.

Permanent Forest Estates and National Parks

Land-use surveys carried out in the 1960s and 1970s have enabled the government to identify Permanent Forest Estates. These areas are protected, with no development or conversion of land use allowed. Large areas of forest are, however, used for commercial logging. Some 10 per cent of the forested land (essentially the primary forest areas) has special **conservation** status ensuring the survival of the rainforest habitats and species.

Forest Stewardship Council

The Forest Stewardship Council (FSC) is an international organisation that promotes sustainable forestry. Products that have been sourced from sustainably managed forests carry the FSC label. The FSC tries to educate manufacturers and consumers about the need to buy wood from sustainable sources. It also aims to reduce demand for rare and valuable tropical hardwoods.

Developing tourism

In recent years, Malaysia has promoted its forests as destinations for **ecotourism** ('green tourism'). This aims to introduce people to the natural world without causing any environmental damage (photo **B**). The great benefit of ecotourism is that it enables the undisturbed natural environment to create a source of income for local people without it being damaged or destroyed.

B | *Ecotourism in Borneo*

Key terms

Conservation: the thoughtful use of resources; managing the landscape in order to protect ecosystems and cultural features.

Ecotourism: tourism that focuses on protecting the environment and the local way of life. Also known as green tourism.

Debt relief: many poorer countries are in debt, having borrowed money from richer countries to support their economic development. There is strong international pressure for the developed countries to clear these debts – this is debt relief.

Debt: money owed to others, to a bank or to a global organisation such as the World Bank.

Features of ecotourism

- Usually involves small groups.
- Local guides used.
- Buildings use local materials and are environmentally friendly (sustainable water, energy and waste management). Their construction and maintenance provides employment for local people.
- Mostly nature-based experiences (walks, birdwatching).
- Limited transport involved.

■ Recent worldwide initiatives

Rainforests are valuable resources particularly for poor countries wishing to expand their economies. Apart from the timber itself, rainforests occupy land that could be used for commercial agriculture such as plantations (e.g. Malaysia) or ranching (e.g. Brazil). Valuable mineral resources such as bauxite, copper or iron may be present in the rock beneath the forests. To expect countries to 'mothball' their rainforests is naïve, however important they are at the global scale.

Debt relief

One approach is to recognise the international importance of rainforests by giving them a monetary value and paying countries to maintain them. This could take the form of **debt relief**, for example, where countries are relieved of some of their **debt** in return for retaining their rainforests.

C *Scientists in Sierra Leone's Gola Forest*

Carbon sinks

In 2008 the Gola Forest on Sierra Leone's southern border with Liberia was protected from further deforestation by becoming a National Park (photo **C**). In recognition of the forest's role in reducing global warming by acting as a **carbon sink**, the 75,000 ha park is supported by money from the European Commission, the French government and **non-governmental organisations (NGOs)** such as the Royal Society for the Protection of Birds (RSPB) and Conservation International.

Activities

1 Study diagram **A**.

a Make a copy of the diagram showing the Selective Management System.

b Use the information in the table to add more detail in the boxes in your diagram.

c Why is the system a good example of sustainable management?

d Can you suggest any modifications that might make it even more sustainable?

e Suggest some possible problems that might exist in trying to implement this approach to forest management.

2 Study photo **B**.

a What is meant by ecotourism?

b What aspects of ecotourism are evident in the photo?

c How does ecotourism offer opportunities to protect rainforests from deforestation?

d Ecotourism has become popular and travel companies are keen to attach this label to many tours. How might this trend cause problems in the future for Borneo's rainforests?

e Use the internet to look for an example of an ecotourism trip to Borneo. Describe the nature of the trip with the aid of photos. Assess whether it is genuinely ecotourism.

∞ links

For further information on the Forest Stewardship Council, visit **www.fsc.org/77.html**.

More details about a National Park, Taman Negara in Malaysia, can be found at **www.geographia.com/malaysia/taman.html**.

Ecotourism information can be found at **www.about-malaysia.com/adventure/eco-tourism.htm**.

4.6 What are the opportunities for economic developments in hot deserts?

The Thar Desert, Rajasthan, India

The Thar Desert is one of the major hot deserts of the world. It stretches across north-west India and into Pakistan (map **A**). The desert covers an area of some 200,000 km², mostly in the Indian state of Rajasthan.

Rainfall in the Thar Desert is low – typically between 120 and 240 mm per year – and summer temperatures in July can reach 53°C. Much of the desert is sandy hills with extensive mobile sand dunes and clumps of thorn forest vegetation, a mixture of small trees, shrubs and grasses (photo **B**). The soils are generally sandy and not very fertile, as there is little organic matter to enrich them. They drain quickly so there is little surface water.

In this section you will learn

the economic opportunities of deserts in rich and poor areas of the world

the challenges faced by desert communities and the management responses.

Key terms

Subsistence farming: farming to produce food for the farmer and his/her family only.

Hunter-gatherers: people who carry out a basic form of subsistence farming by hunting animals and gathering fruit and nuts.

Commercial farming: a type of farming where crops and/or livestock are sold to make a profit.

A *Location map of the Thar Desert*

Economic opportunities in the desert

Subsistence farming

Most of the people living in the desert are involved in farming. The climate presents huge challenges, with unreliable rainfall and frequent droughts. The most successful basic farming systems involve keeping a few animals on the grassy areas and cultivating vegetables and fruit trees. Although a good deal of the farming is **subsistence farming**, some crops are sold at local markets.

Over the border in Pakistan's Thar region, the Kohlis tribe are descendants of **hunter-gatherers** who survived in the desert by hunting animals and gathering fruit and natural products such as honey. This type of subsistence farming is the most basic form of farming and is rarely found in the world today.

Irrigation and commercial farming

Irrigation in parts of the Thar Desert has revolutionised farming in the area. The main form of irrigation in the desert is the Indira Gandhi (Rajasthan) Canal (map **A**). The canal was constructed in 1958 and has a total length of 650 km. Two of the main areas to benefit are centred on the cities of Jodhpur and Jaisalmer, where over 3,500 km² of land is under irrigation. **Commercial farming** in the form of crops such as wheat and cotton now flourishes in an area that used to be scrub desert. The canal also provides drinking water to many people in the desert.

Mining and industry

The state of Rajasthan is rich in minerals. The desert region has valuable reserves of gypsum (used in making plaster for the construction industry and in making cement), feldspar (used to make ceramics), phospherite (used for making fertiliser) and kaolin (used as a whitener in paper).

There are valuable reserves of stone in the area. At Jaisalmer the Sanu limestone is the main source of limestone for India's steel industry. Limestone is also quarried for making cement. Valuable reserves of the rock marble are quarried near Jodhpur for use in the construction industry. Local hide and wool industries form a ready market for the livestock that are reared in the area.

Tourism

In the last few years, the Thar Desert, with its beautiful landscapes, has become a popular tourist destination. Desert safaris on camels, based at Jaisalmer, have become particularly popular with foreigners as well as wealthy Indians from elsewhere in the country. Local people benefit by acting as guides or by rearing and looking after camels.

B   *The natural desert environment near Jaisalmer*

Future challenges

The Thar Desert faces a number of challenges for the future:

- Population pressure – the Thar Desert is the most densely populated desert in the world, with a population density of 83 people per km², and the population is increasing. This is putting extra pressure on the fragile desert ecosystem and leading to overgrazing and overcultivation.

Did you know ??????

The Thar Desert National Park in India is home to the rare great Indian bustard, a large ground-dwelling bird.

- Water management – excessive irrigation in some places has led to waterlogging of the ground. Where this has happened, salts poisonous to plants have been deposited on the ground surface. This is called **salinisation** and is a big problem in deserts (diagram **C**). Elsewhere, excessive demand for water has caused an unsustainable fall in water tables.

- Soil erosion – overcultivation and overgrazing have damaged the vegetation in places, leading to soil erosion by wind and rain. Once eroded away, the soil takes thousands of years to re-form.

- Fuel – reserves of firewood, the main source of fuel, are dwindling with the result that people are using manure as fuel rather than using it to improve the quality of the soil.

- Tourism – although tourists bring benefits such as employment and extra incomes, the environment that they have come to enjoy is fragile and will suffer if tourism becomes overdeveloped.

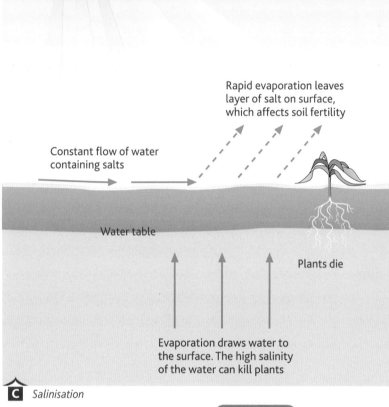

Rapid evaporation leaves layer of salt on surface, which affects soil fertility

Constant flow of water containing salts

Water table

Plants die

Evaporation draws water to the surface. The high salinity of the water can kill plants

C *Salinisation*

Sustainable management

A number of approaches have been adopted to address the challenges of living in the Thar Desert and to provide its people with a sustainable future. In 1977 the government-funded Desert Development Programme was started. Its main aims are to restore the ecological balance of the region by conserving, developing and harnessing land, water, livestock and human resources. In Rajasthan it has been particularly concerned with developing forestry and addressing the issue of sand dune stabilisation.

Forestry

The most important tree in the Thar Desert is the *Prosopis cineraria*. It is extremely well suited to the hostile conditions of the desert and has multiple uses (photo **D**). Scientists at the Central Arid Zone Research Institute have developed a hardy breed of plum tree called a Ber tree. It produces large fruits and can survive in low rainfall conditions. The fruits can be sold and there is the potential to make a decent profit.

Stabilising sand dunes

The sand dunes in the Thar Desert are very mobile. In some areas they form a threat to farmland, roads and waterways. Various approaches have been adopted to stabilise the sand dunes, including planting blocks of trees and establishing shelterbelts of trees and fences alongside roads and canals.

Key term

Salinisation: the deposition of solid salts on the ground surface following the evaporation of water. Also an increase in the concentration of salts in the soil, reducing fertility.

Thar Desert National Park

The Thar Desert National Park has been created to protect some 3,000 km² of this arid land and the endangered and rare wildlife that has adapted to its extreme conditions.

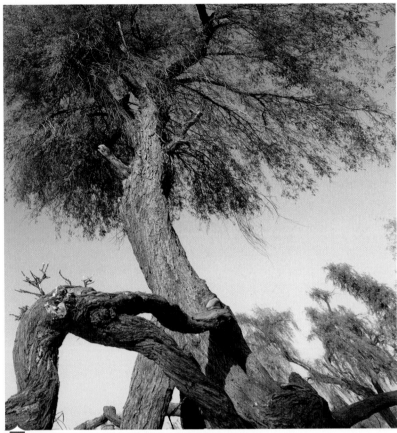

- A lot of foliage is produced, which can be used to feed animals, especially in the drier winter.

- The trees can provide good-quality firewood.

- The wood is strong and can be used as a local building material.

- Its pods provide animal fodder.

- Crops can benefit from shade and moist growing conditions if interspersed between the trees.

- This and other tree species are planted in blocks to help stabilise the sand dunes.

D   *Sustainable qualities of the* Prosopis cineraria *tree*

Activities

1   Study photo **B**.

a   Describe the environment of the Thar Desert as shown in the photo.

b   What are the challenges of this environment for local people?

c   What is the difference between subsistence farming and commercial farming?

d   Describe the characteristics of these two types of farming in the Thar Desert.

e   Apart from farming, what other economic activities take place in the desert?

2   Study diagram **C**.

a   With the aid of a diagram, describe the process of salinisation.

b   Why does salinisation occur in the Thar Desert?

c   Why is salinisation a problem for the future?

d   Suggest ways of reducing the problem of salinisation.

e   Apart from salinisation, what other challenges face the people of the Thar Desert in the future?

3   Study the information in photo **D**. Apart from stabilising sand dunes, what other benefits do trees provide?

4   a   What are the benefits of sand dune stabilisation?

b   Is sand dune stabilisation a form of sustainable management? Explain your answer.

The Sonoran Desert, Arizona, USA

The Sonoran Desert is one of North America's largest and hottest deserts. It is also one of the wettest, with over 300 mm of rain falling in some places. It is located in the south-west of the USA, straddling the lower states of Arizona and California and stretching south into Mexico (map **E**). The Sonoran Desert is stunningly beautiful and is home to a great diversity of flora and fauna including the iconic saguaro cactus (fact file **H**, page 85).

The USA is able to respond somewhat differently to the challenges and opportunities of a desert environment compared with poorer countries such as India (Thar Desert) or the African countries bordering the Sahara Desert. Money enables many of the physical difficulties to be overcome.

The physical extremes of the climate can be overcome to some extent by using air conditioning for vehicles, houses, workplaces and shopping centres. With plentiful supplies of relatively cheap energy, this is perfectly possible in the USA.

Water can be relatively easily piped into the area for irrigating crops, to supply drinking water and for filling swimming pools and watering golf courses.

The clear, clean atmosphere and open spaces form an attraction to short-term holidaymakers and long-term migrants. A recent trend in the Sonoran Desert has been **retirement migration**, where people decide to retire to newly built housing complexes with swimming pools and golf courses.

Marana: the tale of one town in the Sonoran Desert

Marana is a town of some 35,000 people located a few kilometres north-west of the city of Tucson in Arizona (map **E**). Over the years it has developed into a thriving business town and leisure resort.

The town began as a mid-19th century ranching and mining community along the Southern Pacific Railroad. In 1920 a new irrigation system enabled it to become an agricultural centre specialising in cotton, a crop that does well in hot conditions provided it is well watered. Families migrated to the town to work in the cotton fields. Agricultural production increased during the 1940s and expanded to include wheat, barley and pecans.

However, since the 1990s farming in the area has declined. In 2005 only six large cotton farms remained. Durum wheat is grown and exported to Italy to make pasta. A heritage park has been opened to celebrate the town's agricultural heritage.

Migration accounts for much of the growth of the town, which is a thriving and wealthy business community.

In 2007 Marana began hosting golf's PGA Matchplay Championship (photo **F**).

E *Location map of the Sonoran Desert*

Managing the Sonoran Desert

In 1998 the Sonoran Desert Conservation Plan was initiated in Pima County, the administrative region incorporating Tucson in south-west Arizona (map **E**). This is a comprehensive plan to 'conserve the county's most valued natural and cultural resources, whilst accommodating the inevitable population growth and economic expansion of the community'.

The plan resulted from concern about threats to wildlife habitats as housing developments expanded into the desert. An endangered species of pygmy owl was considered to be particularly vulnerable.

Among other initiatives, the plan has led to:

- detailed mapping and inventory of the county's natural and cultural heritage
- development of buffer zones around areas of ecological significance
- native plant protection
- hillside development restrictions
- home design recommendations to conserve energy and water.

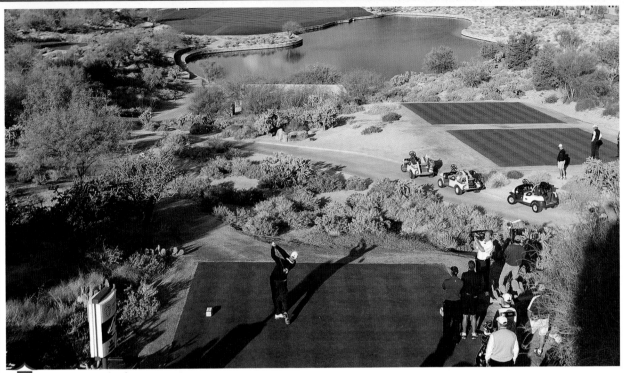

F   *Golf course in the desert near Marana*

Activities

5   Study photo **F** and the information in the text about Marana.

a   Describe the characteristics and location of Marana using the photo to help you.

b   Draw a timeline to describe the development of Marana since the mid-19th century.

6   What is retirement migration and why is it a significant issue in Arizona?

7   What are the current challenges facing the planners in Marana and how does the Sonoran Desert Conservation Plan address some of these issues?

8   To what extent do you think richer countries such as the USA are better able to exploit the opportunities and address the challenges of desert environments than poorer countries such as India?

Study tip

Be sure to separate the themes of economic opportunities, challenges and management options when studying deserts. Think carefully about the contrasts between poor countries such as India and rich countries such as the USA.

⬤⬤ links

Some excellent maps are available at **www.mapsofindia.com/geography** and **www.mapsofindia.com/maps/rajasthan**.

Information about the Sonoran Desert can be accessed at **http://alic.arid.arizona.edu/sonoran**.

Marana Town's website is at **www.marana.com**.

5.1   How and why do river valleys change downstream?

A river valley is subjected to the three main landscape-shaping processes of **erosion**, **transportation** and **deposition**. It is the extent to which they occur and where they dominate that is critical in shaping the valley.

Processes of erosion

A river near to its source concentrates on erosion, and especially downward erosion. Photo **A** of Golden Clough, Edale, shows one such river **channel** and its valley. There are four ways in which a river erodes. These are **hydraulic action**, **abrasion**, **attrition** and **solution**.

- Hydraulic action is the sheer force of the water hitting the bed and the banks. This is most effective when the water is moving fast and there is a lot of it.

- Abrasion occurs when the **load** the river is carrying repeatedly hits the river bed and the banks, causing some of the material to break off.

- Attrition is when the stones and boulders carried by the river knock against each other and over time are weakened, causing bits to fall off and reduce in size.

- Solution occurs only when the river flows on certain types of rock, such as chalk and limestone. These are soluble in rainwater and become part of the water as they are dissolved by it.

Rivers tend to erode in one of two directions: downwards or sideways. The terms for these are **vertical** and **lateral erosion**. As a river gets further down its course, vertical erosion becomes less important and lateral erosion takes over.

Processes of transportation

Having been successful in dislodging parts of the bed and banks, the river then transports the load downstream. There are four methods of transportation. These are **traction**, **saltation**, **suspension** and **solution** (diagram **B**). Photos **C** and **D** show how a river and its valley changes with distance downstream.

> **In this section you will learn**
>
> the processes of erosion: hydraulic action, abrasion, attrition and solution
>
> the processes of transportation: traction, saltation, suspension and solution
>
> how and why deposition occurs
>
> how and why the long and cross profiles are formed and why cross profiles change downstream.

A   Golden Clough, Edale

> **Study tip**
>
> Learn the process terms for erosion and transportation and be certain you use each term in its correct context.

Traction is the method used for moving the largest material. This is too heavy to lose contact with the bed, so material such as boulders is rolled along.

Saltation moves the small stones and grains of sand by bouncing them along the bed. This lighter load leaves the river bed in a hopping motion.

Suspension is a means of carrying very fine material within the water, so that it floats in the river and is moved as it flows.

Solution is the dissolved load and occurs only with certain rock types that are soluble in rainwater. This is true of chalk and limestone and the load is not visible.

B *Processes of transportation*

C *Grindsbrook Clough, Edale*

D *River Noe, Edale*

Key terms

Erosion: the sculpting of a landscape, for example by rivers, involving the removal of material.

Transportation: the carrying of sediment downstream from the point where it has been eroded to where it is deposited.

Deposition: the dumping (deposition) of sediment that has been transported by a river.

Channel: the part of the river valley occupied by the water itself.

Hydraulic action: the power of the volume of water moving in the river.

Abrasion: happens when larger loads carried by the river hits the bed and banks, causing bits to break off.

Attrition: the knocking together of stones and boulders, making them gradually smaller and smoother.

Solution: the dissolving of rocks and minerals by rainwater. This is a means of transportation as well as an erosion process.

Load: material of any size carried by the river.

Vertical erosion: downwards erosion, for example when a river gouges out a deep valley.

Lateral erosion: sideways erosion, for example in a river channel at the outside bend of a meander.

Traction: the rolling along of the largest rocks and boulders.

Saltation: the bouncing movement of small stones and grains of sand along the river bed.

Suspension: small material carried (suspended) within the water.

Deposition

This is where the river dumps or leaves behind material that it has been carrying. It deposits the largest material first as this is the heaviest to carry. The smaller the load, the further it can be transported, so this is deposited much further downstream than the larger load. Thus, large boulders can be seen in photo **A**, whereas they are absent in photo **D**. The river drops some of its load when there is a fall in the speed of the water or the amount of water is less. This often occurs when the gradient changes at the foot of a mountain or when a river enters a lake or the sea.

Long and changing cross profiles

The **long profile** shows how the river changes in height along its course. Diagram **E** shows a theoretical long profile from the source to the mouth. The steep reduction in height near the source gives way to a more gradual reduction further downstream, giving a typical concave profile. The river has much potential energy near the source due to the steep drop. Later on, this is replaced by energy from a large volume of water. However, such a perfect long profile is rare. This is due to land being uplifted, sea level changing and bands of hard and soft rock crossing the path of the river. As the river flows downstream, its valley changes shape and the **cross profile** from one side of the valley to the other clearly shows this. Generally, the cross profile shows the valley becoming wider and flatter, with lower valley sides. Map extract **F** shows part of the course of the River Noe and some of its tributaries, where photos **A**, **C** and **D** were taken. This shows how the valley cross profile changes with distance from the source.

⊙⊙ links

You can find out more facts about large rivers at **http://ga.water.usgs. gov/edu/riversofworld.html** and **http://en.wikipedia.org/wiki/Rivers_ of_England**. On this website, it would be worth searching for Durham and then the Tees as preparation for the next section.

Key terms

Long profile: a line representing the course of the river from its source (relatively high up) to its mouth where it ends, usually in a lake or the sea, and the changes in height along its course.

Cross profile: a line that represents what it would be like to walk from one side of a valley, across the channel and up the other side.

Activities

1. Study photo **A**. Draw a labelled sketch to show the characteristics of the channel and valley of Golden Clough. Include comments about the following in your labels:
   - width/depth of channel
   - size of load
   - profile of bed and banks
   - what water flow is like
   - valley sides.

2. For the terms relating to erosion, produce an illustrated dictionary to give your own clear definitions, supported by a simple diagram.

3. For the four types of transportation, produce a diagram to illustrate all four processes. Write a definition of your own next to the relevant part of the diagram.

Shallow, narrow channel	Wider, deeper channel	Widest, deepest channel
Vertical erosion	Some vertical erosion; lateral erosion more important	Less erosion; only a little lateral
Hydraulic action, abrasion and attrition	Hydraulic action less important	All erosion much less important
Some traction and saltation at high flow	Suspension main transportation; saltation and traction still present	Suspension dominant
Deposition of large material	Deposition more obvious	Deposition of fine material
Large load	Load size reduced	Large amount of load, size now very small

E *A theoretical long profile with cross profiles at points shown*

Activities

4 Study photos **A**, **C** and **D** and diagram **B**.

a How do you think the load shown in photo **A** will be moved? Explain why.

b What process of transportation is likely to be taking place in photo **C**? Give reasons for choosing the process you have selected.

c Describe how the channel and valleys of the two rivers shown in photos **A** and **C** have changed.

d Describe further changes that have occurred between photos **C** and **D**.

5 Study diagram **E**.

a Draw a sketch long profile of a river.

b Mark with a dot where you think the photos in **A** and **D** could have been taken.

c Label your long profile to show how and why the size of deposited material changes downstream.

6 Study map extract **F**.

a Give the approximate height of the rivers where each photo (**A**, **C** and **D**) was taken.

b Describe the gradient of the long profile at each of the locations where photos **A**, **C** and **D** were taken.

c Draw a sketch of the cross profile for each of the three locations.

d Describe how the cross profiles change downstream.

F 1 : 25,000 OS map extract of the River Noe and its tributaries, part of map sheet OL1

5.2 What distinctive landforms result from the changing river processes?

Different river processes lead to different landforms. Therefore, in areas near the source where vertical erosion is dominant, **waterfalls** and **gorges** are characteristic features. Further down, where lateral erosion and deposition become more important, **meanders** and **oxbow lakes** develop. Nearer to the mouth, where deposition is the most significant process, **floodplains** and **levees** become a key aspect of the landscape. The River Tees will be used here to illustrate different landforms and how they change downstream.

Landforms resulting from erosion: waterfalls and gorges

Waterfalls provide some of the most spectacular scenery in mountainous areas. In their wake, they leave gorges as they retreat back up the valley. Diagram **A** shows the sequence of events that occurs in waterfall formation.

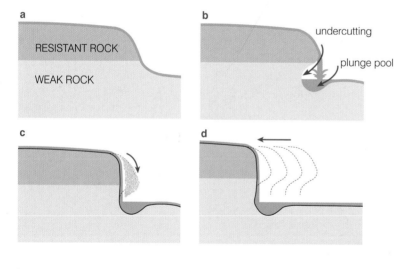

A The formation of waterfalls and gorges

One of the best-known waterfalls in the UK is High Force on the River Tees (photo **B** and map extract **C**). This occurs where whinstone, a resistant igneous rock, overlays softer limestone. Water cascading over the waterfall has formed a deep plunge pool.

B High Force, River Tees

In this section you will learn

how and why waterfalls and gorges form due to erosion

the formation of meanders and oxbow lakes due to erosion and deposition

the development of levees and floodplains, due to deposition

how the formation of some features is linked to the development of others.

Key terms

Waterfall: the sudden, and often vertical, drop of a river along its course.

Gorge: a narrow, steep-sided valley.

Meander: a bend or curve in the river channel.

Oxbow lake: a horseshoe or semi-circular area that used to be a meander. Oxbow lakes are cut off from a supply of water and so will eventually become dry.

Floodplain: the flat area next to the river channel, especially in the lower part of the course. This is a natural area for water to spill onto when the river reaches the top of its banks.

Levees: raised banks along the course of a river in its lower course. They are formed naturally but can be artificially increased in height.

Did you know ??????

Eas a'Chual Aluinn in Scotland is the UK's highest waterfall at 200 m. This is relatively small when compared with the highest waterfall in the world, Angel Falls in Venezuela at a height of 979 m.

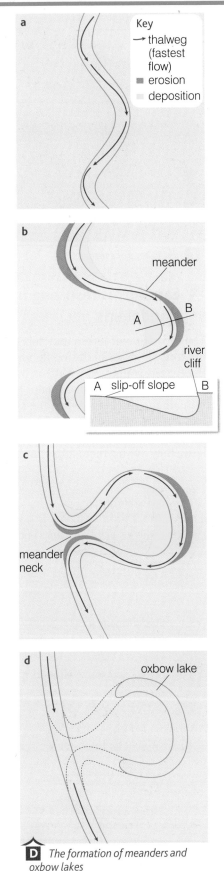

C *1 : 50,000 OS map extract of High Force, part of map sheet 91*

Landforms resulting from erosion and deposition: meanders and oxbow lakes

Meanders and oxbow lakes are characteristic landforms in the middle part of the river. The formation of meanders leads eventually to the development of oxbow lakes, as shown in diagram **D**.

Map extract **E** shows meanders further down the course of the Tees. Can you suggest where an oxbow lake may form?

E *1 : 50,000 OS map extract of the River Tees south-east of Huxworth-on-Tees, part of map sheet 93*

D *The formation of meanders and oxbow lakes*

F *Inside bend of a meander*

Landforms resulting from deposition: levees and floodplains

The formation of levees and floodplains are linked and involve the build-up of material during flooding. Under normal flow conditions, the river is contained within its banks and so no sediment is available to form levees or the floodplain. However, during periods of high rainfall and discharge when the river has burst its banks, both of these features are formed (photo **G** and diagram **H**). Map extract **J** shows the area much nearer the mouth at Thornaby-on-Tees. Levees are present here; they are far more apparent in photo **I**.

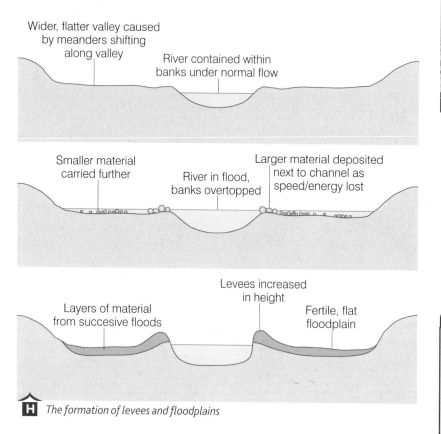

Wider, flatter valley caused by meanders shifting along valley

River contained within banks under normal flow

Smaller material carried further

River in flood, banks overtopped

Larger material deposited next to channel as speed/energy lost

Layers of material from succesive floods

Levees increased in height

Fertile, flat floodplain

H *The formation of levees and floodplains*

G *Extensive flooding at Barje near Ljubljana, Slovenia*

Study tip

When writing answers to questions about the formation of river landforms such as waterfalls and oxbow lakes, ensure that the sequence of formation is correct and refer to river processes.

J *1 : 50,000 OS map extract of the floodplain of the River Tees, part of map sheet 93*

I *Artificial levees on the Mississippi*

Did you know ? ? ? ? ?

The Mississippi River is 3,800 km long. It carries on average 42,002 tonnes of sediment each day and 130 million tonnes a year.

⊙⊙**links**

You can find out more about the River Tees at **http://en.wikipedia. org/wiki/River_Tees**.

Activities

1   Study diagram **A**. Write a series of bullet points to describe the sequence of waterfall formation.

2   Study photo **B** and map extract **C**.

a   Research High Force waterfall using the links suggested to obtain specific facts about the waterfall.

b   Produce an information board about High Force. Include on your board a labelled sketch of the waterfall to describe its features and some facts about it that will interest visiting tourists.

c   Describe the channel and the valley of the River Tees shown in the map extract.

3   Study diagram **D**.

a   Draw simplified copies of the diagrams.

b   Label each diagram to show the stages in the formation of meanders and oxbow lakes.

4   Study map extract **E**.

a   Draw a sketch map of the meanders showing:

■   an inside bend

■   an outside bend

■   the neck of a meander

■   the meander most likely to be cut off first.

b   Describe additional information about the meanders that is present on the map.

c   Locate Low Hail Farm (309097) and The Holmes (325098). Describe the location of the two farms and suggest why they are located here.

d   Comment on the risk of these two farms being flooded by the river.

5   Study photo **F**.

a   Would you expect the deepest water in the river to be on the left or the right side? Explain your answer.

b   Do you think this photo was taken at low flow or during a flood? Justify your answer.

c   What evidence is there that the river rarely flows at a high level?

d   Draw a sketch of the meander and add labels to identify the main landforms, the different river depths and the line of fastest flow.

6   Study diagram **G** and photo **I**.

a   Working in pairs, produce a short PowerPoint presentation to include the following:

■   the formation of levees

■   the formation of floodplains

■   the links between the two landforms.

b   Show your presentation to another group in the class.

5.3 How and why does the water in a river fluctuate?

In this section you will learn

how the amount of water in a river varies

the reasons for this variation.

The **discharge** of a river is the volume of water passing down a river. It can fluctuate a lot in a matter of hours in response to periods of rain. An understanding of the **drainage basin** hydrological cycle (diagram **A**) is useful background in explaining how and why the amount of water in a river is variable.

Key
- Input
- Storage
- Flow (transfer)
- Output

Precipitation: any source of moisture reaching the ground, e.g. rain, snow, frost

Interception: water being prevented from reaching the surface by trees or grass

Surface storage: water held on the ground surface, e.g. puddles

Infiltration: water sinking into soil/rock from the ground surface

Soil moisture: water held in the soil layer

Percolation: water seeping deeper below the surface

Groundwater: water stored in the rock

Transpiration: water lost through pores in vegetation

Evaporation: water lost from ground/vegetation surface

Surface run-off (overland flow): water flowing on top of the ground

Throughflow: water flowing through the soil layer parallel to the surface

Groundwater flow: water flowing through the rock layer parallel to the surface

Water table: current upper level of saturated rock/soil where no more water can be absorbed

A Drainage basin hydrological cycle

The storm hydrograph

The **flood or storm hydrograph** is used to show how a river responds to a period of rainfall (graph **C**). Rivers that respond rapidly to rainfall have a high peak and short lag time and are referred to as **flashy**. A lower peak and long lag time shows a delayed hydrograph. Table **B** gives discharge data for the River Eden in Carlisle between 7 and 9 January 2005.

Did you know ??????

Some places in England received over 380 mm of rain in May, June and July 2007 – more than double the average for the three months. This exceeded the previous high of 349 mm established in 1789.

B *Discharge of River Eden, Carlisle*

Date	Time	Discharge in cubic metres per second (cumecs)
7 January	0000 hours	90
	1200 hours	130
8 January	0000 hours	820
	1200 hours	1,400
	1500 hours	1,520
9 January	0000 hours	1,000
	1200 hours	430

C *Storm hydrograph*

Factors affecting river discharge

River discharge is influenced by a number of factors related to the weather (e.g. rainfall, temperature and previous weather conditions), other physical factors (e.g. **relief** and rock type) and by human land use.

The amount and type of rainfall are important factors. A lot of rain falling causes high river levels, while less rainfall results in lower river levels. The explanation for this lies in the drainage basin hydrological cycle. High amounts of rain saturate the soil and underlying rock. In the case of drizzle, there is time for water to infiltrate the soil and underlying rock, freeing up space for more rain.

Temperature affects the loss of water from the drainage basin and therefore the level of discharge. When temperatures are higher (table **D**), there is greater water loss via evaporation and transpiration, so river levels go down.

D *Average rainfall and temperature in Sheffield*

Month	Rainfall (mm)	Maximum temperature (°C)
January	87	6.4
February	63	6.7
March	68	9.3
April	63	11.8
May	56	15.7
June	68	18.3
July	51	20.8
August	64	20.6
September	64	17.3
October	74	13.3
November	78	9.2
December	92	7.2

Key terms

Discharge: the volume of water passing a given point in a river at any moment in time.

Drainage basin: area from which a river gets its water. The boundary is marked by an imaginary line of highland known as a watershed.

Flood or storm hydrograph: a line graph drawn to show the discharge in a river in the aftermath of a period of rain.

Flashy: a hydrograph that responds quickly to a period of rain so that it characteristically has a high peak and a short lag time.

Relief: height and slope of land.

Impermeable: rock that does not allow water to pass through.

Porous: rock that allows water to soak into it via spaces between particles.

Pervious: rock that allows water to pass through it via vertical joints and horizontal bedding planes.

Urbanisation: the increase in the proportion of people living in cities, resulting in their growth.

Study tip

Ensure that you can explain how physical and human features and processes can affect the amount of water flowing in rivers.

Previous weather conditions also have an impact on river discharge. If it has been dry, it will take longer for the water to reach the river and the amount will be less than if there had been a number of wet days. Table **E** gives the daily totals for Sheffield from 13 June until flooding occurred on the 26th. Notice that a lot of rain had fallen in mid-June before the heavy rain that fell on 24 and 25 June. Steep slopes encourage fast run-off as the water spills rapidly downwards due to gravity.

Rock type is important in determining how much water infiltrates and how much stays on the surface. Areas with impermeable rocks, such as granite, have more surface rivers than permeable rocks such as chalk.

Land use relates to the function of an area. It is a factor that considers the effect of people. Deforestation (photo **F**) and **urbanisation** (photo **G**) are the two most important land-use changes with regard to influencing river discharge. If trees are removed, water reaches the surface faster and the trees do not extract water from the ground. Expanding towns create an impermeable surface. This is made even worse by building drains to take the water away from buildings quickly – and equally quickly into rivers!

E *Rainfall in Sheffield, June 2007*

Date	Rainfall (mm)
13 June	30.3
14 June	88.2
15 June	16.9
16 June	0.0
17 June	2.2
18 June	0.0
19 June	14.7
20 June	0.1
21 June	9.6
22 June	6.9
23 June	0.2
24 June	36.0
25 June	51.1
26 June	0.0

F *Deforestation in Tayside, Scotland*

G *Urbanisation in Leicester*

Activities

1 Study diagram **A**. Work in pairs to produce a series of flash cards for the key terms in the diagram.

a On one side of the card, there should be a definition and an illustration of the term.

b On the other side, the term should be given so that the answer is clear.

c Use your completed flash cards with another pair to see how many terms you got correct and how good your definitions are.

2 Study table **B** and graph **C**.

a Draw a line graph to show the discharge of the River Eden in Carlisle.

b Using the terms in graph **C**, describe the flood hydrograph you have drawn.

c Can the hydrograph be described as 'flashy'?

3 Study tables **D** and **E** and photos **F** and **G**. Work in pairs to produce an A3 spread around the title (placed in the centre) 'The reasons river discharge fluctuates'.

a In the central box, give the meaning of 'river discharge'.

b Place the factors around the central title.

c Add information to each factor to explain how discharge is affected. Each factor should be illustrated by diagrams, sketches or photos. You should use data provided in the tables.

d Your finished spread should be informative and accurate but interesting, colourful and original.

5.4 Why do rivers flood?

Floods occur when a river bursts its banks. Flooding is not a normal condition for the river, but is an extreme situation due to high levels of flow. The extent to which the river exceeds the flow that can be contained in its banks determines the severity of the flood. Floods are common events. Problems and issues arise when people are affected. Building on floodplains results in property being damaged and lives being lost in what becomes a **hazard**.

Causes of floods

Rivers flood due to a number of physical causes such as prolonged rainfall, heavy rain, snowmelt and steep relief (table **A** and extracts **B** and **C**). People often unintentionally increase the likelihood and severity of flooding. This is mainly the result of deforestation and construction work.

A *Rainfall in Sheffield*

Month	Average rainfall (mm), 1971–2000	Actual rainfall (mm), 2007
March	67.9	44.5
April	62.5	5.8
May	55.5	83.8
June	66.7	285.6

In this section you will learn

why flooding occurs – the natural causes and the ways in which people make it worse

where floods have occurred in the UK

how the frequency of flooding seems to be increasing.

Key terms

Floods: these occur when a river carries so much water that it cannot be contained by its banks and so it overflows on to surrounding land – its floodplain.

Hazard: an event where people's lives and property are threatened and deaths and/or damage result.

Soil erosion: the removal of the layer of soil above the rock where plants grow.

News

Home | Contact | Sitemap | News | Forum | Shop

Home
Contact
Sitemap
News
Forum
Shop

Snowmelt is a main contributing factor to flooding. It was partly responsible for floods in Malton (N. Yorkshire) in November 2000 and is frequently important in Bangladesh. An extract from 'Why Bangladesh floods are so bad' (BBC News website news.bbc.co.uk) on the 2004 floods states 'Bangladesh receives enormous amounts of water from four major rivers. All are filled up from melting snow in the Himalayas.' The Himalayas provide some of the steepest relief worldwide and this is also important in ensuring that water reaches the rivers quickly, increasing the flood risk.

Deforestation has an impact on the water cycle in a drainage basin. It is frequently seen as one reason for the increasing severity of flooding in Bangladesh. Chopping trees down in higher-lying areas, including neighbouring countries, such as Nepal, can have unintentional effects elsewhere. As well as increasing rates of surface runoff, **soil erosion** is a consequence. Much of this is washed into rivers, where, when deposited, the amount of water the channel can hold is reduced. Thus, the flood risk is increased.

Building construction can increase flooding. New houses built next to the river in Malton are clearly susceptible to flooding. Building on floodplains is an issue, as outlined in Lincoln.

C *Causes of flooding*

The city experienced the most rain in a single month since records began 125 years ago. A resident said, 'The rain had been almost constant for a week. On the morning the flooding started, the rivers were almost visibly rising. By lunchtime, the city was at a standstill as bridges became impassable and underpasses flooded. We were stranded in the north of the city – it took six hours to travel four miles. By the evening much of the city centre was under water, many roads had collapsed and were impassable and electricity supplies were limited for almost a week. It took well over a year for things to get back to normal.'

Adapted from the Sheffield Star

B *Prolonged rain in Sheffield, 2007*

Frequency and location of flood events

Flooding appears to be becoming an increasingly frequent event. In 1607 a great flood affected Devon, Somerset and South Wales. Major floods, however, were infrequent in the UK. In March 1947 major floods did occur, affecting many areas of southern, central and north-eastern England, including York, Tewkesbury, Shrewsbury, Sheffield, Nottingham and London, following the rapid melting of snow. The combined effects of storm surge and high tides contributed to the floods of January 1953 that hit the east coast, including Suffolk, Essex and Kent, when huge waves washed away sea defences and 307 people died. In 1968 another Great Flood affected counties in south-east England.

After this, there is little reference to major floods until relatively recently, when they have regularly made the headlines. Since 1998 headlines about floods have been an almost annual occurrence. Table **D** summarises some of the most serious floods since 1998.

Did you know

Brize Norton in Oxfordshire recorded 115 mm of rainfall in 12 hours on 20 July 2007; some places received between 30 and 40 mm in one hour. One unofficial rain gauge in Hull recorded 94 mm.

∞ links

You can find out more about causes of flooding at **www.bbc.co.uk**.

D *Major flood events, 2000–2012*

Date	Location	Rivers
May 2000	Uckfield, Petworth, Robertsbridge, Horsham (Sussex)	Uck, Rother
June 2000	Calder Valley, Yorkshire and York	Calder, Ouse
August 2004	Boscastle (Cornwall)	Valency
January 2005	Carlisle	Eden
June 2007	Large areas of south and east Yorkshire including Doncaster, Sheffield and Hull	Don, Hull, Witham,
	Parts of Lincolnshire including Lincoln and Louth	Witham, Ludd
July 2007	Large areas of Gloucestershire including Upton-upon-Severn, Tewkesbury, Gloucester	Avon, Severn
	Oxfordshire including Oxford, Banbury and Witney	Thames, Windrush, Cherwell
November 2009	Cockermouth and the Derwent valley to Workington	Derwent, Cocker
November 2010	Cornwall	River Fowey
November 2012	Severe flooding across SW England, parts of Wales, Cumbria and Scotland	Numerous rivers across the UK burst their banks during the wettest week's weather for 50 years

Activities

1 Study table **A** and extract **B**.

a Draw a comparative bar graph to show the average rainfall between March and June and rainfall that fell in those months in 2007.

b Explain how the figures help to explain the flooding that occurred.

c Consider the comments made by the Sheffield resident in the extract. How do these explain the flooding at the end of June 2007?

2 Study extract **C**.

a Using the example of Bangladesh, explain how snowmelt, relief and deforestation are responsible for flooding. You should include one diagram for each reason.

b Explain why building on floodplains might increase the likelihood of flooding.

c To what extent do you agree with the following statement: 'There is not usually one cause of flooding but a combination of reasons.' Support your answer with evidence.

3 Study table **D**.

a On an outline map of the UK, mark and label the places that flooded.

b Add the major rivers to your map.

c Use internet research to help you add brief facts and figures about each flood as annotations on your map.

5.5 How and why do the effects of flooding and the responses to it vary?

The effects of flooding vary according to their size and location. The impact tends to be more severe in poorer countries. Responses are generally more immediate in countries at further stages of development and the attempts made to reduce the effects come from within the affected area or country. In countries at lesser stages of development, attempts made to reduce the effects may be delayed and require international effort. Long-term responses are likely to show similar differences as a result of variations in wealth and the ability to afford flood protection measures.

In this section you will learn

the effects of flooding and the responses to it in both richer and poorer countries

how and why the effects and responses vary.

Flooding in England (2007)

The flooding of many parts of England in June and July 2007 was the most extensive ever experienced. The depth may not have reached the record levels of 1947, but the scale of the areas affected reached a new high. Diagram **A** shows the main areas affected and the damage done when much of central and southern England suffered the effects of record levels of rainfall.

Did you know ??????

The sale of women's raincoats at John Lewis in July 2007 was over 11 times higher than in July 2006, while the sale of umbrellas was 184 per cent higher.

RISK OF DISRUPTION
21:00 Sun 24 Jun to 23:00 Mon 25 Jun

20%
20%
50%
80%
30%
20%

- Surface water flooding in Hull.
- Widespread disruption and damage to more than 7,000 houses and 1,300 businesses in Hull.
- River Don burst its banks, flooding Sheffield and Doncaster.
- Flooding in Derbyshire, Lincolnshire and Worcestershire.
- Highest official rainfall total was 111mm at Fylingdales (North Yorkshire). Amateur networks recorded similar totals in the Hull area.
- There were fears that the dam wall at the Ulley Reservoir near Rotherham would burst.

B *Flooding in Hull*

RISK OF DISRUPTION
00:00 Fri 20 Jul to 12:00 Sat 21 Jul

20%
20%
30%
20%
50%
80%
30% 70%

- Widespread disruption to the motorway and rail networks.
- In the following days the River Severn and tributaries in Gloucestershire, Worcestershire, Herefordshire and Shropshire broke banks and flooded surrounding areas.
- River Thames and its tributaries in Wiltshire, Oxfordshire, Berkshire and Surrey flooded.
- Flooding in Telford and Wrekin, Staffordshire, Warwickshire and Birmingham.
- The highest recorded rainfall was 157.4mm in 48 hours at Pershore College (Worcestershire).

A *Flooding in England, 2007*

C *Victims of the Tewkesbury floods*

Cockermouth, 2009

Causes of the flood

On 19 November 2009 the highest ever recorded amount of rain in a 24-hour period fell on the hills of the Lake District in NW England. Following a wet autumn, this torrential rain fell on already saturated ground and much of it swept rapidly down the steep hillsides swelling the streams and rivers.

Cockermouth is a small town on the western side of the Lake District 13 km inland from the coast (map **D**). It lies at the confluence of two rivers, the Derwent and the Cocker. The sheer volume of water sweeping down these two rivers overwhelmed the channels and the rivers burst their banks causing widespread and devastating flooding.

D *Location of Cockermouth in the Lake District*

Effects of the flood

In Cockermouth itself a torrent of water some 2.5 m high cascaded down the main road flooding and severely damaging shops, offices and homes (photo **E**). In Workington on the coast, a policeman died when the bridge that he had been warning people not to cross collapsed beneath him.

The flood had a big impact on the local community:

- Over 1,300 people were directly affected by the floods.
- Many homes were without power or water and local schools were forced to close.
- All of Cumbria's 1,800 bridges had to be inspected to check that they were safe to use. Several bridges were completely destroyed by the flood.
- In Workington, the northern part of the town became cut off resulting in a lengthy round trip to reach schools, doctors' surgeries and banks. The dislocation of road communications in rural Cumbria caused immense hardship to local people.

- Insurance companies expected the cost of the damage to be in excess of £100m.
- Farmers suffered greatly from the inundation of their land. Livestock were killed and important pastures became useless, either because they were saturated or because they had become coated with rocks carried down by the swollen rivers. Fences and walls were destroyed, farm buildings damaged and machinery ruined.
- Local businesses, such as shops, pubs and hotels faced a dismal winter with little prospect of making any money. Shop stock had been destroyed and many businesses suffered directly from flood damage with up to 1m of mud and silt needing to be cleared from downstairs rooms.

Responses

Immediately after the flood the main focus was on search and rescue. Some 200 people had to be airlifted from the roofs of their houses by RAF helicopters. People who had been evacuated from their homes were taken to temporary shelters to be looked after. Several people were rescued from their homes by boat.

In the days that followed, flooded buildings were assessed for their safety before residents and shopkeepers were allowed back to assess the damage for themselves. Some small businesses were provided with temporary trading accommodation in the town centre while their shops were refitted. For days, the streets were lined with skips overflowing with damaged shop stock and people's personal belongings, all ruined by the flood.

Most of the residents, whose homes were flooded by up to 6ft of muddy water, had to live in alternative accommodation for several months. The main road bridge over the River Derwent was closed to vehicles for two months to allow for safety checks and repairs. Several roads in the town centre were so severely broken up by the raging floodwaters that they had to be completely re-surfaced.

E *Flooding in Cockermouth 2009*

F   OS 1:25,000 map extract of area shown in Photo E

Case study

Bangladesh, 2004

Bangladesh has experienced particularly severe flooding on a regular basis. Annual flooding is expected in this low-lying country that is located largely on the delta of the Ganges.

The 2004 floods occurred from July to September, inundating over half of the country at their peak. Map **G** shows the areas of Bangladesh under water and the depth of the water.

By July, 40 per cent of Dhaka was under water, 60 per cent of the country was submerged, 600 deaths were reported and 30 million left homeless out of a population of 140 million. Some 100,000 people in Dhaka alone were suffering from diarrhoea as the floodwaters left mud and raw sewage in their wake. As the year progressed, things got even worse as Bangladesh experienced its heaviest rain in 50 years with 35 cm falling in one day on 13 September. The death toll rose to over 750, the airport at Dhaka was flooded as were many roads and railways. Bridges were also destroyed – all of which hampered the relief effort that followed. This damage and that to schools and hospitals was put at $7 billion. In many badly hit rural areas, rice – the main food crop – was washed away and other important food supplies such as vegetables were lost along with cash crops such as jute and sugar.

Key
Depth (cm)
> 400
301–400
201–300
101–200
> 15–100

G   The extent of the floods in Bangladesh

Within Bangladesh, food supplies, medicines, clothing and blankets were distributed. The effects of the floods on the transport system made this difficult (photo **H**). Local communities began to rebuild their homes. Disease from contaminated water remained a major threat. The United Nations launched an appeal for $74 million, but had received only 20 per cent of this by September. An appeal by WaterAid sought to supply water purification tablets and posters highlighting the hygiene risks in flood water. All of these represent immediate responses to the floods.

Longer-term approaches included embankments built along the river, which have not really achieved their goal, whereas flood warning and the provision of flood shelters have been more successful. These are areas of raised land where people can move to temporarily with their cattle and have access to items such as dried food and obtain water before supplies are contaminated.

H *The effects of flooding in rural areas of Bangladesh*

⚭ links

You can find out more about flooding in the UK and Bangladesh at **www.bbc.co.uk**.

The website **www.bangladesh.gov.bd** has information about Bangladesh.

Activities

1 Study diagram **A**. Imagine you are a newscaster presenting a special report on 'The 2007 floods in England'. Write your script, summarising the location of areas hit and the effects. Make sure that you stress the scale of the flooding and refer to evidence to back up what you are saying. You should have a map to refer to in your broadcast.

2 Study photo **E** and map **F**.

a In which direction is the photograph looking?

b What is the name of the area of land at X?

c Describe the extent of the flooding in Cockermouth.

d Describe the likely effects of the flooding on the following people:

■ A shopkeeper on the High Street

■ A homeowner at Y

■ A farmer whose land has been flooded at Z.

e Locate the castle on the map and photo. How does the choice of site for the castle suggest that flooding has been a problem here in the past?

f Despite the flooding of 2009 new houses are being constructed on the floodplain at Y. Do you think this is a wise decision?

3 Study map **G** and photo **H**. Imagine you are working as a volunteer for an aid agency in Bangladesh during the floods of 2004. Write a letter home, describing the situation in the floods in Bangladesh, its effects and responses to it. Try to make your account as real as possible so that the reader can imagine the experience.

4 Consider the Cockermouth flood (2009) and the Bangladesh flood (2004).

a Compare the effects and responses to the floods.

b To what extent do you think the effects and responses reflect the different levels of development of the two countries?

	Cockermouth	Bangladesh
Location		
Date		
Causes		
Effects		
Responses		

5.6 Hard and soft engineering: which is the better option?

Hard engineering strategies involve the use of technology in order to control rivers. **Soft engineering** adopts a less intrusive form of management, seeking to work alongside natural processes. Hard engineering approaches tend to give immediate results but are expensive. Soft engineering is much cheaper and offers a more sustainable option as it does not interfere directly with the river's flow.

Hard engineering

Dams and **reservoirs** exert a huge degree of control over a river. Water can be held up behind a dam following heavy rainfall and then released slowly to prevent flooding. Dams and reservoirs are normally constructed as part of a multi-purpose project rather than with just a single aim in mind.

Straightening meanders represents a smaller-scale approach to managing rivers. Meanders are circuitous courses. Like following a route in a car, a semicircular way is longer and slower than a straight one. Therefore, water in a meander takes longer to clear an area than water in a straight section of a river. A possible solution to flooding in areas where there are many meanders on a river's course is to straighten them artificially. In this way, the river is made to follow a new shorter, straight section and abandon its natural meandering course (diagram **A**).

N

Key
- - - - 1933
▬▬▬ 1975

0   5 km

A *Straightened sections of the Mississippi*

> **Study tip**
>
> Learn the arguments for and against hard and soft engineering strategies used to manage river flow. Back up these arguments with examples.

> **In this section you will learn**
>
> how hard and soft engineering are used to try to manage rivers and flooding
>
> why there is debate about the two options
>
> how to evaluate the two strategies and come to a supported view about them.

> **Key terms**
>
> **Hard engineering:** building artificial structures aimed at controlling natural processes.
>
> **Soft engineering:** this option tries to work with the natural river system and involves avoiding building on areas especially likely to flood, warning people of a possible flood and planting trees to increase lag time.
>
> **Dam:** an artificial structure designed to hold back water to create a reservoir.
>
> **Reservoir:** commonly an artificial lake formed behind a dam and used for water supply.
>
> **Straightening meanders:** making the river follow a more direct, rather than its natural course, so that it leaves an area more quickly.

> **Did you know** ??????
>
> The Hoover Dam over the Colorado river near Las Vegas was the biggest concrete structure when it was completed in 1935. There would have been enough concrete to make a two-lane road between San Francisco and New York.

The Three Gorges Dam, China

The Three Gorges dam was constructed at Yichang on the River Yangtse (map **B**, photo **C** and table **D**). The capacity of the reservoir should reduce the risk of flooding downstream from a 1-in-10-year event to a 1-in-100-year event. Not only will this benefit over 15 million people living in high-risk flood areas, it will also protect over 25,000 ha of farmland.

The dam is already having a positive impact on flood control, navigation and power generation, but it has caused problems. The Yangtse used to carry over 500 million tonnes of silt every year. Up to 50 per cent of this is now deposited behind the dam, which could quickly reduce the storage capacity of the reservoir.

B The location of the Three Gorges dam

The water in the reservoir is becoming heavily polluted from shipping and waste discharged from cities. For example, Chongqing pumps in over 1 billion tonnes of untreated waste per year. Toxic substances from factories, mines and waste tips submerged by the reservoir are also being released into the reservoir.

Most controversially, at least 1.4 million people were forcibly moved from their homes to accommodate the dam, reservoir and power stations. These displaced people were promised compensation for their losses, plus new homes and jobs. Many have not yet received this, and newspaper articles in China have admitted that so far over $30 million of the funds set aside for this has been taken by corrupt local officials.

D The Three Gorges Dam Project fact file

Dimensions	181 m high and 2.3 km wide
Area flooded	632 km^2
Cost	$25.5 billion
Built	Started 1994; finished 2009
Increased depth	110 m (reduced to 80 m when flood risk downstream)

C The Three Gorges Dam

Soft engineering

Soft engineering seeks to work with the natural processes of a river to reduce the risk of flooding. One approach, that may be appropriate in areas where small floods are frequent, is to do nothing! However, there are many other approaches that can reduce the risk of flooding.

Flood warnings and preparation are complementary approaches. Telling people in advance of a flood gives them valuable time to prepare for it. The Environment Agency identifies areas at risk of flooding and issues warnings. For example, information was given on local radio, television and the internet during the Tewkesbury flooding of 2007. Floodline Warnings Direct sends messages to registered users. A flood watch was issued on 20 July at 18.32, followed by a flood warning approximately 20 minutes later. This gave people valuable time to move possessions, turn off services and take precautions. The Environment Agency's website contains general information on how to prepare for a flood and what to do during and afterwards.

Floodplain zoning occurs where the flood risk across different parts of the floodplain is assessed and resulting land use takes this into account. Notice in diagram **E** that the most expensive land uses are located on higher land away from the river.

E *Floodplain zoning*

In some river basins, deliberate flooding is encouraged on low value land (e.g. marshes or grassland). This prevents flooding of more valuable land downstream.

∞ links

You can find out more about the Three Gorges Dam at **www.ctg.com.cn**

The Environment Agency gives extensive advice about flooding, which you can investigate at **www.environment-agency.gov.uk**.

Key terms

Floodplain zoning: controlling what is built on the floodplain so that areas that are at risk of flooding have low-value land uses.

Economic: relates to costs and finances at a variety of scales, from individuals up to government.

Social: refers to people's health, their lifestyle, community, etc.

Environmental: the impact on our surroundings, including the land, water and air as well as features of the built-up areas.

Activities

1 Study diagram **A**.

a Use the scale to estimate the reduction in the course of the river shown in the diagram after it had been straightened.

b Describe in your own words why river straightening reduces flood risk.

c Suggest some environmental effects of river straightening.

d How might river straightening actually increase the flood risk downstream?

2 Study map **B**, photo **C** and table **D**.

a Produce a fact file giving six key items of background information on the Three Gorges Dam. Include such things as its location, when it was completed, etc.

b Create a table to give one **economic**, one **social** and one **environmental** cost and benefit of the project.

3 Access the Environment Agency website from the link above. Working in pairs, produce a leaflet or poster on 'What to do in the event of a flood'. Include information on:

■ warnings available

■ how people can get general and specific information

■ what people should do before, during and after a flood in their home.

Make your leaflet or poster clear, eye-catching, informative and colourful.

4 Study diagram **E**. Vista Homes has submitted a planning application to build on the area labelled 'Playing fields'. Explain why, as the planner considering the application, you have rejected the scheme.

5.7 How are rivers in the UK managed to provide our water supply?

People in the UK use between 124 and 177 litres of water per day. This is an average of 151 litres per person per day. Table **A** shows actual water use, while the maps in **B** show the current and projected demands in England and Wales. The amount of rainfall over England and Wales varies, as does **water stress** (map **C**). Areas with high water stress can be seen as **areas of water deficit** while those with low stress are often **areas of water surplus**.

A *Water use for a selection of activities*

Activity	Average weekly use	Litres used per activity	Total number of litres
Bath	2	80	160
Flushing the toilet	35	8	280
Power shower	7	80	560
Washing machine	3	65	195
Dishwasher	4	25	100
Watering the garden	1	540	540
Washing car with bucket	1	32	32
Washing car with hose pipe	1	450	450

∞ links

You can find out more about water management at **www.environment-agency.gov.uk**. Click on Business and industry, then Water.

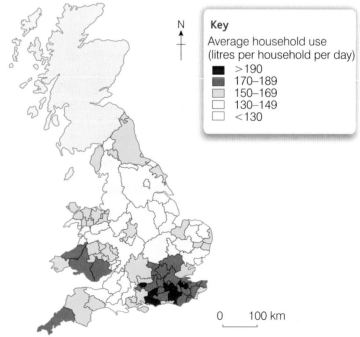

a Actual household use, 2005–06

b Forecast household use, 2029–30

N

Key
Average household use
(litres per household per day)
- >190
- 170–189
- 150–169
- 130–149
- <130

0   100 km

B *Household water use in England and Wales*

Key terms

Water stress: this happens when there is not enough water available. This may be because of an inadequate supply at a particular time or it may relate to water quality.

Areas of water deficit: areas where the rain that falls does not provide enough water and there may be shortages.

Areas of water surplus: areas that have more water than is needed – often such areas receive a high rainfall total, but have a relatively small population.

Sustainable: making sure there is enough water in the long term without harming the environment.

C *Water stress in England and Wales*

It is expected that demand for water will increase due to an increased number of households and population in certain areas. In 2000, the UK's population was 59.4 million. By 2009 this had risen to 61.8 million. Estimates predict a level of about 66 million by 2031. A more affluent lifestyle increases the demand for water as we buy more time-saving goods. We also demand foodstuffs out of season, which contributes to an increase in overall use of water.

There is a need to ensure that demand can be met in a **sustainable** way. A focus on local schemes is one way of ensuring this, rather than large-scale transfers. Generally, households that have a water meter use less water than those that do not – on average 19 litres per person per day less. When supplies are limited during drought, people use less water. Encouraging conservation is another strategy:

- Houses are being designed with better water efficiency.
- Devices are fitted to toilet cisterns to reduce water use.
- Rainwater can be collected.
- Bath water can be recycled to flush toilets.
- More people are taking showers than baths.

A significant amount of water is also lost in leakage.

Did you know ? ? ? ? ? ?

Around 3 per cent of water in the UK is used for drinking, although all water is of drinking quality. Many people in the world survive on less than 10 litres of water a day – a single flush of a toilet uses four-fifths of this.

Water transfer

A traditional solution to unequal supply of water has been to transfer water from areas of surplus to areas of deficit. In the late 1800s the River Vyrnwy in Powys was dammed to supply Liverpool with Welsh water (photo **D** and map **E**). Construction began in 1881 and was completed in 1888. It was the first stone dam in the UK. In front of the new dam, the Liverpool Corporation built the new village ready for when the valley was going to be flooded. In all, 2 chapels, 3 inns, 10 farmhouses and 37 houses were to be lost under the reservoir. The new village, which retained the name Llanwddyn, was built 3 km from the original village.

D   *The dam at Vyrnwy*

Since the dam was built, new transfer schemes have been proposed. In 1973 such an approach was favourably received and three new reservoirs were constructed (Brenig in Wales, Kielder in Northumberland and Carsington in Derbyshire), but the remaining plans never became reality. Predicted demand was never realised and there was over-capacity.

In 1994 the idea of transfer returned, with grand schemes to transfer water from the Severn to the Thames and Trent. However, costs were high and in 2004 it was concluded that local schemes, including small reservoirs, could meet the demand for water in areas such as the south-east. If, in the future, this is not possible, transfers may become a possibility.

E   *The location of Lake Vyrnwy*

Activities

1   Study table **A**.

a   List the number of times you have used water for the activities in the table during the last 24 hours.

b   Multiply the number of times by the litres shown.

c   Add this up to give the total number of litres.

2   Study the maps in **B**.

a   Which parts of England and Wales are forecast to have increased water demands by 2029–30?

b   Suggest reasons why demand in these areas is likely to rise.

3   Study map **E** and photo **D**.

Working in pairs, describe orally one economic, one social and one environmental issue that resulted from the dam over the River Vyrnwy.

4   With the aid of internet research, produce a colourful poster encouraging water conservation in the home.

6 Ice on the land

6.1 How has climate change affected the global distribution of ice?

Temperature fluctuations

We are aware of global warming and the possible impacts it may have on our weather and on sea levels. However, concern about climate change is nothing new. As recently as the 1970s, some scientists suggested that the climate was actually cooling and there was talk of another ice age.

Although the current warming trend may be linked to human activities, climate change in the past has been entirely natural. The most likely causes are to do with subtle variations in the earth's orbit, slight changes in its tilt towards the sun or variations in the global pattern of ocean currents, which move heat around the world. Currently, slight changes in the ocean currents off the west coast of South America result in the **El Niño effect**. This has a significant impact on patterns of rainfall and on the development of tropical storms in some parts of the world.

Climate change during the Pleistocene period

Geological time is divided into periods. The most recent (apart from the present warm Holocene period) is called the Pleistocene period. Sometimes known as the Ice Age, the Pleistocene was a period of some 2 million years when global temperatures fluctuated considerably (graph **A**).

In this section you will learn

the fluctuations of temperature in the recent geological past

changes in the extent and distribution of ice in the world resulting from changes in global temperature.

Key terms

El Niño effect: a periodic 'blip' in the usual global climate caused by a short-term warming of the cold ocean current that normally exists off the west coast of South America. It results in unusual patterns of temperature and rainfall and can lead to droughts and floods in certain parts of the world.

A Fluctuating temperatures during the Pleistocene period

Evidence from ice cores and deep-sea sediments suggests that there may have been as many as 20 cold periods or glacials during the Pleistocene period. During these **glacial periods** ice advanced south in the northern hemisphere to cover large parts of Europe and North America. Just 18,000 years ago ice reached its maximum extent during the last glacial period (map **B**). Map **C** shows how ice spread over the British Isles as far south as the Severn estuary at this time. Try to imagine ice covering almost all of the British Isles to a thickness of hundreds of metres in places. Even southern England would have been completely frozen, rather like parts of northern Canada today.

Did you know ??????

Between 1550 and 1750 the UK suffered a period of severe winters. This period has become known as the 'Little Ice Age'. During this time 'frost fairs' were held on the frozen surface of the River Thames in London.

Between the glacial periods were warmer **interglacials**, which were at least as warm as today's climate if not warmer. There is evidence, for example, that hippopotamuses lived as far north as Leeds. These fluctuations in temperature had nothing to do with human activities – there were no power stations or cars. These changes occurred over thousands of years. You can see why we should treat yearly trends and one-off weather events with extreme scepticism when linking them to climate change.

B Maximum global ice coverage 18,000 years ago

Key
→ Ice movement
▨ Tundra

Key terms

Glacial period: a period when ice advances due to falling temperatures.

Interglacial: a period when ice retreats due to rising temperatures.

Ice sheet: a large body of ice over 50,000 km^2 in extent.

Ice cap: a smaller body of ice (less than 50,000 km^2) usually found in mountainous regions.

Glacier: a finger of ice usually extending downhill from an ice cap and occupying a valley.

Scandinavian ice

Limit of ice 18,000 years ago

Maximum limit of ice sheet during the Pleistocene period

Britain still joined to Europe

0   200 km

C Ice coverage over the British Isles 18,000 years ago

Present-day global ice coverage

Currently there are two large areas of ice in the world called **ice sheets** (map **D**). The largest ice sheet is in Antarctica. It covers an area of 14 million km^2 and holds 90 per cent of all fresh water on the earth's surface. In places it is several kilometres thick. The Greenland ice sheet covers an area of 1.7 million km^2 (over 80 per cent of Greenland) and is currently showing increasing evidence of melting due to global warming.

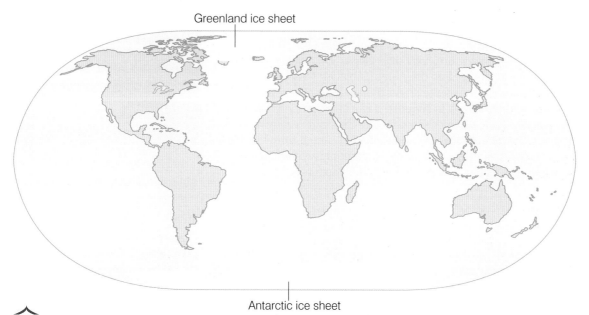

D   *Present-day distribution of ice sheets and ice caps*

Smaller bodies of ice covering an area of less than 50,000 km^2 are called **ice caps** or ice fields. They are usually found in mountainous areas where the temperatures are lower, such as in Iceland and the European Alps. Spreading out from ice caps are individual 'fingers' of ice called **glaciers**. They often follow former river valleys and extend down to an altitude where melting converts the ice to running water. Glaciers are found in every continent in the world and in some 47 individual countries.

∞ links

You can find out more about ice sheets, ice caps and glaciers on the Wikipedia website at **http://en.wikipedia.org/wiki/Ice_sheet**.

Activities

1   Study map **B**.

a   How many ice sheets existed in the northern hemisphere 18,000 years ago?

b   What were the names of the ice sheets in North America?

c   Using an atlas, describe the extent of the ice coverage in North America and Europe 18,000 years ago. Refer to lines of latitude and longitude. Which countries and present-day major cities would have been covered by ice?

d   Suggest why the glacial period 18,000 years ago had little impact on land masses in the southern hemisphere.

2   Study map **C**.

a   On a blank outline map, make a copy of the maximum extent of ice covering the British Isles. Include the arrows to show the direction of ice flow.

b   Using an atlas, label the four upland areas in the British Isles from where ice spread onto lower ground.

c   Why do you think these areas were source areas for ice during this glacial period?

d   Locate your nearest town or city on your map.

e   During this period it would have been possible to walk from the UK to the Netherlands, as there was no North Sea. Explain why.

6.2 | What causes glaciers to move?

Glaciers

A glacier acts as a system with inputs (**accumulation**) and outputs (**ablation**) (diagram **A**). The main input to the system is snow. When snow falls it becomes compacted as more snow settles on top. Air is expelled and the individual snowflakes turn into granular ice crystals. In much the same way that fluffy snow is squeezed into a hard snowball, the ice becomes denser and eventually turns into clear glacier ice. Avalanches of snow and ice also provide inputs into the system. Ablation mostly involves melting. This is likely to occur near the **snout** of the glacier where the air temperature is higher, particularly in summer. It can also occur on the surface of the glacier during summer. Occasionally chunks of ice break away at the snout. This is called calving and is another output from the system. A final output is the loss to the air by evaporation (water liquid to water vapour) and sublimation (water solid to water vapour).

A *The glacial system*

The glacier budget

The **glacier budget** is the balance between the inputs and the outputs. If accumulation exceeds ablation over several years, the glacier will advance. If ablation exceeds accumulation over several years, the glacier will retreat. Note on diagram **A** that accumulation tends to dominate near the top of the glacier whereas ablation dominates at the snout.

The glacier budget varies between the seasons (Graph **B**). In the winter there will be a lot of accumulation with little ablation. In the summer, when it is warmer, ablation will tend to dominate over accumulation.

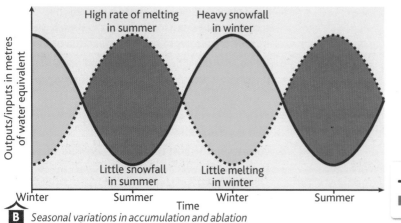

B *Seasonal variations in accumulation and ablation*

The South Cascade Glacier, USA

The South Cascade Glacier in Washington State, USA is one of three 'benchmark' glaciers in the USA that have been monitored by the United States Geological Survey (USGS) for over 40 years. Data have been collected on stream run-off, air temperature and mass balance (glacier budget).

All three glaciers have shown a marked retreat, which may well be caused by global warming. Worldwide, this trend is mirrored by other studies.

Look at the photos in **C**. They show how the South Cascade Glacier changed between 1928 and 2006. Table **D** contains statistics illustrating the changes that have taken place in the glacier budget since 1985.

1928

2006

C Changes in the South Cascade Glacier

D Glacier budget data for South Cascade Glacier, 1985–2005

Year	Winter (metres of water equivalent)	Summer (metres of water equivalent)	Net glacier budget (metres of water equivalent)	Year	Winter (metres of water equivalent)	Summer (metres of water equivalent)	Net glacier budget (metres of water equivalent)
1985	2.18	−3.38	−1.20	1996	2.94	−2.84	
1986	2.45	−3.06	−0.61	1997	3.71	−3.08	
1987	2.04	−4.10		1998	2.76	−4.62	
1988	2.44	−3.78		1999	3.59	−2.57	
1989	2.43	−3.34		2000	3.32	−2.94	
1990	2.60	−2.71		2001	1.90	−3.47	
1991	3.54	−3.47		2002	4.02	−3.47	
1992	1.91	−3.92		2003	2.66	−4.76	
1993	1.98	−3.21		2004	2.08	−3.73	
1994	2.39	−3.99		2005	1.97	−4.42	
1995	2.86	−3.55					

Activities

2 Study the photos in **C**.

a Describe the changes that took place in the South Cascade Glacier between 1928 and 2006.

b Why do you think the lower part of the glacier has melted in 2006?

c Do you think these photos support the concept of global warming? Explain your answer.

d Assuming the melting continues at much the same rate, when do you think the glacier will disappear completely?

3 Study table **D**.

a Copy and complete the table by calculating the figures for the net glacier budget column. The first two have been calculated for you.

b Present the data from the table in the form of a line graph.

c Describe the trends shown by your graph.

d To what extent does your graph support the evidence of glacier retreat indicated by the photos in **C**?

6.3 Which processes operate in glacial environments?

Freeze–thaw weathering

If you visit a glacial area you will notice huge piles of jagged rocks lining the sides of the valleys (photo **A**). These are piles of scree and they result from freeze–thaw weathering (page 37).

Glacial erosion

The angular rock fragments produced by freeze–thaw weathering are vital tools for glacial erosion. They work their way under the ice, acting like sand on a sheet of sandpaper enabling the ice to grind away at the valley floor and sides. The scree fragments themselves become shattered and pulverised by the weight of the ice, turning them into tiny pieces. This material is called rock flour and it causes glacial rivers to look milky.

Although glaciers move slowly – usually at only a few centimetres a year – they are capable of carrying out a tremendous amount of erosion. There are two main types of glacial erosion:

- **Abrasion** – this has a sandpaper effect caused by the weight of the ice scouring the valley floor and sides using the angular rock material trapped underneath (diagram **B**). In the same way that sandpaper smoothes wood, abrasion results in a smooth and often shiny rock surface. Scratches caused by large rocks beneath the ice can often be seen. These are called striations.

Rotational slip in hollow on mountainside

Scree slope

Mer de Glace moves by basal slip and internal deformation

A *Glacier movement in the French Alps and its valley*

- **Plucking** – when meltwater beneath a glacier freezes, it bonds the glacier base to the rocky surface below rather like glue. As the glacier moves, any loose fragments of rock are plucked away, like extracting loose teeth. This process leaves behind a jagged rocky surface as opposed to the smooth surface resulting from abrasion.

Glacial movement

In areas such as the Alps in Europe, melting ice in the summer produces a great deal of meltwater. This water helps to lubricate the glacier, enabling it to slide downhill. This type of movement is called basal slip and it can sometimes cause sudden movements of a glacier. In hollows high up on the valley sides, this movement may be more curved, in which case it is called **rotational slip** (photo **A**).

B *Processes of glacial erosion*

Key terms box on right

Abrasion: a process of erosion involving the wearing away of the valley floor and sides (glaciers) and the shoreline (coastal zones).

Plucking: a process of glacial erosion where individual rocks are plucked from the valley floor or sides as water freezes them to the glacier.

Rotational slip: slippage of ice along a curved surface.

Moraine: sediment carried and deposited by the ice.

Bulldozing: the pushing of deposited sediment at the snout by the glacier as it advances.

Hummock: a small area of raised ground, rather like a large molehill.

In winter, when the glacier is frozen to the rocky surface, the sheer weight of the ice and the influence of gravity cause individual ice crystals to deform in a plastic-like way. This process, called internal deformation, also causes the glacier to slowly move downhill.

Glacial transportation

Rock fragments resulting from freeze–thaw weathering and those that have been eroded by the ice are transported by the glacier, which acts like a giant conveyor belt. This sediment, called **moraine**, can be transported on the ice, in the ice (having been buried by snowfall) and below the ice.

Deposition

Most deposition occurs when the ice melts. As most melting occurs at the snout of a glacier, this is where the bulk of the material carried by the ice ends up. Renewed forward movement of the glacier pushes this debris further downhill rather like a bulldozer, which is why this process is called **bulldozing**.

As a glacier slowly retreats, it leaves behind a sheet of broken rock fragments and pulverised rock flour. Although some of this sediment (moraine) may remain to form **hummocks**, a good deal of it is washed away by meltwater rivers.

Study tip

Make sure that you learn the terminology associated with the glacial processes described.

Activities

1   Study photo **A** and diagram **B**.

a   What is the evidence that freeze–thaw weathering is active in this landscape?

b   Three conditions are required for freeze–thaw weathering to operate. The availability of water is one. Name the other two.

c   Draw a series of simple diagrams to show the process of freeze–thaw weathering. Add annotations to describe what is happening.

d   Why is freeze–thaw weathering absolutely vital if a glacier is going to be able to erode its valley?

2   Study diagram **B**.

a   Make a copy of the diagram.

b   Add labels and annotations to your diagram to describe how abrasion and plucking operate. Use colours to improve the clarity of the diagram.

3   Imagine you are in a glaciated area standing on a rocky surface that has been eroded by a glacier. What evidence would you look for to determine which of the two processes had eroded the rock on which you were standing?

4   Why does most of the material eroded by a glacier end up being deposited at the snout?

6.4   What are the distinctive landforms resulting from glacial processes?

Landforms of glacial erosion

Ice is an incredibly powerful agent of erosion and it can form spectacular landforms in mountainous areas. Look at photo **A**, which shows a glaciated area in the European Alps. Look closely at the labelled landforms. They are commonly found in areas of past and present glaciation.

A *Glaciers with major features of erosion*

Corries

Corries, also known as cirques and cwms, are large, hollowed-out depressions found on the upper slopes of glaciated valleys. They are characterised by having a steep back wall and a raised lip at the front. A corrie may contain a lake called a tarn.

Study diagram **B**, which describes the formation of a corrie. Snow accumulates in a sheltered hollow on a hillside. Gradually the snow turns to ice and a small corrie glacier is formed. Through the process of rotational slip, the glacier scoops out an over-deepened hollow in an action similar to that of an ice cream scoop. Reduced erosion at the front of the corrie due to thinner ice forms a raised lip, allowing a tarn to form behind it.

> **In this section you will learn**
>
> the characteristics and formation of glacial landforms.

> **Key terms**
>
> **Corrie:** a deep depression on a hillside with a steep back wall, often containing a lake.
>
> **Arête:** a knife-edged ridge, often formed between two corries.
>
> **Pyramidal peak:** a sharp-edged mountain peak.
>
> **Glacial trough:** a wide, steep-sided valley eroded by a glacier.
>
> **Truncated spur:** an interlocking spur that has been 'cut off' by ice leaving a very steep cliff.
>
> **Hanging valley:** a tributary glacial trough perched up on the side of a main valley, often marked by a waterfall.
>
> **Ribbon lake:** a long narrow lake in the bottom of a glacial trough.
>
> **Long profile:** this shows the changes in height and shape along the length of a glacier, from its source high in the mountains to its snout.
>
> **Ground moraine:** glacial material deposited on the valley floor, often forming hummocks .
>
> **Lateral moraine:** a ridge of sediment running along the edge of a glacier where it meets the valley side.
>
> **Medial moraine:** a ridge of sediment running down the centre of a glacier formed when two lateral moraines merge.
>
> **Terminal moraine:** a high ridge running across the valley representing the maximum advance of a glacier.

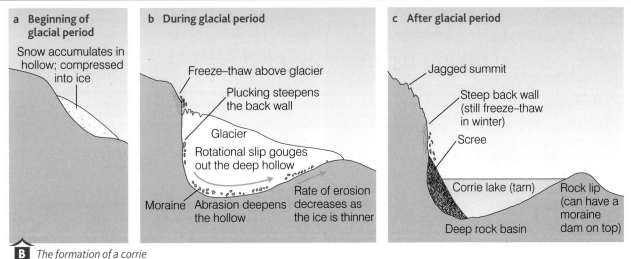

B *The formation of a corrie*

Arêtes and pyramidal peaks

An **arête** is a knife-edged ridge often found at the back of a corrie or separating two glaciated valleys (diagram **C**). Arêtes are often extremely narrow features and, although popular with hill walkers, strong crosswinds can make walking along them hazardous.

A typical arête forms when erosion in two back-to-back corries causes the land in between to become ever narrower. If three or more corries have formed on a mountain, erosion may lead to the formation of a single peak rather than a ridge. This feature is called a **pyramidal peak**.

C *Arêtes and pyramidal peaks*

Glacial valley landforms

Glaciers most commonly flow along pre-existing river valleys. Unable to flow around obstacles, they tend to carve relatively straight courses (diagram **D**). Their incredible strength enables them to form dramatic features including deep **glacial troughs**, **truncated spurs**, **hanging valleys** and **ribbon lakes**.

A glacial trough is a steep-sided, wide and relatively flat-bottomed valley. The process of abrasion is mostly responsible for the formation of glacial troughs – the moving glacier grinds into the base and sides of the valley over a period of many hundreds of years. Unable to flow around previously existing interlocking spurs, the glacier simply cuts straight through them, forming steep-edged truncated spurs. Former tributary valleys, occupied with small glaciers unable to erode down to the same level as the main glacier, are left perched up on the valley side as hanging valleys. Spectacular waterfalls often mark these features.

Erosion of the valley floor is usually erratic and results in an uneven **long profile**. Certain stretches of the valley are prone to increased downcutting, for example where the ice becomes thicker after a tributary glacier has joined or where a weaker band of rock is encountered. At the end of a glacial period, water may occupy this deepened section to form a long, narrow ribbon lake often several tens of metres deep. Ribbon lakes are common in Scotland, with one of the most famous being Loch Ness. Occasionally, a much more shallow ribbon lake forms in a glacial trough behind a dam of deposited moraine.

Activities

1   Study photo **A**.

    Name the glacial features labelled **A**, **B** and **C**.

2   Study diagrams **B** and **C**.

a   Draw a series of simple diagrams to show how the erosion of two back-to-back corries can result in the formation of an arête. Add detailed labels to describe what is happening. Use diagram **B** to help you.

b   Why are arêtes dangerous features to walk along?

a **River valley before glaciation**

Rounded watershed

Source of river

Tributary river

Steep-sided
V-shaped valley

Narrow valley floor

Interlocking spurs

Confluence

Tributary river

b **Same valley after glaciation**

Jagged watershed

Cliff-like U-shaped valley

Truncated spurs

Tributary in a hanging
valley with a waterfall

Long, narrow
ribbon lake

Wide, flat
valley floor

D *Features and landforms in a glacial trough*

Landforms of glacial transportation and deposition

Moraine

Moraine is the general term given to the largely angular rock material transported and then deposited by the ice. It can sometimes be so extensive that it forms a thick blanket of material. Geologists refer to this glacially deposited material as till or boulder clay, on account of the range of sizes of sediment present. Till is found along much of the east coast of northern England. Although it forms fertile soils, it is weak and easily eroded when exposed at the coast.

It is possible to identify a number of types of moraine (diagram **F**):

- **Ground moraine** – material that was dragged underneath the glacier which is simply left behind when the ice melts. It often forms uneven hummocky ground.

- **Lateral moraine** – forms at the edges of the glacier. It is mostly scree that has fallen off the valley sides following freeze–thaw weathering. When the ice melts, it forms a slight ridge on the valley side.

- **Medial moraine** – when a tributary glacier joins the main glacier, two lateral moraines merge to produce a single line of sediment that runs down the centre of the main glacier. On melting, the medial moraine forms a ridge down the centre of the valley.

- **Terminal moraine** – huge amounts of material pile up at the snout of a glacier to form a high ridge, often tens of metres high across the valley. This is a terminal moraine. It represents the furthest extent of the glacier's advance, hence the term 'terminal'.

Meltwater often erodes away moraine features, leaving only fragments.

E *Simplified cross-section of a glacial trough*

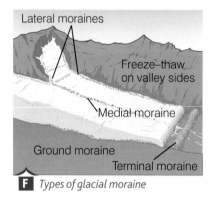

Lateral moraines

Freeze–thaw
on valley sides

Medial moraine

Ground moraine

Terminal moraine

F *Types of glacial moraine*

Activities

3 Study diagram **E**.

a Draw a large copy of the diagram.

b Use diagram **D** to help you label the main features shown on the cross-section.

4 Standing in a glacial trough, you notice a steep rock cliff on the valley side. What evidence would you look for to identify whether it was a truncated spur or a hanging valley?

5 How do ribbon lakes form? Use simple diagrams to help answer this question.

OS map study: glacial features in the Nant Ffrancon valley, Wales

During the last ice advance, North Wales was buried beneath a thick sheet of ice. Glaciers scoured the valleys to create spectacular landforms – none more so than in the Nant Ffrancon valley (map extract **G** and photo **H**). Note that the Welsh term *cwm* denotes a corrie and *llyn* a lake. Take a few moments to orientate the photo on the map and then attempt the following activities.

G   *1 : 50,000 OS map extract of Nant Ffrancon valley, part of map sheet 115*

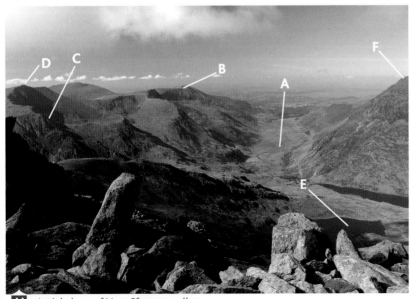

H   *Aerial photo of Nant Ffrancon valley*

Study tip

Practise drawing glacial features and adding labels, including process terms to describe their characteristics and formation.

Did you know ???????

In 1967, in his boat Bluebird K7, Donald Campbell used a ribbon lake called Coniston Water in the Lake District to try to beat his existing world water speed record of 444 kph. Tragically, he was killed as Bluebird flipped and somersaulted at 515 kph.

Drumlins

Drumlins are smooth, egg-shaped hills commonly about 10 m in height and up to a few hundred metres in length, which often occur in clusters on the floor of a glacial trough (photo **I**). They are made of morainic material, but instead of simply being dumped they were actually moulded and shaped by the moving ice. Drumlins usually have a blunt end, which faces up-valley, and a more pointed end facing down-valley. This makes them useful indicators of the direction of glacial movement.

I *Drumlins near Alberta, Canada showing the steep up-valley and the gentler down-valley slopes*

⊂⊃ links

A useful glossary with photos can be found at www.uwsp.edu/geo/faculty/Lemke/alpine_glacial_glossary/glossary.html.

Activities

6 Study diagram **F**.

a What is the difference between a lateral moraine and a medial moraine?

b What sort of deposited material would you expect to find making up a terminal moraine?

7 Study photo **I**. Draw a sketch of the photograph. Add labels to describe its main features. Add an arrow to show the likely direction of movement.

8 Imagine you have discovered two small hills in the centre of a glacial trough. What evidence would you look for to identify whether the feature was a fragment of a medial moraine or a drumlin?

9 Why are moraines often fragmentary?

10 Study map extract **G** and photo **H**.

a What are the names of the landforms labelled **A** to **D**?

b What is the name of the corrie lake (tarn) at **E**?

c What is the name of the peak at **F** and what is its six-figure grid reference?

d In what direction do you think the glacier flowed along the valley? Support your answer with evidence from the map.

e Why do you think some corries have lakes and others do not?

f What attractions are there for tourists to the area? Include references to the map in your answer.

11 Study map extract **G** and photo **H**.

a Draw a cross-section across the Nant Ffrancon valley from grid reference 630620 to the 978 m spot height at grid reference 657620. (If you feel confident about drawing cross-sections, you may choose to take the section further west.)

b Use the same horizontal scale as the map (2 cm = 1 km) and use a vertical scale of 1 cm = 500 m.

c Locate and label the following features:

▪ frost-shattered crags on the east side of the valley

▪ glacial trough

▪ the river (the Afon Ogwen)

▪ the A5 road.

d Complete your cross-section by adding a title and labelling the axes.

12 Study map extract **G**. Complete a summary table to help with your revision. For each of the following features, select an example from the map and draw a simple sketch of the contour patterns. Include scales, contour values and place names. Keep it simple but make it accurate.

▪ corrie (cwm)

▪ arête

▪ ribbon lake

▪ glacial trough

▪ peak (not ideal pyramidal peaks, but not bad examples!)

6.5   What opportunities do glacial areas offer for tourism?

Tourism in the French Alps: Chamonix

Chamonix is situated in the north-westerly part of the Alps, just 15 km from the Swiss border and 15 km from Italy via the Mont Blanc tunnel (map **A**). Chamonix and its valley are dominated by the rounded summit of Mont Blanc, Europe's highest mountain at 4,808 m (photo **B**).

Chamonix has been a centre for tourism for over 250 years. Its stunning landscape has a huge amount to offer outdoor enthusiasts. The resident population of 10,000 is swollen by up to 100,000 visitors a day in summer and about 60,000 a day in winter.

> **In this section you will learn**
>
> the attractions and opportunities available for tourism in the Alps
>
> the need for responsible tourism and sustainable management.

Case study

A *Location map of Chamonix*

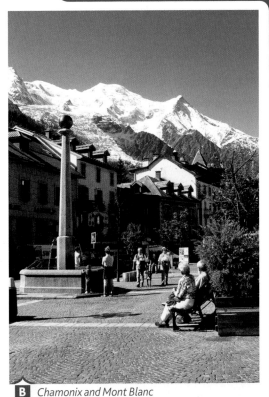

B *Chamonix and Mont Blanc*

Winter attractions

Chamonix provides a huge range of options for skiers and snowboarders of all abilities (map **C** and photo **D**). Cable cars and cog railways provide easy access to the pistes. Cross-country skiing has become popular and two local courses have been established nearby. There are opportunities for ice climbing, free riding and paragliding. Snowshoe trails offer hikers the opportunity to walk in the area. Chamonix itself caters for winter tourists by providing hotels, restaurants, heated swimming pools and spas. With its museums, shops and historical buildings, there is much to do away from the slopes.

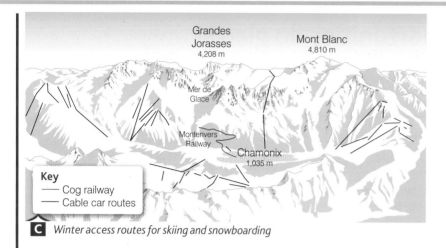

Grandes
Jorasses
4,208 m

Mont Blanc
4,810 m

Mer de
Glace

Montenvers
Railway

Chamonix
1,035 m

Key
— Cog railway
— Cable car routes

C *Winter access routes for skiing and snowboarding*

Summer attractions

In summer, the mountain landscapes offer tremendous potential for outdoor activities. The famous Montenvers railway takes visitors to the Mer de Glace, where visitors can witness the awesome scale of the glacier and the valley that it has carved (photo **A**, page 128). An ice cave allows visitors to step inside the glacier (photo **E**).

The Chamonix area boasts 350 km of marked hiking trails, 40 km of mountain bike tracks, rock climbing, mountaineering, paragliding, rafting, canyoning, pony trekking and summer luging. The town comes alive in the summer with live music, outdoor cafés and colourful flowers.

Impacts of tourism in the French Alps

Tourism to Chamonix and the surrounding area brings both benefits and problems.

Benefits of tourism:

■ Tourists bring huge economic benefits, providing employment for local people in hotels and restaurants, in sports facilities and as guides and instructors. Construction and maintenance provides jobs for local people.

■ The extra income supports local services such as shops. Local people benefit from improvements in public transport and health care.

■ Chamonix is maintained as an attractive town. Pedestrian streets give people safe access to shops and the town is clean and well lit.

Problems of tourism:

■ The town can become noisy and congested at peak times. Access to Chamonix via motorway is good, but in Chamonix itself the roads are narrow and become jammed easily.

■ Mountain footpaths have become eroded due to the sheer volume of visitors, both walking and using mountain bikes.

D *Winter sports in Chamonix*

E *Tourists explore the ice grotto in the Mer de Glace*

- The shops, cafés and restaurants are tourist-orientated and expensive. Local people often have to pay more for everyday items. Houses are expensive and many are second homes for wealthy visitors.

- Conflicts can arise between different groups of people. Mass tourism activities can create unwelcome noise and damage to the environment, which can detract from the enjoyment of those seeking more peaceful activities such as walking or bird watching. Tourism can conflict with local people. Farm animals can be harmed by thoughtless actions of tourists, such as leaving gates open or dropping litter.

Managing tourism in Chamonix

- Chamonix is keen to promote **responsible tourism** as a means of balancing the demands of tourism with the need to conserve and protect the environment.

- The Chamonix municipality (local authority) provides an environmentally friendly transport service with clean energy buses and free public transport.

- An initiative called Espace Mont-Blanc involves cooperation between France, Italy and Switzerland on issues of international transport, nature conservation, forests and water resources.

- A further initiative called Tomorrow's Valley brings together representatives from the local community and tourist groups to plan for **sustainable management**. Current projects include:

  - burying service networks such as electricity lines underground

  - renovating and preserving historic buildings and monuments

  - preserving natural wetlands and peat bogs

  - minimising the impact of skiing on the landscape by planting trees and using local building materials that blend in with the natural environment

  - maintaining and way-marking footpaths and cleaning rivers – this provides seasonal employment for local people

  - supporting local traditional employment sectors, particularly farming.

Activity

1 Study the photos, maps and text.

a   In the form of a table, draw up two lists of the activities available to visitors in winter and summer. (You could add illustrations to your table using pictures from the internet and present your information electronically if you wish.)

b   Why do you think Chamonix promotes the area as both a winter and a summer destination?

c   Suggest some possible conflicts that might arise between different groups of tourists in winter and summer.

d   How might conflicts arise between tourists and local people?

e   In what ways does tourism have a negative impact on the environment?

f   What management measures have been adopted to protect the environment?

g   Why is it important to involve local people in designing management plans for the local area?

Key terms

Responsible tourism: the idea of encouraging a balance between the demands of tourism and the need to protect the environment.

Sustainable management: a form of management that ensures that developments are long lasting and non-harmful to the environment.

⃝links

The main Chamonix tourism site, which has plenty of excellent information, is at **www.chamonix.com**.

The Espace Mont-Blanc website is at **www.espace-mont-blanc.com**.

A detailed map of Chamonix can be found at **www.skifrance.com/chamonix/resortmap.html**.

6.6 What is the impact of climate change on Alpine communities?

Evidence for recent climate change

Many of the Alps' most popular resorts, such as Morzine and Megève, lie at relatively low levels in France – about 1,000 m. They are all in danger of running out of snow as the world warms up.

The UN estimates that in 30 years' time the snowline will have risen by 300 m and that up to half of all resorts in Europe will be forced to close by 2050. This will cause a great deal of hardship as hotels, restaurants and shops are forced to close due to lack of business. Switzerland could lose up to £1bn a year if its resorts close down.

Responses in lower-level resorts

Lower-level resorts have responded in a number of ways in order to cope with the problem:

- Tourists have been transported by bus to higher-level resorts for skiing.
- Artificial snow is cannoned onto the slopes (photo **A**). In low-level parts of Austria and Italy, up to 40 per cent of resorts now have to make their own snow. This is expensive and can have a serious effect on vegetation, which may take 30 years to recover.
- Resorts have had to re-invent themselves. Some have started to promote themselves as centres for cross-country skiing, hiking, climbing, sledding or snowshoeing.
- There are plans to build new ski lifts to link resorts, but this could cause considerable damage to the environment.

In this section you will learn

how climate change poses a threat to communities dependent on tourism

how Alpine environments are fragile and need careful sustainable management.

Key terms

Fragile environment: an environment that is easily unbalanced and damaged by natural or human factors.

Did you know ??????

The snow cannon was developed in 1950. It uses over 1 million litres of water to cover 0.4 ha to a depth of 30 cm.

A A snow cannon in action on the Alps

Abondance, France

Abondance is a typical Alpine ski resort in the Haute-Savoie region of France (photo **B**). It is one of several traditional ski resorts in the area that depends on income from winter skiers for the survival of its many hotels, restaurants and shops.

In 2007, following 15 years of unreliable snowfall, the ski lifts in Abondance closed for the last time. The local council is considering two options in an attempt to secure its future and provide employment for its local population:

- To develop other forms of winter sports, such as ski touring, snowshoeing and snow-mobiling that are less dependent on deep snow than traditional skiing.

- To develop its summer programme of activities to include hiking, water sports and mountain biking. This would enable the town to become more of an all-year round resort rather than just a winter one.

New developments

The High Alps form a pristine landscape rich in wildlife and free from pollution. With low-level resorts in decline, there is considerable pressure from developers to develop these wilderness areas. However, tourism developments can harm **fragile environments** in a number of ways:

- Road construction and the building of ski lifts, houses and hotels can have a big impact on natural ecosystems and habitats.

- Trees are often cut down to make way for developments. They have an important function in binding the soil on steep slopes and breaking up avalanches.

- Overuse of slopes for skiing can strip a hillside of its natural vegetation, which can take many years to re-establish. Mountain biking can lead to gullies, which can be enlarged following heavy rain or snowmelt to form scars on the landscape.

- With increased levels of pollution (e.g. noise, visual), the natural landscape loses some of its appeal and this may reduce the attractiveness of the area for tourism.

B *The Abondance valley in the French Alps*

In Austria new ski lifts and cable cars are being constructed to open up the Gepatsch Glacier to skiers above 3,500 m. However, with almost all Alpine glaciers retreating, there is no guarantee that glacier skiing will last for long. At Lisenser Fernerkogel new cable cars and pistes are being developed (photo **C**). In other areas there are plans to construct cable cars to link resorts, which would enable lower-level resorts to remain viable even if tourists have to travel by cable car to another higher-level resort to ski.

Should the environment be protected at all costs or should some development be allowed in order to provide employment for local people and secure the region's economic future?

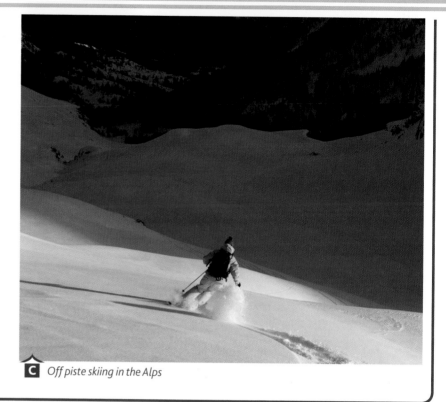

C   *Off piste skiing in the Alps*

Activities

1   Study photo **B**.

a   Why are low-level ski resorts like Abondance suffering from a decrease in winter tourism?

b   How has this affected the lives of local people living in these resorts?

c   What strategies can low-level resorts adopt to respond to the problem?

d   Imagine that you are the mayor of Abondance. Which of the two options do you favour and why? Perhaps you think that both options should be adopted.

2   Study photo **C**.

a   What is meant by 'off piste' skiing?

b   Why are many people attracted to this type of skiing?

c   Imagine that the area in the photograph was to be developed as a permanent ski resort. What developments would you expect to take place and how would they impact on the environment?

d   Make a list of the advantages and disadvantages of developing new areas such as photo **C** as ski resorts.

e   Do you think the area in photo **C** should be developed as a ski resort? Explain your answer.

Study tip

Be aware of the arguments for and against developments in the Alps. Be prepared to express your own opinion.

∞ **links**

The BBC has information at **www. bbc.co.uk**. Type 'Alpine future' into the search box.

6.7   What is the avalanche hazard?

What are avalanches?

Avalanches are masses of snow, ice and rocks that move downhill at speeds of up to 300kph. They occur naturally in mountain environments and only pose a hazard when they impact on people or human activity, such as transport routes or houses.

There are two main types of avalanche:

■ **Loose snow avalanche** – this type of avalanche usually starts from a single point on the hillside and involves loose, powdery snow (photo and diagram **A**).

■ **Slab avalanche** – this tends to be a more deadly type of avalanche. It involves a large slab of ice and snow shearing away from a hillside and moving rapidly downhill, carrying rocks and trees as it does so (photo and diagram **B**). It has immense power and can cause a great deal of damage.

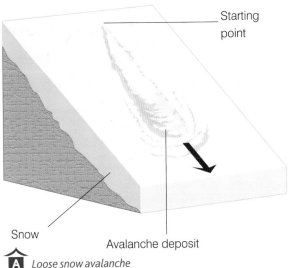

Starting point

Snow

Avalanche deposit

A *Loose snow avalanche*

B *Loose snow avalanche that may trigger the collapse of the huge slab in the top left*

C *Slab avalanche*

Labels on diagram C: Starting zone, Crown, Flanks, Bed surface, Track, Run-out/debris toe

Causes of avalanches

There are a number of factors that contribute to the risk of avalanches:

- Heavy snowfall – this adds weight to earlier snowfalls. Uneven rates of freezing, together with occasional melting, can create distinct layers within the snow and ice making slab avalanches more likely to occur as one layer slips over another.
- Steep slopes – avalanches are more likely to occur on steep slopes in excess of 30°.
- Tree removal – the removal of trees for ski developments enables avalanches to move downhill unimpeded. When present on a hillside, trees can break up an avalanche and prevent it becoming too large.
- Temperature rise – sudden rises in temperatures and associated melting often lead to avalanches in the spring.
- Heavy rainfall – this can lubricate a slope and trigger an avalanche.
- Human factors – almost all deaths from avalanches kill the people who actually triggered them. Off-piste skiing is a major cause of avalanches because it often involves skiing in areas of fresh snow that have not been assessed for the avalanche risk.

Avalanches as hazards

Deaths, injuries and property damage due to avalanches have increased in the last 50 years. This is mainly due to the growth of winter sports and the expansion of ski resorts to cater for increasing numbers of visitors. In Switzerland an average of 40 people die each year from avalanches, over 80 per cent of whom are involved in winter sports. In 2007–08, avalanches in France killed 15 people. Four were climbing and the rest were skiing or snowboarding.

> **Study tip**
>
> Be aware that avalanches usually result from a combination of factors, although there is usually a single trigger such as heavy snowfall or an earthquake. Use the internet to update your case studies.

⚭ links

Up-to-date case studies are important, so make use of online resources and the internet. The main media sites, such as **www.bbc.co.uk** are excellent sources of information.

Increasing numbers of people are putting themselves at risk from avalanches. If avalanches become more frequent as the climate warms, the death toll and damage to property may well increase.

∞links

The Avalanche Center is an excellent source of information at **www.avalanche-center.org**.

D *Reducing the avalanche hazard*

Recent avalanches

Europe, 2006 and 2009

The winter of 2005–06 was a record year for fatalities in the French Alps, with 49 people being killed in off-piste avalanches alone. Irregular weather patterns, with fluctuating temperatures and variable amounts of rain and snow, led to a greater number of avalanches than usual. The fashion for extreme sports was also thought to put more people at risk from avalanches. In 2009 heavy snow triggered avalanches across Europe killing over 20 people who were skiing, climbing and hiking.

Salang, Afghanistan 2010

A freak snowstorm in the Hindu Kush mountains in Afghanistan led to a series of at least 36 avalanches at Salang, north of Kabul. The avalanches buried 3.5 km of road, killing over 170 people and trapping over 2,000 travellers on the road (Photo **E**). Strong winds and heavy rain in the area contributed to the cause of the avalanches.

Case study

E *Rescuers search for survivors in avalanche debris at Salang*

Activities

1   Study figures **A** and **C**, and diagram **D**.

a   With the aid of simple diagrams and sketches, describe the differences between a loose snow avalanche and a slab avalanche.

b   Why do you think slab avalanches pose a greater threat than loose snow avalanches?

c   Present the information describing the factors contributing to the risk of avalanches in the form of a large diagram of a mountain slope similar to that in diagram **D**. Use labels to identify the various factors on your drawing.

d   For each scenario in the case study, which factors seemed to have been important in triggering the avalanches that caused the death and destruction?

2   Study diagram **D**.

a   Draw a simplified version of the diagram.

b   For each of the measures identified, add an annotated label to describe how it reduces the avalanche threat.

c   Which of the measures in your diagram do you think are most appropriate for poor mountainous parts of the world such as Afghanistan? Give reasons for your answer.

3   Use the internet to research recent avalanches. The Planet Ski website at www.planetski.eu/news is a good place to start.

7 The coastal zone

7.1 How do waves shape our coastline?

How waves form

Waves are usually formed by the wind blowing over the sea. Friction with the surface of the water causes ripples to form and these develop into waves. The stretch of open water over which the wind blows is called the **fetch**. The longer the fetch, the more powerful a wave can become.

Waves can also be formed more dramatically when earthquakes or volcanic eruptions shake the seabed. These waves are called tsunamis. In December 2004 giant tsunami waves devastated the countries bordering the Indian Ocean and 240,000 people were killed (photo **A**).

> **In this section you will learn**
>
> how waves are formed
>
> why waves break at the coast
>
> the characteristics of constructive and destructive waves.

> **Did you know** ??????
>
> When the volcano Krakatoa erupted in 1883, a tsunami said to be 35 m high killed 36,000 people on the Indonesian island of Sumatra.

A The Indian Ocean tsunami 2004, Sri Lanka

When waves reach the coast

In the open sea, despite the wavy motion of the water surface, there is little horizontal transfer of water. It is only when the waves approach the shore that there is forward movement of water as waves break and wash up the **beach**. Diagram **B** shows what happens as waves approach the shore. Note how the seabed interrupts the circular orbital movement of the water. As the water becomes shallower, the circular motion becomes more elliptical. This causes the **crest** of the wave to rise up and then eventually to topple onto the beach. The water that rushes up the beach is called the **swash**. The water that flows back towards the sea is called the **backwash**.

C Surfers on a beach in Newquay

Circular orbit in open water

Friction with the seabed distorts the circular orbital motion

Top of wave moves faster

Increasingly elliptical orbit

Wave begins to break

Water from previous wave returns

Water rushes up the beach

Shelving seabed (beach)

B Waves approaching the coast

Types of wave found at the coast

It is possible to identify two types of wave at the coast: **constructive waves** and **destructive waves**.

Constructive waves are waves that surge up the beach with a powerful swash. They carry large amounts of sediment and 'construct' the beach, making it more extensive. These are the waves that are loved by surfers (photo **C**). They are formed by distant storms, which can be hundreds of kilometres away. The waves are well spaced apart and are powerful when they reach the coast. Diagram **D** shows the typical characteristics of a constructive wave.

Destructive waves are formed by local storms close to the coast. They are so named because they 'destroy' the beach. Destructive waves are closely spaced and often interfere with each other, producing a chaotic, swirling mass of water. They rear up to form towering waves before crashing down onto the beach (diagram **E**). There is little forward motion (swash) when a destructive wave breaks, but a powerful backwash. This explains the removal of sediment and the destruction of the beach.

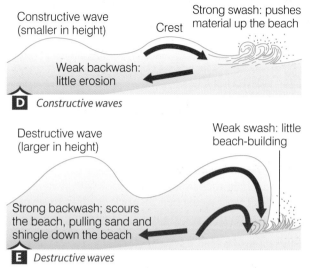

D   *Constructive waves*

E   *Destructive waves*

Key terms

Fetch: the distance of open water over which the wind can blow.

Beach: a deposit of sand or shingle at the coast, often found at the head of a bay.

Crest: the top of a wave.

Swash: the forward movement of a wave up a beach.

Backwash: the backward movement of water down a beach when a wave has broken.

Constructive wave: a powerful wave with a strong swash that surges up a beach.

Destructive wave: a wave formed by a local storm that crashes down onto a beach and has a powerful backwash.

Activities

1   Study photo **A**.

a   What evidence is there in the photo that tsunamis are extremely powerful?

b   Are there any safe places in the photo?

c   Many of the people who died in 2004 lived in small coastal communities around the Indian Ocean. Why do people choose to live close to the sea?

2   Study diagram **B** make a copy of it.

a   Draw an arrow to show the waves approaching the coast.

b   Write the labels 'swash' and 'backwash' in the correct places.

c   What causes the waves to rise up and break on the beach?

d   When waves break on a sandy or pebbly beach, the amount of backwash is often less than the amount of swash. Why do you think this is?

e   On a pebble beach, larger pebbles are often found near the top of the beach with smaller ones near the bottom. Use your answer to d to suggest why this happens.

3   Study photo **C**, which shows a constructive wave. They are sometimes known as a surging waves because they 'surge' up the beach.

a   Why do surfers prefer constructive waves to destructive waves?

b   Are constructive waves generated by storms close to the coast or a long way off?

c   Wave power is being considered as a source of renewable energy off the north Cornwall coast. Do you think this is a good idea? Explain your answer.

Study tip

Practise drawing a labelled sketch of a wave type. It is a good way to learn its features.

∞ links

You can find out more about the Indian Ocean tsunami at **www. guardian.co.uk/world/tsunami2004**.

Watch the surfers in action by webcam at **www.fistralsurfcam.com**.

7.2 Which land processes shape our coastline?

Weathering

Processes of weathering affect rocks exposed at the coast. Look at pages 37 to 39 to find out how common weathering processes operate. At the coast, freeze–thaw weathering is particularly effective if the rock exposed is porous (contains holes) and permeable (allows water to pass through it). Look at photo **A**. The autumn of 2000 was exceptionally wet and the chalk rock became saturated with water. During late winter, long periods of frost weakened the rock, leading to several dramatic **rockfalls** along the south coast of England, including the one shown.

A Rockfall at Beachy Head, Sussex

Key terms

Cliff: a steep or vertical face of rock often found at the coast.

Rockfall: the collapse of a cliff face or the fall of individual rocks from a cliff.

Did you know ? ? ? ? ? ?

The Belle Tout lighthouse at Beachy Head was built in 1832 and decommissioned in 1907. It was moved inland by 17 m in 1999 to prevent it succumbing to coastal erosion. It is now bed and breakfast accommodation.

Mass movement

The rockfall shown in photo **A** is one example of mass movement. Mass movement is the downhill movement of material under the influence of gravity. In 1993, 60 m of **cliff** slid onto the beach near Scarborough in North Yorkshire, taking with it part of the Holbeck Hall Hotel (photo **B**). Teetering on the brink, the hotel had to be demolished. Diagram **C** describes some of the common types of mass movement found at the coast.

B Landslip at Holbeck Hall, Scarborough

a **Rockfall** – fragments of rock break away from the cliff face, often due to freeze–thaw weathering

Cliff face

Scree

b **Landslide** – blocks of rock slide downhill

Slide plane

Detached rock

Bedding of rocks

c **Mudflow** – saturated soil and weak rock flows down a slope

Soil

Stream

Saturated soil and rock debris

Lobe

Bedrock

d **Rotational slip** – slump of saturated soil and weak rock along a curved surface

Head

Scarp

Foot

Curved slip plane

Toe

C *Types of mass movement at the coast*

Both mass movement and weathering provide an input of material to the coastal system. Much of this material is carried away by the waves to be deposited elsewhere along the coast.

Activity

Study photo **A** and the section about chalk on pages 42–43.

a Why is chalk vulnerable to freeze–thaw weathering?

b How does freeze–thaw weathering operate?

c What other weathering processes affect chalk? Describe how these processes work.

d How might rockfalls such as that shown in the photo be a hazard to people?

e What do you think will happen to the pile of rocks at the base of the cliff in the photo?

f Imagine the local council has decided to place an information board at the top of the cliff to warn people of the dangers of cliff collapse. It wants to inform people why the cliff is dangerous. Design an information board explaining why the cliff is vulnerable to rockfalls. Use diagrams to illustrate your board and do not forget to warn people to keep well away from the cliff edge!

Study tip

Weathering processes take place over long periods of time and often require many repetitions before changes occur. Always refer to the correct geographical terms when writing about weathering and mass movement.

∞ links

You can find out more about a Beachy Head rockfall in 1999 at **www.bbc.co.uk**. Enter 'Beachy Head rockfall' into the search box.

There is a spectacular video of a rockfall in Cornwall at **www.guardian.co.uk** search for 'massive Cornwall rockfall'.

7.3 Which marine processes shape our coastline?

Coastal erosion

When a wave crashes down on a beach or smashes against a cliff, it carries out the process of erosion (photo **A**). There are several processes of coastal erosion:

- **Hydraulic power** – this involves the sheer power of the waves as they smash onto a cliff (photo **A**). Trapped air is blasted into holes and cracks in the rock, eventually causing the rock to break apart. The explosive force of trapped air operating in a crack is called cavitation.
- **Corrasion** – this involves fragments of rock being picked up and hurled by the sea at a cliff. The rocks act like erosive tools by scraping and gouging the rock.
- **Abrasion** – this is the 'sandpapering' effect of pebbles grinding over a rocky platform, often causing it to become smooth.
- **Solution** – some rocks are vulnerable to being dissolved by seawater. This is particularly true of limestone and chalk, which form cliffs in many parts of the UK.
- **Attrition** – this is where rock fragments carried by the sea knock against one another, causing them to become smaller and more rounded.

Coastal transportation

Four main types of sediment transportation can be identified (diagram **B**). The size and quantity of sediment transported by the sea depends on the strength of the waves and tidal currents. During storms, quite large pebbles can be flung up on to seawalls and promenades where they can cause damage to buildings and cars.

In this section you will learn

the processes of coastal erosion, transportation and deposition.

Key terms

Hydraulic power: the sheer power of the waves.

Corrasion: the effect of rocks being flung at the cliff by powerful waves.

A Waves crashing onto cliffs in Iceland

Solution: dissolved chemicals often derived from limestone or chalk

Suspension: particles carried (suspended) within the water

Traction: large pebbles rolled along the seabed

Saltation: a 'hopping' or 'bouncing' motion of particles too heavy to be suspended

B Types of coastal transportation

The movement of sediment on a beach is largely determined by the direction of wave approach. Look at diagram **C**. Note that where the waves approach 'head on', sediment is moved up and down the beach. However, if the waves approach at an angle, sediment moves along the beach in a zig-zag pattern. This is called **longshore drift**.

Key terms

Longshore drift: the transport of sediment along a stretch of coastline caused by waves approaching the beach at an angle.

Bay: a broad coastal inlet often with a beach.

Headland: a point of usually high land jutting out into the sea.

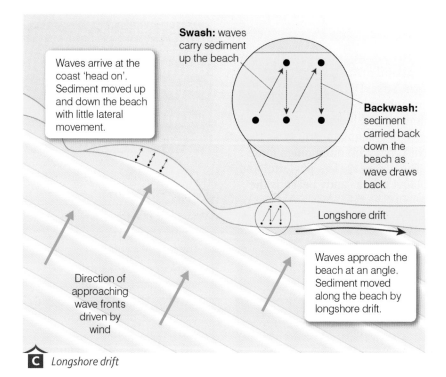

Waves arrive at the coast 'head on'. Sediment moved up and down the beach with little lateral movement.

Swash: waves carry sediment up the beach

Backwash: sediment carried back down the beach as wave draws back

Longshore drift

Direction of approaching wave fronts driven by wind

Waves approach the beach at an angle. Sediment moved along the beach by longshore drift.

C   *Longshore drift*

Coastal deposition

Coastal deposition takes place in areas where the flow of water slows down. Sediment can no longer be carried or rolled along and has to be deposited. Coastal deposition most commonly occurs in **bays**, where the energy of the waves is reduced on entering the bay. This explains the presence of beaches in bays and accounts for the lack of beaches at **headlands**, where wave energy is much greater.

Study tip

It is important to use the correct terms when describing coastal processes and to make sure that you can say what each one involves. Diagrams work well here.

Activities

1   Study diagram **B**. Draw an annotated diagram similar to this diagram to describe the processes of coastal erosion. Draw a simple diagram of a wave breaking against the foot of a cliff. Add detailed labels (annotations) in their correct places to describe the five processes of erosion.

2   Study diagram **C**.

a   What is meant by the term 'longshore drift'?

b   Why does longshore drift occur on some beaches but not on others?

c   Draw your own diagram or a series of diagrams to show how the process of longshore drift operates. Add labels to describe what is happening.

d   Imagine that you are going to carry out a fieldwork investigation to look for evidence of longshore drift along a stretch of coastline. What evidence would you look for? Explain your reasons.

⬤⬤links

A good summary of coastal processes and landforms can be found at **www.georesources.co.uk/leld.htm**.

A fun animation using a rubber duck to show the process of longshore drift can be found at **www.geography-site.co.uk/pages/physical/coastal/longshore.html**.

7.4 What are the distinctive landforms resulting from erosion?

Headlands and bays

Cliffs rarely erode at an even pace. Sections of cliff that are particularly resistant to erosion stick out to form **headlands**. Weaker sections of coastline that are more easily eroded form **bays**. Diagram **A** shows the changes that take place to a coastline where rocks of different resistances meet the coast. Headlands are most vulnerable to the power of the waves, which explains the presence of erosional features such as cliffs and **wave-cut platforms**. In contrast, bays are often much more sheltered from the full fury of the sea. The waves are less powerful and deposition tends to dominate. This explains why a sandy beach is the most common feature found in bays.

A *The formation of headlands and bays*

a
- Less resistant (softer) clay
- Resistant (harder) sandstone
- Waves
- Clay
- Resistant (harder) chalk or limestone
- Clay

b
- Less resistant rock worn away to leave a bay
- Resistant (harder) rock left as a headland
- Waves
- Sheltered bay – sand is deposited
- Headland
- Bay

In this section you will learn

the formation and characteristics of features of coastal erosion (headlands and bays; wave-cut platforms and caves; caves, arches and stacks).

Key terms

Wave-cut platform: a wide, gently sloping rocky surface at the foot of a cliff.

Wave-cut notch: a small indentation (or notch) cut into a cliff by coastal erosion roughly at the level of high tide.

Cave: a hollowed-out feature at the base of an eroding cliff.

Arch: a headland that has been partly broken through by the sea to form a thin-roofed arch.

Stack: an isolated pinnacle of rock sticking out of the sea.

Cliffs and wave-cut platforms

When waves break against a cliff, erosion close to the high-tide line takes a 'bite' out of the cliff to form a feature called a **wave-cut notch**. Over a long period of time – usually hundreds of years – the notch gets deeper until the overlying cliff can no longer support its own weight and it collapses. Through a continual sequence of wave-cut notch formation and cliff collapse, the cliff line gradually retreats. In its place will be a gently sloping rocky platform called a wave-cut platform (photo **B**).

A wave-cut platform is typically quite smooth due to the process of abrasion, but in some places it may be pockmarked with rock pools. During long periods of constructive waves, the wave-cut platform may become covered by sand or shingle. Destructive waves associated with local winter storms remove the beach once again, exposing the wave-cut platform.

B *Wave-cut platform and cliff near Beachy Head*

Caves, arches and stacks

Lines of weakness in a headland, such as joints or faults, are particularly vulnerable to erosion. The energy of the waves gouges out the rock along a line of weakness to form a **cave** (diagram **C**). Over time, erosion may lead to two back-to-back caves breaking through a headland to form an **arch**. Gradually, the arch is enlarged by erosion at the base and sides and by weathering processes acting on the roof. The roof collapses eventually to form an isolated pillar of rock known as a **stack**.

Did you know ??????

In 1990 a well-known arch in South Australia called London Bridge collapsed, leaving a car and its passengers stranded on the newly formed stack. They had to be airlifted to safety.

Headland, e.g. **the Foreland, Dorset**

4 Roof of arch becomes too heavy to be supported and collapses

5 A stack is an isolated portion of the cliff

1 Joint or fault in resistant rock

6 The stack is undercut and collapses to leave a stump, which is covered up at high tide

2 Corrasion and hydraulic action of waves widens the weakness in the cliff to form a cave

3 Waves cut through headland to form an arch, which is continually widened at its base

N = wave-cut notches

C Arch and stack formation

Activity

Study photo **B**.

a Draw a simple sketch of the cliff and wave-cut platform in the photo.

b Add labels to identify the cliff and the wave-cut platform. Suggest where you think the wave-cut notch is located at the foot of the cliff.

c Add labels to indicate where the processes of erosion operate at high tide. The rock in the photo is chalk.

d Use a series of simple annotated diagrams to show how a cliff (such as the one in the photo) is undercut by the sea and then collapses to form a wave-cut platform. Include reference to the processes and landforms in your annotations.

e Under what conditions might a wave-cut platform become covered by sand or shingle?

f Is it a good time to go rock-pooling after a period of stormy weather? Explain your answer.

Study tip

Practise drawing annotated diagrams to describe the formation of these features of erosion.

links

Good diagrams of coastal features can be found at www.georesources. co.uk/leld.htm.

Check out Geography at the Movies at www.gatm.org.uk.

7.5 Coastal erosion at Swanage, Dorset

OS map study: coastal erosion at Swanage, Dorset

The coast at Swanage in Dorset is a classic stretch of coastline in the UK. It exhibits several of the key features of erosion that you have been studying, including headlands, bays, cliffs, arches and stacks (photo **B**).

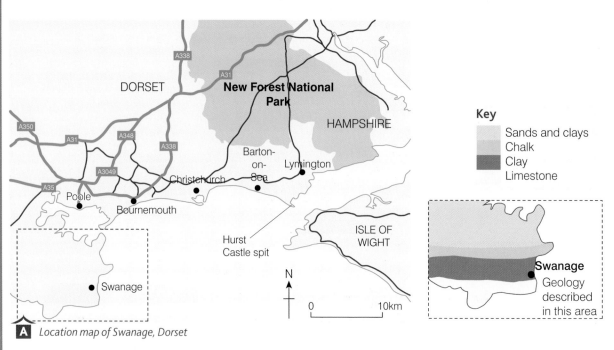

Key
- Sands and clays
- Chalk
- Clay
- Limestone

A *Location map of Swanage, Dorset*

B *Old Harry Stacks and the Foreland, Dorset*

C *1 : 50,000 OS map extract of the Swanage coast, part of map sheet 195.*

Activities

1 Study map extract **C**.

a The Foreland, Peveril Point and Durlston Head are all examples of which coastal landform?

b In which grid square is the Foreland?

c Locate Swanage Bay. Approximately how wide is the bay from Ballard Point to Peveril Point?

2 Study map **A** and map extract **C**.

a Use map **A** to explain the formation of Swanage Bay. Include simple diagrams to support your explanation.

b What map evidence is there that deposition is occurring in Swanage Bay?

c How does this deposition help to explain the growth of Swanage as a tourist resort?

3 Study photo **B** and map extract **C**.

a What are the features labelled **A**, **B** and **C** on the photo?

b Why do you think feature **A** has been formed in this position?

c What processes of erosion have led to the formation of feature **A**?

d Use map extract **C** to give the local name of feature **C**.

4 Design an information board to be located at the Foreland to explain the formation of feature **C**. Draw a series of annotated diagrams to describe its formation. Refer to the processes of erosion in your annotations. Your information board is aimed at the general public, so make sure it is clear and colourful.

7.6 What are the distinctive landforms resulting from deposition?

Beaches

Beaches are accumulations of sand and shingle (pebbles) found where deposition occurs at the coast. Sandy beaches are often found in sheltered bays, where they are called bay head beaches. When waves enter these bays, they tend to bend to mirror the shape of the coast. This is called wave refraction (photo **A**). The way the water gets shallower as the waves enter the bays causes this to happen. Wave refraction spreads out and reduces the wave energy in a bay, which is why deposition occurs here.

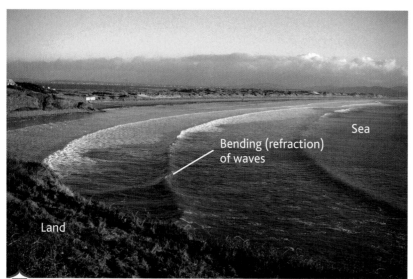

Sea

Bending (refraction) of waves

Land

A *Wave refraction at the head of a bay*

Elsewhere along the coast, pebble beaches may form. These are most commonly found in areas where cliffs are being eroded and where there are higher-energy waves, such as along the south coast of the UK.

Ridges or berms are common characteristics of a beach (photo **B**). They are small ridges coinciding with high-tide lines and storm tides. Some beaches may have several berms, each one representing a different high-tide level.

Spits

A **spit** is a long, narrow finger of sand or shingle jutting out into the sea from the land (diagram **C**). Spits are common features across the world. As sediment is transported along the coast by longshore drift, it becomes deposited at a point where the coastline changes direction or where a river mouth occurs. Gradually, as more and more sediment is deposited, the feature extends into the sea. Away from the coast, the tip is affected by waves approaching from different directions and the spit often becomes curved as a result.

In this section you will learn

the formation and characteristics of features of coastal deposition (beaches, spits and bars).

Key terms

Spit: a finger of new land made of sand or shingle, jutting out into the sea from the coast.

Salt marsh: low-lying coastal wetland mostly extending between high and low tide.

Bar: a spit that has grown across a bay.

B *Berms on a beach at Deal on the Kent coast*

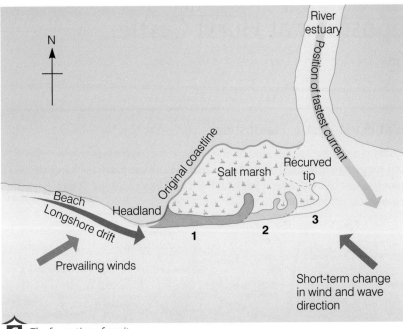

C *The formation of a spit*

D *Coastal bar at Slapton Ley, Devon*

Over time, the sediment breaks the surface to form new land and a spit is formed. It soon becomes colonised by grass and bushes, and eventually trees will grow. On the landward sheltered side of a spit where the water is a calm, mudflats and **salt marshes** form. These are important habitats for plants and birds. Being close to sea level, spits are vulnerable to erosion, especially during storms.

Bars

Occasionally, longshore drift may cause a spit to grow right across a bay, trapping a freshwater lake or lagoon behind it. This feature is called a **bar** (photo **D**). In the UK some offshore bars have been driven onshore by rising sea levels following ice melt at the end of the last glacial period some 10,000 years ago. This type of feature is called a barrier beach. Chesil Beach in Dorset is one of the best examples of this feature.

Study tip

A spit is a land feature, so it does not get covered at high tide. On a map, it will be clearly bordered by the high tide line. Be careful not to confuse it with sediment exposed only at low tide.

links

Information on Dungeness spit in Washington State in the USA, can be found at **www.reefnews.com/reefnews/oceangeo/washngtn/dnwr.html**.

Activities

1 Study photo **A**.

a What is wave refraction? Draw a simple sketch based on the photo to support your answer.

b How does wave refraction explain the formation of a bay head beach?

c A sandy beach is more likely to be found in a sheltered bay, whereas a shingle (pebble) beach is more likely to be found on an open and exposed stretch of coastline. Explain why.

2 Study photo **B**. What are berms and how do they form on a beach? Use a simple diagram to help your explanation.

3 Study diagram **C** and photo **D**.

a What is a spit?

b Draw a series of three simple diagrams to show the formation of a spit. Add detailed labels to describe what is happening using the text and the diagram to help you.

c What is the difference between a spit and a bar?

d What is the difference between a bar and a barrier beach?

7.7 Coastal deposition at Hurst Castle, Hampshire

OS map study: coastal deposition at Hurst Castle, Hampshire

Hurst Castle spit (map extract **A** and photo **B**) is a shingle spit located on the Hampshire coast close to the city of Southampton. Its formation is complex, but longshore drift has been actively shaping the landform for hundreds of years. Henry VIII built a castle near the tip of the spit to help defend England from possible invasions. Today, English Heritage manages the castle and it is a popular tourist destination.

A 1:25,000 OS map extract of Hurst Castle spit, part of map sheet OL22

B *Hurst Castle spit, Hampshire*

Activities

1 Study map extract **A** and photo **B**.

a In what direction is the photo looking?

b How long is the spit? Is it roughly 1 km, 2 km or 3 km in length?

c Use a ruler to measure the width of the spit in grid square 3090. Give your answer to the nearest 50 m. Remember that the spit is the area of land above the high-tide line, shown by the bold blue line on the map.

d Which symbol is used to indicate that the spit is made of shingle (pebbles)?

e Use the key to describe the nature of the land behind the spit in grid square 3090.

f What is the name of the spit feature at **A** on the photo?

g How has this feature been formed?

h In what direction do you think longshore drift is operating? Explain your answer.

i Summarise the answers you have given by writing a paragraph describing the spit. Use facts and figures in your description.

2 Study map extract **A**.

a Draw a sketch map to show the spit and its main features. Use a pencil for the sketch and a pen for adding labels.

b Begin by drawing a grid of squares to represent the grid squares on the map. This will enable you to copy the spit accurately. Use the same scale: 4 cm = 1 km or enlarge it if you wish.

c Carefully draw the spit. Remember to follow the bold blue high-tide line. This marks the outline of the spit.

d Locate Hurst Castle on your map and label it.

e Add the following additional labels to your sketch:

■ spit

■ recurved tip

■ salt marsh

■ direction of longshore drift.

f Complete your sketch by adding a north point, scale and title.

7.8 How will rising sea levels affect the coastal zone?

The causes of rising sea levels

One of the effects of global warming is sea-level change. Over the last 15 years, global average sea levels have risen by 3 mm a year. The latest estimates from the Intergovernmental Panel on Climate Change (IPCC) suggest a rise in global sea levels of between 28 and 43 cm by the end of the century.

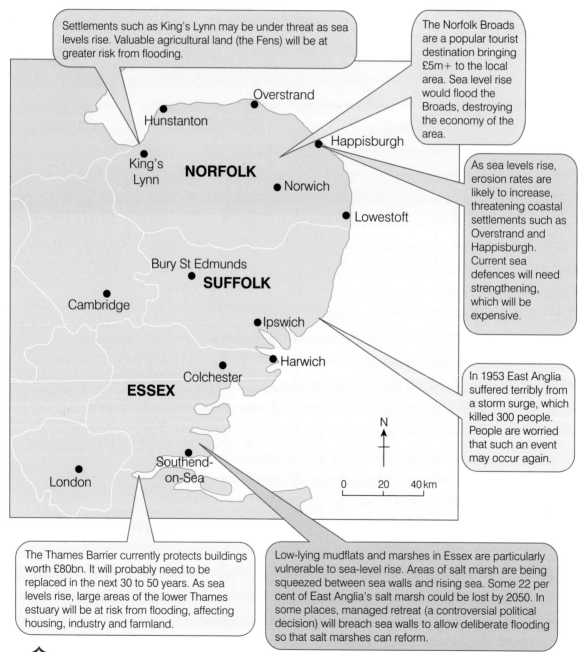

Settlements such as King's Lynn may be under threat as sea levels rise. Valuable agricultural land (the Fens) will be at greater risk from flooding.

The Norfolk Broads are a popular tourist destination bringing £5m+ to the local area. Sea level rise would flood the Broads, destroying the economy of the area.

As sea levels rise, erosion rates are likely to increase, threatening coastal settlements such as Overstrand and Happisburgh. Current sea defences will need strengthening, which will be expensive.

In 1953 East Anglia suffered terribly from a storm surge, which killed 300 people. People are worried that such an event may occur again.

The Thames Barrier currently protects buildings worth £80bn. It will probably need to be replaced in the next 30 to 50 years. As sea levels rise, large areas of the lower Thames estuary will be at risk from flooding, affecting housing, industry and farmland.

Low-lying mudflats and marshes in Essex are particularly vulnerable to sea-level rise. Areas of salt marsh are being squeezed between sea walls and rising sea. Some 22 per cent of East Anglia's salt marsh could be lost by 2050. In some places, managed retreat (a controversial political decision) will breach sea walls to allow deliberate flooding so that salt marshes can reform.

Overstrand · Hunstanton · King's Lynn · **NORFOLK** · Happisburgh · Norwich · Lowestoft · Bury St Edmunds · **SUFFOLK** · Cambridge · Ipswich · Harwich · Colchester · **ESSEX** · London · Southend-on-Sea

N

0   20   40 km

A *Possible impact of sea-level rise in East Anglia*

The main cause of sea-level rise is thermal expansion of the seawater as it absorbs more heat from the atmosphere. The melting of ice on the land, for example from glaciers on Greenland, will increase the amount of water in the oceans but scientists do not believe that this will significantly affect sea levels. Melting sea ice, such as from the Arctic, will have no direct effect on sea levels.

The actual amount of sea-level rise will vary from place to place. It is complicated by relative rises and falls in the level of the land as well as variations in the amount of deposition occurring at the coast. The amount of sea-level rise will also depend on the rate of global warming. However uncertain the future may be, most scientists agree that sea levels will rise and that coastal zones will be at an increasing risk from wave attack and flooding.

In the UK, East Anglia (diagram **A**) is likely to be hardest hit as rising sea levels threaten coastal defences and natural ecosystems. Elsewhere in the world, vast areas of low-lying coastal plains such as Bangladesh and whole chains of islands such as the Maldives and Tuvalu could disappear.

Already, two Pacific islands have been submerged, and many others have been flooded. Since more than 70 per cent of the world's population live on coastal plains, the effects of rising sea levels are likely to be devastating.

Did you know ?????

If sea levels rise by 1 m, several major cities of the world will be affected by flooding including London, Tokyo and New York.

Study tip

Be sure to understand the meaning of economic (money), social (people), environmental (natural world) and political (decision-making) when describing the possible impacts of sea-level rise.

Activities

1 Study diagram **A**.

a Describe some of the likely economic impacts of sea-level rise in East Anglia.

b Suggest some likely social and political (decision-making, often by the government) impacts of sea-level rise. Some of these will be linked to the economic factors identified in a.

c With the aid of a diagram, describe how salt marshes could be lost as sea levels rise.

d Why is there concern about loss of salt marsh environments in East Anglia?

2 This activity will involve internet research.

a Select a coastal zone under threat from sea-level rise, such as Bangladesh, the Mississippi delta in the USA or the Maldives.

b Conduct an internet search ('sea level rise + Maldives', for example) to find out about the economic, social, environmental and political impacts of sea-level rise on your chosen locality.

c Draw a diagram similar to diagram **A**, using a photo or map of your locality in the centre.

B   *The islands of the Maldives are under threat from sea-level rise*

⬯links

http://thelondonflood.com is an excellent source of information. **www.floodlondon.com** looks at what might happen if London was flooded.

7.9 How can cliff collapse cause problems for people at the coast?

Various factors can contribute to cliff collapse. These include weathering processes such as heavy rainfall that can saturate the land and make it unstable, mass movement such as **sliding** and **slumping**, which is more likely if the land is made of soft weak rock types, and of course the power of the waves continually crashing against the cliffs and undercutting them from below. Various stretches of UK coastline are vulnerable to cliff collapse, including Christchurch Bay in Hampshire, where Barton-on-Sea is sited.

> **In this section you will learn**
>
> the causes and consequences of cliff collapse for people living in the coastal zone.

Case study

Barton-on-Sea, Hampshire

Locate the small settlement of Barton-on-Sea on map **B**. This stretch of coastline in Christchurch Bay has long been affected by coastal erosion and cliff collapse. Over the years a number of buildings, and most recently a café, have been lost to the sea.

Extensive coastal defences have been built to try to prevent coastal erosion. However, in 2008 a fresh **landslip** occurred (photo **A**). This has once again raised concerns among local residents about the vulnerability of this part of the coast to cliff collapse. An older development of houses in Barton Court is just 20 m from the cliff edge. The local authority predicts that the houses will be lost in the next 10 to 20 years.

The cliffs at Barton-on-Sea are prone to collapse due to a number of factors:

- The rocks are weak sands and clays. They are easily eroded by the sea and have little strength to resist collapse.
- The arrangement of the rocks (permeable sands on top of impermeable clay) causes water to 'pond-up' within the cliffs. This increases the weight of the cliffs. The increase in water pressure within the cliffs (called pore water pressure) encourages collapse.

A *Cliff collapse at Barton-on-Sea, 2008*

- This stretch of coastline faces the direct force of the prevailing south-westerly winds. With a long fetch, the waves approaching Barton-on-Sea are powerful and can carry out a great deal of erosion. Rates of erosion have been as much as 2 m a year in places.

- Several small streams (with the local name 'Bunny') flow towards the coast but disappear into the permeable sands before they reach the sea. This adds to the amount of water in the cliffs.

- Buildings on the cliff top have increased the weight on the cliffs, making them more vulnerable to collapse. They can also interfere with drainage.

∞ links

A website with fantastic photos is www.southampton.ac.uk/~imw/barteros.htm.

B *Location of Barton-on-Sea on England's south coast*

Activity

Study photo **A**.

a What evidence is there that there has been a cliff collapse?

b Estimate the drop in the grass surface due to the collapse.

c Look closely at the rock material forming the cliffs. How strong do you think it is? Explain your answer.

d What action has been taken to keep people at a safe distance from the cliff?

e Using evidence from the photo, suggest how this and future cliff collapses might affect people living in the area.

f How does the cliff collapse affect the local environment?

g Draw a simplified sketch of the cliffs at Barton-on-Sea and add annotations to identify the factors that have led to the cliff collapse.

Key terms

Sliding: a type of mass movement involving material moving downhill on a flat surface (a landslide).

Slumping: a type of mass movement involving material moving downhill under its own weight.

Landslip: a type of mass movement common at the coast involving material slipping downhill usually along a curved slip surface.

Study tip

Cliff collapse usually results from the interaction of several factors. Make this clear in any explanation you are required to give.

7.10   How can coastlines be managed?

The coastal zone needs to be managed in order to maintain a balance between the forces of nature and the demands of people. The coastline is under threat from cliff collapse, flooding and future sea-level rise. With millions of people living in the coastal zone, sustainable management is an important consideration.

Shoreline Management Plans

The coastline of England and Wales has been divided into a number of self-contained sediment cells. A **Shoreline Management Plan (SMP)** has been developed for each area, which details the natural processes, environmental considerations and human uses. Coastlines at risk from erosion or flooding have been identified and plans put in place to cope with the issues.

In most cases, a decision has been made to 'hold the line'. This means taking action to keep the line of the coast as it is now. Occasionally, planners decide to 'advance the line' of the coast to afford greater protection by, for example, increasing the size of the beach. In taking action, authorities have the option of hard or soft engineering approaches.

Hard engineering approaches

Hard engineering involves using artificial structures to control the forces of nature. For many decades people have used hard engineering structures such as sea walls (photo **A**) and groynes (photo **B**) to try to control the actions of the sea and protect property from flooding and erosion. Table **C** outlines the common hard engineering approaches used in coastal management.

In this section you will learn

the options of coastal management including hard and soft engineering and managed retreat.

Key terms

Shoreline Management Plan (SMP): an integrated coastal management plan for a stretch of coastline in England and Wales.

Hard engineering: building artificial structures such as sea walls aimed at controlling natural processes.

Soft engineering: a sustainable approach to managing the coast without using artificial structures.

Did you know ??????

In 1902 a sea wall was constructed at Galveston, USA following the devastating hurricane of 1900. The wall is 16 km long, 5.2 m high and 4.9 m thick at its base. So far, it has never been overtopped.

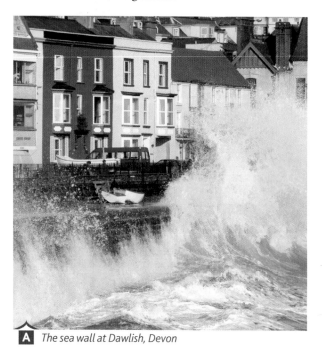

A *The sea wall at Dawlish, Devon*

B *Groynes at Eastbourne*

C *Hard engineering schemes*

Hard engineering	Description	Cost	Advantages	Disadvantages
Sea wall	Concrete or rock barrier built at the foot of cliffs or at the top of a beach. Has a curved face to reflect the waves back into the sea, usually 3–5m high.	Up to £10 million per km (south sea zones).	• Effective at stopping the sea. • Often has a walkway or promenade for people to walk along.	• Can be obtrusive and unnatural to look at. • Very expensive and has high maintenance costs.
Groynes Beach sand	Timber or rock structures built out to sea from the coast. They trap sediment being moved by longshore drift, and broaden the beach. The wider beach acts as a buffer to the incoming waves, reducing wave attack at the coast.	Up to £5,000 per metre.	• Result in a bigger beach, which can enhance the tourist potential of the coast. • Provide useful structures for people interested in fishing. • Not too expensive.	• In interrupting longshore drift, they starve beaches downdrift, often leading to increased rates of erosion elsewhere. The problem is not so much solved as shifted. • Groynes are unnatural and rock groynes in particular can be unattractive.
Rock armour	Piles of large boulders dumped at the foot of a cliff. The rocks force waves to break, absorbing their energy and protecting the cliffs. The rocks are usually brought in by barge to the coast.	Approximately £1,000 –£4,000 per metre.	• Relatively cheap and easy to maintain. • Can provide interest to the coast. Often used for fishing.	• Rocks are usually from other parts of the coastline or even from abroad. Can be expensive to transport. • They do not fit in with the local geology. • Can be very obtrusive.

Hard engineering approaches are less commonly used today. Not only are they expensive and involve high maintenance costs, they are also obtrusive and unnatural. They tend to interfere with natural coastal processes and can cause destructive knock-on effects elsewhere. In altering wave patterns, for example, erosion can become concentrated further down the coast leading to new problems of cliff collapse.

Soft engineering approaches

Soft engineering approaches (table **D**) try to fit in and work with the natural coastal processes. They do not involve large artificial structures. Often more 'low key' and with low maintenance costs – both economically and environmentally – soft engineering approaches such as beach nourishment (photo **E**) are more sustainable. They are usually the preferred option of coastal management.

> **Key terms**
>
> **Sea wall:** concrete or rock barrier built at the foot of cliffs or at the top of a beach.
>
> **Groyne:** timber or rock structure built out to sea to trap sediment being moved by longshore drift.
>
> **Rock armour:** piles of large boulders dumped at the foot of a cliff to protect it by forcing waves to break and absorbing their energy.

D *Soft engineering schemes*

Soft engineering	Description	Cost	Advantages	Disadvantages
Beach nourishment	The addition of sand or shingle to an existing beach to make it higher or broader. The sediment is usually obtained locally so that it blends in with the existing beach material. Usually brought onshore by barge.	Approximately £3,000 per metre	• Relatively cheap and easy to maintain. • Blends in with existing beach. • Increases tourist potential by creating a bigger beach.	• Needs constant maintenance unless structures are built to retain the beach.
Dune regeneration	Sand dunes are effective buffers to the sea yet they are easily damaged and destroyed, especially by trampling. Marram grass can be planted to stabilise the dunes and help them to develop. Areas can be fenced to keep people off newly planted dunes.	Approximately £2,000 per 100 m	• Maintains a natural coastal environment that is popular with people and wildlife. • Relatively cheap.	• Time-consuming to plant the marram grass and fence off areas. • People do not always respond well to being prohibited from accessing certain areas. • Can be damaged by storms.
Marsh creation (managed retreat)	This involves allowing low-lying coastal areas to be flooded by the sea to become salt marshes. This is an example of managed retreat. Salt marshes are effective barriers to the sea.	Depends on the value of the land. Arable land costs somewhere in the region of £5,000 to £10,000 per hectare	• A cheap option compared with maintaining expensive sea defences that might be protecting relatively low-value land. • Creates a much-needed habitat for wildlife.	• Land will be lost as it is flooded by sea water. • Farmers or landowners will need to be compensated.

Managed retreat

A further option for coastal management is to allow for some retreat of the coastline. This is called **managed retreat** or coastal realignment. It is a real option if there is a high risk of flooding or cliff collapse and where the land is relatively low value. Poor quality grazing land, for example, is seldom worth protecting if the costs of defences outweigh the benefits of protection (see Marsh creation in table **D**). This appraisal is known as a cost–benefit analysis. With sea levels forecast to rise, this approach is likely to become an increasingly popular option.

Key terms

Managed retreat: allowing controlled flooding of low-lying coastal areas or cliff collapse in areas where the value of the land is low.

Study tip

Be clear about the differences between hard engineering and soft engineering. Appreciate that there is a great deal of debate about the option of managed retreat. Make sure that you know both sides of the argument.

E *Beach nourishment in operation at Poole in Dorset*

Activity

Use photos **A**, **B** and **E**, and tables **C** and **D**, to help you answer the following questions.

a   Why is a sea wall an example of hard engineering?

b   What is the purpose of a sea wall?

c   What are the advantages and disadvantages of a sea wall?

d   What are groynes and what is their purpose? Draw a simple diagram to support your answer.

e   How effective do you think the groynes are in photo **B**?

f   Beach nourishment is a good example of soft engineering. What is soft engineering?

g   With reference to photo **E**, outline some of the advantages of beach nourishment.

h   Imagine a local council wishes to defend a 1 km stretch of coastline. Use tables **C** and **D** to calculate comparative costs for a sea wall, groynes, rock armour and beach nourishment.

i   Why is the economic cost only one of several considerations when deciding which coastal defence measure to adopt?

Coastal defences at Minehead

Minehead on the north coast of Somerset is one of the region's premier tourist resorts. It is home to a large Butlin's resort and every year it is visited by many thousands of tourists.

By the early 1990s it became clear that the current sea defences were going to be inadequate in the future. Storm damage was estimated to be £21m if nothing were done. The Environment Agency developed a plan to defend the town and improve the amenity value. Work started in 1997 and the sea defences were officially opened in 2001. The total cost was £12.3m, which represents a considerable saving on the potential losses due to storm damage.

The main features of the scheme (diagram **F**) are:

- A 0.6 m high sea wall with a curved front to deflect the waves. It has a curved top to deter people from walking on it and its landward side is faced with attractive local red sandstone.

- Rock armour at the base of the wall to dissipate some of the wave energy.

- Beach nourishment (sand) to build up the beach by 2 m in height. This forces the waves to break further out to sea and provides an excellent sandy beach for tourists.

- Four rock groynes to help retain the beach and stop longshore drift moving sand to the east.

- A wide walkway with seating areas alongside the sea wall. This is popular with tourists and local people.

The scheme has been extremely successful. Not only does it protect the town from storms and high tides, but it has also enhanced the seafront by creating an attractive beach environment (photo **G**).

Case study

F   *Coastal defences at Minehead*

G   *The beach at Minehead*

Coastal defences at Wallasea Island

Wallasea Island is a low-lying coastal island formed at the confluence of the River Crouch and River Roach in Essex (map extract **H**). Protected from the sea by a ring of embankments, until recently it has been mostly used for growing wheat.

With the north coast defences falling into disrepair, the government decided to realign the northern part of the island by constructing a new embankment inland and allowing the old sea defences to be breached (map extract **H**). The new mudflats and salt marsh will help to protect the new sea wall and offer additional protection to land and property to the south.

The £7.5m scheme aims to replace bird habitats lost to development, improve flood defences on the island and create new leisure opportunities. In July 2006 the old sea wall was breached in three places to allow 115 ha of land to be flooded (photo **I**). Eventually the flooded area will contain islands and a number of salty lakes. Much of it will revert to salt marsh, providing a much-needed breeding ground for birds. The site is managed by the RSPB.

I *Managed retreat on Wallasea Island*

H *1 : 50,000 OS map extracts of Wallasea Island, part of map sheets 168 and 178*

⃝links

The Geography Site has information at
www.geography-site.co.uk/pages/physical/coastal/defences.html.

7.11   What are salt marshes and why are they special?

Salt marshes are areas of periodically flooded low-lying coastal wetlands. They are often rich in plants, birds and animals (photo **A**).

A   *Keyhaven Marshes*

A salt marsh begins life as an accumulation of mud and silt in a sheltered part of the coastline, for example in the lee of a spit or bar. As more deposition takes place, the mud begins to break the surface to form mudflats. Salt-tolerant plants such as cordgrass soon start to colonise the mudflats. These early colonisers are called **pioneer plants**. Cordgrass is tolerant of the saltwater and its long roots prevent it from being swept away by the waves and the tides. Its tangle of roots also helps to trap **sediment** and stabilise the mud.

As the level of the mud rises, it is less frequently covered by water. The conditions become less harsh as rainwater begins to wash out some of the salt and decomposing plant matter improves the fertility of the newly forming soil. New plant species such as sea asters start to colonise the area and gradually, over hundreds of years, a succession of plants develops. This is known as a **vegetation succession** (diagram **B**).

In this section you will learn

the characteristics of a salt marsh environment

sustainable approaches to the management of salt marshes.

Key terms

Pioneer plant: the first plant species to colonise an area that is well adapted to living in a harsh environment.

Sediment: loose rock debris that has been weathered or eroded before being transported and then deposited.

Vegetation succession: a sequence of vegetation species colonising an environment.

Did you know ??????

In France, salt is produced commercially from salt marshes.

B   *Salt marsh vegetation succession*

Keyhaven Marshes, Hampshire

Keyhaven Marshes is an area of salt marsh formed in the lee of Hurst Castle spit (map **A**, page 156). It supports a range of habitats including grassland, scrub, salt marsh and reed beds. This variety of habitats accounts for a rich diversity of wildlife in the area (table **C**).

C *Common wildlife species found at Keyhaven Marshes*

Species detail	Image	Species detail	Image
Plant: cordgrass – spiky, untidy-looking grass that grows fast on mudflats		Bird: ringed plover – feeds intertidally and nests on the salt marsh	
Plant: sea lavender – attractive, colourful flowers attract wildlife		Butterfly: common blue – resident butterfly commonly found on higher marshes	
Bird: oystercatcher – feeds and nests in salt marshes		Spider: wold spider – clings for hours to submerged stems of cordgrass waiting for low tide and food	

In common with many areas of salt marsh in the UK, Keyhaven Marshes is under threat:

- The salt marsh is retreating by up to 6 m a year. Although the causes of this are not yet fully understood, further sea-level rise threatens a 'squeeze' of the salt marsh as it lies between a low sea wall built in the early 1990s and the encroaching sea.

- The salt marsh has been under threat from the breaching of Hurst Castle spit during severe storms. In December 1989 storms pushed part of the shingle ridge over the top of the salt marsh, exposing 50 to 80 m to the full fury of the sea. It was eroded in less than three months.

- Increasing demands for leisure and tourism have meant that increasing numbers of people wish to visit the marshes. Careful management is required to prevent damage by trampling, parking and pollution. The area is popular with mariners who use the many creeks to moor their boats.

- In 1996 rock armour and beach nourishment were used to increase the height and width of the spit in an attempt to stop breaching. Since the completion of the £5m sea defences, the spit has not been breached and Keyhaven Marshes seems safe … at least for the time being.

- Keyhaven Marshes has been nationally recognised as an important site for wildfowl and wading birds. The area is officially a Site of Special Scientific Interest (SSSI) and part of the salt marsh is also a National Nature Reserve. This means that the area is carefully monitored and managed to maintain its rich biodiversity. Access is limited and development restricted.

- For the future, with sea levels expected to rise by 6 mm a year, the big issue concerns the 'squeeze' between the low sea wall and the rising sea.

D *The salt marsh at Keyhaven*

∞ links

An excellent case study based on Chichester harbour can be accessed at **www.conservancy. co.uk/learn/wildlife/saltmarsh.htm**.

Activities

1 Study photo **A**, diagram **B**, table **C** and photo **D**.

a What is a salt marsh and what makes it a special habitat?

b Why do salt marshes often develop in the shelter of spits?

c Why is cordgrass well suited to be a pioneer species?

d How does cordgrass improve the salt marsh environment to enable other plant species to grow?

e What is meant by a vegetation succession?

f How do the environmental conditions of a salt marsh change as the vegetation succession proceeds?

g Suggest ways that people's actions might affect a natural salt marsh vegetation succession.

2 Study the OS map extract of Hurst Castle spit and Keyhaven Marshes (map extract **A**, page 156).

a What symbol is used on a 1:25,000 map to depict an area of salt marsh?

b Locate the large area of salt marsh in grid square 3090. Would you expect this area to be flooded at high tide? Explain your answer.

c Locate Keyhaven Marshes in grid square 3191. What is the evidence from the map that there is a variety of habitats here?

d What is the evidence of human activity in Keyhaven Marshes (3191)?

e Locate the area of salt marsh just to the south-east of the village of Keyhaven (306912). What is the evidence of a vegetation succession here?

f Imagine that a major breach destroyed most of the spit in grid square 3090. With the aid of an annotated sketch map, suggest the possible impacts of such a breach on the natural salt marsh.

8.1   How does population grow?

■ Exponential growth

In 2011 the world's population topped 7 billion people. Since about 1900 the world's population has grown exponentially. This means that the rate of growth has become increasingly rapid. Between AD 1 and AD 1000 growth was slow, but in the last thousand years it has been dramatic. By 2000, there were 10 times as many people living as there had been 300 years before in 1700. Not only is population increasing, but the rate of increase is becoming greater.

Population grew especially quickly during the late 20th and early 21st centuries. Between 2008 and 2009, 220,980 people were added to world population *every day*. Growth is predicted to continue, but now the rate is slowing down. Population is likely to rise to 8.92 billion by 2050 and finally peak a century later in 2150 at 10.8 billion. This should be followed by a more stable period of **zero growth** or even **natural decrease (ND)**.

Population growth is usually shown as a line graph. **Exponential growth** produces a line that becomes steeper over time, taking the shape of a letter J. Today, growth rates are slowing down (although the numbers being added daily are still high), so the shape of the graph is levelling off into an S curve (graph **A**).

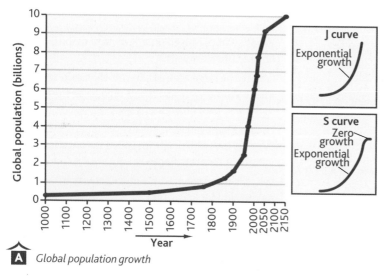

A *Global population growth*

■ Birth rate, death rate and natural change

Birth rate (BR) is the number of babies born alive per 1,000 people per year. Today, birth rates vary at between 5 per 1,000 per year and 40 per 1,000 per year, depending on the country concerned. In the past, figures have been as high as 50 per 1,000 per year, but availability of birth control means such high rates rarely occur now.

In this section you will learn

definitions of key terms involved in measuring population change

how to calculate population change by country

how to interpret population change calculations and compare countries.

Key terms

Zero growth: a population in balance. Birth rate is equal to death rate, so there is no growth or decrease.

Natural decrease (ND): the death rate is greater than the birth rate.

Exponential growth: a pattern where the growth rate constantly increases – often shown as a J-curve graph.

Birth rate (BR): the number of babies born per 1,000 people per year.

Death rate (DR): the number of deaths per 1,000 people per year.

Natural change: the difference between birth rate and death rate, given as a percentage.

Natural increase (NI): the birth rate is greater than the death rate.

Life expectancy: the number of years a person is expected to live, usually taken from birth.

Death rate (DR) is the number of deaths per 1,000 people per year. Typically, death rates lie between 5 per 1,000 per year and 20 per 1,000 per year unless there is an epidemic, famine or war, which increase levels significantly.

Birth and death rates are expressed per 1,000 so that figures for countries of different sizes can be compared. Huge nations such as China and India, with 1.3 and 1.2 billion people each, can be compared with smaller countries such as Singapore (4.7 million) and Luxembourg (503,302) (2011 figures).

Natural change is the difference between birth and death rates in a country. It is a useful measure of a population's growth or decline and, once we compare countries, we can to find reasons to explain their population statistics.

Until recently, all countries have been in a situation of **natural increase (NI)**, except in periods of epidemic, famine or war. In Europe between 1348 and 1353 the Black Death killed about a third of the population. Today, some countries have reduced their birth rates so much that they are now experiencing **natural decrease (ND)** and population is declining.

Data on birth rates, death rates and natural increase or decrease give us information on the level of development of a country. Whatever their stage of development, all countries now have low death rates. People often assume that DR in countries at lesser stages of development must be high because people are poor and **life expectancy** may not be long, but this is not true. Two factors affect the level of DR:

- health care has improved in poorer countries, lowering DR
- having so many people under the age of 15 reduces the chance of death.

Death rates in countries at further stages of development are often higher because their populations are older, causing DR to rise slightly. Birth rate is a better indicator of development. Although family size has reduced in most countries at lesser stages of development, parents in wealthier parts of the world still have fewer children.

Did you know ??????

According to United Nations estimates, the 7 billionth person was born on 31 October 2011. An organisation called Plan International, which works for more rights for children, chose a girl born on that day as a symbol for this 7 billionth person. They picked a baby called Nargis, born just after midnight (UK time) on 31 October, in India.

Examples

Natural change calculations

UK

BR = 10.7 per 1,000 per year

DR = 10.1 per 1,000 per year

$NI = BR - DR$

$= 10.7 - 10.1$

$= 0.6$

Natural change is always expressed as a percentage, so the answer must be divided by 10.

Therefore:

NI = 0.06% per year

Czech Republic

BR = 9.0 per 1,000 per year

DR = 10.6 per 1,000 per year

$ND = DR - BR$

$= 10.6 - 9.0$

$= 1.6$

ND = 0.16% per year (sometimes written as –0.16%)

B *Birth rate is a good indicator of development*

C *All countries today have low death rates*

D *European population, 1800–2010*

Year	Population (millions)
1800	203
1900	408
1950	547
1975	676
1985	706
1995	727
2005	725
2010	830

E *Birth and death rates for selected countries, 2011*

Country	Continent	Birth rate (per 1,000)	Death rate (per 1,000)
Afghanistan	Asia	37.8	17.4
Brazil	South America	17.8	6.7
China	Asia	12.3	7.0
Czech Rep.	Europe	8.7	10.9
Ethiopia	Africa	43.0	11.0
France	Europe	12.3	8.8
Germany	Europe	8.3	10.9
Hong Kong	Asia	7.5	7.1
India	Asia	21.0	7.5
Ireland	Europe	16.1	6.3
Italy	Europe	9.2	9.8
Nigeria	Africa	35.5	16.1
Pakistan	Asia	24.8	6.9
Romania	Europe	9.6	11.8
South Korea	Asia	8.6	6.3
UK	Europe	12.3	9.3
USA	North America	13.8	8.4

Key terms

Newly industrialising countries (NICs): these include the Asian 'tigers' as well as other emerging industrial nations such as Malaysia, the Philippines and China.

Asian 'tiger': one of the four east Asian countries of Hong Kong, South Korea, Singapore and Taiwan, where manufacturing industry grew rapidly from the 1960s to the 1990s.

Activities

1 Study table **D**.

a Use the data from the table to draw a growth curve for Europe. Plot the year along the *x*-axis and the population along the *y*-axis.

b Name the shape of the graph you have drawn. Why is this name used?

c Describe the population growth pattern that you have drawn. Give details of the graph's shape and quote figures from the graph to support your answer. Use key terms such as *exponential, J-shaped, S-shaped, levelling off, zero growth* and *population decline*.

2 Study table **E**.

a Choose five countries and calculate the natural change for each country. Set out your calculation clearly so that your teacher can follow each stage of your working.

b Classify all the countries in the table as one of the following:

■ country at a further stage of development

■ recent **newly industrialising country (NIC)**

■ **Asian 'tiger'** (or older NIC)

■ improving country at lesser stage of development

■ extremely poor country at lesser stage of development.

c Draw a summary table listing each country, its rate of natural change (in percent) and the type of country it is using your answers to questions 2a and b.

d Is there a relationship between population change (NI or ND) and level of economic development? Use your summary table to help you discuss this. Refer to figures from your calculations and your table to support your answer.

8.2   What is the demographic transition model?

Demography is the study of population. Transition simply means change. The **demographic transition model (DTM)** is shown in diagram **A**.

The model explains birth and death rate patterns across the world and through time. It includes the main period of a country's development and shows the links between demographic and economic changes. The diagram is divided into five stages, showing change from high birth and death rates in Stage 1 to much lower ones in Stages 4 and 5. Originally, the model was designed to explain population change in countries at further stages of development, but it has since been used to explain events in all countries. This allows us to compare different patterns of demographic and economic development.

In this section you will learn

the trends in the demographic transition model

how to interpret the demographic transition model and use it to compare the situations of different countries.

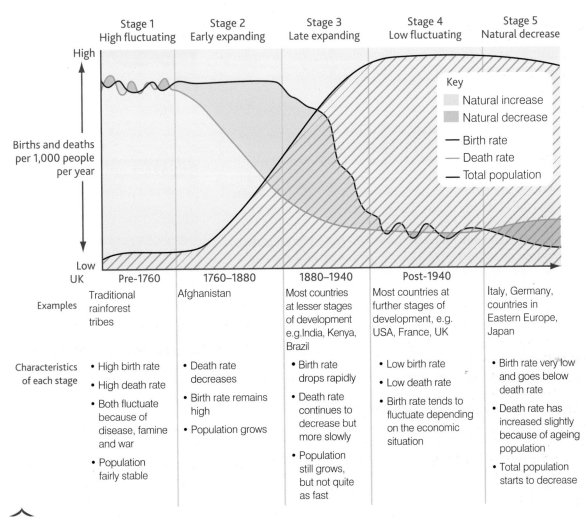

A *Demographic transition model*

Key term

Demographic transition model (DTM): a theoretical model that shows changes in population information (birth and death rates and population growth) over a period of time.

Characteristics of each stage

Stage 1 – high fluctuating

The high fluctuating stage occurs in societies where there is little medicine, low life expectancy and no means of birth control. Remote rainforest areas of Amazonia and Indonesia are the only locations where this stage might happen today. These are traditional societies, largely cut off from the rest of the world. The UK was at Stage 1 before around 1760.

Stage 2 – early expanding

The key factor that indicates the change from Stage 1 to Stage 2 is a decrease in death rate. Improvements in medicine and hygiene cure some diseases and prevent others. Life expectancy increases. The gap between birth rate and death rate results in population growth. The farther apart the lines are on the graph, the greater the rate of growth. Most economies in Stage 2 are agricultural. Children are needed to work the land, as they can produce more food than they eat. This keeps birth rates high. From 1760, new agricultural and industrial inventions and medical discoveries in the UK led to the start of Stage 2.

Stage 3 – late expanding

Death rate continues to fall, but more slowly. The key factor at the start of Stage 3 is a decrease in birth rate, which is often quite rapid. This is due to both the availability of birth control and economic changes, which mean people benefit from having smaller families. As a country develops, children become economic costs instead of economic assets. In other words, they cost the family money rather than earning it! When children have to go to school, they can no longer work and their education may cost the family money. In the UK, the 1870 Education Act made children up to the age of 12 go to school at a cost of one penny a week per child. The UK entered Stage 3 around 1880.

Stage 4 – low fluctuating

Birth and death rates are both low. The lines on the graph are close to each other and birth rate varies according to the economic situation. When the economy is growing and people have jobs and earn a good living, they are more likely to afford children. In times of unemployment and low wages, people tend to postpone having a family until times are better. In the UK in the 1960s, the economy was growing and the birth rate rose slightly. But, in the 1970s, with world economic recession, the birth rate fell again. Overall, there is still population growth, but it is slow. Birth rates in the USA have been declining since a record high in 2007. It is thought that this decline could be explained by the economic recession that began in 2008.

B *The introduction of machines heralds the start of the agricultural revolution*

Did you know ??????

A model is a diagram used by geographers to help explain a system or process. It simplifies what is happening in the real world, leaving out detail so that the basic ideas are clear. The demographic transition model is a geographical model, simplifying changes in birth and death rates over time so that the pattern becomes clearer and the factors affecting these changes can be explored.

Stage 5 – natural decrease

Many Eastern and a few Western European countries are at Stage 5, but for different reasons. The UK remains at Stage 4. Death rate rises (as indeed it has in the UK too) because the population includes more elderly people. In Eastern Europe an uncertain economy discourages people from having babies, while Western European economies give young women so many career opportunities that they decide to be childless or to postpone motherhood. For these reasons, birth rate dips below death rate and there is a natural decrease in the population.

Investigating countries

Case study

Stage 1: Traditional rainforest tribes

In parts of Indonesia, Brazil and Ecuador, small numbers of people live separately with little contact with the outside world (photo **C**). They retain high birth and death rates, making them the people closest to a true Stage 1 situation in the world today.

Stage 2: Afghanistan

Afghanistan is an extremely poor country, held back by political instability. In table **E** on page 172 it has one of the world's highest birth rates at 37.8 and a much lower death rate of 17.4. Natural increase is therefore 2.04 per cent per annum. Some 79 per cent of people are farmers, often nomadic (photo **D**), so need children to help with crops and livestock. Cities such as Kabul, the capital, have even higher rates of natural increase because easier access to medical care reduces the death rate while high numbers of young adults (who have migrated to the cities) increase the birth rate.

Stage 3: Brazil

Brazil is a newly industrialising country (NIC). Although it is a country at a lesser stage of development, it is developing fast economically. Brazil's population will have almost doubled between 1975 and 2015, from 108 million to 210 million people. As a Roman Catholic country, it has a high birth rate, but rapidly improving standards of living mean people can see the benefits from having fewer children.

Stage 4: USA

The USA is the largest and most developed economy in the world. The world's third largest population (after China and India) with over 313 million people in 2011, its growth is quite high for a Stage 4 country. This is mostly due to immigration. Many immigrants come from Catholic Central America, but the USA is now encouraging a more highly trained Asian workforce who are likely to have lower birth rates.

Stage 5: Germany

Germany is almost as well developed as the USA, but it has moved a stage further in the demographic transition model. Women achieving high-powered positions at work, plus an ageing population, are factors that have brought Germany clearly into Stage 5. One of the first countries to enter this stage, Germany's birth rate is well below **replacement rate**. The government has to cope with the costs of a large elderly population and a declining workforce.

C   *Rainforest tribeswoman, Ecuador*

D   *Afghan nomads*

Key terms

Replacement rate: a birth rate high enough for a generation to be the same size as the one before it.

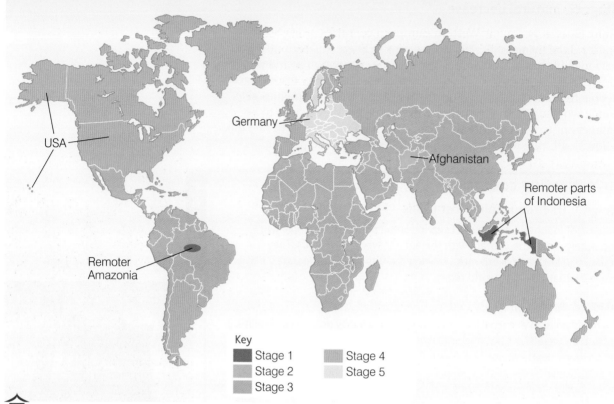

E *Countries at different stages of the demographic transition model*

Key

- Stage 1
- Stage 2
- Stage 3
- Stage 4
- Stage 5

Major factors affecting population growth

Agricultural change

Changes in agriculture occur early in a country's development. Even at intermediate levels, technology improves yields and saves labour. This frees some workers for industry and more rapid economic growth. In the Industrial Revolution in the UK, factories needed a large workforce, so for a while larger families were a benefit. Soon, however, technological advantages reduced the need for labour, making smaller families more desirable and reducing population growth.

Urbanisation

Rural-to-urban migration is common in poorer countries as cities are believed to have greater opportunities, and generally do. One major reason for such migration is to seek better educational opportunities for children. Children's labour is therefore of less value in cities than in rural areas. Highly urbanised societies tend to have lower rates of population growth.

> **Study tip**
>
> Learn the characteristics of the five stages carefully and be able to identify the differences. Know examples of countries in each stage today and know when the UK was at each of Stages 1 to 4.

> **Key terms**
>
> **Urbanisation**: the growth in the proportion of people living in towns and cities
>
> **Rural-to-urban migration**: moving home from a rural area to settle in a town or city.

Education

As levels of educational achievement increase, bringing improved standards of living, children become an economic disadvantage. Fewer children means parents have more money to be spent on each one, giving them better future chances. Many parents in poorer countries see education as their children's best chance in life. Increased educational opportunities tend to result in lower rates of population growth.

Emancipation and status of women

As economies develop and education improves, opportunities for girls increase alongside those for boys. With development a larger workforce is required, so women must participate more in paid work outside the home. Reaching a good standard of living in a household requires two incomes.

Over time, prejudice against women holding more senior positions at work reduces. Equality increases and is perceived as not only acceptable but desirable. Countries like Sweden have changed the law to increase the proportions of women in management and government (photo **F**). Improvements in the status of women, leading to lower birth rates, slows down the rate of population growth.

However, achieving highly in any career demands a large time commitment, leaving less opportunity for taking maternity leave or caring for children. Some women make deliberate choices regarding not having children or having them later, and these increase as an economy develops. Larger families, or even having a family at all, may be rejected. One in five women in the UK today is childless, compared with one in ten in their mothers' generation. Another issue for working women is childcare, which can be expensive.

F *Women at work*

Activities

1 Study diagram **A**.
a Describe how birth and death rates change through the five stages of the demographic transition model.
b How do these changes affect population growth?
c Why is Stage 1 really a thing of the past?
d What is likely to happen to the number of countries at Stage 5 in the future?

2 Study map **E**.
a Research the internet for birth and death rates by country and suggest at least two more countries for each of Stages 3, 4 and 5.
b Describe the distribution of countries at each stage of the demographic transition model.

3 Imagine you are a factory worker in an urban region of Brazil. Are you more likely to have a small or a large family? Explain your reasons, not forgetting that individuals may hold varying opinions.

4 Why might women in Germany and other Stage 5 countries have a very small family?

8.3 How do we use population pyramids?

▍Population pyramids

A population pyramid is a type of bar graph used to show the **age** and **gender structure** of a country, city or other area. The horizontal axis is divided into either numbers or percentages of the population. The central vertical axis shows age categories: every 10 years, every 5 years or every single year. The lower part of the pyramid is known as the base and shows the younger section of the population. The upper part, or apex, shows the elderly.

Interpreting population pyramids tells us a great deal about a population, such as birth rates, to a lesser extent death rates, life expectancy and the level of economic development (or stage in the demographic transition model).

Population pyramids and the demographic transition model

In this section you will learn

how to construct a population pyramid

how to interpret population characteristics from a pyramid

how to predict likely future changes in a population.

Stage 1

The Stage 1 pyramid has a very wide base due to its extremely high birth rate (up to 50 per 1,000 per year). However, **infant and child mortality rates** are high (only 50 per cent may reach their fifth birthday), so the sides of the pyramid curve in very quickly. Death rate is high in all age groups, so life expectancy is low. The result is a very narrow apex and the shortest of all the pyramids.

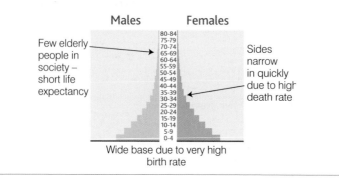

Few elderly people in society – short life expectancy

Males   Females

Sides narrow in quickly due to high death rate

Wide base due to very high birth rate

Stage 2

Stage 1 and 2 pyramids are similar in shape. Death rate begins to fall, making the sides of the Stage 2 pyramid slightly less concave. The apex shows a few extra elderly people as life expectancy begins to rise.

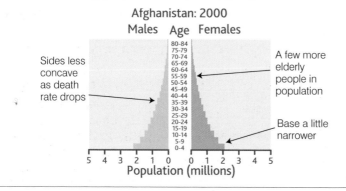

Afghanistan: 2000

Males   Age   Females

Sides less concave as death rate drops

A few more elderly people in population

Base a little narrower

5 4 3 2 1 0   0 1 2 3 4 5
Population (millions)

Key terms

Age structure: the proportions of each age group in a population. This links closely to the stage a country has reached in the demographic transition model.

Gender structure: the balance between males and females in a population. Small differences can tell us a great deal about a country or city.

Infant mortality: the number of babies that die under a year of age, per 1,000 live births.

Child mortality: the number of children that die under five years of age, per 1,000 live births.

B *A Stage 5 family*

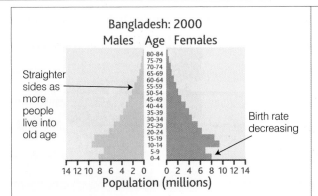

Straighter sides as more people live into old age

Birth rate decreasing

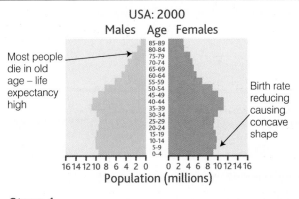

Most people die in old age – life expectancy high

Birth rate reducing causing concave shape

Stage 3

The narrowing base shows the decrease in birth rate typical of Stage 3 countries. The sides become straighter. Birth rate decreases quickly. Health improvements allow even more people to live into old age.

Stage 4

This pyramid has become straight-sided, showing a steady low birth rate. High life expectancy allows most people to live into their 60s and 70s and a significant minority into their 80s.

Stage 5

Germany has been at Stage 5 since the 1970s – one of the first countries to reduce its birth rate to this extent (photo **B**). When today's middle-aged people become elderly, there will be few adults of working age to support them. A Stage 5 population is not sustainable.

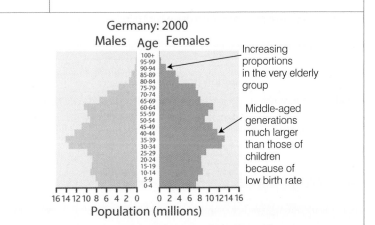

Increasing proportions in the very elderly group

Middle-aged generations much larger than those of children because of low birth rate

A   *Population pyramids and the demographic transition model*

■ Future population change

Diagram **C** shows population pyramids for India in 2000, 2025 and 2050. Computer programs can predict future population patterns from today's statistics. Although India's birth rate has fallen, its base remains wide because there are so many young adults in their child-bearing years. By 2025 the number of babies born each year will have stabilised, reducing slightly by 2050. Increasing numbers live into old age, and the 90–94, 95–99 and 100+ age groups are included on future graphs. By 2050 most people will live into their 70s and India will have all the characteristics of a Stage 4 population.

Urban areas of many countries at lesser stages of development are predominantly male in all age groups up to 60–64. Usually more boys are born than girls, explaining the differences at the base (diagram **E**). Rural-to-urban migration in search of work remains common in countries at lesser stages of development. Men and older boys leave the women, younger children and elderly behind in rural areas. Cities offer greater opportunities to earn money, which can be sent back to improve the family's standard of living (photo **D**). Sometimes whole families make the migration.

Study tip

Some tips to help you create or complete a population pyramid:

- Be careful to correctly annotate the horizontal scale.
- Mark the ends of the horizontal bars accurately.
- Use a sharp pencil and a ruler.
- If you have been asked to complete a population pyramid, make your bars as similar as possible to those that have already been drawn.

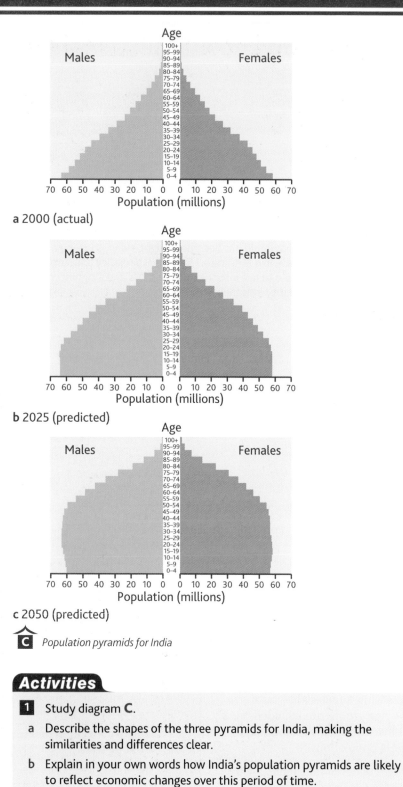

a 2000 (actual)

b 2025 (predicted)

c 2050 (predicted)

C Population pyramids for India

D Men queuing for work in Kolkata, India

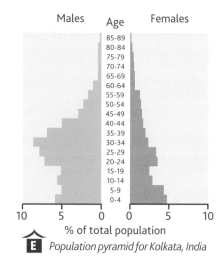

E Population pyramid for Kolkata, India

Activities

1 Study diagram **C**.

a Describe the shapes of the three pyramids for India, making the similarities and differences clear.

b Explain in your own words how India's population pyramids are likely to reflect economic changes over this period of time.

2 Study diagram **E**. Label a copy of Kolkata's population pyramid to show its unusual characteristics.

3 Research the pyramids for two countries at different stages of development in the early 21st century. Try to predict likely changes in population and development in the future.

⬭ links

India's population pyramids can be used to predict future changes in the country, both demographically and economically. The same can be done for other countries.

See **http://populationpyramid.net**.

8.4 How can a population become sustainable?

A **sustainable population** is one whose growth and development is at a rate that does not threaten the success of future generations. Countries at Stage 4 of the demographic transition model, with low birth and death rates, are the most sustainable. The economy is stable or growing and the standard of living is maintained or improving.

Stage 5 populations are not sustainable because numbers are decreasing. In Japan, calculations were done to predict how long it would take the country to die out if current low birth rates continued well into the future. Although it is highly unlikely to happen, the fact that it was even thought about was worrying.

> **In this section you will learn**
>
> the reasons for the one-child policy in China from 1979
>
> the severity of the rules imposed
>
> how the one-child policy has changed over recent years and the outcomes of these changes.

Will China have a sustainable population?

The early days of the one-child policy

During the 1970s the Chinese government realised that the country was heading for famine unless severe changes were made quickly. Change to an industrial economy at the expense of farming had already caused a catastrophic famine from 1959 to 1961, with 35 million deaths. A 'baby boom' followed and population was growing too fast to be sustainable. The government stepped in to avoid another crisis. However, its methods have been considered too strict, even cruel.

Beginning in 1979, the one-child policy said that each couple:

- must not marry until their late 20s
- must have only one successful pregnancy
- must be sterilised after the first child or must abort any future pregnancies
- would receive a 5 to 10 per cent salary rise for limiting their family to one child
- would have priority housing, pension and family benefits, including free education for the single child.

Any couples disobeying the rules and having a second child were severely penalised:

- a 10 per cent salary cut was enforced
- the fine imposed was so large it would bankrupt many households
- the family would have to pay for the education of both children and for health care for all the family
- second children born abroad are not penalised, but they are not allowed to become Chinese citizens.

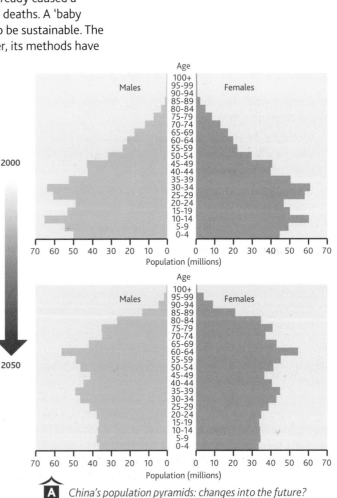

A *China's population pyramids: changes into the future?*

Case study

182

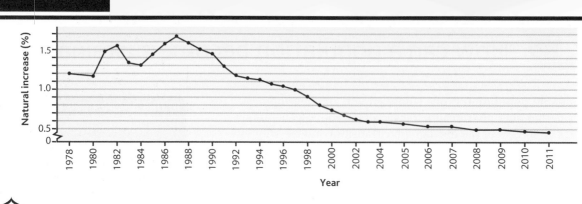

B *China's population growth through the one-child policy*

Pressure to abort a second pregnancy even included pay cuts for the couple's fellow-workers so they would make life unbearable. The 'Granny Police' – older women of the community entrusted with the task of keeping everyone in line – kept a regular check on couples of childbearing age, even accompanying women on contraception appointments to make sure they attended.

China is racially mixed but over 80 per cent of the population is of the Han race. Minority groups could become unsustainable under the one-child policy, so they were exempt. In rural areas, where sons are essential to work the family land, a second pregnancy was allowed if the first child was a girl, in the hope of getting a boy.

The problems and benefits of the policy

The one-child policy has been controversial for many reasons:

- Some women were forced to have abortions as late as the ninth month of pregnancy.
- Women were placed under tremendous pressure from their families, workmates, the 'Granny Police' and their own consciences and feelings.
- Local officials and central government had power over people's private lives.
- Chinese society prefers sons over daughters. Some girls were placed in orphanages (photo **C**) or allowed to die (female infanticide) in the hope of having a son the second time round.
- Chinese children have a reputation for being over-indulged because they are only (single) children, hence the name 'Little Emperors' (photo **D**).

China's one-child policy has brought important benefits to the country, however. The famine previously forecast has not happened. Population growth has slowed down sufficiently for people to have enough food and jobs. It is estimated that 400 million fewer people have been born. Increased technology and exploitation of resources have increased standard of living for many. New industries have lifted millions out of poverty. This is partly the result of the one-child policy, but new technology from other countries has helped.

Study tip

This topic has given you a detailed case study of China's one-child policy. Points have been made in favour of and against the policy. When you write your answer to question 4, remember to use lots of detail and make plenty of points on both sides. Clearly state your conclusion, for or against, giving your reasons or evidence.

C *Children in a Chinese orphanage*

D *Only children are often spoiled*

Changes to the one-child policy in the 1990s and 2000s

- Young couples who are both only children are allowed two children, but government officials are expected to set an example by only having a single child.
- As people have become wealthier, some are choosing to have larger families and simply pay the fines.
- Couples no longer need to obtain permission to have a first child.
- The Shanghai government is considering introducing incentives to encourage couples to have two children.
- It is now illegal to discriminate against women who give birth to baby girls and has prohibited sex-selective abortions.
- In 2008, following a devastating earthquake that killed lots of children, the policy was relaxed in Sichuan Province.

Consequences of the one-child policy

- With less time needed for childcare, women have been able to concentrate on having a career.
- The policy will not change until at least 2015. In 2008, China still had 1 million more births than deaths every five weeks and half the population lived on less than $2 a day.
- With boys being favoured rather than girls, China has a serious gender imbalance. There are now 60 million more young men than young women.

Did you know ???????

There are over 15 million orphans in China, most healthy girls, abandoned as a result of the one-child policy and Chinese society's economic and social preference for boys. Missionary-run orphanages are usually very good, but in state institutions the girls are neglected and sometimes treated cruelly.

Did you know ???????

Chinese couples had to apply for permission to try to become pregnant and take their turn. If they did not succeed in a six-month period, they had to wait for another opportunity.

We cannot just be content with the current success. We must make population control a permanent policy.

Adapted from the People's Daily (China's Communist Party newspaper), 2000

Beijing mother-of-one, Zhao Hui, who has a four-year-old daughter called Zhang Jin'ao, says she never wanted more than one child. 'One child is enough. I'm too busy at work to have any more,' says the 38-year-old.

*Adapted from BBC News website **news.bbc.co.uk**, 20 September 2007*

E *News items about the policy*

Activities

1 Study diagram **A**.

a Describe the shape of each pyramid.

b On copies of the pyramids, label the key features, paying particular attention to any similarities and differences.

2 Study graph **B**.

a Describe the shape of the graph.

b Do you think the one-child policy has been a success in controlling population growth? Explain your answer.

3 Study the extracts in **E**.

a Make a list of the controversial aspects of the one-child policy. Remember that the Chinese government and people may not see everything in the same way as outsiders.

b What were the successful outcomes of the policy during the 1980s?

4 Make a decision – was the Chinese government wise to introduce the one-child policy? Have the benefits outweighted the disadvantages? There is no right or wrong answer here – you simply need to justify your opinion clearly.

8.5 What alternative birth control programmes exist?

Case study

Transmigration in Indonesia

Indonesia is a rapidly developing country in south-east Asia (map **A**). It comprises a group of some 17,500 islands (known as an archipelago), two of the largest being Sumatra and Java. With a population of about 240 million, it is the 4th most populous country in the world. The population is growing at a rate of just over 1 per cent per year, with the birth rate at 18.1 per 1000 (2011) and the death rate at a very low 6.3 per 1000 (2011). Look back to diagram A (page 173) to consider what stage of the demographic transition model Indonesia is in.

A *Location of Indonesia*

What is transmigration?

Whilst population growth is now slowing down in Indonesia, back in the 1950s and 1960s, it was growing rapidly and the islands of Java, Bali and Madura were in danger of becoming over-populated. This occurs when there are not enough resources (for example, food, water, jobs and housing) to adequately support the number of people.

In 1969, in an attempt to re-distribute the population, the Indonesian government embarked on an ambitious project called **transmigration**. This involved encouraging people to move from densely populated islands such as Java to the more sparsely populated outer islands, such as West Papua (Irian Jaya). Transmigration was a chance for people to escape from the poverty of overcrowded urban slums to become land owners elsewhere and earn money through farming. Between 1979 and 1984, at the height of the programme, more than 2.5 million people were involved. In total, over a million people have resettled in West Papua (Irian Jaya) alone.

Financed by the World Bank and the Asian Development Bank, transmigration continued through the 1980s but recent financial difficulties and changes in government have led to the policy being scaled down.

B *Transmigration settlement near Geumpang, Aceh in Indonesia*

In this section you will learn

how all birth control programmes in the developing world do not take the same approach

how to compare China's one-child policy and other birth control programmes.

Key terms

Transmigration: a population policy that aims to move people from densely populated areas to sparsely populated areas and provide them with opportunities to improve the quality of their lives.

Industrialisation: a process, usually associated with the development of an economy, where an increasing proportion of people work in industry.

Recent developments

In 2006, an estimated 20,000 families took advantage of the transmigration programme, supported by the Department of Manpower and Transmigration. By 2010, there were about 250,000 families who wanted to move, the government was only able to sponsor 10,000 families at a cost of some $US160.5 million.

Following the eruption of Mount Merapi in 2010, the government offered to re-locate tens of thousands of displaced people from Java to Kalimantan. By 2011, some 2,000 families had taken up the offer encouraged by free transportation and the promise of two hectares of land and living costs for six months.

What have been the effects of transmigration?

Whilst transmigration has probably eased overcrowding in some towns and cities, the policy has led to problems.

Economic

- Rather than reducing poverty, critics suggest that transmigration has simply re-distributed poverty.
- Many new migrants lacked the necessary farming skills to make productive use of their new land and some abandoned their new homes to become refugees.
- Settlements were often poorly planned, with few shops, roads and services such as water, sanitation and electricity (photo **B**).
- Re-settlement was extremely expensive, costing $US7,000 per family in the 1980s.

Environmental

- Transmigration has been blamed for accelerating the rate of deforestation in previously sparsely populated regions.
- Poor land use practises, such as over-cultivation, have led to issues of soil erosion.

Social

- Clashes have occurred between migrants and the indigenous populations, particularly in more remote islands. In 2001, hundreds died when the local Dayaks and the transmigrant Madurese (from Madura) clashed.
- Traditional land rights were often ignored as land ownership was granted to the new settlers.
- There have also been religious clashes between the Islamist migrants and the largely Christian local people

Political

- Some critics have suggested that transmigration was encouraged by the government primarily to increase national security and control indigenous people in the outer islands.

Despite the problems, the transmigration policy has resulted in the re-settlement of an estimated 20 million people, mostly to Sumatra and Kalimantan. Whilst the population pressures have continued to increase in cities such as Jakarta, the situation would probably have been much worse if transmigration had not occurred.

Industrialisation: another approach to coping with population pressures

For the future, as birth control programmes have led to a slowing down of population growth in Indonesia (families are encouraged to have two children only), the transmigration programme will probably continue to decline. In its place, as Indonesia expands its programmes of resource exploitation (for example, minerals, timber, oil palm and shrimp farming) and **industrialisation**, more and more poor people will migrate to the remoter islands looking for work. Since the 1990's the government has encouraged industrialisation in the remoter islands through its 'Eastward Development Policy'. By encouraging resource development and industrialisation, workers will naturally be attracted. This can be considered another approach to coping with a rapidly growing population.

Activities

1 Study the information in the case study and answer the following questions.

a What is transmigration?

b How does transmigration address the issue of rapid population growth?

c What are the advantages of the transmigration programme to the migrants?

d How have local indigenous people been affected by the influx of new migrants?

e Do you think transmigration has been a success? Explain your answer.

2 Use the information in this case study together with your own internet research to find out more about the environmental impacts of the transmigration programme. You might choose to focus on the Mega Rice Project in Kalimantan. Use maps and photos to support your study. Assess the success of the transmigration programme – did the economic benefits outweigh the environmental damage?

8.6 What are the issues and opportunities for an ageing population?

Populations in richer countries are ageing. Low birth rates and smaller families result in fewer children and adolescents. Better health care and more advanced medicines allow people to live longer, increasing the proportion of elderly people. Today's older people in countries at further stages of development tend to be wealthier, fitter and have wider interests, with the spare time to enjoy these. This is, however, the age group with the most expensive needs, especially in terms of health care. The 85+ age group – the very elderly – is growing fastest, increasing stress on health and social welfare systems (photo **A**).

A *The 85+ age group is growing fast. This couple is living in a care home*

In this section you will learn

the ways in which an ageing population is different from younger populations

the demands on a country that has an ageing population

how, as the proportion of elderly people increases, the costs to the government increase dramatically

different ways of solving the problem of an ageing population

how to evaluate different approaches to coping with an ageing population.

▌ The issues

Health care

The demand for health care increases because more illness occurs in old age. The elderly visit their GP (doctor) more often. They have more hospital appointments and more time in hospital than younger or middle-aged people. The government has to find more funding to support older people and this comes from taxation of present workers.

Social services

Elderly people need other services such as nursing homes, day-care centres and people to help them to care for themselves at home. These special needs put financial pressure on a country.

The pensions crisis

Life expectancy is higher in developed countries than in developing countries. In wealthier countries, people expect to be able to retire from work and have a pension (an income) for the rest of their lives. As there are more elderly people and the proportion of working people is decreasing, so the taxes must increase to pay the pensions bill.

The state pension began in 1908 when male life expectancy was 67 and retirement age was 65. The average person would therefore receive their pension for only two years. Today, the situation could not be more different as life expectancy has risen to 80. In response to this, the retirement age is set to increase over the next few years.

Key terms

European Union (EU): a group of countries across Europe that work towards a single market, i.e. they trade as if they were one country, without any trade barriers.

Did you know ??????

With the second lowest birth rate in Europe, Italy faces population decline in the 21st century. Projections suggest that 40 per cent of Italians will be over 60 and only 15 per cent under 20 by the end of this century.

1 Study diagram **A** on pages 178–179.

a Describe how the numbers and proportions of elderly people change as a country passes through the demographic transition model.

b Look at the pyramids for Stages 4 and 5. What has happened to the gender ratio?

■ The opportunities

The situation has a positive side too. Younger retired people (those in their later 60s and early 70s) contribute a great deal to the economy (photo **B**). They are relatively wealthy and have lots of leisure time. They spend money on travel and recreation, providing jobs in the service sector. Many do voluntary work and some still do paid work and therefore pay taxes.

B *Younger retired people contribute a lot to the UK's economy*

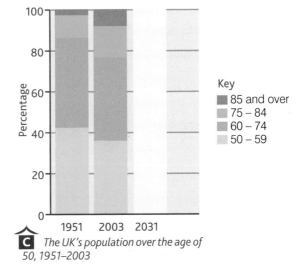

Key
- ■ 85 and over
- ■ 75 – 84
- ■ 60 – 74
- ■ 50 – 59

C *The UK's population over the age of 50, 1951–2003*

As soon as my hair turned white, people started to ignore me. It was as if I had become invisible.

Anna, 90, and still coping in her own home with no outside help

Britain's elderly are being neglected, poorly treated and marginalised by the country's health system. Inspectors found that many older patients were hungry because meals were taken away before they could eat them.

The Independent, *27 March 2006*

It's horrid having to rely on other people for the most basic things. It's bad enough when it's your own family and friends, but when it's strangers from social services it's so much worse.

Barry, 95, who has four carers every day to get him up, washed, dressed and, later, back to bed

How bad is the UK's pension crisis? Every day seems to bring fresh warnings that Britons will not have enough money to live on when they retire.

Adapted from BBC News website **news.bbc.co.uk**, *23 September 2005*

D *Quotes on being elderly, pensions and the health crisis*

■ Ageing in the EU

Table **E** shows **European Union (EU)** birth rates are very low – in fact, they have never been so low and they may decrease even more. Smaller families and later motherhood could soon result in a noticeable decline in population in some countries. In each generation there are fewer parents, so fewer children are born. In 2008, 1.6 babies were born in the EU for every woman, but 2.1 are needed for a population to be sustainable. Western European birth rates are higher than those in Eastern Europe, but Germany – a Western European country – has an even lower birth rate (table **E**).

Case study

France's solution

France is tackling its ageing population with a strong **pro-natal policy** – it encourages people to have children to produce a more favourable age structure and **dependency ratio**. This has had some effect, but has not been entirely successful as graph **F** shows.

Couples are given a range of incentives to have children:

- three years of paid parental leave, which can be used by mothers or fathers
- full-time schooling starts at the age of three, fully paid for by the government
- day care for children younger than three is subsidised by the government
- the more children a woman has, the earlier she will be allowed to retire on a full pension.

Nicole Falcou is 53. She lives in Muret, close to Toulouse in south-west France. She is married with three daughters aged between 14 and 22 and works locally with disabled children. She has three children of her own, so she is entitled to extra benefits from the government, including retiring in her early 50s on a full state pension if she chooses. Although a pension is always less than a salary, as her children grow up and become less financially dependent this is a tempting offer.

E Selected EU birth rates (2011)	
Country	**Birth rate (per 1,000)**
Ireland (W)	16.1
France (W)	12.3
UK (W)	12.3
Netherlands (W)	10.2
Poland (E)	10.0
Bulgaria (E)	9.3
Latvia (E)	10.0
Germany (W)	8.3

The average global birth rate was 19.95 per 1000 in 2009.
Note: (W) Western European country
(E) Eastern European country

F French birth and death rates, 1960–2007

Activities

2 Study graph **C** on page 187.
a Copy and complete the graph, adding a similar bar for 2031 by using the data in table **G**.
b Describe the changes shown by the bars between 1951 and 2031.
c Explain why these changes are happening.
3 Study graph **F**.
a Describe the pattern of the birth rate line.
b List the problems affecting a country with a very low birth rate.

G UK population aged over 50, 2031	
Age group	%
50–59	28
60–74	44
75–84	20
85 and over	8

Key terms

Dependency ratio: the balance between people who are independent (work and pay tax) and those who depend on them. Ideally, the fewer dependents for each independent person, the better off economically a country is. Here is the formula (figures can be in numbers or percentages):

$$\frac{\text{number of dependent people}}{\text{number of independent people}} \times 100$$

8.7 What are the impacts of international migration?

■ Push–pull factors

People move home for many different reasons. Every individual's decision to move is the result of **push–pull factors**. Negative aspects of a person's home area push them away from it and make them look for somewhere better. Positive characteristics of new places, which attract people to move there, are called pull factors.

■ Impacts of international migration

The impacts of **migration** on the **country of origin** and the **host country** can be positive or negative.

Economic

Migrant workers often send money back to their country of origin to help their families. This means that money leaves the host economy – a disadvantage – but the country of origin can benefit enormously.

Housing

Finding accommodation can be difficult for migrants in the UK. Some have been helped by social services and this causes resentment from UK citizens who feel they are being treated as second-class citizens in their own country. Demand for housing has grown immensely in the UK during the early 21st century, fuelled by high levels of migration. The demand for housing is greater than supply, so property prices rose quickly in the early 2000s and immigration has contributed to this.

Labour and skills

Migration brings labour and skills, and the economies of the UK and the EU have grown as a result. Most migrants are more successful than they would have been at home, although some are less fortunate. Exploitation does happen and not everyone earns as much as they had expected. Tragedies have occurred when gang masters, who often control large numbers of workers in agriculture and shellfish harvesting, have been negligent. The deaths of 23 Chinese cockle-pickers in Morecambe Bay in February 2004 was perhaps the worst example.

Social

Too many migrants can be a burden. Schools taking many **immigrant** children may be under pressure. British parents sometimes feel this reduces opportunities for their own children because teachers are too busy with those whose first language is not English. On the other hand, cultural mixing is often seen as positive as long as racial prejudice does not become a problem.

In this section you will learn

- the concept of migration and people's reasons for moving home (push–pull factors)
- the positive and negative impacts of international migration
- who moves within the EU and why
- who comes to the EU and their reasons for wanting to live here
- the differences between voluntary economic migrants and refugees
- the benefits and difficulties of international migration for EU countries.

Key terms

Push–pull factors: push factors are the negative aspects of a place that encourage people to move away. Pull factors are the attractions and opportunities of a place that encourage people to move there.

Migration: the movement of people from one permanent home to another, with the intention of staying at least a year. This move may be within a country (national migration) or between countries (international migration).

Host country: the country where a migrant settles.

Country of origin: the country from which a migration starts.

Immigrant: someone entering a new country with the intention of living there.

Emigrant: someone leaving their country of residence to move to another country.

A Slovak girl working in Sussex

Jana Susinkova came to the UK in 2002 with her Czech boyfriend. She was only 18 and he a little older. She worked as a domestic cleaner, undercutting the level local women charged by at least £1 per hour. She had enough work to keep busy six days a week. Her boyfriend was a mechanic and odd-job man, and his job provided accommodation for them.

Late in 2007 Jana returned home to Slovakia. Her boyfriend had already left to find a job in the Czech Republic, where the growing economy offered increasing opportunities for skilled people. While in the UK they had saved enough money to buy the materials and labour to build a four-bedroom house in the Czech Republic, giving them an excellent start to their married life. Jana's English had become fluent, so she quickly found a well-paid job where she uses it every day.

A *Working as a cleaner*

B *Push–pull factors for a family in West Africa*

Family member	Situation
Father	Subsistence farmer – crops unpredictable due to climate.
	Part-time fisherman – catches are reducing because of overfishing.
Mother	Housewife with limited primary education.
Adult son	Secondary education completed.
	Would like the chance to go to university or obtain an interesting job.
Daughters	Part-way through school.
	Want to get as well qualified as possible.
	School resources are sometimes in short supply.

Activities

1 Write the factors listed below into two groups of push and pull factors in terms of someone's possible migration:

job prospects   natural disasters

low income   housing shortages

health care   intolerance

high standard of living   high unemployment

improved housing   racial/religious tolerance

attractive environments   high wages

political or social unrest

educational opportunities   difficult climate

2 Study table **B**, which shows the factors affecting a family in West Africa who are considering moving to the EU. The family consists of two parents, an adult son and two younger daughters who are still at school.

a The father is keen to move but the mother wants to stay. Suggest reasons for these opinions.

b Identify the push and pull factors affecting the children.

c If the family moves to the EU how might the individual members benefit?

d Suggest any possible problems or issues that the family might face.

Migration from outside the EU

Europe currently receives over 2 million immigrants from beyond its borders a year – more than any other world region. The ratio between current population and immigrants is higher for Europe than for the USA. European population is changing more in age and racial structure due to immigration than by changes in birth and death rates.

About 9.4 per cent of the EU's people are foreign-born, compared with 10.3 per cent in the USA and almost 25 per cent in Australia. The range of countries around the world from which migrants to Europe come has changed. Africa and Asia are the major sources of immigrants, but not the same regions as previously.

Migration within the EU

There are two categories of migrants within the EU: those moving between countries and those coming in from beyond the borders. Wealthier countries usually receive immigrants searching for work and a better lifestyle. Poland and other Eastern European countries joined the EU in 2004. Since that date, many people have moved temporarily or permanently to the UK and other Western EU countries for work.

Case study

Polish workers migrating to UK

Since 2004, 1.5 million Eastern Europeans have entered the UK, two thirds of whom are Polish. Most have found formal jobs with much better pay than they would receive at home. Polish workers in the UK earn on average five times as much as they would at home, while the UK cost of living is only twice that in Poland. Most migrants pay tax, which contributes to the UK's economy. However, some work in the informal economy – working for cash and not paying tax. Polish workers also use UK health and education services, which add to the government's costs.

Overall, the UK economy has benefited from the influx of migrants from Poland. Poles are now the most numerous of foreign nationals in the UK. There are 545,000 Polish passport holders living in the UK compared with 75,000 in 2003, the year before Poland joined the EU.

D   *Occupations of Polish workers in the UK, 2008*

Occupation	Total
Administration, business, management	33%
Hospitality and catering	22%
Agriculture	10%
Manufacturing	8%
Health service	6%
Food processing	5%
Retail	5%
Construction	5%
Others	6%

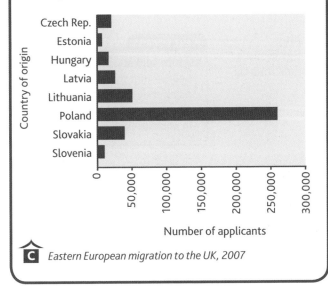

C   *Eastern European migration to the UK, 2007*

Activities

3   Study graph **C** and table **D**.

a   Using figures, describe the dominance of Poland in EU migration to the UK.

b   Use the information in table **D** to draw a pie chart to show the occupations of Polish workers in the UK.

c   Discuss the types of occupations Polish workers undertake. Are there any trends?

4   Suggest the benefits and difficulties of migration within the EU. Who benefits and who does not?

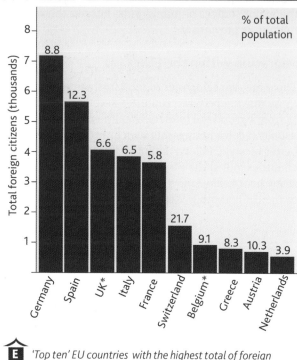

% of total population

Total foreign citizens (thousands)

Germany 8.8, Spain 12.3, UK* 6.6, Italy 6.5, France 5.8, Switzerland 21.7, Belgium* 9.1, Greece 8.3, Austria 10.3, Netherlands 3.9

E 'Top ten' EU countries with the highest total of foreign citizens (2009)(* UK and Belgium 2008)

F Passport control at Heathrow Airport – a popular point of entry for economic migrants

Labour migration

Cheaper travel and more information attract skilled and unskilled labour to Europe. Many EU residents would like the flow of migration to reduce, but the United Nations predicts that immigration into the EU will rise by 40 per cent over 40 years. Immigration is a subject of political debate in all EU countries. Spain's immigrant population grew by 400 per cent in 10 years in the early 21st century. Italy expects 100,000 Romanians in the years following Romania's joining of the EU. Although Italy needs workers, not everyone is happy with such a large influx of new people.

Europe needs immigrants because of its falling birth rate and the resulting lack of workers. Highly skilled workers often come to the EU to take temporary jobs in areas of shortage such as teaching, nursing and high-tech computer jobs. About 20 per cent are graduates. Nevertheless, many people see immigrants as a problem rather than as an opportunity.

Key terms

Asylum seekers: people who believe that their lives are at risk if they remain in their home country and who seek to settle in another (safe) country.

Activities

5 Study graph **E**.

a On a sheet of plain paper, draw proportional circles to scale to show the total foreign citizens as a percentage of total population. Cut them out carefully.

b On a blank outline map of Europe, stick each symbol on or beside the country it represents.

c Give your map a title and explain the scale of your circles in a key.

d Describe the pattern shown in your completed map.

Case study

International labour migration to the EU: Senegal to Italy

Senegalese children love football and support home teams, but many also support Lazio, AS Parma and other Italian teams. The reason for this is that many of these children's fathers and brothers already work in Italy. Patterns of emigration from Senegal are well established and many young men are keen to work in Italy.

G   *Many Senegalese fishing villages have been abandoned*

Opportunities are limited in Senegal, where many people are subsistence farmers. With limited services and high rates of urban unemployment, young men are keen to emigrate to the EU to find work. Money is often sent home to support children's education or improve living conditions. For example, in the villages of Beud Forage money has been used to set up water and electricity supplies.

Refugee movements to the EU

Asylum seekers are people who are at risk if they stay in their own country. They become refugees when they settle in another country. One-third of EU immigrants claim to be asylum seekers. Since EU countries have reduced the number of EU migrants they would allow in, some **economic migrants** have claimed to be asylum seekers, believing this would give them a better chance of being allowed to stay in the EU. Unfortunately, this has sometimes caused strong feelings against genuine asylum seekers.

Despite being criticised by the United Nations for not taking enough genuine refugees, the EU has a good record of accepting those displaced by war. The 1990s Bosnian war produced hundreds of thousands of refugees to the EU. Germany alone took 400,000, many of whom returned home once the situation was peaceful.

Today, the wars in Iraq and Afghanistan provide most asylum claims. Two million Iraqis have already left the country, some for neighbouring countries and some to the EU. Another 1.8 million refugees live away from their homes in Iraq and many feel sufficiently threatened to want to leave.

Sweden is particularly generous to asylum seekers (table **G**). By 2007, 70,000 Iraqis already lived there – half of those coming to the EU. The Netherlands, Germany, Greece, Belgium and the UK have given homes to most of the rest. With the Iraq war coming to an end, asylum requests to EU countries from Iraqis have decreased to 19,176 in 2010 from a peak of 38,286 in 2007. Afghans are now the largest group seeking refuge in the EU with 22,939 asylum requests in 2010.

Annual asylum applications (2010)

H

EU country	Number of applications
Sweden	31,820
Netherlands	13,330
Belgium	19,940
Germany	41,330
Denmark	4,970
Ireland	1,940
UK	22,090
Spain	2,740

Activities

6   a   Who are 'asylum seekers' and how do they differ from economic migrants?

b   Why do wars often produce large numbers of asylum seekers?

c   Represent the data in table **G** in the form of bars on an outline map of Europe.

d   Why do you think the countries in table **G** are popular destinations for asylum seekers?

e   Use the internet to make your own study into asylum seekers associated with a recent world conflict, such as civil war in Libya (2011).

Key term

Economic migrant: someone trying to improve their standard of living, who moves voluntarily.

⃝⃝ links

To investigate further why Eastern European migrants are returning to the UK, visit www.migrationwatchuk.com.

9.1 What are the characteristics and causes of urbanisation?

In 2008, for the first time in history, over half of the world's population lived in towns and cities. **Urbanisation** – where there is an increasing proportion of city dwellers in contrast to those in the countryside – is a worldwide process. It began at different times in different parts of the world and occurred at contrasting paces, as it continues to do so today (graph **A**). The contrasting proportions of people living in towns and cities is shown in map **B**.

In this section you will learn

the process of urbanisation and how it varies throughout the world and over time

the causes of urbanisation.

Key terms

Urbanisation: a process where an increasing proportion of the population lives in towns and cities resulting in their growth.

Rural-to-urban migration: moving home from a rural area to settle in a town or city.

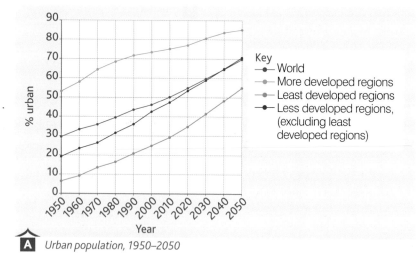

Key
— World
— More developed regions
— Least developed regions
— Less developed regions, (excluding least developed regions)

A Urban population, 1950–2050

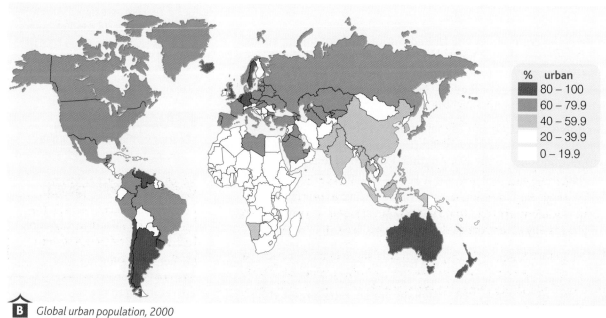

% urban
80 – 100
60 – 79.9
40 – 59.9
20 – 39.9
0 – 19.9

B Global urban population, 2000

Causes of urbanisation

There are two causes of urbanisation: **rural–urban migration** and natural increase. The initial cause of urbanisation is usually rural–urban migration. This is the result of push–pull factors, as shown in the photos in **C**. The people that migrate into the towns and cities are generally young and this results in relatively high levels of natural increase. The high proportion of young adults results in high levels of births. Improvements in medical care mean that babies are more likely to survive. This can lead to an increase in the urban population while birth rates remain high.

> ### Did you know ???????
>
> The largest city in the world (based on the population of the metropolitan area) is Tokyo, with a population of 32,450,000, followed by Seoul (20,550,000), Mexico City (20,450,000) and Mumbai (19,200,000). London is ranked 18th, with a population of 12,875,000.

> 66 Recent droughts have meant yields have been lower and lower, so I've struggled to provide enough food for my family to eat. I have only a small amount of land and can't afford to buy any fertilisers. 99

> 66 I came here because I thought we would be better off. I believed we would have a better house and I would have a good job and some money. My children would be able to go to school and we would get better medical help if we are sick. 99

C   *Reasons why people leave the Ethiopian countryside*

Activities

1   Study graph **A**.

a   Describe the trends shown by each of the lines. Support your answer with evidence from the graph.

b   Give examples of how the process of urbanisation has been important at different times and has occurred at different speeds.

2   Study map **B** and a political map in an atlas. Describe the pattern shown by the map. Try to select areas where rates of urbanisation are very high, high, average, low and very low. Give a clear overview of the locations of places that generally fall into such categories. Can you see any exceptions to the patterns you have described?

3   Study the photos in **C**. Imagine you are a resident of the rural area shown in the photo. Relatives have come back to your village and described the city shown in the second photo to you. Explain why you really want to move there.

> ### Study tip
>
> Ensure that you can explain the process of rural–urban migration with specific reference to push and pull factors.

9.2 How does land use vary in an urban area?

In all towns and cities the **land use** varies. In some areas shops and services may be dominant, whereas other areas may be dominated by housing, industry or recreation. Some areas have mixed land use where the **function** varies. In British cities, certain areas in similar locations tend to have similar characteristics. For example, the central area tends to be the shopping area or **central business district (CBD)**. The area around this is likely to have originally been the oldest part (although more recent building may have changed this) and this is referred to as the **inner city**. Newer areas are generally found on the outskirts, often known as the **outer city or suburbs**. The photos in **A** show the key areas and their features.

In this section you will learn

how urban areas have a variety of functions

the characteristics and locations of some urban areas.

a CBD

b Redevelopment

c Suburbs

d Inner city

A *Characteristics of different parts of Sheffield*

B *1 : 50,000 OS map extract of Sheffield, part of map sheet 110*

Key terms

Land use: the type of buildings or other features that are found in the area, e.g. terraced housing, banks, industrial estates, roads, parks.

Function: the purpose of a particular area, e.g. for residential use, recreation or shopping.

Central business district (CBD): the main shopping and service area in a city. The CBD is usually found in the middle of the city so that it is easily accessible.

Inner city: the area around the CBD – usually built before 1918 in the UK.

Outer city or suburbs: the area on the edge of the city. Many suburbs were built after 1945 and get newer as they reach the edge of the city.

Study tip

Practise drawing a simple sketch map showing typical land uses in a British city. Think about why each land use is found where it is.

Did you know ??????

The Burj Dubai is the world's tallest building, with 141 storeys and 828 m in height. The Freedom Tower at the World Trade Center will be 110 storeys and including the spire, 541 m high (1776 feet commemorating the year of United States indepence) when it is completed in 2013

⦾**links**

Visit www.multimap.co.uk to see a complete range of maps at different scales. You can overlay them with satellite images to see how land use varies in Sheffield or a city near to where you live.

Activity

1 Study the photos in **A** and map **B**.

a What is the evidence that photo **a** shows a CBD?

b Describe the CBD (roughly in the centre of the area within the ring road) from the OS map. You should include reference to its size, shape and functions.

c Using the photo of the inner city, draw a labelled sketch to show the characteristics of the houses and the environment.

d Provide evidence to support the idea that land use in Sheffield varies. You should try to give five different points.

9.3 What are the issues for people living in urban areas in richer parts of the world?

There are many issues in towns and cities, including those relating to housing, traffic, services and provision for a mixed community. The photos in **A** highlight some of the issues.

A *Issues in urban areas in the UK*

Activity

1 Study the photos in **A**. Work in pairs.

a For one of them, write three questions to identify key features shown in the photo. Your partner should do the same for the other photo. Your questions should be designed to obtain clear, detailed and thoughtful answers.

b Swap questions. Answer the questions your partner has written on the photo. You should give full and detailed answers to the questions.

c Swap your answers and read and discuss them. Do you agree with the answers given? How good were the questions asked? How could they be improved?

d Together, summarise the issues you think are shown.

Issue 1: housing

Population in the UK has increased by 10.5 per cent since 1971 and this rate of growth is predicted to continue, giving a population of 65 million by 2025. The number of **households** has risen by 30 per cent since 1971. Most of this increase is because more people live alone – some 7 million (12 per cent in 2009) of the UK's population. New single-person households account for 70 per cent of the increased demand for housing. This is due to people leaving home to rent or buy younger than previously, marrying later, getting divorced and living longer. A third of single-person households are aged over 65.

The government target is to build 240,000 new houses every year by 2016 so that house prices do not spiral out of control as a result of a shortage. Many of these new homes will be built throughout existing towns and cities, with a target of 60 per cent to be built on **brownfield sites** – areas that have been previously built on, usually in the inner city. However, some housing will inevitably be built on **greenfield** sites – areas that have not previously been built on, usually on the edge of the city. Table **B** summarises the points in favour of each of these two alternatives. The photos in **C** show the different types of housing being built to meet the growing demand and contrasting needs of the population in different parts of the city.

B *Advantages of building on brownfield and greenfield sites*

Advantages of building on brownfield sites	Advantages of building on greenfield sites
Easier to get planning permission as councils want to see brownfield sites used	New sites do not need clearing so can be cheaper to prepare
Sites in cities are not left derelict and/or empty	No restrictions of existing road network
Utilities such as water and electricity are already provided	Pleasant countryside environment may appeal to potential home owners
Roads already exist	Some shops and business parks on outskirts provide local facilities
Near to facilities in town centres, e.g. shops, entertainment and places of work	Land cheaper on outskirts so plots can be larger
Cuts commuting	More space for gardens

a Riverside apartments, Bridgewater Place, Leeds

b Gentrified housing, Cambridge

c Retirement bungalows, Scartho, Grimsby

d Family homes, Scartho Top, Grimsby

C *Types of housing*

Key terms

Regeneration: improving an area.

Sustainable community: community (offering housing, employment and recreation opportunities) that is broadly in balance with the environment and offers people a good quality of life.

Quality of life: how good a person's life is as measured by such things as quality of housing and environment, access to education, health care, how secure people feel and how happy they are with their lifestyle.

Park-and-ride scheme: a bus service run to key places from car parks on the edges of busy areas in order to reduce traffic flows and congestion in the city centre. Costs are low to encourage people to use the system – they are generally cheaper than fuel and car parking charges in the centre.

Activities

2 Read the text and study table **B** on page 199.

a Why is the demand for housing likely to increase significantly in the next few years?

b What is meant by the term 'brownfield site'?

c What are the advantages and disadvantages of building new houses on a brownfield site?

d Identify a brownfield site that is being used for housing in your local area.

e What is a 'greenfield site'?

f Why are many people concerned about the use of greenfield sites for building houses?

g Is there a greenfield site near you that is being developed for housing? If so, has it caused concern among local people? Explain your answer.

3 Study the photos in **C** on page 199.

a In groups, take on the following roles:

■ professional accountant working in a city-centre office, aged 26 and single

■ a 68-year-old pensioner, widowed and living alone

■ a couple seeking an old, modernised house as a first home together

■ a family with two children aged 10 and 12.

b For each role, identify which of the four houses shown in **C** would be most suitable and explain the advantages of living there.

Did you know ??????

There were riots in Toxteth, in inner-city Liverpool, and St Paul's in Bristol in 1981 and more recently in Oldham in 2001. These were seen as race riots by the press.

Study tip

Know the arguments in favour of urban development taking place on both brownfield and greenfield sites. Relate this to how an inner-city area has been changed as a direct result of a development strategy.

■ Issue 2: the inner city

Part of the demand for housing will be satisfied in inner-city areas. Over the years governments have had a variety of strategies to improve living in inner cities. In the 1960s and 1970s cheap high rise flats were considered to be the best approach. However, they proved to be unpopular and many have since been demolished. Since the 1980s there have been three main strategies for addressing issues of the inner city.

Strategy 1: UDCs

Urban Development Corporations (UDCs) were a major strategy introduced in the 1980s, with London Docklands Development Corporation (LDDC) and Merseyside Development Corporation (MDC) being established in 1981. Eleven more UDCs followed. These were large-scale projects where major changes occurred with the help of both public and private investment. Although the LDDC ceased to exist after 1998, the area has continued to develop and change. During its lifetime, £1.86 billion of public money was invested along with £7.7 billion from the private sector (diagram **D**). Changes are continuing today, with further improvements in the transport system (such as the eastward extension of the Jubilee Line), and the building of further skyscrapers at Canary Wharf _ron Quay, North Quay) and other locations.

Activity

4 Study diagram **D** and photo **E**. You could work in groups of three for this task, with each member of the group doing one of the strategies.

a For each of the three strategies (UDCs, City Challenge and sustainable communities), complete a fact file including the following information:

■ location

■ dates

■ what was done

■ who was involved

■ where funding came from

■ what has been done to improve housing, the environment and the community.

b Create a table to show the advantages and the disadvantages of each of the three strategies.

c Which of the three strategies do you think is best? Give full justification for your answer. You should stress its advantages and the disadvantages of the other two.

UDC example: The London Docklands Development Corporation

The 1980 Act requires an urban development corporation 'to secure the regeneration of its area, by bringing land and buildings into effective use, encouraging the development of existing and new industry and commerce, creating an attractive environment and ensuring that housing and social facilities are available to encourage people to live and work in the area.'

The LDDC was at work for 17 years. In its final annual report in 1998 it headlined its achievements as follows:

- £1.86 billion in public sector investment
- £7.7 billion in private sector investment
- 431 ha of land sold for development
- 144 km of new and improved roads
- the construction of the Docklands Light Railway
- 2.3 km² of commercial/industrial floorspace built
- 762 ha of derelict land reclaimed
- 24,046 new homes built
- 2,700 businesses trading

- contributions to 5 new health centres and the redevelopment of 6 more
- funding towards 11 new primary schools, 2 secondary schools, 3 post-16 colleges and 9 vocational training centres
- 94 awards for architecture, conservation and landscaping
- 85,000 people now at work in London Docklands.

D   *London Docklands*

Strategy 2: City Challenge

City Challenge was a big initiative of the 1990s. It had a holistic approach to **regeneration**, where local authorities, private companies and the local community worked together from the start. The focus of projects varied. The Hulme (Manchester) City Challenge Partnership sought to improve the housing that had been built in the 1960s to replace the old terraces that had once stood there. Integral to this was an attempt to improve the environment, community facilities and shopping provision (photo **E**).

City Challenge example: Hulme, Manchester

- Crescents were built in the 1960s and demolished in the 1990s
- Through City Challenge, Hulme received £37.5 million
- Some old buildings were retained
- Homes were designed to conserve water, and be energy efficient and pleasant
- There was a return to a traditional layout – Stretford Road (at the end of which is Hulme Arch) was rebuilt after demolition of crescents (original course was through the middle of these)
- Local schools and a new park have been built
- The views of local people were taken into account

E   *Hulme, Manchester*

Strategy 3: Sustainable Communities

Sustainable communities allow people to live in an area where there is housing of an appropriate standard to offer reasonable **quality of life**, with access to a job, education and health care. This initiative began in 2003 and one area affected by it is an area of east Manchester, formerly known as Cardroom and now renamed New Islington Millennium Village. As diagram **F** shows, it seeks to provide for an appropriate quality of life in inner-city Manchester in the 21st century.

Sustainable communities example: New Islington Millennium Village

What's coming to New Islington?

New homes
- 66 houses, 200 ground-floor apartments
- 500 two- and three-storey apartments
- 600 1- and 2-bed apartments
- 34 urban barns
- workshops
- refurbishment of Ancoats hospital and Stubbs Mill
- new office space

Waterways
- 3,000 metres of canalside
- 12 bridges
- 3 giant canopies
- 50 moorings for narrow boats and canalside facilities

Urban amenities
- 10 new shops
- 2 pubs, 2 restaurants, cafés and bars
- Metrolink stop in 10 minutes' walking distance
- New bus lines and bus stops
- 200 on-street and 1,200 underground car-parking spaces
- a safe Old Mill Street

Parks and gardens
- 300 new trees
- 2 garden islands, an orchard, a beach
- play areas and climbing rocks
- secured courtyard gardens
- private gardens and patios

Community facilities
- a primary school and play areas
- a health centre with 8 GPs
- 2 workshops
- a crèche
- an angling club and a village hall
- a football pitch

Sustainability Agenda
- boreholes will provide up to 25 litres per second of naturally filtered water
- central heat and power to generate 600 kW electrical energy and 1,000 kW thermal energy
- recycling collection points that allow occupants to recycle 50 per cent of domestic waste

F *Living in New Islington, Manchester*

▪ Issue 3: traffic

As we demand greater mobility and accessibility, the number of cars has increased, as has the problem of traffic congestion. More people have more money and welcome the door-to-door service that comes with having a car. Many households (approx. 30 per cent) have more than one car, while 45 per cent have one car. Photo **G** shows some of the environmental problems this creates. Diagram **H** shows strategies designed to reduce the use of cars by encouraging cycling, making public transport more attractive, introducing **park-and-ride schemes** and congestion charging.

- Air pollution from vehicles
- Noise from heavy vehicles
- Buildings discoloured
- Impact on health – respiratory conditions, asthma
- Unsightly

G *Environmental problems resulting from traffic congestion*

a

Central London congestion charging zone (£10 per day)

Shoreditch

Marylebone

City

Holborn

River Thames

Southwark

Westminster

Lambeth

N

Chelsea

0   1km

b Park and Ride, York

B1363 HELMSLEY

A64 SCARBOROUGH MALTON PICKERING

A19 TEESSIDE DARLINGTON

2

9

MONKS CROSS PARK AND RIDE SITE
P + 🚌
7 days a week

RAWCLIFFE BAR PARK AND RIDE SITE
P + 🚌
7 days a week

A59 HARROGATE SKIPTON

GRIMSTON BAR PARK AND RIDE SITE
P + 🚌
7 days a week

A166 DRIFFIELD BRIDLINGTON

B1242 WETHERBY

8

A1079 BEVERLEY HULL

ASKHAM BAR PARK AND RIDE SITE
P + 🚌
7 days a week

3

A64 TADCASTER LEEDS M62, M1, A1

McARTHURGLEN PARK AND RIDE SITE
P + 🚌
7 days a week

7

A19 SELBY DONCASTER

H   *Attempts to solve the problem in London (top) and York (below)*

c

d

e

Issue 4: the central business district (CBD)

During the 1960s to the early 1980s, the CBD struggled to attract businesses. Out-of-town shopping areas and regional shopping centres became more favourable destinations as they offered pleasant shopping opportunities with ample parking. In contrast, city centres appeared busy and crowded. The air quality was poor, with the smell of diesel and lead concentrations in certain areas a cause for concern.

However, there have been significant changes in CBDs and their image is now, once more, a positive one. They have become vibrant and pleasant places as a result of a number of initiatives (photo **J**).

Activities

5   Study diagram **H**.

a   Produce a poster to show the good and bad points of the options available to solve the environmental impact of traffic.

6   Study photo **J** on page 204.

a   Use evidence from the photo to suggest how the CBD has been revitalised (improved).

b   Can you suggest any further improvements that would make the CBD an attractive area to visit?

I *Revitalising the image of Leeds CBD*

J *The CBD in Leeds*

Issue 5: multicultural mix

Despite the apparent racial mix in many cities, a significant number of immigrants choose to live with people from similar areas and away from others with different ethnicity and culture. This is called **segregation**.

Here are some of the reasons why people choose to cluster in the same area as their fellow immigrants:

- Support from others

People feel safe and secure when they can associate with other people from the same background. There is a sense of belonging and protection from racial abuse.

- A familiar culture

In a strange country, there is comfort from being with people who have similar ideas and beliefs and speak the same language.

- Specialist facilities

In many areas these are provided so that, for example, Sikhs can worship in a *gurdwara* and Moslems in a mosque. Familiar foodstuffs will be available in shops.

- Safety in numbers

People have a stronger voice if they are heard as a group, rather than individually.

- Employment factors

Immigrant groups tend to do low-paid jobs or have a high rate of unemployment. They have limited money and so can only afford cheaper housing in certain parts of the city, usually inner city areas.

There is an attempt to integrate different ethnic groups and reduce segregation. In Leeds, this has involved the following measures:

- increasing children's achievement by improving educational provision and opportunities in deprived areas; and seeking to improve literacy in areas where English can be a second language
- increasing employment through initiatives to ensure basic skills and access to information and training
- increasing community involvement by ensuring that the needs of minority groups are understood and met
- providing facilities that encourage meetings of all sections of a community rather than separate ethnic groups.

∞ links

Find out more about Leeds CBD and its plans for the city and Chapeltown at **www.leeds.gov.uk**.

Key terms

Segregation: occurs where people of a particular ethnic group choose to live with others from the same ethnic group, separate from other groups.

9.4   What are the issues for people living in squatter settlements in poorer parts of the world?

The speed of urbanisation in many poorer areas of the world results in **squatter settlements** being built and the evolution of an **informal sector** of the economy. The pace of rural–urban migration is too fast to allow the time needed to build proper houses. New arrivals to the city find unoccupied areas of land and building materials and begin to build their own makeshift shelters. As there are few official jobs available, people create their own employment by selling items, making and repairing things and becoming couriers, cleaners and gardeners.

In this section you will learn

why squatter settlements have developed, their characteristics and effects on people's lives

different strategies to try to improve squatter settlements and evaluate them

how to apply general concepts relating to squatter settlements to a case study.

a Roçinha, the largest favela in South America

Key terms

Squatter settlements: areas of cities (usually on the outskirts) that are built by people from any materials they can find on land that does not belong to them. They have different names in different parts of the world (e.g. *favela* in Brazil) and are often known as shanty towns.

Informal sector: that part of the economy where jobs are created by people to try to get an income (e.g. taking in washing, mending bicycles) and which are not recognised in official figures.

b Close-up of Roçinha

c Mumbai

A   *Typical shanty towns*

Living in squatter settlements

No preparation for the building of these areas is done. The houses are not provided with basic infrastructure such as sanitation, piped water, electricity and road access. The photos in **A** (page 205) include views of Roçinha, a *favela* in Rio de Janeiro, which has a population of over 100,000. Close-up views give a clearer impression of conditions in the *favela*. The houses are made of any materials available nearby – corrugated iron, pieces of board – haphazardly assembled to provide a basic shelter. There is a simple layout that may have a living area separate from a sleeping area.

Parents and large families inhabit a small shack in an area that is very overcrowded. There are no toilets. Water must be collected from a nearby source – often at a cost – and carried back. Rubbish is not collected and the area quickly degenerates into a place of filth and disease. The inhabitants tend to have poorly paid jobs where the income is unreliable.

The quality of life for many people is poor. Houses are densely packed together with few open spaces and green areas or trees. Poor environmental conditions lead to disease and, with many people living in poverty, crime is a major issue.

Strategies to improve living conditions

Improvement by residents involves the residents seeking to 'do up' their original shelters (photo **B**). This means replacing flimsy, temporary materials with more permanent brick and concrete, catching rainwater in a tank on the roof, and obtaining an electricity supply (often illegally by tapping into a nearby source). Such improvements are slow and not all the problems can be solved.

Self-help occurs where local authorities support the residents of the squatter settlements in improving their homes. This involves the improvements outlined above, but it is more organised. There is cooperation between residents to work together and remove rubbish. There is also cooperation from the local authority, which offers grants, cheap loans and possibly materials to encourage improvements to take place. Standpipes are likely to be provided for access to water supply and sanitation. Collectively, the residents, with help from the local authority, may begin to build health centres and schools. Legal ownership of the land is granted to encourage improvements to take place, marking an acceptance of the housing.

B *DIY improvements in Roçinha*

Key terms

Self-help: sometimes known as assisted self-help (ASH), this is where local authorities help the squatter settlement residents to improve their homes by offering finance in the form of loans or grants and often installing water, sanitation, etc.

Site and service: occur where land is divided into individual plots and water, sanitation, electricity and basic track layout are supplied before any building by residents begins.

Site and service schemes are a more formal way of helping squatter settlement residents. Land is identified for the scheme. The infrastructure is laid in advance of settlement, so that water, sanitation and electricity are properly supplied to individually marked plots. People then build their homes using whatever materials they can afford at the time. They can add to and improve the structure if finances allow later.

Local authority schemes can take a number of different forms. There may be large-scale improvements made to some squatter settlements or new towns may be constructed. In Cairo, new settlements such as 10th of Ramadan City were built to reduce pressure on the city (photo **C**). High-rise blocks of flats were built, together with shops, a primary school and a mosque. Industries were also planned to provide jobs for the new inhabitants.

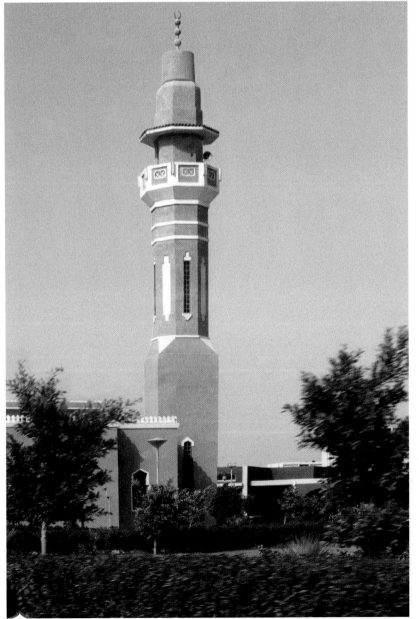

C *10th of Ramadan City, Cairo*

Kibera, a squatter settlement in Nairobi, Kenya

Map **D** shows the situation of Kibera in the capital city of Nairobi in Kenya. Some 60 per cent of Nairobi's inhabitants live in slums, over half of them in Kibera. Specific facts about Kibera are uncertain. It is believed that between 800,000 and 1 million people live in the shanty town, in an area of 255 ha. This gives extremely high densities, with people only having 1 m² of floor space each. Over 100,000 children are believed to be orphans as a result of the high incidence of HIV/Aids. Photos **E** and **F** show the squatter settlement. The homes are made of mud, plastered-over boards, wood or corrugated iron sheeting. The paths between the houses are irregular, narrow and often have a ditch running down the middle that has sewage in it. Rubbish litters the area as it is not collected. The area smells of the charcoal used to provide fuel and of human waste. A standpipe may supply water for up to 40 families; private operators run hosepipes into the area and charge double the going rate for water. Crime is rife and vigilante groups offer security – at a price. Police are reluctant to enter. However, homes are kept clean and the residents welcome visitors.

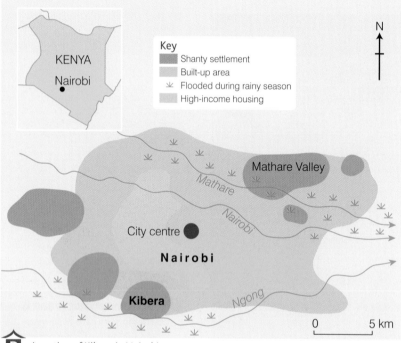

D *Location of Kibera in Nairobi*

E *General view of Kibera*

Finding solutions

There are signs that things are improving.

- Practical Action, a British charity, has been responsible for developing low-cost roofing tiles. Made from sand and clay, and using natural fibres and lime, building blocks can be made as a cheaper alternative to concrete. These allow self-help schemes to progress.

- The United Nation's Human Settlement Programme (UN-Habitat) has provided affordable electricity to some parts at 300 Kenyan shillings (about £2.25) per shack.

- There are two mains water pipes – one provided by the council and the other by the World Bank – at a cost of 3 Kenyan shillings (about 2 pence) for 20 litres. Improving sanitation is more difficult and progress is slow.

- Medical facilities are provided by charities.

- Gap-year students are encouraged to go to Kibera to oversee the spending and to help coordinate efforts.

- In a 15-year project that began in 2003, there are plans to re-house thousands of residents of Kibera. This is a joint venture between the Kenyan government and UN-Habitat. In its first year, 770 families were rehoused in new blocks of flats with running water, toilets, showers and electricity.

F *Close-up view of Kibera*

Activities

3 Study map **D** and photos **E** and **F**. Produce a fact file on Kibera by completing the following tasks:

a Draw a labelled sketch map to show the location of Kibera in Nairobi.

b Write a summary of the key points about the Kibera squatter settlement.

c Draw a labelled sketch from one of the photos to show the characteristics of the squatter settlement and the living conditions there.

d Summarise the attempts that have been made to improve Kibera.

e In your opinion, is Kibera a slum of hope (where things are getting better) or a slum of despair (where there is no improvement and no hope for the future)? Justify your views.

⊘⊘ links

Investigate Kibera at **www.bbc.co.uk** and **www.mojamoja.org**

9.5   What are the problems of rapid urbanisation in poorer parts of the world?

■ Examples of problems

Environmental disasters

During the early hours of 3 December 1984, the world's worst industrial accident unfolded in the Indian city of Bhopal. Poisonous gas escaped from a chemical plant and killed at least 3,000 people (photo **A**). Around 50,000 suffered permanent disabilities and more died later. This is one example of how rapid urbanisation and **industrialisation** can lead to environmental problems in poorer parts of the world. Expanding cities lead to problems of air and water pollution and **disposal of waste**, including toxic waste from plants like the one at Bhopal. Non-existent or poor regulations and a lack of planning for an environmental emergency make problems worse.

Electronic waste

Creation of electronic waste is another major problem in a rapidly industrialising country like India. The country imports more than 4.5 million new computers a year, plus many second-hand ones with shorter lifespans. Computer waste is known as electronic waste or e-waste. In the cities, India's poor scrape a living by breaking down PCs and monitors (photo **B**). They boil, crush or burn parts in order to extract valuable materials like gold or platinum. But what they do not realise is that the toxic chemicals inside like cadmium and lead can pose serious health risks. India's hospitals are starting to see patients with ten times the expected level of lead in their blood. Dumping and unsupervised recycling of e-waste is literally leading to a brain drain.

Water polution

The Ganges River contains untreated sewage, cremated remains, chemicals and disease-causing microbes. Cows wade in the river. People wash their laundry in it and drink from it (see Photo **D**).

Waste and polution

In Shanghai, the construction boom is creating 30,000 tonnes of waste per day. Industry there is responsible for 70 per cent of the country's carbon dioxide emissions. Some 73 per cent of electricity is produced by coal-fired power stations. These factors are responsible for 400,000 deaths annually.

Key terms

Industrialisation: a process, usually associated with the development of an economy, where an increasing proportion of people work in industry.

Disposal of waste: safely getting rid of unwanted items such as solid waste.

A   Deaths caused by the industrial accident in Bhopal

B *Breaking down PCs and monitors in India*

Reducing the problems

In order to seek to reduce the environmental problems resulting from rapid urbanisation and industrialisation, there need to be guidelines to indicate what is allowed and what is not. Limits must be monitored and enforced to ensure that industries, for example, do not exceed the stated limits.

Waste disposal

Waste provides a resource and a means of making a living for many shanty dwellers in poor countries.

- In São Paulo, Brazil, two huge incinerators burn 7,500 tonnes of waste a day, resulting in a problem caused by a management strategy. There were only two landfill sites in 1990. Children and adults alike scavenge and extract materials and then reuse or resell them. For example, car tyres may be made into sandals and food waste is fed to animals or used as a fertiliser on vegetable plots.

- In Shanghai, China, an effective solid waste disposal unit has been installed in most houses and the waste is used as a fertiliser in surrounding rural areas.

- Toxic waste and its safe disposal is a key issue in areas where the manufacturing industry is increasing. In the aftermath of the Bhopal accident in 1984, the site was covered in toxic waste. This could not be disposed of safely in India. This meant that the waste was packed up and sent to the USA.

- Large companies need to take responsibility for safely disposing of electrical goods in areas such as Bangalore in India, where there are many call centres. The large amount of e-waste in Bangalore is covered by one enforcement order, which is inadequate. There are not enough people employed to make sure the law is obeyed.

- Recycling plants are becoming more common in cities throughout the world as an attempt to reduce the need to dispose of waste in landfill sites (photo **C**).

Air pollution

Air pollution is an issue in many industrial cities. There is a need to encourage the use of new technologies that can reduce emissions of sulphur dioxide and nitrogen oxide. Switching to cleaner, alternative sources of energy is an option. However, given the plentiful supplies of coal in countries such as China (where 80 per cent of electricity is from this source) and India, this may need the introduction of a carbon tax to induce a change. In Shanghai, China, industries use low sulphur coal to try to reduce pollution. Limits need to be set and enforced on emissions, and companies, including **transnational corporations (TNCs)**, must be monitored to ensure that emissions of carbon dioxide and sulphur dioxide are reduced. Transport also needs to be considered and strategies such as allowing odd-numbered cars into Mexico City on one day and even-numbered on another day can reduce traffic in towns. Other strategies include improving public transport, limiting the number of cars and introducing congestion charging to discourage car owners from entering city centres.

Water pollution

As with air pollution, limits relating to **water pollution** need to be identified and enforced if quality is to be improved. In 1986, the Ganga Action Plan sought to introduce water treatment works on the River Ganges in India, which it did successfully. However, the increasing population was not taken into account and water quality has since deteriorated. Such attempts have been replicated in other countries. In Shanghai, the Huangpu and Suzhou rivers have been the target for improving water quality. A World Bank loan of $200 million was granted to this cause in 2002.

⚭ links

For information on Union Carbide, the Bhopal disaster and toxic e-waste, go to **www.bbc.co.uk**.

For reducing air pollution in Asia and the Pacific, visit **www.unep.org**.

Look into the dumping of toxic waste in poor countries such as Ivory Coast at **www.npr.org** and research more about e-waste at **www.bbc.co.uk**.

C   *A recycling centre in Beijing, China*

D   *The River Ganges, India*

Activities

1
  a   Describe the sources of pollution in the rivers Ganges and Huangpu.

  b   Explain why they present a hazard to health.

  c   Produce a fact file to summarise the events at Bhopal on 3 December 1984.

  d   What is your view of the events of that night? Give reasons for your opinion.

  e   Why do many poorer countries use coal as a source of energy?

  f   Describe how some people living in cities in India make a living from discarded computers.

  g   Explain the dangers of making a living in this way.

2   Study the text on the strategies to reduce the environmental effects of rapid urbanisation.

Produce a diagram to summarise the strategies adopted to manage the environmental problems in poorer parts of the world. Use case studies and illustrations as part of your work.

9.6 How can urban living be sustainable?

A **sustainable city** has certain characteristics that relate to its long-term future. It enjoys a clean environment, has a sound economic base with plenty of jobs and has a strong sense of community with local people involved in decision making. Sustainable cities make use of public transport, manage waste efficiently and create green spaces and gardens. Sustainable cities are cities of the future! Photos **A** and **B** show two contrasting urban scenes in Los Angeles and Belfast.

> ### In this section you will learn
>
> attempts made to ensure that city life is environmentally and socially sustainable
>
> the characteristics of a sustainable city.

A Los Angeles: non-sustainable urban living?

> ### Key terms
>
> **Sustainable city:** an urban area where residents have a way of life that will last a long time. The environment is not damaged and the economic and social fabric are able to stand the test of time.

B Belfast: sustainable urban living?

> ### Activity
>
> **1** Study photos **A** and **B**.
>
> a Describe the characteristics of the urban scenes from the photos.
>
> b In which of the photos do you think life is sustainable? Explain reasons for your choice.

◼ Seeking environmental sustainability

Conserving the historic environment

The Liverpool Maritime Mercantile City provides an example of conserving an area of previous industrial use and historic commercial and cultural areas. The Liverpool waterfront and areas associated with its development were designated a World Heritage Site in 2004. The award recognised the importance of the area as a port and associated buildings of global significance during the heyday of the British Empire in the 18th and 19th centuries. Many of the buildings are architecturally as they were then, although their function has changed. The photos in **C** show some of the many faces of the sites that gained recognition, conserving an environment so rich in history and heritage.

a Liver Building

b Cunard Building

c Albert Dock Warehouse

d St George's Hall

C *Liverpool maritime mercantile city*

Activity

2   Study the photos in **C**. Produce a leaflet for Liverpool City Council or another city near where you live. Produce an illustrated report to show how the city has used and conserved its industrial heritage in a sustainable way. Use the internet to help you with your research.

Conserving the natural environment

E   *Advantages of building on a brownfield site*

- Provides an economic use of derelict land
- Provides jobs
- Foundations often in place for new construction
- Improves environment
- No need to develop greenfield sites
- Prevents **urban sprawl**

D   *Green belts in England*

The natural environment can be conserved by restricting development on the edge of a town or city. **Green belts** exist around many large towns in England (map **D**). They were established to protect the surrounding countryside from development. This often provides recreational open space for urban residents. Limiting available sites on the edge of the city means that alternative locations for development must be offered if growth is to continue. This means that building on brownfield sites is encouraged. There are several advantages of building on brownfield sites (diagram **E**).

Reducing and safely disposing of waste

By 2008, the UK was producing 400 million tonnes of waste each year – enough to fill the Royal Albert Hall in London *every hour*. Much of this was from mining and quarrying, but 30 million tonnes was from households, many of them in cities. There is a need to reduce the amount of waste produced. A great deal of domestic waste can be composted (20 per cent of household waste is garden waste and 17 per cent kitchen waste) or recycled (18 per cent is paper/card). In 2011, around 40 per cent of UK household waste was recycled. That is a big improvement from 2001, when only 11 per cent was recycled. But the UK still sends more waste to landfill than most European countries.

Key terms

Green belt: land on the edge of the built-up area, where restrictions are placed on building to prevent the expansion of towns and cities and to protect the natural environment.

Urban sprawl: the spreading of urban areas into the surrounding rural/rural–urban fringe areas.

Sustainability: development that looks after future resources and considers the needs of future generations.

Did you know ??????

In the UK we produce 275 kg of waste per person every year.

It is important to reduce waste so that fewer plastic bags are used. Consumer pressure could reduce packaging in general – do apples need to come in plastic bags? Do red peppers need individual packaging? Packaging can be made so that it can be returned and reused, such as milk bottles and 'bag for life' carrier bags.

At present, over 80 per cent of household waste is disposed of in landfill sites (photo **F**). However, in the future, there will be a shortage of suitable sites. Incineration (burning) is another option, accounting for 8 per cent of waste disposal. Although incineration can produce energy (photo **G**), it is a controversial strategy. For example, a new facility planned for Kings Lynn is unpopular with local people due to fears about pollution and increased traffic.

Providing adequate open spaces

The presence of official green belts or areas where local authorities choose to restrict buildings around cities offers open space for recreation purposes. In addition, many areas within cities have designated areas of open space in the form of parks, playing fields and individual gardens. Map **H** shows the distribution of open space in Greater London and some of the types of open space available.

F *A landfill site in Liverpool*

G *Incineration: Sheffield energy recovery facility*

Lea Valley Park

N

River Thames

Key
■ Park
■ Green belt

Regent's Park

Hyde Park

Richmond Park

0   10 km

H *Open space in London*

Activities

3 Study map **D** and diagram **E**. Imagine you are a town planner on a visit to a local school where you have to explain how green belt policy and the use of brownfield sites can help in conserving the natural environment. Design a presentation using Powerpoint to outline the advantages of green belts and using brownfield sites for development.

4 Work in pairs. Produce a radio advert for your local council encouraging residents to 'reduce, reuse and recycle'. Make the advert clear and informative, and try to introduce a catchy slogan to promote a more responsible attitude to waste.

5 Study photos **F** and **G**. Summarise the advantages and disadvantages of:

- landfill
- incineration

as a means of waste disposal.

6 a   What materials are collected by the council from your home?

   b   What other items do you recycle at home?

   c   How do you reuse items at home?

   d   Describe how you try to reduce waste at home.

   e   What efforts are made at school to reduce, reuse and recycle?

   f   How effective do you think efforts are at home and at school? In what ways could they be improved?

7 Study map **H**.

   a   Describe the distribution of the different types of open space in Greater London.

   b   London was designed to have many central parks. How do you think these parks are used by people?

   c   Do you think cities should have open spaces such as parks? Justify your answer.

Involving local people

If people have ownership of ideas and feel involved and in control of their own destiny, they are much more likely to respond positively and care for the building and environment in which they live. Consulting people at planning stages – before decisions are made – is essential. Planners increasingly survey opinions before putting forward plans and consult after they have been produced. Residents form associations to give them a stronger collective voice (photo **I**).

Providing an efficient public transport system

The volume of cars as a means of private transport is a problem and a barrier to a city being sustainable. London has sought to make parts of the city unattractive to drivers by congestion charging. However, an alternative form of transport needs to be available in the form of fast and efficient public transport. This means a focus on the Underground and improvements in buses and rail links. The 2012 Olympics has added impetus to improvements. The Tube is undergoing extensive upgrading, not just to the lines, but also to the trains and stations. London overground links will be extended to form a complete circuit around London – the railway equivalent to the M25. Buses are being improved and will be more frequent to reduce overcrowding.

All buses now have CCTV to increase feelings of security and bus shelters have been added at more bus stops. The extension of bus lanes has led to quicker journeys and cash fares have been frozen. Schemes such as the Oyster card, which allows for the advanced purchase of up to £90 worth of journeys on a swipe card, offer journeys at reduced rates.

I *Resident's meeting*

Did you know ??????

Between three and a half and four million journeys are made on the Underground (Tube) in London every weekday. The Tube is the oldest of its kind in the world – some parts dating back to the 1860s.

London 2012: the sustainable Olympics?

The London Olympics 2012 has been designed to create a sustainable legacy for local communities. Not only will this result in an improvement to the physical environment but it will seek to ensure the long-term sustainability of the economy, retailing and transport.

During the Olympics:

- The vast Olympic Park has been built in a formerly largely derelict and neglected industrial area in Stratford, East London. The physical environment has been hugely improved with the creation of parks and landscaped areas.

- Some 70% of the events will take place on the one site and the vast majority of athletes and coaches will be accommodated in the Olympic Village, reducing the need for transport to and from the Games. This will reduce traffic congestion and pollution.

- No car parking will be provided, forcing spectators to use the massively improved public transport systems

- 97% of materials from demolished buildings have been re-used in the construction of the Olympic Park. Timber has been sourced from sustainable forests.

- Several buildings, such as the Velodrome, have been designed to minimise energy use by making use of natural light and ventilation.

- Rainwater will be collected and used to flush toilets and irrigate the gardens and lawns

- Green spaces have been created, especially along the River Lea, which has been cleared of thousands of tonnes of rubbish. Waterside footpaths have been laid and tracks created for cyclists. Some 4,000 new trees have been planted and bird and bat boxes have been installed.

After the Olympics:

- The Olympic Park Legacy Committee intends the sports stadiums to be used in the future. The Olympic Stadium itself will host the 2017 World Athletics Championships. New bids for the tenancy of the stadium were being taken in 2012 after a deal for the stadium to become the home of West Ham United collapsed in October 2011. The Aquatic Centre is to become a swimming facility for local residents.

- The high-tech International Broadcast Centre may be used in the future by media and IT companies and could create up to 3,000 jobs.

- Some of the housing used to accommodate athletes in the Olympic Village will become affordable housing for local people.

- Developments such as the massive Westfield Shopping Centre will be a permanent legacy of the Olympics, providing local jobs and retail opportunities.

Only the future will tell quite how sustainable the London Olympics 2012 will turn out to be. You will have to judge for yourself!

K *The 2012 Olympic site.*

Activities

8   Use the internet to conduct your own research into sustainability at the London Olympics 2012. Produce a Powerpoint presentation or an information poster identifying aspects of sustainability both during and after the Olympics. To what extent do you think the Olympics will leave a sustainable legacy?

⊂⊃links

For more information about the 2012 Olympics, visit
www.london2012.com

Sustainable urban living in Curitiba

Curitiba is the capital city of the Brazilian state of Parana. It is the seventh largest city with a population of 1.8million. The city is seen as a role model for planning and sustainability in cities worldwide. In 1968, the Curitiba Master Plan was adopted to controlurban sprawl, reduce traffic in the city centre, develop public transport and preserve the historic sector. The emphasis has been on ensuring an appropriate quality of life for the residents of Curitiba with concern for the environment and the need to leave a suitable area for future generations living in the city.

There is now a network of 28 riverside parks creating almost 100 miles of city trails. Lakes have been created within these parks that fill and flood the surrounding parkland in periods of heavy rain reducing the risk of flooding in the city itself.

The 'green exchange' programme involves low-income families in shanty towns exchanging rubbish for bus tickets and food. 70 per cent of the city's rubbish recycled by its residents.

The Bus Rapid Transport (BRT) System

Curitiba was the first Brazilian city to have dedicated bus lanes. The BRT system has four elements:

- direct line buses operate from key pick-up points
- speedy buses operate on the five main routes into the city and have linked stops
- inter-district buses join up districts without crossing the city centre
- feeder mini-buses pick people up from residential areas.

Housing in Curitiba

In Curitiba, COHAB, the city's public housing programme, believes that residents should have 'homes – not just shelters'. They have introduced a housing policy that will provide 50,000 homes for the urban poor.

L *The innovative bus system in Curitiba*

Activities

9 Study the information in this case study and use the internet to find out more about Curitiba.

a Describe how Curitiba's bus system works and assess how successful it is.

b Explain why it was a good idea to preserve part of the old area of Curitiba.

c In Curitiba, 'planners come up with creative and inexpensive ways to go about solving universal problems for cities'. Provide evidence to support this statement.

10 Working in pairs, summarise the characteristics of a sustainable city.

10 Changing rural environments

10.1 What pressures are being placed on the rural–urban fringe?

As you travel out of a town or city, urban land uses, such as housing and industry, become replaced with signs of the countryside, such as fields and woodlands. This broad zone of transition is called the **rural–urban fringe**.

Pressures on the rural–urban fringe

Demands for land in the rural–urban fringe

The rural–urban fringe is under intense pressure due to the growth of urban areas (urban sprawl) and the increasing mobility of the population because of car ownership. The main demands on the land are for retail developments, leisure (golf courses, horse-riding, etc.), residential (growth of villages) and transport (ring roads, airports, etc.).

Retail outlets

The areas of land on the outskirts of cities are prime land for the development of out-of-town **retail parks**. A retail park is a huge area of shops and leisure facilities such as cinemas and restaurants. The shops are often under cover and are served by large car parks. Most of the shops are well-known stores such as Next, Marks & Spencer, and WHSmith, but there may be parades of smaller shops and markets.

Commuting/commuter villages

Commuting is increasingly common. More people are prepared to spend time, money and energy travelling a greater distance to work to be able to live in the countryside. Rural areas not only depend on the urban zone for jobs, but also for services and administration. Rural-based businesses thrive because of the larger urban market close by. Garden centres and market gardens are examples.

Leisure

The rural–urban fringe serves the city as a leisure area. Box Hill, in the Surrey North Downs, lies in the commuter belt of London. Small towns like Leatherhead and Dorking have expanded and villages like Bookham house commuters. Local people use Box Hill for walks and cycling, and people come for days out from London, placing great pressure on a small green area (diagram **A**).

In this section you will learn

what is meant by the rural–urban fringe and know why people are attracted to live there

the impacts of out-of-town retail outlets and leisure provision

how transport networks have expanded in the rural–urban fringe

what is meant by commuting and its impacts on landscape and settlement

the characteristics of a suburbanised village, how they grow, their characteristics and the type of people who live there.

Key terms

Commuting: people travelling between home and work and back again every day.

Rural–urban fringe: an area around a town or city where there is a mix of urban and rural land uses.

A Pressures on the rural–urban fringe around London

Bluewater Park, Kent

Bluewater Park is the largest and most recent of the five out-of-town **regional shopping centres** built in the UK. It is located in Kent just beyond the M25 close to its major junction with the A2 (map **B**). It is a **high-access location** within London's rural–urban fringe. Some 12 million people live within two hours' drive of Bluewater, and just 4 km from the recently opened Ebbsfleet station on the Channel Tunnel rail link, it attracts customers from France.

Bluewater was built in a disused chalk quarry. Many would consider this development an improvement on what was there before. Close by, just to the north of the River Thames, is Lakeside, a similar shopping development. Surrounding it is a huge area of retail parks, which include large stores like IKEA. The buildings themselves and the necessary infrastructure place immense pressure on the rural–urban fringe. This part of Kent is much more urbanised and congested than it used to be. Massive engineering works took place in 2008 to improve the link from the M25 to Bluewater.

Since 1999 when Bluewater opened, three other large centres have been categorised as being on a regional scale: the Trafford Centre in Manchester, Braehead in Glasgow and the Westfield Centre in west London. However, these are all within an existing urban area. Due to recent planning restrictions, it is unlikely that any more edge-of-town developments like Bluewater will be built in the rural–urban fringe.

Case study

C Bluewater Park regional shopping centre

Key
- === M25 motorway
- == Primary route
- = Main A road
- ⊢⊢⊢ Railway line

B *The location of Bluewater Park*

Suburbanised villages

Villages that have grown in recent decades and have housing estates with more recent residents than long-term ones are called **suburbanised villages**. They are most likely to be found in the rural–urban fringe as the reason they grow is because of access to both the city and the countryside. They are part of the process of **counter-urbanisation**, i.e. moving out of the city. These villages develop in stages (diagram **D**):

Key terms

Suburbanised village: a village with easy access to a large urban area much in demand. Housing estates attached to the village edges aim to fulfil this demand.

Counter-urbanisation: the process of people leaving towns and cities to live in more rural areas such as the rural–urban fringe.

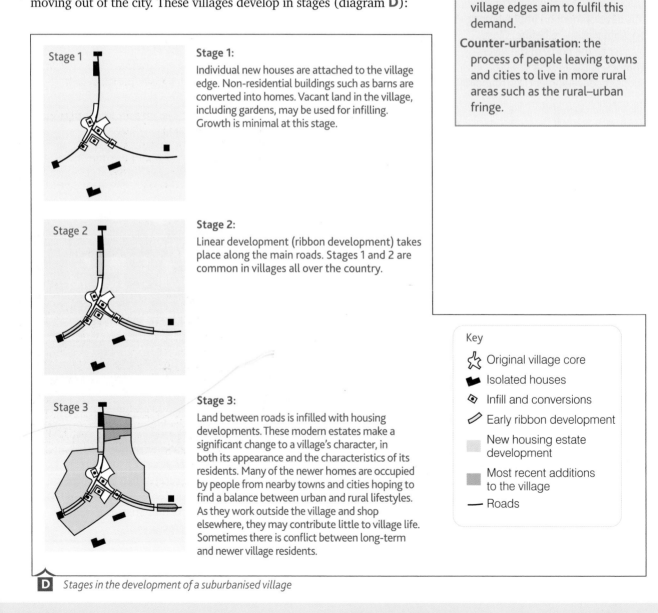

Stage 1:
Individual new houses are attached to the village edge. Non-residential buildings such as barns are converted into homes. Vacant land in the village, including gardens, may be used for infilling. Growth is minimal at this stage.

Stage 2:
Linear development (ribbon development) takes place along the main roads. Stages 1 and 2 are common in villages all over the country.

Stage 3:
Land between roads is infilled with housing developments. These modern estates make a significant change to a village's character, in both its appearance and the characteristics of its residents. Many of the newer homes are occupied by people from nearby towns and cities hoping to find a balance between urban and rural lifestyles. As they work outside the village and shop elsewhere, they may contribute little to village life. Sometimes there is conflict between long-term and newer village residents.

Key
- Original village core
- Isolated houses
- Infill and conversions
- Early ribbon development
- New housing estate development
- Most recent additions to the village
- Roads

D Stages in the development of a suburbanised village

Chalgrove, Oxfordshire

Chalgrove lies on the edge of the rural–urban fringe between Oxford and London (map **E**) . Its residents can commute to work in either city. Although some Oxfordshire villages are growing, others are declining. Location and planning regulations are key factors. Reasons for the growth of Chalgrove include the following:

■ The village is close to the M40 motorway, allowing access to London.

■ It has A-road access to Oxford (for much of the route).

■ Mainline railway stations are accessible in nearby Thame and Wallingford.

■ These towns provide a range of local services, including health and education.

■ New job opportunities are growing in the Didcot–Thame development axis.

■ Chalgrove is outside both the green belt and the Area of Outstanding Natural Beauty, so is not limited by their planning restrictions.

■ Since 1993 the South Oxfordshire Development Plan has actively encouraged the further development of larger villages like Chalgrove.

Chalgrove's typical 'suburban' residents:

■ are highly mobile (90 per cent of households have cars)

■ work in the professions or in management (40 per cent)

■ have lived in the village for less than 10 years.

Did you know ??????

The rural–urban fringe should serve the needs of both city and countryside. It should include parks and continuous green corridors with limited development. Public transport should be more efficient and attractive to allow access and daily travel. The rural–urban fringe should serve the city for recreation and sustainable waste management. More woodland could be planted.

∞ links

Find out more about Chalgrove at **www.chalgrove-parish.org.uk**.

Average house prices in Chalgrove

Beds	2008	2011	
All	£415,000	£404,540	–2.5% ⬇
2	£259,000	£234,700	–9.4% ⬇
3	£348,000	£294,400	–15.4% ⬇
4	£575,000	£449,000	–21.9% ⬇

Key

═══ M40 motorway

═══ Main roads

▬ Didcot–Thame development axis

☐ Green belt

☐ Chilterns, Area of Outstanding Natural Beauty (AONB)

☐ City

■ Small to medium-sized towns

● Village

0 — 10 km

E   *Factors affecting the development of Chalgrove*

F   *Chalgrove*

Transport developments

Rail and road networks are of good quality in the rural–urban fringe, so transport is relatively quick and efficient. As people move into the rural–urban fringe, infrastructure must increase to serve their needs. More people leads to more cars and therefore an expanded road network. The M25 motorway around London was primarily built to help movement around the city and within the rural–urban fringe. It is said, however, that traffic volume expands to fill any new roads developed.

G   *M25 was built on green belt land*

> **Did you know** ??????
>
> Car pooling is becoming more common, sharing with someone going in the same direction. This cuts costs, is sociable and environmentally friendly. Councils and companies are increasingly running sharing schemes.

Activities

3   Write a short definition of the term 'suburbanised village'.

4   Study diagram **D** and map **E** on pages 222-223.

   a   With the aid of simple sketches, describe the characteristics of a village at each of the three stages of suburbanisation.

   b   What characteristics does Chalgrove have that make it a suburbanised village? Refer to the three stages of suburbanisation in your answer.

   c   Would you prefer to live in a suburbanised village like Chalgrove or a village that has not grown in this way? Give your reasons.

5   Study table **F**.

   a   Using the data in the table, describe the house price changes in Chalgrove between 2008 and 2011.

   b   Since 2008 the UK was affected by an economic recession which caused house prices to fall. What effect do you think this had on Chalgrove?

10.2 / What social and economic changes have happened in remote rural areas?

Locations of remote rural areas in the UK

There is a close link between uplands, hill farming zones and remote rural areas (map **A**). Hill sheep farming uses land that is too poor for most other agricultural activities. It is **marginal land** with severe physical limitations. Snowdonia's climate is harsh, with low temperatures, and high rain and snowfall. Glacial troughs have steep rock sides with bare rock or thin, stony soil. The landscape is both dramatic and physically attractive, but these remote areas can make people's lives extremely difficult.

Remote farming areas, usually used for hill farming

North-west Highlands

Grampian Mountains

Southern Uplands

Lake District

Pennines

SNOWDONIA

Cambrian Mountains

Brecon Beacons

Exmoor

Dartmoor

N

0   200 km

A Remote rural farming areas in the UK

In this section you will learn

the reasons for rural depopulation and the impacts it brings

how village characteristics change during decline

the growth of second homes and the impact this has on village decline.

Key terms

Marginal land: land that is only just good enough to be worth farming. It may be dry, wet, cool, stony or steep.

Rural depopulation: people leaving a rural area to live elsewhere, usually in a town or city.

Rural depopulation in Snowdonia

Rural depopulation is the net emigration of people from a rural area. The 2001 Census showed a decline of 3 per cent in the number of residents in Snowdonia compared with 1991. During the 1980s there had been a 6.2 per cent growth, but the 1990s saw zero growth.

As one of the highest and steepest regions in the UK, Snowdonia has never been densely populated, but today it continues to lose population. Those leaving are local people whose families have lived there for generations.

People have left Snowdonia for a number of reasons:

1 Decline in hill farming

The number of hill sheep farmers is decreasing nationally, mainly due to economic pressures. In the 1990s, the lamb prices were below the cost of production and, with rising fuel costs, many farmers went out of business. Since 1996 farm incomes have fallen by 60 per cent.

Did you know ??????

The 1990s saw the worst agricultural recession for almost 100 years in the UK. The average family farm suffered a 90 per cent drop in income over five years.

2 Competition from abroad

Competition from abroad was also a problem. New Zealand can produce cheaper lamb and ship it round the world to undercut Welsh lamb in British supermarkets. To increase income, hill farmers have tried to diversify by working in other rural industries such as tourism and forestry. This has worked well in the Lake District because it is an important tourist and leisure destination. However, Snowdonia is an even more remote rural area and so has fewer tourists, providing less opportunity for **diversification**. Some farms run B&B businesses, but this is not a secure income.

3 Job losses

Agriculture is not the only sector experiencing job losses. Quarrying has reduced its labour force and the closure of Trawsfynydd Nuclear Power Station in 1993 caused a disastrous 500 job losses. For any chance of re-employment, people were forced to move to the towns.

4 Better job opportunities elsewhere

Emigration of young adults for higher education, training and employment has long been a trend in remote rural areas like Snowdonia. Once educated, young people seek well paid jobs elsewhere in the UK. The National Park employs some graduates of suitable subjects, as do health and education services, but most must look to urban areas for suitable careers.

5 Housing shortage

Snowdonia National Park Authority does not allow planning permission for building new homes within the park in order to preserve the traditional landscape. Many houses are bought as second homes by people living outside the area. This reduces the housing stock and inflates prices putting houses out of reach for local people.

6 Loss of services

The trend towards loss of services in remote rural areas has accelerated in recent years. With decreasing local populations, services such as shops, post offices, schools and health centres have been forced to close leaving communities to suffer. Unless new sources of employment and income can be put in place, as well as new housing being developed, many villages have little chance of being regenerated.

7 Growth in ownership of second homes

A **second home** is a local property bought by someone whose main home is outside the region. Used for holidays and weekends, the houses' occupants are rarely part of the community, so they are not well accepted. They tend not to use local services, often bringing all they need with them. The average figure across Wales for houses that are second homes is 1.2 per cent. Within Snowdonia National Park it is a huge 13.7 per cent (photo **B**).

B *Snowdonia: a remote rural area with limited economic opportunities*

News

Home | Contact | Sitemap | News | Forum | Shop

Home
Contact
Sitemap
News
Forum
Shop

Controls on second homes reviewed

Radical plans which would require second home buyers to apply for planning permission could be introduced in Wales to protect rural communities. If the proposals are approved the authority [Snowdonia] would become the first national park in the UK to stop outsiders from buying a holiday home in the region due to the sharp rise in property prices. 'It raises very interesting questions about civil rights and people's rights to live anywhere in the UK.'

C *From the BBC News website*   *Adapted from BBC News website **news.bbc.co.uk**, 5 September 2001*

Study tip

Think of the social and economic changes that have taken place in remote rural areas.

Rhyd, Snowdonia

Rhyd is a small Snowdonian village linked to other settlements by a minor road. Local jobs used to be in farming, lead mining and clay works, but all have been in decline. In 2003 the village contained only 15 homes with 37 residents. Five were holiday homes. Rhyd has no services and no jobs within the village, whereas in the past it had a primary school, chapel, post office and shop. The only service now is two buses passing daily.

D *Distances to essential services for Rhyd's population*

Service	Distance (km)
Primary school	3
Pub	3
Doctor's surgery/ pharmacy	7
General store	11
Clothes shop	11
Bank	11

Case study

E *The village of Rhyd*

Activities

1 Define these terms:

a marginal land

b rural depopulation

c diversification

d second homes.

2 Write a list of the characteristics of declining villages in remote rural areas.

3 Study extract **C**. Does Snowdonia National Park Authority have the right to prevent outsiders buying cottages as second homes? Discuss your ideas in a group and either:

a present your argument to the class, or

b hold a class debate.

Remember, your ideas and opinions must be justified.

4 a Write a paragraph to describe the difficulties faced by the population of Rhyd in Snowdonia.

b Living in Rhyd has its advantages too. Consider whether you would like to live there or not. Explain the reasons for your answer.

10.3 How can rural living be made sustainable?

Conserving resources and protecting the environment

To live sustainably involves conserving resources. If we waste what we have, and do not protect our environment (an important resource in itself), not only will our economy and standard of living suffer, but so will the generations that follow us.

There are several government schemes and initiatives aimed at protecting the rural environment.

1 Environmental Stewardship Scheme

This scheme is open to all farmers to improve their sustainability. Run by the Department for Environment, Food and Rural Affairs (Defra), it aims to:

- conserve wildlife
- increase biodiversity (photo **A**)
- improve landscape quality
- provide flood management
- promote public access to the countryside.

Annual payments from UK government to farmers vary from around £30 to £60 per hectare or more, depending on the level of involvement of the farmer.

2 Rural Development Programmes

The England Rural Development Programme (ERDP) was designed to support sustainable farming methods and greater environmental responsibility between 2000 and 2006. £1.6 billion of EU and UK government money was put into a wide variety of schemes.

A Meadow land developed under the Environmental Stewardship Scheme

The new Rural Development Programme for England (RDPE) replaced this in 2007 and will run until 2013 to distribute £3.9 billion to make rural life more sustainable. Most funding (£3.3 billion) will help farmers to manage their land more sustainably, and encourage biodiversity and good water quality while combating climate change. Money became available from January 2008.

The remaining £600 million will make agriculture and forestry more competitive and sustainable, as well as increasing rural job opportunities. Three types of project grants exist:

- the Forestry Commission can support sustainable woodland schemes
- Natural England operates the Energy Crops Scheme
- the Regional Development Agencies deliver new economic and social funding in rural areas.

Supporting the needs of the rural population

People need to be able to get to work and to access services as easily as possible. Some schemes have been put in place to help improve the quality of rural life.

1 Rural Transport Partnership

Rural transport is a difficult issue. Distances are longer and customers fewer. Making public transport networks pay can be almost impossible. The Devon Rural Transport Partnership began in 1999 to address these problems in the county. Financial grants support and advise local transport groups on the practicalities of setting up services.

B   *The Buses4U scheme*

In rural east Surrey there is support for students aged over 16 who need to travel to college courses. The moped loan scheme allows them travel where public transport routes do not serve. Safety helmets and clothing are provided. Student discounts on bus, coach and train fares are also supported by this funding.

Buses4U is a minibus scheme open to all members of rural communities in east Surrey. Journeys need to be booked at least an hour in advance and the minibus routes are then planned (photo **B**).

2 Village Shop Development Scheme

This grant scheme aims to help village and farm shops and other local services to provide for their communities more efficiently and discourage people from getting in their cars and driving to the nearest town. This is important because:

- people save time and energy
- carbon emissions are lowered
- those without cars retain local accessible services
- a sense of community is enhanced.

In supporting local services, the scheme helps rural communities to become more sustainable. Opportunities for employment are also created. In some villages pubs and village halls have been converted to enable a shop or post office to operate in addition to the main use of the building. Community groups are often involved in maintaining services.

- Redmire, North Yorkshire lost both its shop and post office. The scheme has enabled both to re-open in the local garage run by community volunteers.

Harting village store, West Sussex

With their shopkeepers anxious to retire and no new buyer in sight, the villagers of Harting set up an action committee. They formed a Village Shop Association, which gave them access to government funding and raised £60,000. A new shop owner was then able to pay the rest of the value of the premises, so Harting retained its services and social lifeline (photo **C**). The store is increasingly being used by people from the surrounding area. Environmentally it is also a success. People drive less often to towns, saving 'shopping miles'.

C   *Harting village store*

Supporting the rural economy

There are two important programmes aimed at supporting the local economy in rural areas.

1 Rural Challenge

Rural Challenge involved 11 rural regeneration schemes in the 1990s to generate jobs, improve **living standards** and tackle social disadvantage. The schemes, worth £75m, provided training for thousands of people and created over 3,000 jobs. Around 200 new community facilities were set up. One example is in Bishop's Castle, Shropshire, which has 37 small business units with an IT resource centre and childcare facilities.

Latest initiatives by the government to support the economy of rural areas include:

- £100m of funding from the Rural Development Programme for England aimed at rural businesses
- £530m spent on superfast broadband
- £25m used to promote tourism in rural areas
- £15m to help communities tap into the renewable energy potential of rural areas.

2 Objective 1

'Objective 1' regions are those parts of the EU considered to be the most deprived areas. They have average incomes of 75 per cent or less of the EU average and are eligible for considerable financial support from the EU. Money comes from four funds:

- the European Regional Development Fund
- the European Social Fund
- the Agricultural Guidance and Guarantee Fund
- the Financial Instrument for Fisheries Guidance.

These funds must be matched by the national government concerned.

The aim is to revive failing traditional industries and improve local economies by supporting new projects and investing in education and training.

South Yorkshire (2000–2008)

Case study

In 2000 South Yorkshire was one of Europe's most deprived regions. For a period of 8 years, £2.4 billion was invested in the region, boosting the local economy and creating jobs. Some 250 organisations and 650 projects were supported in both urban and rural parts of the county. Examples of investment in rural South Yorkshire included:

- providing training in rural crafts and skills, such as dry stone walling
- funding for farm diversification, e.g. the conversion of a farm building at Loversall Farm, near Rotherham, into a childcare facility
- support for a local tourist attraction, the 'Maize Maze' in Cawthorne, Barnsley and the development of 'Maizie Moo' ice cream on the farm (2007)
- £2 million invested in South Yorkshire Forest Partnership, which has planted 1 million trees and supported over 50 timber-related businesses.

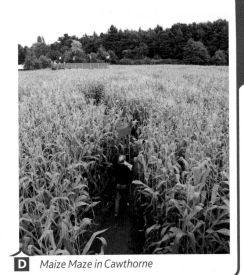

D *Maize Maze in Cawthorne*

Activities

1. a Name two ways in which the UK government promotes protection of the environment.
   b Choose **one** of the schemes named in **a** and explain briefly how it works.

2. If you live in a rural area, this question applies directly to you. If you are an urban person, put yourself in the position of someone living in the countryside.
   a What are the most difficult things about living in a rural area? Consider shopping, getting to school or college, transport in general and finding a job.
   b Choose any of these problems. How might the projects discussed on pages 229–31 help you with this difficulty?
   c Are there any ways in which you would improve the existing schemes?

10.4 How does commercial farming operate in the UK?

Factors affecting farming

All agriculture is affected by both physical and human/economic circumstances. Farmers make decisions on land use based on quality of land, climate, supermarket pressure and people's choice of what to buy.

The operations of a farm can be described as a **farm system**. **Inputs** to the system include climate, land, labour, seeds and livestock. The farmer **processes** the inputs by carrying out tasks such as ploughing, harvesting and milking. Having been processed, there are a number of farm **outputs**, which include milk, crops (e.g. wheat), eggs and 'waste' such as straw. Profit from the farm can be re-invested, for example, in buying new machinery.

Key terms

Farm system: the operation of a farm, where inputs are processed to produce outputs.

Inputs: anything entering the farm system, e.g. climate, soil, seed, labour.

Processes: jobs done on the farm to produce outputs.

Outputs: products leaving the farm system, usually for sale.

Intensive farming: high inputs of capital and/or labour to achieve maximum productivity.

Livestock farming: rearing animals.

Mixed farming: farming both crops and animals.

Arable farming: growing crops.

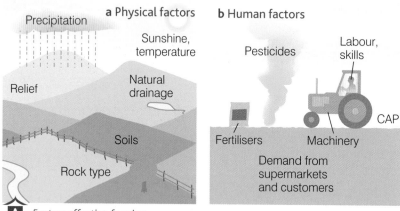

a Physical factors — Precipitation, Sunshine, temperature, Relief, Natural drainage, Soils, Rock type

b Human factors — Pesticides, Labour, skills, Fertilisers, Machinery, CAP, Demand from supermarkets and customers

A *Factors affecting farming*

Activities

1   Define the following terms:
a   intensive farming
b   livestock farming
c   mixed farming
d   arable farming.

2   Draw a flow diagram to show the **inputs**, **processes** and **outputs** of a commercial mixed farm.

3   Describe the outputs typical of an East Anglian farm. Support your answer with facts and figures.

Study tip

You can achieve a much better answer to a question if you use facts and figures to support what you say. Using numbers like this gives a much clearer picture and allows you to compare more accurately.

∞ links

Research in your school library and on the internet into different types of farming areas in the UK. Try the NFU's FACE website at **www.face-online.org.uk**. Look particularly at Lynford House Farm, Cambridgeshire.

Commercial farming in East Anglia

As a farming region, East Anglia covers Norfolk, Suffolk, Essex and Cambridgeshire. The landscape varies from undulating grazing land to fertile fenland, which is farmed **intensively**. In fact, East Anglia is one of the most productive agricultural landscapes in the world. Three-quarters of its land area is used for farming.

Crops

The region is well known for its cereal crops, growing more than a quarter of England's wheat and barley.

- Almost one-third of East Anglia's 1.4 million hectares is used for wheat alone.
- Well over half the UK's sugar beet crop and a third of all potatoes come from Norfolk, Suffolk and Cambridgeshire, much being processed locally.
- Market gardening and horticulture are also important: peas, beans, salad crops, strawberries and other fruits, as well as flowers, are cultivated.

Livestock

In terms of **livestock**, the UK's pig and poultry industry centres on East Anglia. Animals are fed directly on local grain.

- Some 2.2 million eggs and 25 per cent of chickens consumed weekly in the UK are produced in the region, mainly indoors under intensive systems.
- More than 1 million pigs live on 1,900 farms.
- Beef and dairy cattle herds and sheep flocks are small compared with other regions that specialise in these, such as the south-west peninsula. Nevertheless, grazing land is still an important part of the East Anglian landscape. Raising crops, feed and livestock is known as **mixed farming**.

Physical factors

East Anglia's climate is ideal for intensive **arable** production. Low rainfall (around 650 mm per year) comes mainly in spring and summer, when it proves most useful to growing crops. Warm summers (July = 18°C), with plenty of sunshine hours, ensure rapid ripening.

Human factors

Large farm machinery is essential to production on this scale. Most farms are hundreds of hectares in size – some of the largest in Europe. Farms often share the most expensive equipment such as combine harvesters, so during harvest time in August farmers work all day and at night using floodlights.

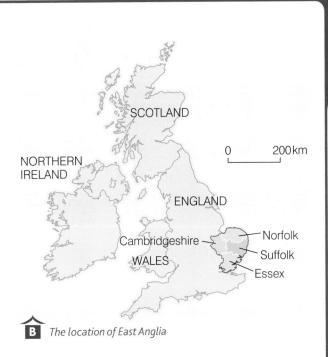

B   *The location of East Anglia*

C   *Sugar beet factory in East Anglia*

Many farms are owned by large companies that employ a manager to run one or more farms. Financial inputs are high. Much is spent on chemical fertilisers, pesticides and weed killers.

10.5 What are agribusinesses in the UK?

Agribusiness is large-scale farming of crops or livestock, aiming for high yields. Products usually supply major supermarkets. Farms are highly mechanised and **capital intensive**. Little labour is needed. Farms may be owned by companies and several farms can be operated by one company.

■ Impacts of agribusiness

Agribusiness is sometimes criticised for damaging and polluting the British landscape because of the following reasons.

1 Use of chemicals

Environmental groups oppose this system of farming. Chemical usage is high and much criticised.

- Pesticides are used to control pests, diseases and weeds. Without them, yields would be 45 per cent lower. This is why yields on **organic farms** are always lower. However, chemicals kill important wildlife such as bees, which are essential for crop pollination.
- Artificial fertilisers are mineral compounds that increase plant growth. Most soils do not contain enough nutrients for the high yields we want. Problems include cost (most are oil-based) and leaching of chemicals into rivers and the water table, leading to **eutrophication**.
- Phosphates released from farm slurry (animal manure) pollute water supplies and can be up to 100 times as damaging as household effluent.

2 Damage to ecosystems

Intensification of agriculture has caused the loss of important wildlife **habitats**, such as:

- wetlands
- hedgerows.

Wetlands act as sponges, soaking up excess rainwater and preventing floods. When drained, they make high-quality farmland, but flooding has increased as a result.

Although hedgerows are manmade (they were mostly planted in the 18th century), they are an important wildlife habitat (photo **A**). Large machinery is more efficient in big fields, as less turning is necessary. Hedgerows also take up valuable cropland. Between 1945 and 1990, over 25 per cent of UK hedges were destroyed, but in the most commercial arable areas like East Anglia, the figure was over 60 per cent. However, attitudes have now changed and hedges are being replaced, even on very large farms. They act as windbreaks and their roots bind soil together, which reduces soil erosion. Trees within hedges act as a windbreak and provide added wildlife habitat.

Key terms

Agribusiness: running an agricultural operation like an industry. Inputs and outputs are both high.

Capital intensive: farming to achieve maximum production through buying fuel, fertilisers and buildings that will allow maximum output.

Organic farm: a farm that does not use chemicals in the production of crops or livestock.

Eutrophication: pollution of fresh water from agricultural waste or excess fertiliser run-off.

Habitat: the home to a community of plants and animals.

Genetically modified (GM) crops: involves putting genes from other species (sometimes animals) into a crop to give it certain characteristics that increase yield.

A *A hedgerow in winter*

3 Use of genetically modified (GM) crops

Agribusiness farms are more likely to use **genetically modified (GM) crops**, which aim to prevent food shortages and reduce costs for the customer. Their use in the UK is still experimental, but is much opposed by environmental groups. If the added genes transfer into the natural environment, ecosystems could be irreversibly altered. GM development is controlled by multinational companies with a great deal of power.

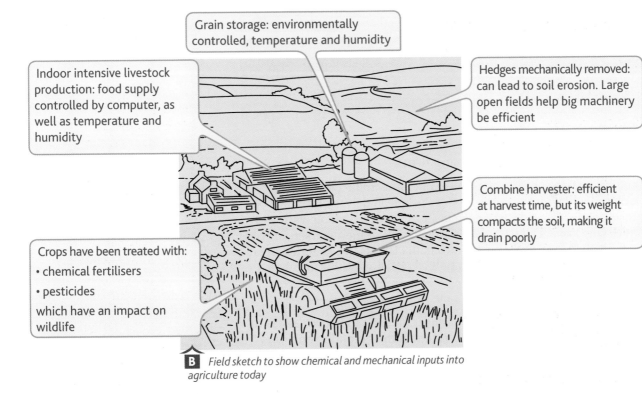

Grain storage: environmentally controlled, temperature and humidity

Indoor intensive livestock production: food supply controlled by computer, as well as temperature and humidity

Hedges mechanically removed: can lead to soil erosion. Large open fields help big machinery be efficient

Combine harvester: efficient at harvest time, but its weight compacts the soil, making it drain poorly

Crops have been treated with:
• chemical fertilisers
• pesticides
which have an impact on wildlife

B Field sketch to show chemical and mechanical inputs into agriculture today

The influence of supermarkets on UK farming

The major supermarkets have considerable power and control over the whole food supply system. Almost all our food is purchased in supermarkets. One-tenth of all spending (and not just on food) is in Tesco alone, now one of the world's largest retail outlets. If farmers want to sell their produce, they often have to take what the supermarkets offer them.

UK dairy farmers receive one of the lowest prices for their milk in the EU. In 2010 they received 25p per litre. Milk is a daily basic food and people do not want to pay more than they have to, giving supermarkets an incentive to reduce the price. Supermarkets put pressure on dairy food processing companies for lower prices, so they in turn pay farmers less for milk too.

People who feel strongly about these issues have demonstrated outside and inside supermarkets (photo **C**). Bad publicity can have a great influence. Some companies now offer farmers a better deal and they use this in their advertising.

C *What can the customer do?*

The influence of food processing firms

Food processing converts raw foods from farm production into packaged, often ready-cooked food for people and livestock. The food processing industry in East Anglia alone is worth £3 billion. Factories are usually located close to their raw materials or their market. British Sugar processes all sugar beet grown in the UK. Its five factories are all within the growing region (map **D**). Shaw Bakery, Warburton's bread factory in Oldham, Lancashire, manufactures 750,000 loaves every week. All are sold within 48 km of the factory.

Food processing companies are put under pressure by supermarkets to produce food at a certain price. To maintain their profit margin, they try to buy their raw materials as cheaply as possible from farmers. Everyone wants to make a profit. Farmers are at the end of the chain and so find themselves having to accept low prices rather than not sell their produce at all.

D *British Sugar factory locations*

Activities

1. Draw a mind map (concept map) to show the main features of agribusiness.

    a   Write 'agribusiness' in the centre of your page and define it. Use a photo from the Internet too.

    b   Around the edges, add information using text and photos to describe the main features and impacts of agribusiness.

2. Discuss the impacts of supermarkets and food processing companies on farmers and customers.

3. a   Write lists of advantages and disadvantages of using chemical fertilisers and pesticides on farms.

    b   Consider the environmental issues involved.

    c   Make a decision: When is it right to use these chemicals, and when not so?

10.6   How can we reduce the environmental effects of high impact farming?

The importance of organic farming

Organic farming is a type of farming that does not involve the use of chemicals, such as artificial fertilisers and pesticides. It is generally considered to be more sustainable because it looks after the soil and natural habitats, as well as producing healthier food for people. However, yields per hectare are significantly lower than in non-organic farming, making produce more expensive to buy.

Since 1990 the market for organic produce has been growing by 20 to 25 per cent each year, despite prices being higher. In 2010 organic produce was worth £36 billion in the UK. The amount of organic land is also growing: 0.9 per cent globally and 4.3 per cent in the UK.

A certain level of pest damage is accepted as organic methods are less effective. Beneficial organisms are introduced, such as ladybirds to eat aphids. Bees and other insects thrive without the chemicals that kill them, in turn improving pollination. Weeds are controlled mechanically, which is more time-consuming, and by mulching (adding a layer of organic material on top of the soil to prevent weed germination).

Some people argue that organic foods are not what they seem – they are an indulgence the world cannot afford. Organic pesticides such as copper stay in the soil for ever and are toxic. This may be worse for the environment than some modern, biodegradable pesticides.

Dairy production is a major source of greenhouse gas emissions, mainly methane, which is more than 20 times as powerful as carbon dioxide. Organically reared cattle produce twice the amount of methane of conventional cattle because of their diet. Organic crops produce less per hectare but cost the same amount of energy to harvest.

The Department for Environment, Food and Rural Affairs (Defra) estimates that organic tomato production in the UK takes 25 per cent more water than non-organic production. On the other hand, organic wheat uses less water and less energy per kilogram harvested than non-organic wheat.

> **In this section you will learn**
>
> government policies to reduce environmental effects of high impact farming
>
> how to compare and contrast intensive and organic farming systems.

> **Key terms**
>
> **Crop rotation**: changing the use of a field regularly to help maintain soil fertility.

A *Organic produce in a supermarket*

How do government policies affect farming today?

Environmental Stewardship Scheme

Farmers are the main people working to conserve the countryside. The UK government aims to support them in several ways, including paying grants under the Environmental Stewardship Scheme. By March 2011, 6.4 million hectares of British farmland were included in this scheme. Farmers restore wildlife habitats by:

- replacing hedgerows and keeping them well trimmed
- leaving a strip of land along both sides of a hedge to increase wildlife habitat
- planting trees and managing woodland
- looking after ditches and ponds (photo **B**)
- maintaining hay meadows and grassland.

The National Farmers' Union (NFU) has calculated that farmers carry out £400 million of unpaid work in maintaining the British landscape.

Single Farm Payment Scheme

In 2005, the Single Farm Payment Scheme was introduced to provide European Union support enabling farmers to maintain their land in good condition agriculturally and environmentally. Calculated according to farm size, the payment is dependent on land being farmed in an environmentally sensitive way with careful use of chemicals. Farmers are, for example, encouraged to retain 2 m of uncultivated land around their fields to act as wildlife corridors.

Study tip

To compare and contrast effectively it is useful to plan your ideas first by listing the characteristics of the material being reviewed.
Compare means to point out the similarities. **Contrast** means to highlight the differences.
Finally, consider where the balance lies and draw a conclusion.

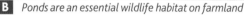

B *Ponds are an essential wildlife habitat on farmland*

Activities

1 Study photo **A** on page 237.
a Can you identify some organic produce being sold?
b What is meant by 'organic farming'?
c How do organic farmers cope with pests?
d Why is organic food often more expensive than intensively grown food?
e Would you buy organic food? Explain your answer.

2 a How does the Environmental Stewardship Scheme help farms to restore wildlife habitats?
b Suggest reasons why wildlife habitats should be preserved.

3 Research some of the problems in the UK farming industry such as BSE and foot-and-mouth disease. These are often associated with farming too intensively. Since demand for food is increasing, farming is likely to become even more intensive. Discuss some of the problems this may bring and consider some possible solutions.

10.7 How do countries change from subsistence to cash crop production?

Most poor countries are in debt. One solution is to turn land currently used for subsistence crops to cash crop production. Cash crops can be exported for foreign currency to help repay debt and some of the profit might pay for development benefits for the country.

Whilst this may sound an attractive option, poorer subsistence farmers can suffer when their land is converted to cash crop production. Also, the production of food crops can be reduced as a country focuses more on cash crops.

In this section you will learn

how cash crop cultivation impacts on subsistence food production.

Cash crop production in Kenya: flowers

Poorer countries like Kenya are committing more land to cash crop production for export to generate hard currency income (map **A**). The land involved was previously used for growing subsistence crops for local people or belonged to small-scale producers of tea and coffee. Many benefits and costs result for the communities involved and the country as a whole.

Kenya's flower industry is the oldest and largest in Africa. It accounts for 10 per cent of Kenya's exports by value. Kenya's main flower crops are roses and carnations. No other country exports as many roses as Kenya. Just look at your local supermarket – they will almost certainly have Kenyan roses (photo **B**).

Main flower-producing areas

⊗ Nairobi – main airport for exports

A   *Major flower-producing areas in Kenya*

B   *Kenyan roses on sale in a UK supermarket*

Today, Kenya's flowers have an export value of $250m a year, second after earnings from tea. There is an annual growth rate of 20 per cent. The busiest time of year is the first half of February because of Valentine's Day in Europe. Some 20 per cent of annual business takes place then and hours worked are at a maximum. Millions of roses are flown from Nairobi to Europe every year. The USA is also an expanding market.

Case study

C *Worker in Kenya's flower cash crop industry*

Kenya has some of the largest flower farms in the world, even compared with the Netherlands – a country famous for its flower production. Even though Kenya has a good climate for flower growing, most roses are grown in greenhouses to protect them from rain, which rots them, and wind and hail, which damage them. Flowers are grown close to the Rift Valley lakes because they are a reliable source of water and cultivated flowers need vast quantities of water.

The business employs tens of thousands of workers (photo **C**). Two-thirds of them are casual labourers with no job security or benefits – pregnancy usually means loss of employment. Wages of £1 per day – Kenya's minimum wage – are just above the globally accepted poverty level of $1 per day.

Study tip

There are always at least two points of view to any issue. You need to put your own opinion to one side initially and write about all sides of the situation. In your conclusion, state your own opinion but it must be backed up with reasons.

∞ links

See p.292 for more on flower production in Kenya. This will help inform your activity answers.

Activities

1 Study map **A** on page 239.

a Describe the location of the flower-growing area in Kenya.

b Explain the advantages of this location. Think about workforce, market and transport.

2 a List the advantages and disadvantages of flower farming in Kenya for local labourers.

b How might their lives have changed working on flower farms rather than in subsistence production?

c What other types of job are created by new flower businesses? Who profits?

3 a How is the land affected by flower production? Be careful to include both positive and negative impacts in your answer.

b Write a conclusion in favour of or against flower farm expansion in Kenya. Use your answers to earlier questions to justify your point of view.

10.8 How do forestry and mining impact on the traditional farming economy?

Traditional farming in the Amazon Basin

Shifting cultivation (also called 'slash and burn' agriculture) is the traditional form of rainforest subsistence farming. Native tribes have practised the system for thousands of years. Rainforest soils are poor quality as most nutrients in this rich ecosystem are stored in the vegetation. The soil takes at least 20 years to regenerate after use for only 2 or 3 years. Typically one family has three or four plots under cultivation each year and ten times as many **fallow** ones.

Tribal people often have no legal right to the land they cultivate and governments can sell it off to transnational corporations (TNCs). Once the forest is opened up, whether for logging or mining, the ecosystem breaks down. Vegetation is cleared and the soil quickly loses its structure. Heavy rain then washes it away. Once clearance has happened, traditional farming cannot restart because the most basic resource – the soil – has been ruined. Regeneration is almost impossible, so shifting cultivators cannot return to this land.

Rainforest destruction

There are four main causes of rainforest destruction.

1 The impact of cash crops and ranching

Economic pressures force the governments of poorer countries to grow and export cash crops. Land is needed and rainforest is cleared. This is called deforestation. In the Amazon, huge areas have been cleared for soya production, mainly to feed beef cattle in the USA or Brazil itself to produce beef for export. In Indonesia, cassava – another fodder crop – is grown for export to the EU. Large areas of forest have been cleared for cattle ranching, especially in the Amazon Basin. On average one animal requires two hectares of land.

In this section you will learn

the scale of deforestation for forestry and mining in the Amazon Basin

the impacts of this on traditional farmers

whether some forms of large-scale exploitation are more acceptable than others.

Key terms

Fallow: land that has been left unseeded to recover its fertility.

A *Deforestation*

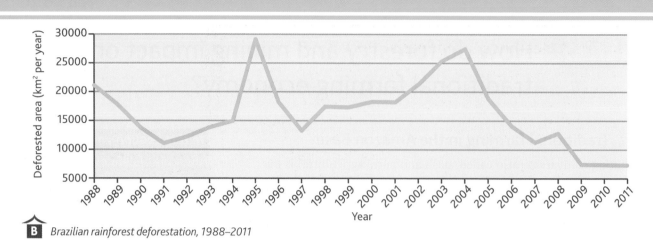

B *Brazilian rainforest deforestation, 1988–2011*

2 The impact of forestry

Logging has devastated local tribes in Indonesia such as the Moi people. Their way of life threatened, they tried to stand up to the major Intimpura Timber Company. The government sent in the army to support the company over its own people. Land, air and water pollution were the results of this over-exploitation. Rivers were silted up due to soil erosion and machine oil polluted the soil and water.

3 The impact of mining

Carajas Iron Ore Mine in Brazil is one of the largest operating open-pit mines in the world. Rainforest has had to be cleared on a large scale to make way for the mining operators and for transport (photo **D**). The landscape has been completely changed, ecosystems destroyed and rivers polluted.

4 The impact of growing infrastructure

Road construction in the Amazon has led to great losses too. Roads provide access to logging and mining sites, as well as allowing poor farmers to penetrate deeper into the forest. The Trans-Amazonian Highway was a huge project 3,200 km long bisecting the rainforest region. Some 100 tonnes of soil per hectare were eroded due to clearance for this highway. (Remember, a hectare is a square with sides of 100 m.)

Malaysia's controls on deforestation have been relatively strict. Nevertheless close to Kuala Lumpur, the capital city, rapid industrialisation is still causing increased deforestation.

C *A farmer burns the rainforest*

D *Large-scale mining in the Amazon Basin*

Case study

Rainforest clearance in Indonesia, 1997–1998

From September 1997 to June 1998, much of South-east Asia suffered major pollution caused by thousands of rainforest fires. An area as large as Western Europe had visibility reduced to as little as 50 m. Some fires were started by new farmers clearing land and they were largely blamed. However, 80 per cent were due to large forestry companies taking advantage of the dry El Niño conditions to clear land for large-scale mining and agriculture projects.

Indonesia has lost 20,000 plant species and 17 per cent of the world's birds. Thousands more species face extinction due to deforestation. From 1997 to 1998, rainforest fires polluted the whole region.

Did you know ??????

Between 1970 and 2006, over 600,000 km^2 of Amazon rainforest were destroyed, mostly by logging and some by mining concerns. Speed of clearance has increased. From May 2000 to August 2006, nearly 150,000 km^2 were lost, a quarter of the total losses in one-sixth of the time period. A peak clearance year was 2004. Since then there has been some evidence of a decline in annual deforestation.

E *Advantages and disadvantages of large-scale exploitation*

Advantages	Disadvantages
Timber and minerals produce foreign exchange for the country, which can pay for development projects	Local people are thrown off land they use for traditional farming activities and have nowhere else to go
TNCs bring expertise to the country – new skills are learned by local people	Businesses are often owned by TNCs and the profits go abroad
Jobs are provided and income for local people	Senior workers are brought in from outside and local workers are often low paid
Infrastructure is improved to provide access to exploited sites	New roads and railways are cut through the rainforest, leading to soil erosion

∞links

Research deforestation in the Amazon Basin at **www.mongabay. com/brazil.html**.

Activities

1. a Use the data below to draw a pie chart to show the causes of deforestation in the Amazon Basin. The diameter of your pie chart should be at least 6 cm for clarity.

Causes of deforestation in the Amazon Basin, 2000–2005	
Cattle ranching	60 per cent
Small-scale subsistence agriculture	30 per cent
Fires, mining, urbanisation, road construction and dams	4 per cent
Logging, legal and illegal practices	4 per cent
Large-scale commercial arable agriculture	2 per cent

   b Why do you think cattle ranching is by far the main cause of deforestation?

   c Why has rainforest been cleared for roads?

   d Do you think the government should spend money stopping illegal practices? Explain your answer.

2. Study graph **B**. Do you agree that rainforest clearance has increased over the years? Use data from the graph to support your answer.

3. Study photo **C**.
   a Why is the farmer burning the rainforest?
   b Suggest some environmental consequences of what he is doing.

4. Study photo **D**.
   a What is happening in the photo?
   b What might be the environmental consequences of this mining operation?

10.9 What are soil erosion issues?

What is soil erosion?

Soil erosion occurs when the soil is either blown away by wind or washed away by rain (photo **A**). It is common in areas with steep slopes. Deforestation removes the roots that bind the soil together and the shelter that limits the impact of the wind. Poor farming techniques make the problems worse because they weaken soil structure and make it more likely to erode. Population increase puts pressure on farmers to grow more.

What are the impacts of soil erosion?

Traditional agriculture has continued for centuries, so it ought to be in balance with its environment. This is not always true. Iraq was part of the Fertile Crescent, where agriculture began 10,000 years ago. It was the wealthiest and most technologically advanced region in the world. Today, it has the worst soil problems in the world: erosion, salinisation and deforestation. The USA, Australia and China also have serious widespread soil erosion problems. In the world as a whole, an area 10 times the size of the UK has become so severely degraded that it can no longer produce food – a serious problem as world population continues to grow.

A Severe soil erosion in East Africa

Where does soil erosion occur?

In Madagascar, the best farmland is used for export coffee production, so people have had to clear more and more forest for their subsistence crop production. Half the island's forest vanished between 1950 and 1985. Losses of topsoil are huge. Air and satellite photos show red staining in the Indian Ocean due to topsoil being washed out to sea (photo **B**).

In Democratic Republic of Congo and Nigeria, increased population and food demand meant shifting cultivators could not leave soil plots long enough to regenerate between crops. They cleared too many areas too close together, which allowed heavy rain to wash the soil away. This whole farming system has broken down as a result.

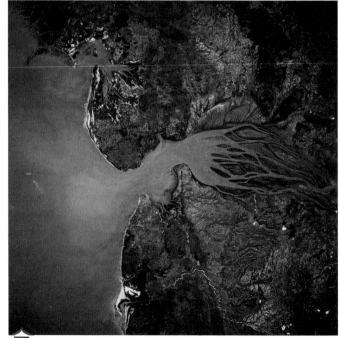

B Satellite photo showing eroded soil washed into the Indian Ocean

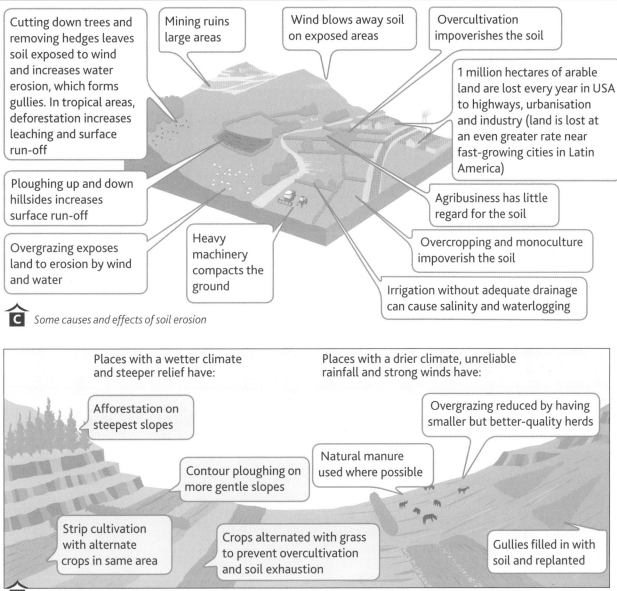

Cutting down trees and removing hedges leaves soil exposed to wind and increases water erosion, which forms gullies. In tropical areas, deforestation increases leaching and surface run-off

Mining ruins large areas

Wind blows away soil on exposed areas

Overcultivation impoverishes the soil

1 million hectares of arable land are lost every year in USA to highways, urbanisation and industry (land is lost at an even greater rate near fast-growing cities in Latin America)

Ploughing up and down hillsides increases surface run-off

Agribusiness has little regard for the soil

Overgrazing exposes land to erosion by wind and water

Heavy machinery compacts the ground

Overcropping and monoculture impoverish the soil

Irrigation without adequate drainage can cause salinity and waterlogging

C   *Some causes and effects of soil erosion*

Places with a wetter climate and steeper relief have:

Places with a drier climate, unreliable rainfall and strong winds have:

Afforestation on steepest slopes

Overgrazing reduced by having smaller but better-quality herds

Natural manure used where possible

Contour ploughing on more gentle slopes

Strip cultivation with alternate crops in same area

Crops alternated with grass to prevent overcultivation and soil exhaustion

Gullies filled in with soil and replanted

D   *Some attempts to reduce and prevent soil erosion*

Activities

1   Write a definition of the term 'soil erosion'.

2   Study photo **A**.

a   Make a list of annotations you could write for the photo.

b   Describe the photo, making clear what has happened to the landscape and its usefulness to people.

3   Study diagram **C**.

a   What are the causes of soil erosion?

b   Which causes do you think are more responsible for soil erosion, physical or human factors? Justify your answer.

c   Draw your own version of diagram **D**. Choose items from the list below to add extra labels:

■   terracing on steep slopes

■   stone lines laid to trap surface water run-off and soil

■   hedgerows replanted to hold the soil together and act as windbreaks.

10.10 How do irrigation schemes increase food production?

What is irrigation?

Irrigation is the artificial watering of the land. It has played an important role in increasing agricultural output worldwide. As global population is predicted to rise to 10 billion by 2150, food production must rise dramatically. More than half of rice and wheat are already grown using irrigation. One-third of the world's food is grown on 17 per cent of its land, all of which is irrigated.

What problems does irrigation bring?

California and Australia have employed irrigation schemes on a vast scale. Yields were dramatically increased, but after several years problems such as **salinisation** emerged. Up to half the irrigated land in these developed world regions suffers from this, putting it out of production until the problem can be solved – an expensive process. Some 40 per cent of Australian soils are affected, especially in South Australia and Victoria where large areas are cultivated using irrigation. California has similar problems while Syria, a neighbour of Jordan, has 50 per cent of land affected. In Uzbekistan, a staggering 80 per cent of soils are damaged by salt.

Two solutions have been tried in Egypt's Nile Valley:

- Underground drainage systems take the saline water away, but they are expensive to build.
- Changing land use is a cheaper alternative. Some grasses are salt-tolerant, so turning arable land to pasture keeps it productive while the salt washes away slowly with the rain.

Irrigation in sub-Saharan Africa

Sub-Saharan Africa suffers from erratic, unreliable rainfall patterns and includes many of the world's poorest countries. Only 3.5 per cent of land is currently irrigated (photo **A**). Africa lags behind Asia and the rest of the world in all aspects of irrigation. In West Africa, 1 in 20 of Senegal's farmers has irrigation and this is one of the better-served countries. In Asia, one in three farmers has irrigation. The lack of irrigation results in lower than average calorie intake and occasional food shortages.

Due to lack of technology, most African irrigation systems utilise the water only once. It is not recycled within the system. Most technology improvements are funded by aid.

In this section you will learn

how irrigation schemes can change agriculture.

Key terms

Salinisation: the deposition of solid salts on the ground surface following the evaporation of water. Also an increase in the concentration of salts in the soil, reducing fertility.

Did you know ??????

By 2025, 80 per cent of food is expected to come from irrigated land.

A An irrigation scheme in sub-Saharan Africa

Types of irrigation

For a drip irrigation scheme, pipes are laid across the fields. Water flows through them slowly and drips out through holes in the pipe. It soaks gradually into the soil over a long period of time (diagram **B**). With sprinkler irrigation, water is piped to one or more central locations within the field. Pressure sprinklers then distribute water to the crops (photo **C**). Countries at further stages of development, including the UK, favour this method but it is expensive to set up and run and is therefore less valuable in poorer countries.

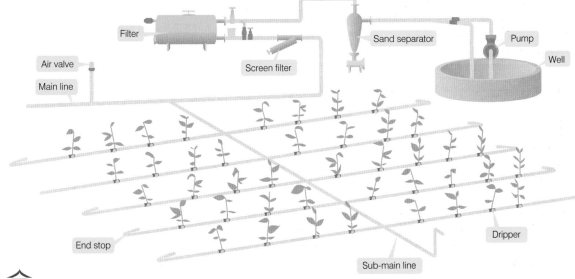

Filter · Air valve · Main line · Screen filter · Sand separator · Pump · Well · End stop · Sub-main line · Dripper

B   *A drip irrigation scheme*

C   *Sprinkler irrigation*

	Drip	Sprinkler
Advantages	• Uses a small amount of water • Little chance for water to evaporate • Can be laid in the ground, so even less water is wasted • Plants have regular supply of water • Easy to control • Inexpensive to set up • Can use recycled water • Farmer can control soil moisture • Minimises soil erosion • Leaves stay dry; no rot	• Flexible – can be fed by hose from water source • Can be moved easily around a field • Can use recycled water
Disadvantages	• Only works with crops grown in rows • Needs gently sloping land to work efficiently • Pipes can become clogged with silt • Needs a pump to flow well on flat land	• Expensive to start up • May need a pump to run • Leaves get wet and might rot • Uses more water • Higher rate of evaporation

D   *Advantages and disadvantages of drip and sprinkler irrigation*

Water use in Jordan

Jordan is a particularly dry country in the Middle East. With very low rainfall and a rapidly growing population, Jordan has concentrated on using as much water for irrigation as possible. Only 6 per cent of the country is farmed. Irrigation is essential and 70 per cent of all water resources are already used for food production (photo **E**). Treated waste water is now used to provide extra irrigation water. Sixteen treatment plants put 60 million m³ of clean water directly into irrigation schemes or into the river systems of the River Jordan basin to be extracted for use further downstream. The World Bank financially supports the companies involved. Other countries might be able to learn from Jordan's experience.

E   Intensive production of tomatoes using pumped water in the Badia desert, Jordan

Appropriate technology

Poorer countries need affordable technology at a level suitable for the purpose which can be realistically maintained. This is appropriate technology.

Sometimes in the past aid projects have introduced technology at too high a level to be practical in the circumstances. To repair machinery needs tools that must be available and those using them must have sufficient training. Machinery needs fuel, which can be expensive to buy. Just as small, handheld ploughs may be more appropriate in a remote part of rural Africa than tractors, so simple irrigation systems, like the drip method, may turn out to be more effective than more expensive and complex systems.

Activities

1 a Write a short definition of 'irrigation'.
 b Explain briefly why irrigation is important in world farming today.

2 a Explain what is meant by the term 'salinisation'.
 b What problems does salinisation cause for the farmer?
 c How can the problems be solved or reduced?

3 a Write a brief definition of 'appropriate technology'.
 b Explain why any new irrigation scheme in sub-Saharan Africa would need to be based on appropriate technology.
 c How do you think irrigation in Africa could be much more effective?

4 Read the case study of water use in Jordan and look at the photo **E**.
 a How is the expansion of irrigation in Jordan likely to help the country's people and economy?
 b Do you think Jordan's new irrigation scheme is sustainable?

5 Imagine you are a consultant on a new irrigation scheme in a less well-off country. What advice would you give on the following points?
 ▪ the best type of scheme to be used
 ▪ the construction of the scheme
 ▪ avoiding future problems of salinisation.

Present your advice in the form of a short report using photos and diagrams.

10.11 How does rural-to-urban migration affect rural areas?

Reasons for rural-to-urban migration

Rural-to-urban migration is caused by rural push factors and urban pull factors. The rural push begins the process.

Poor rural standards of living make people want to do better for themselves and their children. Rural areas often lack opportunities for improvement. As a country develops, more opportunities become available, but most of these are in the cities. People begin to look elsewhere for improvement. The pull factors, or attractions of the cities, become important at this stage in a person's decision-making process.

Impacts of rural–urban migration on the rural area

Rural areas may benefit from this migration flow. Migrants send money home to those remaining in the villages. This can be used to improve farming – increasing livestock, buying new tools or better seed – or to help the family by paying school fees.

However, it also brings some problems. Wives, children and the elderly are less able to carry out the hard physical labour involved in farming. Crop yields may reduce and rural development may become limited. Children are brought up with less influence from their fathers. They may have to help more on the farm, which can affect their education. Although the money sent home helps, the family and farming system are put under pressure.

> **In this section you will learn**
>
> the reasons for rural-to-urban migration
>
> the impact rural-to-urban migration may have in the rural areas from which people move
>
> why some agricultural systems are failing.

> **Study tip**
>
> With reference to specific places, you need to be able to explain the main causes of soil degradation and possible solutions.

A *Poor quality land in Lesotho, Africa acts as a 'push' factor encouraging rural–urban migration*

Crisis in Lesotho

Farming employs 57 per cent of Lesotho's labour force, mostly on small subsistence farms. This figure is low compared with other poor countries. The reasons vary:

- Lesotho's mountainous environment limits the amount of agricultural land available. Much of the land suffers from serious soil erosion, partly the result of drought.

- Some 35 per cent of adult males leave home to work in the cities and mines of neighbouring South Africa (map **B**). If they were all at home on the land, farm labour would be a much higher 86 per cent of the national workforce.

- It is difficult to manage efficient and productive farming in such circumstances. In addition, since the area of productive land has decreased, 40 per cent of families are landless.

Table **C** shows the main crops produced in Lesotho. Maize is the staple carbohydrate. Notice how along with other crops its production has declined since 2000/01. Crop production in Lesotho is high risk and low yield because of poor soil quality and the harsh, unpredictable climate (photo **A**). About 10 per cent of the country is arable land, but only 1 per cent is high quality. Lesotho has to import much of its grain as well as some other food. Livestock production is important to rural income because animals cope better with poor land than crops, although drought in the 1980s and 1990s limited the amount of pasture.

With so many men and older boys leaving to find paid work elsewhere, much of the farm labour is left to women, children and the elderly.

On a more positive note, Lesotho has one of the most advanced soil conservation programmes in Africa. It is beginning to solve some of the problems by terracing the land and introducing irrigation systems.

B The location of Lesotho in southern Africa

1 Study table **D**.

a Draw the data in the table as a line graph, with one line for each crop. Plot the years on the x-axis and agricultural production on the y-axis.

b What is the general trend shown by your graph?

c Suggest reasons for the trend you have described.

C Agricultural production, 2000–2007 (thousands of tonnes)

Crop	2000/01	2001/02	2002/03	2003/04	2004/05	2005/06	2006/07	2007/8
Maize	158.2	111.2	82.1	81.0	75.0	76.9	60.3	59.6
Sorghum	45.4	11.9	12.0	10.3	10.3	12.1	7.8	10.1
Wheat	37.3	19.0	13.1	11.7	11.1	2.9	1.2	3.7
Beans	7.9	4.4	3.7	4.8	5.2	5.3	5.3	3.1
Peas	3.7	3.0	3.0	1.5	1.4	0.7	0.7	1.0

11   The development gap

11.1   What are the traditional ways of dividing up the world?

First, second and third worlds

One early method of dividing up the world was from a Western European perspective. Europeans saw themselves as the **first world**. The wealthier regions they colonised, such as North America and Australia, were referred to as the **second world**. This system had no clear place for Communist countries such as the former Soviet Union, which were quite well developed, and had never been colonies or part of Western Europe. They were added into the second world group, but this was always unsatisfactory. Poorer countries were then grouped together as the **third world**.

North/South

The Brandt Report on the state of world development was published in 1971. It made a simpler division, contrasting economically wealthier and industrialised countries with poorer, less mature and largely agricultural ones. A line called the North-South divide was drawn on a world map to make this difference clear. The development indicator used was GNP (Gross National Product) per capita which is a measure of a country's wealth. This over-simplistic system is now seen as out of date.

> **In this section you will learn**
>
> the traditional ways of dividing up the world in terms of development
>
> a modern division based on wealth.

> **Did you know** ???????
>
> Gross Domestic Product (GDP) is an indication of the value of goods produced within a country's borders. Gross National Product (GNP) relates to the value of goods produced by citizens of the country.

> **Did you know** ???????
>
> Map **A** shows GDP per capita (per head) across the world. The type of map used to show this is called a choropleth map. It is a shaded map where the depth of colour increases as the value gets higher. Also, the shades are close to each other in the colour wheel. Choropleths give a clear visual impression of the pattern of values. We naturally associate darker colours with higher values and paler ones with lower values. The appearance of the map helps us to understand it easily and quickly.

NORTH
SOUTH

GDP per capita
(US$) 2007

■ 12000 or more
■ 3500–11999
■ 1000–3499
□ less than 1000
□ no data

A *Choropleth map showing GDP per capita, 2007*   Source: International Monetary Fund 2008

Countries at different stages of development

More recently a simple twofold division involved the use of 'less developed country' (LDC) and 'more developed country' (MDC). This was not widely accepted because development is not only economic but also social and cultural. Many poor countries have a rich culture and society. It was negative to suggest that culture was at a low level just because the country was economically poor. LDC therefore became 'less economically developed country' (LEDC) and MDC became 'more economically developed country' (MEDC).

Since the late 20th century the world order has changed tremendously. Globalisation means there are more contacts and trade between countries than ever before. Some LEDCs are growing more rapidly than most developed economies. A new category had to be introduced to cover those developing fastest. They became known as **newly industrialising countries (NICs)**.

Within any country there are increasing differences between people and regions. The middle class is growing in many poor countries. Their capital cities, along with their surrounding regions, are often well developed and almost indistinguishable from any MEDC city. The LEDC/MEDC division is therefore becoming much less useful.

> ### Key terms
>
> **Newly industrialising countries (NICs)**: these include the Asian 'tigers' as well as other emerging industrial nations such as Malaysia, the Philippines and China.

The five-fold division based on wealth

The five categories are based on wealth (map **B**):

1 rich industrialising countries
2 oil-exporting countries
3 newly industrialising countries
4 former centrally planned economies (those previously having a Communist political system)
5 heavily indebted poor countries.

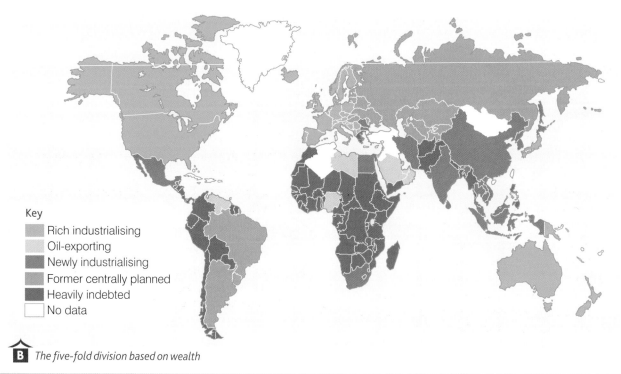

Key
- Rich industrialising
- Oil-exporting
- Newly industrialising
- Former centrally planned
- Heavily indebted
- No data

B *The five-fold division based on wealth*

1 Rich industrialising countries

The UK would be classed as a rich industrialising country. We are still wealthy, but our manufacturing industry has declined over recent decades.

2 Oil exporting countries

Oil-exporting countries have a great spread of wealth in their societies. Huge amounts of money are made from exporting oil. Rich people and companies are investing their money in businesses abroad. Some UK football clubs have been bought by Middle Eastern oil billionaires (photo **C**). Nevertheless, the majority of people remain poor in oil-exporting countries such as the United Arab Emirates (UAE) and Venezuela. Some profit is used for development projects, so eventually everyone may benefit.

3 New industrialising countries

The newly industrialising countries (NICs) such as India, China and Mexico have developed rapidly in recent years and will probably become category 1 countries in the near future.

4 Former centrally-planned economies

The category of former centrally planned economies covers a wide variety of countries today. Former Communist states have become more like Western European countries with Latvia, Lithuania, Estonia, Romania, Poland and the Czech Republic becoming member states of the European Union. China still has its Communist government, but it is one of the world's fastest growing economies and its speed of industrialisation has been phenomenal.

5 Heavily indebted poor countries

Some of the world's poorest countries borrowed large amounts of money in the past and are now in serious debt. Many African countries are in this position. Once in debt, it is very hard for countries to develop.

> **Study tip**
>
> Remember that a choropleth map involves density shading, with darkest shading representing the highest values. These maps give a general representation, as two countries with the same density shading may have wide variations between them and within them.

C *Manchester City football club was bought by a Middle Eastern company*

Activities

1 Study map **A**.

a Use an atlas to help you name two countries with less than $1000 per person per year and two with $12,000 or more.

b Describe the pattern of GDP per capita across the world in 2007. Identify clusters of similar countries.

c Describe the pattern made by the North/South divide line. Can you see anything odd about the shape of the line?

d Does the line separate countries of similar choropleth shading? Name some countries that are exceptions to the rule.

2 Study maps **A** and **B**.

a What is the evidence that Africa is the poorest continent in the world?

b Suggest reasons for the recent rapid growth of the NICs.

c Compare and contrast the pattern on the two maps.

3 Consider, using Internet research, the cultural richness (music, art, etc.) that exists in many of the poorer countries of the world.

11.2 How can we measure development?

Correlating different measures of development

Indicators of development tell us a great deal about a country and allow us to compare them. Any **development measure** that tells us about wealth, poverty or economic development should correlate with similar indicators. For example, a country with low **GNP** per capita is likely to have most of its people surviving on subsistence agriculture with low levels of income. Money is limited to pay for education and health, so living standards for most people are low.

Birth rate is closely correlated with level of development. The more developed a country, the lower its birth rate. The demographic transition model gives us evidence that birth rate decreases as countries become more developed (map **A**). A country at a further stage of development is likely to have a high **human development index (HDI)** (see p256), low **infant mortality** rate and widespread access to clean water. There are likely to be many doctors for the number of people and **literacy rates** will be high because the government has sufficient money to spend on health and education. Poorer governments do not have enough funds to provide high-level services. Often even the basics like clean water and a living wage are not possible (table **B**).

In this section you will learn

a range of measures of development and interpret what they tell us about a country

how these measures correlate.

Key terms

Development measure: statistics used to show the level of development, which allows countries to be compared.

GNP: is the total value of all goods and services produced by a nation in a particular year.

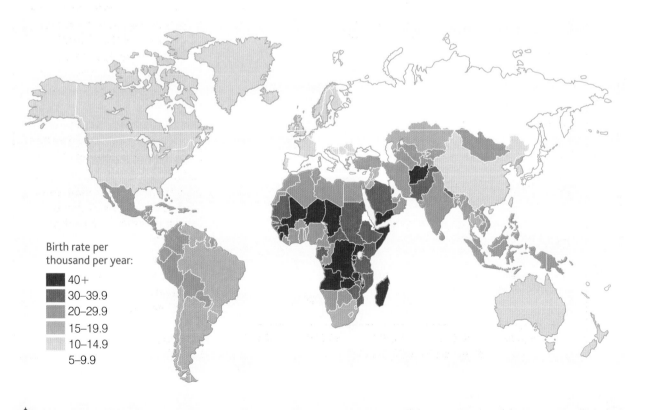

Birth rate per thousand per year:
- 40+
- 30–39.9
- 20–29.9
- 15–19.9
- 10–14.9
- 5–9.9

A Birth rate as a development indicator

B   *A range of development indicators for selected countries*

Country	GNI per capita (US $) (2010)	HDI (2010)	Birth rate per 1,000 per year	Death rate per 1,000 per year	Infant mortality per 1,000 live births per year	Number of doctors per 1,000 people	Literacy rate (%)	Percentage of population with access to clean water
USA	47,020	0.902	13.8	8.4	6.1	2.3	99.0	99
Japan	34,790	0.884	7.3	10.1	2.8	2.0	99.0	100
UK	36,580	0.849	12.3	9.3	4.6	2.2	99.0	100
Turkey	14,580	0.679	17.9	6.1	23.9	1.3	88.7	99
Romania	14,050	0.767	9.6	11.8	11.0	1.9	97.6	61
Brazil	10,920	0.699	17.8	6.4	21.2	2.1	90.0	97
China	7,570	0.663	12.3	7.0	16.1	1.5	95.9	89
Ivory Coast	1,650	0.397	31.0	10.2	64.8	0.1	48.7	80
Bangladesh	1,620	0.469	23.0	5.8	50.7	0.3	53.5	80
Zimbabwe	460	0.140	30.0	15.0	56.0	0.6	90.7	82

Graph **C** shows a clear correlation between two development indicators, although there are a few anomalies. An anomaly is a figure that does not fit in with the pattern. For example, Romania has a lower birth rate than expected, given its low **GNI**.

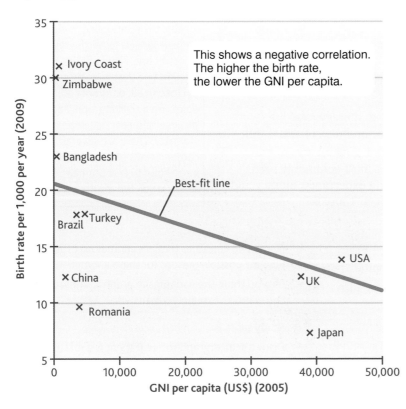

This shows a negative correlation. The higher the birth rate, the lower the GNI per capita.

C   *GNI per capita (2005) and birth rate (2009)*

Key terms

Human development index (HDI): an index based on three variables: life expectancy at birth; level of education, including both literacy rate and years spent in school; income adjusted for purchasing power (how much it will buy). Maximum HDI = 1. Wealthy countries like Japan have an HDI of over 0.9, whereas poor countries are around half that figure or less.

Infant mortality: the number of babies that die under a year of age, per 1000 live births.

Literacy rate: the percentage of adults in a country who can read and write sufficiently to function fully in work and society.

GNI: Gross National Income – the total value of goods and services produced within a country including income received from and payments made to other countries.

Limitations of using a single development measure

Birth rate

Birth rate is an excellent measure of development. In rich industrialising countries, women achieve high levels of education and career prospects. As it is difficult to pursue a high-flying career and bring up several children, having children is often sacrificed for success in the working world. Some countries such as France have tried to encourage career women to have children, using tax advantages and benefits.

Death rate

Death rate is a poor indicator of development. Almost all countries have low death rates today. The more economically developed the country, the higher is the death rate. This is because improved health care allows most people to live longer. With more elderly people, the death rate will be higher. As the population in rich countries ages, so the death rate inevitably increases, often bringing it into line with poorer countries where death rates reflect poor health care and high infant mortality (see **Table E**, page 172).

GNP/GNI

GNP or GNI per capita are only economic measures so give no clear indication of people's personal living standards. They do not tell us what people earn or how much that buys. Nor do they touch directly on how educated people are and the cultural quality of their lives.

All indicators of development are averages across a country. Within any society there are extremes of wealth and opportunity, which a single figure hides.

Multi-variable indicators

Combining several indicators gives a better view of a country's economic and social status.

- **Physical Quality of Life Index (PQLI)** uses literacy rate, life expectancy and infant mortality to provide an index of social well being and quality of life.
- **Human Development Index (HDI)** is the most commonly used indicator of overall development, using life expectancy, literacy and incomes to calculate an index value between 1 and 0.

> **Key terms**
>
> **Physical quality of life index (PQLI):** the average of three social indicators: literacy rate, life expectancy and infant mortality.

> **Study tip**
>
> The relationship between development indicators can be shown clearly on a scattergraph. Ideally, the relationship is close enough for you to be able to draw a best fit line. A best fit line is a straight line that goes through or close to all, or almost all, the points on a scattergraph. Each axis shows a different development indicator. There are several combinations of data sets. It is interesting to test out pairs of data sets and see the results achieved.

Activities

1. Study table **B**.
   a. Which country has the highest GNI per capita?
   b. Find evidence to show how the country named in a uses its wealth to benefit its people.
   c. Which country has the lowest GNI per capita?
   d. In which ways is the poverty of the country named in c obvious from other development indicators?

2. Study graph **C**.
   a. Describe the relationship between GNI and birth rate.
   b. What is meant by the term 'anomaly'?
   c. Name two countries that are anomalous in graph **C**. Suggest possible reasons for these anomalies.
   d. Do you think the variables in graph **C** show a clear correlation? Explain your answer.

3. Study table **B**.
   a. Draw a scattergraph to see if there is a relationship between GNI (on the horizontal axis) and another development indicator of your choice.
   b. Try to draw a best-fit line for your graph.
   c. Discuss how closely your data sets correlate. Remember to point out any anomalies. Give reasons for the patterns you have identified.

11.3 What factors make global development inequalities worse?

■ Physical factors

The physical geography of some countries does not favour development, these include mountainous terrain, swamp land, deserts, etc. Africa has more landlocked countries than any other continent and this makes trade less easy due mainly to the inability to have coastal ports. Tropical Africa, South America and Asia tend to be the poorest world regions and these areas suffer from more climate-related diseases than cooler parts of the world. Many people in the Tropics are debilitated by malaria and other diseases. HIV/Aids is a recent health problem from which sub-Saharan Africa has suffered particularly badly. People cannot improve their standard of living when they are so ill, and many children are orphaned.

Climatic hazards such as drought regularly strike Africa, especially Ethiopia, Eritrea and Somalia in the east. These limit future development and destroy what may already have been achieved.

Water

Poor water quality causes disease, which debilitates people and prevents economic development. Many tropical countries suffer from endemic malaria, yellow fever, bilharzia and river blindness. Diseases are carried in water and water quality is unreliable.

In some countries, rainfall amounts vary hugely through the year and irrigation may not be an option.

■ Economic factors

Poverty causes poverty. Low life expectancy and low standard of living, as well as factors like corruption, make an almost impossible base from

> **In this section you will learn**
> different factors that contribute to development inequalities.

> **Did you know** ??????
> As a rule, Africa exports raw materials (mainly minerals and petroleum) and imports manufactured goods. The production of export goods employs around 2 million people over the whole continent, a fraction of the total population of over 934 million. Companies involved are transnational corporations (TNCs), so profits go to their bases abroad. African governments have sometimes squandered their profits, so trade has been of little help towards true development.

∞ links
Find out more about the importance of clean water at **www.wateraid.org.uk**

A *Drought in Somalia*

which to develop and expand. The poorest countries are those in, or just emerging from, civil wars, e.g. Democratic Republic of the Congo, Burundi, Somalia and Sierra Leone. Ethiopia had a successful history yet today it is one of the world's poorest nations due to famine and war. Global trade policies have not favoured the poorest countries. Sometime **tariffs** are placed on goods by the purchasing country.

Africa is the least industrialised continent. Even though it has really cheap labour, processing and value-adding is usually done in the purchasing country. Most African exports are primary goods (raw materials) and these are less valuable than processed products.

Companies have been reluctant to invest in Africa due to political instability, unreliable services (such as electricity) and a poorly skilled workforce.

A country's income is primarily measured by its **gross domestic product (GDP)** per capita and the welfare of its people by the human development index (HDI). In general, when the income is low, so is the level of welfare (table **B**).

■ Environmental factors

Occasionally people abuse the land, but there are often understandable reasons for doing so. Farmers on the verge of starvation are unlikely to be concerned about the rainforest they are cutting down to try to feed their families. Throughout the Sahel region just south of the Sahara, deforestation and overgrazing have increased desertification. Wildlife have been sacrificed to poachers when they could have been the basis of a successful tourist industry. Poor governments have little spare money or resources to protect and develop environmental resources.

■ Social factors

Education

A poor country finds it difficult to fund education for all children to a good level. Investors are put off by the lack of an educated workforce.

Health

When Sierra Leone got its independence in 1963 it had a health system in place, but as a poor country it has not been able to maintain this. It is difficult for sick people to work hard, so Sierra Leone's economy has spiralled downwards. It is one of the most distressed countries in the world, with an HDI of only 0.0317 (2010).

B GDP per capita and HDI compared, 2010 *2001 data

Continent/ country	GDP per capita ($) (2010)	HDI (out of 1) (2010)
Africa:		
Chad	1,600	0.363
Comoros	1,000	0.428
DR of Congo	300	0.305
Ethiopia	1,000	0.412
Ghana	2,500	0.492
Somalia	600	0.284*
Sudan	2,300	0.475
Zimbabwe	500	0.181
Asia:		
India	3,500	0.585
Indonesia	4,200	0.686
Iran	10,600	0.739
Malaysia	14,700	0.766
Pakistan	2,500	0.527
Philippines	3,500	0.681
Latin America:		
Mexico	13,900	0.793
Peru	9,200	0.758

Key terms

Gross Domestic Product (GDP): the total value of goods and services produced by a country divided by its total population. Foreign income is not included.

Tariffs: government taxes on imported or exported goods.

Activities

1 List two physical and two human factors that make global inequalities worse.

2 Study table **B**.
a Draw a scattergraph to show HDI and GDP per capita for the selected countries shown in the table. Put GDP on the horizontal axis and HDI on the vertical axis.
b Draw a best fit line and describe the relationship.
c To what extent do the countries cluster closely together? Does one continent stand out as being especially different from the others?

11.4 How do physical and human factors increase global inequalities?

Hurricane Ivan

Hurricane Ivan was one of the Caribbean's most powerful and destructive hurricanes. Ivan struck the island of Grenada on 7 September 2004 (map **B**). Winds of 200 km per hour lashed the island causing extensive damage. At its peak in the Gulf of Mexico Ivan reached the size of Texas and was the tenth most intense Atlantic hurricane ever recorded.

Hurricane Ivan affected the entire island of Grenada. Trees were broken and uprooted, services and buildings were destroyed (photo **A**). Roads were seriously blocked by fallen trees, although the coastal defences provided some protection from the storm surge. Thirty-seven people were killed and 90 per cent of houses were damaged or destroyed, including the residence of the Prime Minister. Water, power and telecommunications systems were disrupted and almost all schools were destroyed.

In the short term, people lacked food, clean water and medical care, but these shortages were overcome. In the long term, agriculture, tourism and infrastructure were badly hit and took much longer to repair and replace, and at much greater cost. Hurricane Ivan had a significant impact on the economic and social development of Grenada. It created severe hardship for many people that lasted for several years.

In this section you will learn

the impacts of a natural hazard on development (a physical factor)

the unfairness of world trade (an economic factor)

the effects of water quantity and quality on standards of living (a social factor)

how unstable and corrupt governments limit economic development (a political factor).

Case study

A Hurricane Ivan's damaged landscape

B Hurricane Ivan: a path of destruction

Economic factors

World trade is often unfair. Richer countries want to pay as little as possible for their raw materials, many of which come from developing countries. There is often more supply than demand, which keeps prices low. Poorer countries find themselves competing against each other for business and have lowered their prices to attract buyers for commodities such as tea, bananas, sugar, etc. The result is that poor farmers do not receive enough to support their families.

Social factors

Clean water is essential to ensure good health and enable people to work effectively to earn a living. It also means good crop production. If water is in short supply, people have to spend time searching for it and wasting valuable energy carrying it. If water is dirty and contaminated, people become ill and less able to work and support their families. Great improvements in standard of living have been experienced by villages whose water supply has been made secure and clean.

C *Collecting water from a burst water pipe in Iraq*

Political factors

Corrupt politicians enrich themselves illegally at the expense of their country's development. When this happens, money is not available for education, health services, roads, clean water and sanitation. People in the Solomon Islands and Zimbabwe have suffered from corrupt governments. In Zimbabwe, highly productive land that was previously owned by large-scale white farmers was taken over by government officials and 'war veterans'. The country's economy has been almost completely destroyed and inflation has exceeded 1,000 per cent.

Corrupt governments are unstable. Foreign investors and aid providers are discouraged from putting funds into such a country because they cannot rely on the money reaching the target. Economies that are already weak cannot afford to miss out on this income.

Activities

1 Study map **B** on page 259.

a Make a list of the countries affected by Hurricane Ivan in September 2004.

b Describe the impacts of Hurricane Ivan on Grenada.

c Why was it difficult for individuals, families and the Grenada government to recover from the physical impacts of Hurricane Ivan?

2 Study photo **C**

a What are the people in the photo doing?

b Do you think the water is safe? Explain your answer.

c How would clean water supplied directly to their homes improve the quality of life of the people in the photo?

3 Undertake some Internet research into the economic and developmental impacts of another physical hazard on poorer parts of the world. Try earthquakes, volcanoes and river floods. Consider the impact of your choice on the future development of the country(ies) concerned.

11.5 How can international efforts reduce global inequalities?

■ Loans and aid

Loans are sums of money that at some time in the future have to be paid back with interest. Brazil borrowed huge sums in the 1970s. The aim was to build factories, manufacture goods for export and make a profit. Loans were to be repaid from that profit. This policy was successful but not all countries have been so lucky.

Aid is gifts of money, goods, food, machinery, technology and trained workers. True aid is not a loan that needs to be repaid. However, in the real world some 'aid' really is a loan because some form of payback is required. Many people in the richer world want to relieve the poorer world of its debt burden. There is popular support for attempts to reduce poverty, as shown by the marches that took place in London and Edinburgh in 2005 (photo **A**).

Loans and their impacts

A country in need of funds for development projects can borrow from other countries, world financial organisations (e.g. IMF, World Bank) or international banks. If the project is a success, the debt is repaid. However, often things do not go according to plan and the country defaults on the debt, which then has to be paid back over a longer period. People in the debtor country have to work hard to produce goods for export to fund the interest on the loan. Standard of living and level of development simply cannot improve.

Debt relief and abolition

Poorer countries can be helped by debt relief. This means reducing the interest rate or the amount of the loan. Sometimes debts are abolished or written off. Debtor nations (those who have borrowed) benefit hugely as they can begin to improve life for their citizens. Today, there is pressure for some richer countries to write off debts to poorer countries who are unlikely to be able to repay them.

Loan solutions

Micro-enterprises may be the way forward. Non-profit groups in the USA have been lending money to individuals in poor countries. Sara Garcia in Lima, Peru borrowed $1,845 in 1984. She invested in equipment to make patterned handkerchiefs. She hired extra workers and family members to help. Output has risen from 20 to 500 items per day. She met her repayments on time. The technology used was appropriate, allowing the business to become sustainable and successful.

In this section you will learn

the key differences between loans and aid

how debt results from loans and how individuals and countries are affected

the concept of Fairtrade, and its advantages and disadvantages for producers and consumers

the different types of aid

the advantages and disadvantages of aid for both recipient and donor countries.

Did you know ??????

Each year Africa sends more money to Western bankers in interest on its debts than it receives in foreign aid from these countries. Relieving at least some of the debt would help these economies grow, as long as they are well managed.

 Make Poverty History march, 2005

Did you know ??????

Loans from governments, world organisations and banks from countries at lesser stages of development total $1.2 trillion.

Conservation swaps

Conservation swaps are agreements whereby a proportion of a country's debts are written off in exchange for a promise by the debtor country to undertake environmental conservation projects. These were first set up by environment groups in the 1980s to reduce the debt problem of poor countries and to promote the conservation of important environments.

Between 1987 and 2001, 50 countries took part. The first swap took place in Bolivia, South America. A North American conservation group took over $650,000 of Bolivia's national debt in return for the Bolivian government setting aside a large area of rainforest as a nature reserve (Photo **B**). Other countries that have taken part in such schemes include Guatemala, Peru, Ecuador, Costa Rica and Poland.

B *Bolivian rain forest*

Fairtrade

Fairtrade is an international movement ensuring producers in poor countries get a fair deal. They receive a minimum guaranteed price for their crop, which provides them with a living wage, long-term contracts for security and skills training to develop their businesses.

Table **D** shows the rapid growth in Fairtrade goods consumed in the UK between 1999 and 2009. The volume of goods produced increased by 150 per cent in 2006/07 alone. Around 7 million farmers, farm workers and their families in 58 poorer countries benefit from the improved trading conditions brought about by Fairtrade. Recognition of the Fairtrade Mark has grown rapidly in the 21st century. Almost 70 per cent of adults in the UK know what it means.

Aid: positives and negatives

Short-term aid in the form of disaster relief can help to save lives, particularly after a natural disaster. **Long-term aid** can build schools and hospitals, and invest in industry and agriculture. There are many successes, both large and small scale.

During the 1990s it was realised that many poorer countries were not improving with aid and many richer countries cut their contributions. Some aid is lost to corrupt governments and individuals. A lack of infrastructure can prevent development happening as planned, for example schools and hospitals cannot operate without roads and power. Trained staff may not be available. Too much aid has been tied, which means the **donor country** gains more than the **recipient country**.

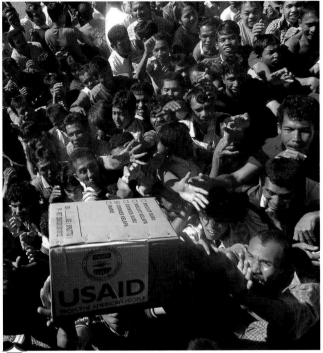

C   *Disaster relief in Indonesia*

D   *Fairtrade goods consumed in the UK, 2002 – 2012 (£ millions)*

Product	Year						
	2002	2005	2008	2009	2010	2011	2012
Coffee	23.1	65.8	137.3	160	179.8	193	192.4
Tea	7.2	16.6	64.8	70.3	82.6	87.1	79.7
Cocoa/chocolate	3.9	13.2	25.6	44.5	162	212.8	320.9
Honey	4.9	3.5	5.2	3.6	6.8	3.8	3.6
Bananas	17.3	47.7	184.6	215.5	206.6	210.9	242.5
Flowers	n/a	5.7	33.4	30	27.6	26.4	23.7
Wine	n/a	3.3	10	18.1	18.5	21.8	23.9
Cotton	n/a	0.2	77.9	73.2	51.7	41	39.6
Other	n/a	6.4	21.8	26.2	23.5	27	28
Total	56.4	162.4	560.6	641.4	759.1	823.8	954.3

∞ **links**

More on Guatemala's debt for nature swap can be found at **www.wildlifeextra.com/go/news/guatemala-debt.html**.

You can find out more about Kuapa Kokoo by entering the name of the organisation into the search box on **www.fairtrade.org.uk**.

Possible effects of the recent global recession

The recent global economic recession has affected most countries in the world, though at differing rates. The problems of the wealthier countries will spread to all those with whom they trade or exchange loans or debts. Countries that normally donate aid will have less to give away in aid or to lend. As world prices decrease, poorer countries will receive less for their exports. These countries will no longer be able to repay the interest on their debts to richer countries and to global financial institutions. They may therefore go even further into debt.

E *Advantages and disadvantages of aid for donor and recipient countries*

Type of aid	Donor countries		Recipient countries	
	Advantages	Disadvantages	Advantages	Disadvantages
Short-term aid	People give willingly in a disaster – 'feel-good factor'	None	Immediate help – lives saved Flow of aid may continue following publicity of the disaster	Occasionally, well-meaning governments and organisations fail to provide exactly what is needed
Long-term aid	Companies and individuals find satisfying and well-paid work in projects overseas Trade may continue into the future	None	New industries improve skills and employment Agricultural improvements – new and better crops New infrastructure such as schools and hospitals built Trade may continue into the future	Tied aid – makes recipient country reliant on donor country Local people may not have sufficient skills and training to reach senior posts Agricultural change may not be sustainable – level of technology too high Lack of money for fuel, spare parts, etc. May not be sufficient funding to maintain schools and hospitals to an adequate level Local people may lose their land to large-scale projects
Top-down aid	Coordinated by government or international organisations – makes donor feel in control	Projects swallow large amounts of money – donors may feel it is wasted	Capital-intensive – aims to improve country as a whole Large projects, e.g. dams, improve national infrastructure	Most ordinary people do not benefit directly
Bottom-up aid	NGO aid, so individuals give to charity – 'feel-good factor' Feeling of direct link between donor and recipient – e.g. sponsorship schemes like ActionAid	None	NGOs work with recipient communities, who have input into the project Money not lost to corruption Appropriate technology used, so projects are sustainable	Charity funds may reduce in economic recession

Activities

1. Study photo **A**.
   a. Make a list of possible reasons for going on this march.
   b. Several moves have been made to improve both debt and aid problems. Suggest why these are likely to be successful or unsuccessful.

2. Study table **D**.
   a. Draw a series of line graphs to show the consumption of Fairtrade goods in the UK. Notice that some of the lines will be longer than others! Use different colours and a key. Plot the years on the x-axis and consumption on the y-axis.
   b. Describe the overall trend shown by the lines and comment on differences between the lines.
   c. Do you and your family choose to buy Fairtrade products? Why?

11.6 How successful are development projects?

A large-scale aid project

The Cahora Bassa dam, Mozambique – an example of bilateral aid

The project

The Cahora Bassa dam was begun by the Portuguese government of Mozambique in the 1960s. It was completed three decades later. Civil war (1977–1992) prevented development and use of the scheme, as well as damaging its infrastructure. Renewal work did not begin until 1995, ending in 1997.

It is the largest HEP scheme in southern Africa, with five huge turbines and a surface area second only to Nasser behind Egypt's huge Aswan dam. Three major dams have been constructed in the River Zambezi Basin.

Who has benefited?

Despite this huge resource, only 1 per cent of Mozambique's rural homes have a direct electricity supply and this level has hardly changed during the life of the dam. Most of the power is sold to South Africa, which makes money for the Mozambican economy but does little for its citizens. The Cahora Bassa dam has much greater potential than what it produces today. It could provide the whole of Mozambique with all the power it needs for the foreseeable future as long as some natural gas, solar and wind projects are also developed to serve the most rural areas.

Environmental impact

Having three dams in one basin has caused environmental damage. River flow is low because so much water is held in reservoirs. The shrimp fishing industry in the lower valley has been almost destroyed. A new dam, the Mepuna Uncua, was planned in 2005 downstream from Cahora Bassa, even though the existing dam is not operating at anywhere near its full capacity. The environmental consequences of this are uncertain, but risky.

Success?

Has Cahora Bassa been a success as a development project? Certainly it has much greater potential than has ever been realised. Perhaps if it had concentrated on serving Mozambique, its success would have been much greater. Also, if it was to work in harmony with other dams, its total potential might serve the whole region of Mozambique plus its neighbouring countries. It was hoped that the Cahora Bassa dam would bring major river flooding under control. Some success has been experienced, but with more careful control much more could be achieved.

In this section you will learn

detailed case studies of aid at different scales and from different donors

Case study

Fact file

- Catchment area: 56,927 km²
- Length of lake: 292 km
- Maximum width of lake: 38 km
- Surface area of lake: 2,739 m
- Average depth of lake: 20.9 m
- Maximum depth of lake: 157 m

A *Cahora Bassa dam fact file*

B *The Cahora Bassa dam*

A medium-scale aid project

ActionAid, Mumbai, India

ActionAid is a UK charity working in local communities in the developing world to alleviate poverty. Its six target areas of relief are:

- HIV/Aids
- hunger and food
- women's rights
- the right to education for all
- the right to security
- the right to good government.

ActionAid works in the poorest districts of Mumbai such as Dharavi, known as the world's worst slum. This area has unimaginably high population densities and few services.

Some of ActionAid's work is done through sponsorship schemes. Donors are encouraged either to give monthly to general projects or to sponsor a child and his or her family or community. This is a successful approach. Donors like the idea of improving the life chances of an individual, especially that of a child.

ActionAid's donors feel they are doing something worthwhile for real people. Low technology is used. Local people benefit, both individuals and communities, but costs remain low. Environmental quality is improved as sustainability is an important aspect of ActionAid's work.

A small-scale aid project

Community Youth Empowerment Programme, Uganda

Restless Development (formerly Student Partnership Worldwide (SPW)) is a UK-based organisation placing gap-year students in development projects in countries like Uganda. They work with school pupils and farmers. Volunteer UK and Ugandan students work together to:

- raise awareness of the Aids risk in order to prevent as many infections as possible, especially among young people, through non-formal education techniques in school such as role-play and drama
- improve knowledge of environmental health concerns such as nutrition, sanitation and waste management
- teach energy conservation methods such as how to construct a fuel-efficient stove or how to start a tree nursery to provide precious fuelwood
- promote sustainable organic farming ideas.

Projects have included the following examples:

1   In Kebager village, the three natural springs were polluted. Restless Development students constructed a covered water tank to keep pollution out. People took their supplies from this by tap, so water never

C *Restless Development works with school pupils in countries like Uganda*

lay open to risk. Appropriate technology has improved living standards as well as enhancing the environment.

2   In Bwanyanga village, both the primary and secondary schools received Restless Development students as volunteer teachers, who provided a number of lessons and workshops over the course of six months. These focused on sexual health awareness and improving life skills. These projects were well received but suffered setbacks due to issues with school fees affecting the attendance of pupils.

Activities

1   Study the case study on the Cahora Bassa dam.

a   Who are the winners and who are the losers in this project? Make two lists to show who has benefited and who has suffered.

b   Decide whether the dam should have been built, giving reasons for your answer based on your answer to a.

2   a   Why do you think medium- and small-scale projects are considered to be more appropriate than large-scale projects?

b   Consider the short-term and long-term benefits of improving water quality and education in Uganda.

11.7 How do levels of development vary within the EU?

A The 28 EU member countries

There are marked variations in levels of development in the EU (map **A**). Table **B** (page 268) shows three measures of development for all 28 EU countries. They have been selected to show you that there are many similarities and some differences. HDI is high for every member country and life expectancy is always over 70 years. GDP per capita is the indicator that really shows up the clearest differences. Luxembourg's GDP per capita is almost seven times higher than that of Bulgaria. The older members of the EU have higher GDP per capita than the newer ones.

Contrasting two EU countries: Bulgaria and Ireland

Bulgaria

Bulgaria's population in 2011 of 7,364,570 was lower by almost 1 million than in 1998. People are leaving to find better opportunities in the rest of the EU, which Bulgaria joined in 2007. Today it is a democracy, but previously it was politically and economically dominated by the USSR and was a Communist country. With the break-up of the Communist bloc in the 1990s, its standard of living fell by 40 per cent. Although Bulgaria is the second poorest country in the EU and on its **economic periphery**, new funding and projects are improving quality of life.

Ireland

Ireland's 2011 population of 4,581,269 is growing slowly because of natural increase and migrant labour. Until it joined the EU in 1973, it was a poor country within Europe. Membership has benefited Ireland enormously, changing its focus from agriculture to a high-tech service economy. Its 10 per cent per annum economic growth rate from 1995 to 2000 earned it the title 'Celtic tiger' and brought it from being on the economic periphery to be very much part of the **economic core.**

B *EU comparative development indicators (2010/2011)*

Country	HDI rank in the world	Human Development Index (HDI) (2010)	Life expectancy at birth (years) (2011 est.)	GDP per capita ($) (2010)
Ireland	5	0.895	80.2	37,300
Sweden	9	0.885	81.1	39,100
Netherlands	7	0.890	79.7	40,300
France	14	0.872	81.2	33,100
Finland	16	0.871	79.3	35,400
Spain	20	0.863	81.2	29,400
Denmark	19	0.866	78.6	36,600
Austria	25	0.851	79.8	40,400
UK	26	0.849	80.1	34,800
Belgium	18	0.867	79.5	37,800
Luxembourg	24	0.852	79.6	82,600*
Italy	23	0.854	82.0	30,500
Germany	10	0.885	80.1	35,700
Greece	22	0.855	79.9	29,600
Slovenia	29	0.828	77.3	28,200
Cyprus	35	0.810	77.8	21,000
Portugal	40	0.795	78.5	23,000
Czech Rep	28	0.841	77.2	25,600
Malta	33	0.815	79.7	25,600
Hungary	36	0.805	74.8	18,800
Poland	41	0.795	76.1	18,800
Slovakia	31	0.818	75.8	22,000
Lithuania	44	0.783	75.3	16,000
Estonia	34	0.812	73.3	19,100
Latvia	48	0.769	72.7	14,700
Bulgaria	58	0.743	73.6	13,500
Romania	50	0.767	74.0	11,600
Croatia	46	0.796	77.0	18,200

* Third highest in the world

■ EU policies to reduce inequalities

The Common Agricultural Policy (CAP)

The CAP includes a system of subsidies paid to EU farmers. Its main purposes are to:

- guarantee minimum levels of production so that there is enough food for Europe's population
- ensure a fair standard of living for farmers
- ensure reasonable prices to customers.

Supporters of the CAP say it guarantees the survival of rural communities, where more than half of EU citizens live, and preserves the appearance of the countryside. Critics say that as only 5 per cent of EU citizens work in agriculture, which generates only 1.6 per cent of GDP, the CAP costs too much (extract **C**).

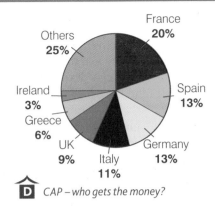

D   *CAP – who gets the money?*

E   *Common Agricultural Policy supports sheep farming in the EU*

News

Home | Contact | Sitemap | News | Forum | Shop

The Common Agricultural Policy is regarded by some as one of the EU's most successful policies, and by others as a scandalous waste of money.

A series of reforms has been carried out in recent years, the most significant being the Single Payment Scheme introduced in 2003, intended to break the link between farm aid and production.

In the latest reforms, announced in November 2008, farmers are to have more of their subsidies for food production diverted towards rural development. Milk quotas will be boosted before being scrapped in 2015.

Instead of paying farmers to produce more, the EU now makes payments conditional on farmers meeting environmental and animal welfare standards and keeping their land in good condition.

C   *From the BBC News website*   *Adapted from BBC News website* **news.bbc.co.uk**, *20 November 2008*

The addition of 10 new member countries in 2004, together with Bulgaria and Romania three years later, brought another 7 million farmers into the EU. In 2009 there was a total of 12 million farmers in the EU. CAP cannot possibly maintain them at the previous Western European level.

European Investment Bank (EIB)

Money from the European Investment Bank is invested in regional development. Some regions are suffering difficulties because of the decline of local industry or reduced farm incomes. Projects are usually locally based and funds are used to train people with new skills and to help set up new businesses.

Did you know ??????

CAP costs about £34 billion (€43 billion in 2008) a year, just over half the total EU budget of £60 billion. Most of this goes straight to farmers. Another £5 billion (€7.7 billion) is spent on rural development. This adds £9 to a family of four's weekly food bill.

Urban II fund

Most Europeans live in urban areas because they are the centres of economic activity and hold greater opportunities. However, all cities have concentrations of social, environmental and economic problems. Urban II fund money comes from the European Regional Development Fund and it is for **sustainable development** in troubled districts of European cities. It aims to provide economic and social regeneration. Any successful idea in one city is shared with others to try to improve living conditions as widely as possible.

Social and economic urban regeneration includes:

- improving living conditions (e.g. renovating older buildings)
- creating new jobs in services that benefit the whole population
- integrating less-favoured groups of people into education and training so that they can find satisfactory employment
- developing environmentally friendly transport systems
- making greater use of renewable energy
- using the most up-to-date ICT systems to make work more efficient and to improve people's skills and therefore their job prospects.

Urban II has 70 different programmes that affect 2.2 million people. Its budget was €728.3 million between 2000 and 2006. Money is divided according to need, which is measured by population numbers and unemployment rates. See table **F**.

Structural funds

Structural funds support poorer regions of Europe and improve infrastructure, particularly transport. Together with CAP, it makes up most of EU spending. Regions whose GDP per capita is less than 75 per cent of the EU average are targeted. The aim is to accelerate economic development so they catch up with other regions. The budget for 2007–13 is €347.41 billion. In addition, the most deprived regions will receive extra money from other funds.

F Urban II fund across Europe, 2000–06

Country	Urban II fund (Euros)
Austria	8,400,000
Belgium	21,200,000
Denmark	5,300,000
Finland	5,300,000
France	102,000,000
Germany	148,700,000
Greece	25,500,000
Ireland	5,300,000
Italy	114,800,000
Netherlands	29,800,000
Portugal	19,200,000
Spain	112,600,000
Sweden	5,300,000
UK	124,300,000

Key terms

Sustainable development: this allows economic growth to happen over a long period of time without harming the environment. It benefits people alive today but does not compromise future generations.

Case study

Teruel, Spain

The people of the town of Teruel in northern Spain have a new ring road, paid for by Urban II funds. It will reduce traffic flows through the town by at least 20 per cent, cutting congestion and improving travel times and air quality in the town. The new road also links previously isolated neighbourhoods. There are paths for cyclists and joggers. The project cost €16.6 million.

Activities

1 Study Table **B**.
a Which countries have the highest life expectancy in Europe?
b Suggest possible reasons for this.

2 Use the Internet and the information in this section to carry out a comparative study of Bulgaria and Ireland. Try to identify how and why the two countries differ in terms of their development.

3 Describe the effects of the Urban II fund on the town of Teruel. Try to find some information and photographs from the Internet to support your study.

4 Work in small groups to suggest how deprived regions of the EU could be best helped to enable them to catch up with the wealthier regions. Present your research in the form of a large information poster.

12 Globalisation

12.1 What is globalisation?

Have you heard the phrase 'The world is shrinking'? It's often used to describe the way that technology such as satellites, the Internet and high speed travel have reduced the 'distance' between places. Everywhere seems closer together and more interconnected. Consider all the world brands in the High Street. This increasing connectivity and interdependence in the world is what is meant by **globalisation**.

This has been made possible by the relaxation of laws allowing foreign investment in countries (which encouraged the rise of transnational corporations, or TNCs), the increased provision and speed of international transport and developments in communication with the use of fax, telephone and e-mail.

Nike is a TNC that manufactures footwear and clothing. It has 124 plants in China, 73 in Thailand, 35 in South Korea, 34 in Vietnam and others elsewhere in Asia. In addition, it has factories in South America, Australia, Canada, Italy, Turkey and the USA. Africa is the only inhabited continent not represented.

In this section you will learn

what is meant by the term 'globalisation'

about the increased interdependence and interrelationships that result from greater connectivity between the different countries.

Key terms

Globalisation: the increasing links between different countries throughout the world and the greater interdependence that results from this.

Interdependence: the relationship between two or more countries, usually in terms of trade.

Study tip

Ensure that you explain the meanings of the terms 'globalisation', 'interdependence' and 'transnational corporation' (defined on page 276).

A *Nike shoes on sale in China*

■ The production of a Wimbledon tennis ball

Slazenger has supplied the All England Club since 1902. Dunlop Slazenger is responsible for making the 48,000 balls that supply the showpiece tournament in June each year. From the 1940s to 2002, the tennis balls were made at Barnsley, south Yorkshire. However, in an attempt to boost profits by cutting labour costs, production shifted to Bataan in the Philippines in 2002.

Table **B** shows the ingredients for making the tennis balls and their origin. Many of the components are used to vulcanise the rubber so that the balls have the correct amount of bounce. They are all transported to Bataan for manufacture, before being despatched to London.

B *The manufacture of a Wimbledon tennis ball*

Ingredient	Origin	Destination
Wool	New Zealand	UK
Cloth (made from wool)	UK	Philippines
Dyes	UK	Philippines
Silica	Greece	Philippines
Zinc oxide	Thailand	Philippines
Rubber	Malaysia	Philippines
Tins	Indonesia	Philippines
Clay	USA	Philippines
Magnesium carbonate	Japan	Philippines
Sulphur	South Korea	Philippines
Tennis balls (product)	Philippines	UK

C *A Wimbledon tennis match*

Activities

1 a Write down a definition of 'globalisation' and give one example to illustrate it.

b Compare your answer with a partner's and agree on a definition.

c Now work together to make a list of international companies that have shops or businesses in your local town or city centre.

2 Study table **B**.

a On a world political map outline, draw flow lines to show the movement of materials to the Philippines and then the completed tennis balls to the UK.

b Describe how your map illustrates the concept of 'globalisation'.

c Why might it be said that the production of the cloth to cover the tennis balls is the best example of the globalisation process?

∞ links

Find out more about globalisation by typing the word into the search box at **www.bbc.co.uk**.

12.2 How has globalisation changed manufacturing and services worldwide?

■ The influence of developments in ICT

Improvements in transport and communications have been largely responsible for the spread of manufacturing and services worldwide. Look at Graph **A**. Notice how transport and communication costs have fallen over the years.

Much of the advances made in communication are the result of developments in satellites. A satellite is an object that revolves around the earth following a particular path or orbit. It is usually built for a specific purpose, for example, weather or communications satellites (Photo **B**) . Consider how much the media depends on satellite for television (i.e. Sky) and for transmitting sports fixtures 'live' around the world.

1930 costs = 100   **1970 costs = 100**

Legend:
- Transatlantic phone call [1]
- Sea freight [2]
- Air transport [3]
- Satellite charges

Costs / Date

Original source: HM Treasury

[1] Cost of three-minute telephone call from New York to London
[2] Average ocean freight and port charges per short ton of import and export cargo
[3] Average air transport revenue per passenger mile

A *Falling transport and communication costs*

The development of submarine cables has been important in allowing global operations for both manufacturing and service industry. These underwater cables link western Europe with SE Asia, the Middle East and Australia, providing high speed transmission of data.

Did you know ??????

Submarine cables can be accidentally damaged. On 26 December 2006, an earthquake damaged SEA-ME-WE3 cables off Taiwan and, on 30 January 2008, a ship's anchor damaged the SEA-ME-WE4 off Egypt.

B *Satellites are used for high-speed communications*

■ Small industrial region with global connections

Developments in ICT have allowed immediate access to people all over the world and fostered developments in small areas, knowing that communication across the world is possible. This has led to a cluster of world-famous companies associated with motor racing in an axis between Northampton and Oxford in the southern part of the British Midlands (map **C**). This area is known as Motorsport Valley®.

① Aston Martin Lagonda
② Cosworth
③ Force India F1
④ Fortec Motorsport
⑤ Lotus Renault
⑥ Mercedes AMG Petronas
⑦ Prodrive
⑧ Red Bull Racing
⑨ Ricardo
⑩ Williams F1
✈ Airport
＼ Motorways
■ Silverstone

C The location of Motorsport Valley®

Fact file

Motorsport Valley® fact file

• Almost 40,000 people employed including over 25,000 world-class engineers.

• 2,200 businesses relating to design, research and development, and event organisation.

• Over 80 per cent of the world market in high-performance engineering.

• Sales of around £6 billion, of which 60 per cent are exports.

• About one third of the total profits are reinvested into research and development.

D Sebastian Vettel, Red Bull Racing

Did you know ??????

Several F1 teams are based in Motorsport Valley® including the 2010 and 2011 Constructor's Champions, Red Bull Racing. Silverstone is the home of the British Grand Prix and attracts many racing-based industry including the Force India F1 team. Rockingham Motor Speedway near Corby, Mallory Park near Leicester and Donington Park near Derby also host major race meetings.

■ The development of call centres abroad

A **call centre** is an office where people respond to telephone enquiries, often relating to banking, communications (Internet, telephones, etc.) and the media. Call centres are big business and in the UK they employ 400,000 workers, often in small towns such as Harrogate, Carlisle, Gateshead and Warrington. Banks and other finance companies such as insurance were among the first to develop centralised call centres and the first to look abroad. Household names such as ASDA, Tesco, BA, BT, Barclays, Lloyds TSB, HSBC and Virgin Media have all set up call centres in India. It is the big cities that house these, such as Mumbai, Delhi, Hyderabad and Bangalore (map **E**). Other important destinations for call centres abroad are South Africa and the Philippines.

About 10 per cent of the population (some 100 million people) speak English fluently

Of the 787 million living in towns, about 80 per cent are literate and 18 per cent of these are graduates

Operating costs are between 10 and 60 per cent lower than in the UK

Salaries are lower, e.g. £1,200 per year in contrast to £12,000 per year in the UK

Low staff turnover, working nine-hour shifts at times to fit in with origin country of company

Development of ICT allows fast and clear communication

E Telephone call centres in India

Activities

1 Study graph **A** on page 273.

a What is the significance of the 100 value on the y-axis?

b What happened to the cost of a transatlantic phone call between 1930 and 1950?

c State two changes in communication costs between 1930 and 2000.

d Give evidence from the graph to support the changes described in c.

2 Study map **C** and the fact file. Produce a leaflet on Motorsport Valley® to illustrate the cluster of motor sports industry and the reasons for it. Your leaflet should include the following:

■ a labelled sketch map to show the advantages of the location

■ a labelled photo of one of the companies present

■ five good reasons for locating an automotive industry here, including one that relates to ICT developments and the need for international communications.

3 Study map **E**. Work in pairs for this activity. Imagine you are director of customer relations for a call centre in India. You are being interviewed about your reasons for choosing to locate abroad for national television news. Present the questions you were asked and your answers to them.

∞ links

You can find out more about submarine cables at **www.telegeography.com**.

More information on Motorsport Valley® can be found at **www.thebritishmidlands.com**.

Visit **www.call-centres.com** for more on call centres.

12.3 What are the advantages and disadvantages of TNCs?

Transnational corporations (TNCs) are large, wealthy international organisations. They are companies that have their headquarters in one country, but often have many other branches spread across much of the world. As a result of improvements in transport and communications, TNCs have grown steadily over the last 30 years.

Most TNCs have their headquarters in richer areas of the world, especially the USA, UK, France, Germany and Japan. Research and development is usually centred here. Production often occurs in poorer areas where labour costs are lower, laws more lenient or where governments want to seek investment. Production also occurs in richer areas where benefits include a skilled workforce. Table **A** shows the biggest TNCs according to their value.

A *The top ten non-financial TNCs, 2008*

Rank	TNC	Headquarters	Product
1	General Electric	USA	Electrical/electronic equipment
2	British Petroleum	UK	Petroleum
3	Toyota	Japan	Motor vehicles
4	Royal Dutch/Shell	UK/Netherlands	Petroleum
5	ExxonMobil	USA	Petroleum
6	Ford	USA	Motor vehicles
7	Vodafone	UK	Telecommunications
8	Total	France	Petroleum
9	Electricité de France	France	Electricity/gas/water
10	Wal-Mart	USA	Retail

Advantages of TNCs

TNCs offer many advantages to the countries where they set up branches. They provide jobs in factories making supplies and in services where products are sold. The additional income benefits local businesses, creating a **multiplier effect**. Training of the workforce leads to the development of skills. Often, the infrastructure is improved as better access, both within and between countries, and communications are needed.

Disadvantages of TNCs

A significant disadvantage is that of **leakage**, as well as the fact that in some locations wages are very low and key jobs go to outsiders. If there are problems worldwide economically or within the company, the branch plants may be closed. In some areas, working conditions can be poor and the labour force is expected to work long hours. Health and safety may be an issue and pollution may be a problem in countries where there are less strict rules and regulations.

In this section you will learn

what advantages and disadvantages result from the presence of TNCs in countries

the characteristics of Toyota as a case study of a TNC.

Key terms

Transnational corporation (TNC): a corporation or enterprise that operates in more than one country.

Multiplier effect: where initial investment and jobs lead to a knock-on effect, creating more jobs and providing money to generate services.

Leakage: where profits made by the company are taken out of the country to the country of origin and so do not benefit the host country.

Did you know ??????

The income of Ford and General Motors added together is greater than the GDP of all of sub-Saharan Africa.

Did you know ??????

On 3 December 1984 a gas leak from a chemical factory in Bhopal, India killed 3,000 people immediately and has since led to the deaths of 15,000 others. Some 100,000 people suffered chronic illness as a result of one of the world's worst industrial accidents.

Toyota

Toyota began in Toyota, Aichi, Japan in 1937. Seventy years later, it had become the biggest producer of cars in the world, with profits of $11 billion in 2006. Map **B** shows (in red) the countries where Toyota plants are present and table **C** shows production in different regions in 1996 and 2005.

 B *The global location of Toyota*

Toyota began to develop overseas in the late 1950s in Brazil. From its headquarters in Tokyo, a huge operation is managed with 250,000 workers employed in 26 countries. The company decided to seek to develop production in the UK in the early 1990s. The reasons for this are given in a statement on the company's website (extract **D**). The UK's Burnaston factory, which started production in 1992, is shown in photo **E** and located on the map extract (map **F** p.278).

C *Toyota production by region, 1996 and 2009 (1 = 1,000 vehicles)*

Region	1996	2009
North America	782.9	1,189.1
Latin America	3.2	181.5
Europe	150.3	507.3
Africa	85.0	102.8
Asia	257.0	1,501.4
Oceania	67.6	96.8
Overseas total	1,346.0	3,579.0
Japan	3,410.1	2,792.2
Worldwide total	4,756.1	6,371.3

◄ ► C + http:// ⊙ ⌃ Q▾

Home | Contact | Sitemap | News | Forum | Shop

News

Home
Contact
Sitemap
News
Forum
Shop

So, having established the logic behind building in Europe, why the UK? High up on the list of reasons was the strong tradition of vehicle manufacturing in Britain and the large domestic market for our product. In addition, the UK offered us solid industrial transport links to our customers and our 230 British and European supply partners. Another reason was the excellent workforce and favourable working practices.

There was also a supportive positive attitude to inward investment from the British government at both local and national level. Also of course the English language is very much the second language in Japan, making communication and integration so much easier. In December 1989 Toyota Manufacturing UK was established. Another point to remember is that the location of the engine plant alongside the vehicle manufacturing plant at Burnaston would have reduced Toyota's long-term capacity to expand at that site and indeed would have restricted the opportunity for both plants to expand.

D *Reasons for a UK location, taken from www.toyotauk.com*

E *The Toyota plant at Burnaston*

F 1 : 50,000 OS map extract showing the Burnaston area, part of map sheet 128

⚭ links

You can find out more about Toyota at **www.toyotauk.com**.

Activities

1 Study table **A** on page 276. Work with a partner.

a Find out the identity of a further 10 large TNCs.

b Produce a collage to display the name, logo and line of business in which they are involved. Try to do this in a limited amount of time – say, 20 minutes – to see how you can work under pressure.

2 On a large copy of the table below, summarise the economic, social and environmental advantages and disadvantages of TNCs. One category has been partly done for you to illustrate the types of answers you could include.

3 Study map **B** and table **C** on page 277.

a With the help of an atlas, on an outline world map label 10 countries where Toyota is present. Make sure your labels reflect the global presence of Toyota.

b On your map, draw located bars to show production in each region for 1996 and 2009.

c Describe the pattern shown by your map in 2009.

d Summarise the changes made between 1996 and 2009.

e Where and why do you think Toyota should locate future new branches?

4 Study extract **D** on page 277, photo **E** and map extract **F**.

a Draw and label a sketch map to describe and explain why the location at Burnaston is a good one.

b What advantages did Toyota believe existed in deciding to locate in UK?

c What advantages and disadvantages have resulted from Toyota coming to the UK? Present your answer in the form of a table (see below).

Category	Advantages	Disadvantages
Economic		
Social	People may feel more secure with a job and regular income.	Working conditions are poor. Workers have to suffer crowded, hot conditions and work for many hours at a stretch.
Environmental		

12.4 How and why is manufacturing in different countries changing?

■ Changes in relative importance of world regions

Manufacturing industry has declined in importance in some regions, while it has become more significant in others. The changes in high-tech manufacturing are shown in graph **A**. In many of the richest areas of the world, manufacturing has declined. For example, in Britain the number of people employed in manufacturing fell from just over 6 million in 1981 to 2.49 million in 2010. This is the result of **de-industrialisation**, which has occurred because of increased mechanisation and the need for industry to be competitive.

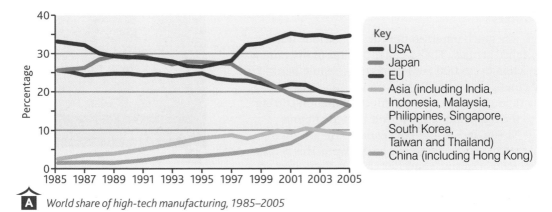

A *World share of high-tech manufacturing, 1985–2005*

Reasons for changes

There are many reasons why some areas have experienced growth in manufacturing industry whereas others have suffered a decline.

1 Government legislation

This can take many forms, such as:

- setting up areas (**assisted areas/enterprise zones**) where conditions are favourable for new industry, for example lower taxes
- providing **advanced factories** of various sizes
- offering retraining and removal expenses
- ensuring educational reform is high on the list in areas such as the four Asian 'tigers'.

Some countries have a minimum wage. In the UK, this is currently £6.08 per hour for those aged 21 years and older (2012 figures), but in Sri Lanka garment workers are often paid a fraction of a much lower minimum wage.

An EU directive limits the maximum number of hours worked per week to 48 (except in the UK). The average South Korean works 2,390 hours a year in contrast to 1,652 in UK. This has real implications for production. In Sri Lanka, garment workers should not work after 10pm

Key terms

De-industrialisation: a process of decline in some types of industry over a long period of time. It results in fewer people being employed in this sector and falling production.

Assisted areas/enterprise zones: areas that qualify for government help. Enterprise zones are on a smaller scale than assisted areas.

Advanced factories: where buildings for production are built in the hope they will encourage businesses to buy or rent them.

due to International Labour Organization rules, but they are often forced to do so by their employers.

2 Health and safety regulations

Working conditions tend to vary globally. In the UK, adult employees working over six hours are entitled to a 20-minute break. Workers have the right to:

- know how to do their job safely and to be trained to do so
- know how to get first aid
- know what to do in an emergency
- be supplied with protective clothing.

Such regulations often do not exist in some poorer countries or are not enforced. Some workers – unable to travel home after a shift and arrive back on time for the next shift – sleep on the factory floor, although this is illegal.

3 Prohibition of strikes

In the 1970s, there was much unrest in the UK and various trade unions frequently called **strikes**. The so-called 'winter of discontent' began with strike action by 15,000 Ford workers in September 1978. There were many groups that joined in and power cuts became the norm. Such disruption had an adverse effect on manufacturing industry and led to the reduction of the power of trade unions. Companies such as Nissan and Toyota only came to the UK on the understanding that strike action would not be allowed. This is also true of many newly industrialising countries (NICs). Trade unions are allowed in Sri Lanka, but workers are likely to be threatened if they join one.

4 Tax incentives and tax-free zones

Tax incentives take a variety of forms, but all seek to offset costs. For example, One NorthEast (the development agency responsible for the north-east of England) offered job-creation grants, business rate or rent-free periods and help in preparing a business plan. Regional development agencies closed in 2012 with some of their functions now carried out by local enterprise partnerships.

Tax-free zones are areas where new businesses do not need to pay tax, e.g. parts of Dubai (photo **B**).

■ China: the new industrial giant

China has been dubbed 'the new workshop of the world' (photo **C**), a phrase that was first used to describe Britain during the 19th century. China makes 60 per cent of the world's bicycles (photo **D**) and 72 per cent of the world's shoes. Between 2000 and 2006, cloth manufacture more than doubled and car production increased by more than six times. Mobile phone ownership increased nine times. The National Bureau of Statistics of China is predicting economic growth of at least 7 per cent to 2018. China is currently ranked 2nd in industrial output and is expected to take over 1st place from USA during 2012.

B   *Burj Al Arab Hotel, Dubai*

C   *In 2010 China became the world's largest exporter*

D   *60 per cent of the world's bicycles are made in China*

E   *Chinese knitwear factory, part of a rapidly growing textile sector*

Reasons for China's rapid growth

There are many reasons why China is emerging as the new economic giant.

1 Government legislation

In 1977, Deng Xiaoping sought to end China's isolation and stimulate Chinese industry. Foreign investment was encouraged but the government maintained overall control over the economy so that China would gain maximum benefit.

Between 1980 and 1994 special economic zones (SEZs) were set up. These paved the way for foreign investment by providing tax incentives to foreign companies.

2 The home market

The one-child policy, introduced in 1979, successfully reduced population growth and, as families become wealthier, consumer demand increased. Today China has a large and relatively rich urban population demanding electrical houshold goods, air conditioning, cars and computers. China's massive home market will continue to grow.

Special Economic Zones (SEZ)
1 Pudong District, Shanghai Muncipality
2 Xiamen, Fujian Province
3 Shantou, Guangdong Province
4 Shenzhen, Guangdong Province
5 Zhuhai, Guangdong Province
6 Hainan Province

F *China's Special Economic Zones (SEZs)*

3 The Olympics factor

The 2008 Olympics were held in Beijing. This provided China with the perfect opportunity to showcase the nation. The opening ceremony, based on the theme 'One World, One Dream', was important in an attempt to convey China as a modern, open and friendly country.

4 Energy

Industrial development on a large scale demands large resources of energy. China currently generates two-thirds of its electricity at coal-fired power stations. Many new plants are being built. Hydroelectric power (HEP) accounted for 13.9 per cent of electricity in 2010. China produces more HEP than any other country in the world and is keen to develop new sources of energy. The Three Gorges Dam is the biggest in the world, generating 22,500 mW. Together with the development of navigation along the Yangtse, the dam has led to much development.

G *The Olympics in Beijing*

5 Labour

Cheap labour is a key reason why the economy has been thriving. Wages are 95 per cent lower than in the USA.

H The Three Gorges Dam

Activities

1 Study graph **A** on page 279.

a What percentage of high-tech manufacturing was produced in the EU in 1985 and 2005?

b What percentage of high-tech manufacturing was produced in China in 1985 and 2005?

c Using evidence from the graph, summarise the trends shown.

2 Study map **F** and the text on pp. 281–283.

Produce an information poster (preferably A3 size) identifying the main factors responsible for China's recent economic growth. Use the Internet to find maps and photos to support text boxes. Choose a striking image for the centrepiece of your poster.

∞ links

There are many statistics relating to China that can be found in the National Bureau of Statistics of China at **www.stats.gov/cn/english**.

Research information about China and economic policy, including SEZs, at **www.china.org.cn**.

You can find out more about the Three Gorges Dam at **www.bbc.co.uk**.

12.5 What are the causes and effects of increasing global demand for energy?

There are a number of reasons why there is an increase in demand for energy. Some of these reasons will be considered separately but, in reality, there are links between them. The increasing world population is getting richer and advances in technology increase the availability of products and create an insatiable thirst for energy.

1 World population growth

Table **A** and graph **B** show the overall global increase in population and the relative importance of different regions. Notice how the global population has increased dramatically since 1950 accounting for the recent rapid surge in demand for energy. The rapid rise in the populations of Asian countries combined with their economic growth also accounts for the increase in energy use.

A *Overall global increase in population, 1750–2050*

Year	1750	1800	1850	1900	1950	1999	2050
World population (billions)	0.79	0.98	1.26	1.65	2.52	5.98	8.91

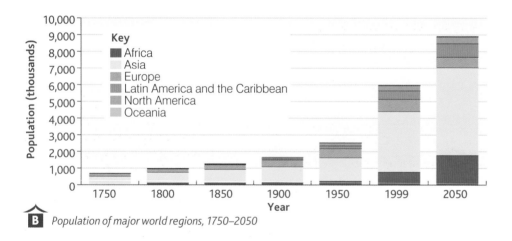

B *Population of major world regions, 1750–2050*

2 Increased wealth

As people become wealthier they demand more products and consumer items, such as electrical devices. These require energy to make and to use.

Consider the following facts and the impact of these on demand for energy:

- The average wage in China has risen to 1750 yuan a month, four times higher than in 1995.
- Private car ownership in China increased from virtually zero in 1997 to 26 million in 2009.
- In the UK, the number of families not owning a car fell from 32 per cent to 27 per cent. In 2009 more households owned two cars than owned no cars at all.

3 Technological advances

Technological advances have supplied us with increasing amounts of energy and a wide variety of goods that we can purchase. The development of steam using coal led to large-scale production in the UK. It is the use of coal in power stations that has fuelled the Chinese economy. Modern technology allows the development of other sources of energy, such as nuclear power. Resources can now be exploited from deep below the sea and in very inhospitable regions, such as the Arctic. Research and development is big business. Companies strive to compete with each other and produce smaller mobile phones, faster laptops, in-house entertainment systems that offer best-quality pictures, most innovative games, etc. People see these and want to buy them. This requires energy to develop, make and run the consumer products that are so much a part of our lives today.

C   *Smog in Beijing, home of the 2008 Olympics, before the games*

■ Social, economic and environmental impacts

The social effects of increased energy use have an impact on people's health. In countries like the UK, the incidence of lung-related diseases such as emphysema and bronchitis was traditionally associated with industrial areas where coal provided the basic source of energy. The incidence of these diseases will increase in areas that are experiencing industrialisation today.

People may also choose to leave cars at home and cycle to work for economic and environmental reasons. Where we go on holiday could also be affected if air fares increase substantially because of rising fuel costs. More people could choose to holiday at home which may benefit the home economy. As energy sources are used up, energy becomes more expensive and new sources of energy need to be found.

In addition, some cities are shrouded in a haze that blocks out the sun and contains a dangerous mix of chemicals, including those from coal smoke and ozone. Photo **C** shows Beijing before the 2008 Olympic Games, when 1.3 million of the city's 3 million cars were taken off the road and 100 factories were closed. Poor air quality leads to asthma and other respiratory diseases.

Other environmental impacts include:

- on land, where spoil heaps have built up adjacent to coal mines when unneeded material has been dumped
- on water, where the transportation of oil has led to major pollution incidents such as the *Exxon Valdez* oil spill off Alaska in 1989 and the *Prestige* sinking off the coast of north-west Spain in 2002
- on air, where poor quality is responsible for ill health on a local scale and for substantial effects on a global scale, where global warming is seen to be the main result (diagram **D**).

Did you know ??????

At the opening ceremony of the Beijing Olympics on 8 August 2008, a British smog monitoring team had to close down its website after it recorded an air pollution index (API) of between 101 and 150 micrograms per m^3 (100 is regarded as safe), whereas the official Chinese figures showed 95.

⚭ links

The Environment Agency gives extensive advice at **www. environment-agency.gov.uk**.

You can investigate air quality at **www.airquality.co.uk** and global warming at **www. worldviewofglobalwarming.org**.

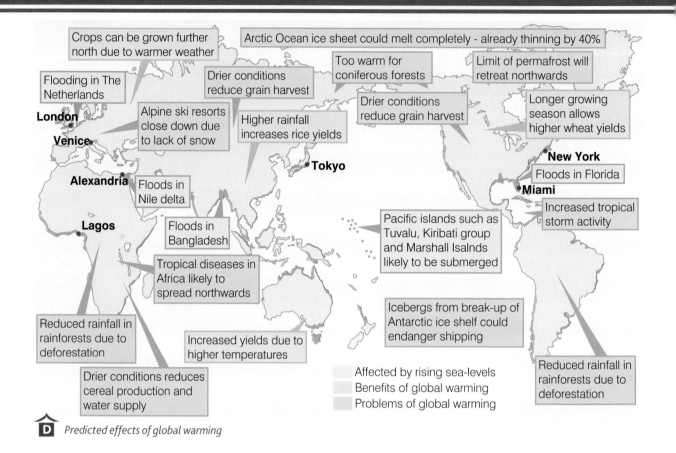

Crops can be grown further north due to warmer weather

Arctic Ocean ice sheet could melt completely - already thinning by 40%

Too warm for coniferous forests

Limit of permafrost will retreat northwards

Flooding in The Netherlands

Drier conditions reduce grain harvest

Drier conditions reduce grain harvest

Longer growing season allows higher wheat yields

London

Alpine ski resorts close down due to lack of snow

Higher rainfall increases rice yields

Venice

Tokyo

New York

Floods in Florida

Alexandria

Floods in Nile delta

Miami

Increased tropical storm activity

Lagos

Floods in Bangladesh

Pacific islands such as Tuvalu, Kiribati group and Marshall Isalnds likely to be submerged

Tropical diseases in Africa likely to spread northwards

Icebergs from break-up of Antarctic ice shelf could endanger shipping

Reduced rainfall in rainforests due to deforestation

Increased yields due to higher temperatures

Reduced rainfall in rainforests due to deforestation

Drier conditions reduces cereal production and water supply

Affected by rising sea-levels
Benefits of global warming
Problems of global warming

D *Predicted effects of global warming*

Activities

1 Study table **A** on page 284.

a Draw a line graph to show the total world population figures from 1750 to 2050.

b Describe the trends shown by the graph you have drawn.

2 Study graph **B** on page 284.

a Summarise the changes in population in the different world regions.

b Explain how the trends account for an increase in the demand for energy. (You may want to refer to section 12.4 on China here.)

3 **a** List the products you and your family own that use energy.

b Ask your parents to highlight the items they would not have owned 10 and 20 years ago.

c How will the amount of energy used by you and your family have changed?

4 Explain how increasing levels of wealth and technological advances have resulted in an increasing demand for energy. Try to illustrate your answer using your own experience.

5 Study photo **C** and diagram **D**. Work in pairs. Produce a poster that summarises the social, economic and environmental impacts of increased energy use. You should include at least one map, one photo and evidence of further research. There should be reference to at least two effects in each category. Try to include facts, figures and information as evidence wherever possible.

12.6 / How can energy use be sustainable?

■ The use of renewable energy

Renewable energy promises sustainable development. Our reliance on fossil fuels to meet our energy needs is only short term. Supplies of coal, oil and natural gas are limited and renewable alternatives have been used for some time, albeit on a relatively small scale. Hydroelectric power (HEP), solar, tidal and wind power are sustainable options (fact file **A**). They share similar advantages over the use of fossil fuels, but are not without their opponents. The recent surge in the use of **biofuels** also appears at first to offer this possibility, but there is debate about this.

> **In this section you will learn**
>
> how the use of renewable energy is sustainable
>
> why some locations are more suited to the development of renewable energy than others and the debate over locations and costs
>
> the importance of international directives and local initiatives in the drive to ensure sustainability.

A

Fact file

Wind power in the UK

- **Aims**: to generate 10 per cent of power by renewable energy sources.

- **Role**: to be responsible for one-third of electricity generated.

- **Number of wind farms and turbines operational in July 2011**: 306.

- **Location**: mostly onshore.

- **The future**: offshore wind farms to become more important, with 8 GW to be generated by 2016.

- **Size of a modern wind turbine**: 100 to 120 m, including the blades. Offshore wind turbines tend to be the largest. For comparison, the London Eye is 135 m high.

- **Offshore operations**: these are usually within 4 to 6 km off the coast, but some planned developments will be over 18 km.

- **Location requirements**: the shallow waters off the coast of the UK are an advantage. Wind farms require an exposed location, whether onshore or offshore, clear of any obstructions (such as buildings onshore). Small differences in distance can mean a real difference in the potential of the site, e.g. a site that is 10 per cent less windy means 20 per cent less energy is generated.

- **Opinions – against**: noise levels for a distance of 350 m are measured at 35 to 45 dB, while a busy office is measured at 60 dB. Research suggests that turbines are avoided by migrating birds. House prices nearby may reduce. The cost of generating electricity is more expensive than traditional methods (more than double per kW hour). Turbines can be very tall and an eyesore.

  Opinions – for: wind is free and can now be captured efficiently. The energy it produces does not cause green house gases or other pollutants. Although wind turbines can be very tall each takes up only a small plot of land (a small footprint). This means that the land below can still be used, for example for agriculture. At sea the turbines can attract fish and have no long term affects on sea life. Some people find wind farms an interesting feature of the landscape. Wind turbines can be used to produce electricity in remote areas that are not connected to the National Grid. Individuals could also choose to generate their own energy.

- Operational
- Under construction

N

Aberdeen

Glasgow • Edinburgh

Newcastle upon Tyne

Belfast

Isle of Man

Manchester

Dublin

Norwich

Birmingham

London

Cardiff

Southampton

0   100km

Plymouth

B *The location of wind farms in the UK*

C *Burbo Bank wind farm, Liverpool Bay*

The importance of international directives

Air pollution knows no bounds. It does not stop at international borders and therefore cooperation is needed between countries worldwide if air quality and global warming issues are to be effectively addressed. The Earth Summit in Rio de Janeiro in 1992 marked the first real international attempt to cooperate to reduce emissions. Richer countries agreed there would be no increase in emissions.

The **Kyoto Protocol** in 1997 went further, with an agreement by industrialised countries to reduce greenhouse gas emissions to 5 per cent below 1990 levels between 2008 and 2012. EU countries as a whole should show an 8 per cent reduction, but individual countries have their own targets. The treaty became legally binding in 2005, when enough countries responsible for 55 per cent of the total emissions had signed. The USA has declined to sign the agreement but by August 2011 there were 191 signatories. The poorer nations, including those with many industries, do not have to reduce their emissions. Countries can trade in their carbon credits – the amount of greenhouse gases they are allowed to emit. Countries putting more pollution into the atmosphere than they should can buy carbon credits from a country below its agreed level.

The Bali Conference in December 2007 sought to establish new targets to replace those agreed at Kyoto. No figure was decided, only a recognition that there would need to be 'deep cuts in global emissions'.

The Durban Conference in December 2011 agreed to a legally binding deal comprising all countries, including USA, China and India, which will be prepared by 2015, and take effect in 2020.

Key terms

Biofuels: the use of living things such as crops like maize to make ethanol (an alcohol-based fuel) or biogas from animal waste. It is the use of crops that has become especially important.

Did you know ? ? ? ? ? ?

Biofuels are sometimes known as 'deforestation diesel'. The grain needed to fill the tank of a large Range Rover is enough to feed one person for a year. The EU has a target of 5.75 per cent biofuels for transport by 2010.

Key terms

Kyoto Protocol: an international agreement to cut CO_2 emissions to help reduce global warming.

Local initiatives

The phrase 'think globally, act locally' indicates the need for individuals and groups to seek to reduce pollution and to take responsibility for this. Reducing the use of resources not only increases their life, it also reduces pollution and energy in production. We can seek to seize the initiative by conservation and recycling, and therefore reducing waste and the need for landfill.

Conservation

Conservation can involve simple things like turning off lights and appliances when they are not being used, filling a kettle with only the water that is needed rather than to the top and buying reusable carrier bags rather than accepting free plastic bags.

Recycling

Local authorities provide a variety of recycling containers for paper, cans, glass, plastic, cardboard and garden waste, and many encourage composting in an attempt to reduce waste thrown into bins. This in turn reduces the amount that is put into landfill. Figures from the Department for Environment, Food and Rural Affairs (Defra) show that in 2009–10, 40.1 per cent of household waste was recycled. By 2015 the government want only 35 per cent of waste to go into landfill sites.

Study tip

Be able to give examples of attempts at achieving sustainable development operating at international and local scales.

⚭links

You can investigate biofuels by searching **www.bbc.co.uk**. This website is also useful for information on offshore wind farms.

The British Wind and Energy Association website at **www.bwea. com** gives lots of information on wind farms in the UK.

Local authority websites provide information on recycling and waste disposal.

Activities

1 Study map **B**.

a Describe the distribution of wind farms shown on the map.

b Explain reasons for the distribution you have described.

2 Study photo **C**. Draw a labelled sketch to show the characteristics of an offshore wind farm and the advantages of its location.

3 Different people have contrasting views on the development of wind farms such as Burbo Bank (photo **C**) and onshore wind farms.

a Choose one of the following who you think would support wind farms and one who you think would oppose them.

   i   a resident overlooking the new development in favour of renewable energy

   ii   a NIMBY ('Not In My Back Yard') supporter of wind energy

   iii an electricity-generating company director

   iv a member of the Royal Society for the Protection of Birds (RSPB)

   v   a member of Greenpeace for action against climate change

   vi a resident who wants cheap electricity.

b From the point of view of each person, give your views explaining fully why you are for or against the development of wind farms.

4 a Explain the importance of an international approach to reduce air pollution.

b In your view, how successful have international initiatives been? Provide evidence to back up your answer.

5 Use your own experience of where you live and research what your local authority does to encourage energy conservation. Work in pairs. You have been commissioned by your local council to produce a leaflet encouraging people to conserve energy. Design and present your leaflet so that it is informative, clear, well illustrated and eye-catching.

12.7 What are the effects of increasing global food production?

Food production has increased significantly throughout the world in the last 50 years (graph **A**). The quest to increase food production worldwide – whether out of necessity for survival or to sell to areas where food items are needed – has had significant impacts. These can be categorised as environmental, political, social and economic.

■ Environmental impacts

Transporting food longer distances – the idea of **food miles** – increases our **carbon footprint**. People in the UK demand out-of-season produce and this demand is met by importing food. One half of vegetables and 95 per cent of fruit comes from abroad out of season. We import 1 per cent of food by air, but this accounts for 11 per cent of carbon emissions resulting from transportation of UK food. Therefore, the more we rely on imported food – especially air-freighted food – the more we are contributing to air pollution and global warming.

Whilst it may seen logical to suggest that food flown thousands of miles to the UK is bad for the environment, it's not quite so simple. For example, Kenyan green beans are produced efficiently using manual labour and natural fertilisers. British beans are grown in oil heated greenhouses or grown in fields sprayed and ploughed by tractors. According to Gareth Thomas, Minister for Trade and Development (2008–2010): 'Driving six and a half miles to buy your shopping emits more carbon than flying a pack of Kenyan green beans to the UK.'

Apples are harvested in September and October. Some are sold fresh while the rest are chill stored. For most of the following year, they still represent good value (in terms of carbon emissions) for British shoppers. However, by August those Cox's orange pippins and Braeburns will have been in store for 10 months. The amount of energy used to keep them fresh for that length of time will then overtake the carbon cost of shipping them from New Zealand. It is therefore better for the environment if UK shoppers buy apples from New Zealand in July and August rather than those of British origin.

In this section you will learn

how efforts to meet the global demand for food can have both positive and negative effects

how these impacts can be classified as environmental, political, social and economic, and that at times the categories overlap.

Key terms

Food miles: the distance that food items travel from where they are grown to where they are eaten.

Carbon footprint: the amount of carbon generated by things people do, including creating a demand for out-of-season food.

Did you know ??????

A quarter of Europe's cut flowers are supplied by Kenya in an industry that was worth £77 million in 2003 and 10 per cent of Kenya's export earnings.

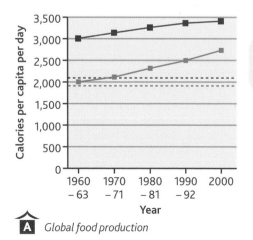

A *Global food production*

As populations increase in certain areas of the world, there is pressure to increase food production. This may involve farming on marginal land that is not really suitable. Photo **B** illustrates the difficult conditions in which people try to grow food in order to survive. Here, the already poor-quality land is likely to become even poorer. As the meagre crops are harvested, no goodness is returned to the soil and so it becomes exhausted. The lack of vegetation cover makes the area prone to soil erosion, where it is easily washed or blown away (photo **C**). This is known as **environmental degradation**.

B   *Marginal land in Darfur*

C   *Soil erosion caused by growing crops on marginal land*

■ Political impacts

Water is essential for farming and food production. In areas where water is limited or available only seasonally, irrigation is essential.

The River Indus flows through northern India and Pakistan. The flow of the Indus is seasonal. A huge amount of water results in flooding in summer, whereas flows are much less in winter due to seasonal variation in rainfall. The Indus supplies the fertile Punjab, which crosses the India–Pakistan border.

After the Independence Act of 1947, it took 13 years of negotiation before the Indus Waters Treaty was signed by the two countries (map **D** on page 292). The disputed region of Kashmir lies within the drainage basin and there had been concerns that during times of conflict India could build dams and cut off water to Pakistan. The signing of the Indus Waters Treaty in 1960 meant that Pakistan had the westward-flowing rivers and India had the eastward-flowing rivers. The construction of two dams on the Jhelum and Indus Rivers gave Pakistan water independent of upstream control by India. However, there is resentment in that part of Kashmir in India as people believe that farming and irrigation has been limited due to them being deprived of water that should have been theirs. In June 2006, talks about the Wuller Barrage that India wants to build on the Jhelum River for navigation raised fears about India controlling Pakistan's water.

Did you know

The River Indus is 3,200 km in length, making it the 24th longest river in the world.

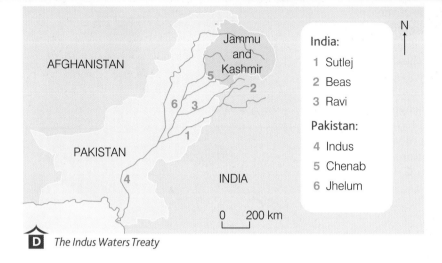

D *The Indus Waters Treaty*

India:
1 Sutlej
2 Beas
3 Ravi

Pakistan:
4 Indus
5 Chenab
6 Jhelum

AFGHANISTAN

Jammu and Kashmir

PAKISTAN

INDIA

N

0   200 km

E *The Indus River*

Social impacts

Social issues relate to aspects such as health, safety and quality of life, and include the right to a clean water supply. Growing **cash crops** for a source of income can offer economic benefits. However, socially there are potentially more problems. The areas around Lake Naivasha in Kenya and north of Mt Kenya are home to the profitable flower industry (diagram **F**).

links

See spread 10.7 on p.240 for more on flower production in Kenya

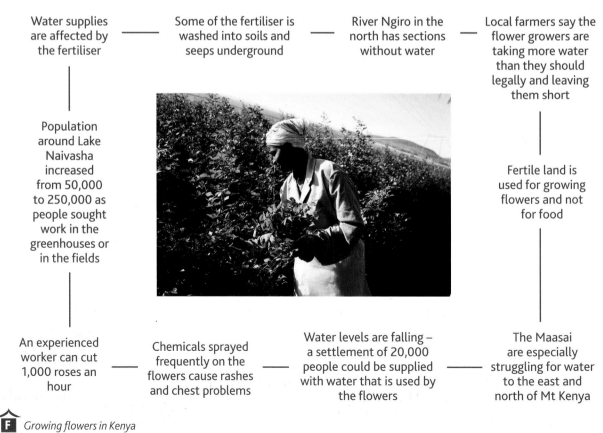

Water supplies are affected by the fertiliser — Some of the fertiliser is washed into soils and seeps underground — River Ngiro in the north has sections without water — Local farmers say the flower growers are taking more water than they should legally and leaving them short

Population around Lake Naivasha increased from 50,000 to 250,000 as people sought work in the greenhouses or in the fields

Fertile land is used for growing flowers and not for food

An experienced worker can cut 1,000 roses an hour — Chemicals sprayed frequently on the flowers cause rashes and chest problems — Water levels are falling – a settlement of 20,000 people could be supplied with water that is used by the flowers — The Maasai are especially struggling for water to the east and north of Mt Kenya

F *Growing flowers in Kenya*

Economic impacts

Growing cash crops as well as food crops is often the way forward for many small-scale farmers – some even seek to sell any surplus of food they produce. Additional cash allows investment in the farm and other items to be bought. However, there are problems. There is often a need to intensify production, which means increasing the use of fertilisers and pesticides. These cost money and a vicious circle can be set up creating **rural debt** (diagram **G**).

Key terms

Cash crops: crops grown in order to sell to make a financial profit.

Rural debt: money borrowed and now owed by farmers to banks or other organisations.

G *The effects of borrowing money*

Study tip

Ensure that you are able to argue both for and against transporting food very long distances to satisfy demand.

Buying locally produced food

In the UK, farmers benefit from local people buying food they produce. Buying from local, or indeed regional or national sources, should benefit the domestic farming industry and address environmental concerns. Others might argue from a different perspective. What would the effect on Kenya be if the UK stopped importing strawberries, for example?

In the UK, we can ensure that we support local produce by:

- looking at labels in supermarkets, which increasingly give the specific origin of foods
- visiting specialist local shops
- buying online from 'local' producers
- supporting local farmers' markets (photo **H**)
- attending regional agricultural shows, which celebrate and sell local produce
- heeding the advice of celebrity chefs such as Gordon Ramsay who joined the debate in May 2008 by saying 'There should be stringent licensing laws to make sure produce is only used in season. I don't want to see strawberries from Kenya in the middle of March. When we haven't got it, we take it off the menu.'

H *Fresh, local produce from a farmers' market*

Activities

1 Working in small groups, choose at least two different types of non-seasonal fruit and vegetables each. Visit one (or more) supermarkets, making sure in advance that they stock the produce you have decided on. If not, you will need to change your choice of items.

a Write down the origin of the items you have selected and whether they have been brought in by air. Many supermarkets now give this information.

b Display the origins of the fruit and vegetables on a world map.

c Summarise what you have discovered about the origin of fruit and vegetables eaten in the UK.

d Describe the environmental impact of this.

2 Study photos **B** and **C** on page 291.

a Give the meaning of 'marginal land'.

b Use the photos to illustrate the difficulties of farming on marginal land.

c Use photo **C** to explain the negative effects of farming on marginal land.

3 Study map **D** (and photo **E**) on page 292.

a Draw a sketch map to show the Indus and its five tributaries, international boundaries, main regions and places.

b Label the map to show the cause of conflict linked to water.

c Draw a timeline to show the sequence of events described that contributed to the conflict.

4 Working in pairs, produce an advert for locally produced food in your area.

a Decide whether your advert is to be printed in a newspaper or spoken on the radio.

b Carry out some research to discover which foods are grown locally. Your local newspaper, library, farm shops, farmers' markets and the internet may be useful.

c Produce your advert. It needs to be informative but hard-hitting if it is to be successful.

d Present your advert to the rest of the class.

∞ links

The case study on 'Flower growing in Kenya' on **www.learningafrica.org.uk** is particularly useful, as is **www.farmersmarkets.net**.

13 Tourism

13.1 Why has global tourism grown?

Growth in tourism

Tourism is the world's largest industry, worth $500 billion dollars in 2007. There were 940 million international tourist arrivals in 2009 and this is set to rise to a massive 1.6 billion by 2020. In most countries, domestic tourism (people going on holiday in their own country) is between four and five times greater than international tourism.

A *International tourist arrivals (millions)*

Region	2006	2010	Percentage change 2006–10	Percentage of world tourism (2010)
Africa	50	49	–2.0%	5.2%
Americas	136	151	+11.0%	16.1%
Asia and Pacific	168	204	+21.4%	21.8%
Europe	461	471	+2.2%	50.5%
Middle East	41	60	+46.3%	6.4%
World	856	935	+9.2%	100.0%

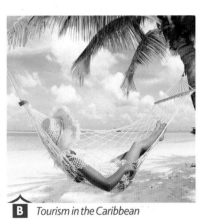

B *Tourism in the Caribbean*

The tourism industry is one of the greatest providers of jobs and income in all countries. Many countries rely heavily on income from tourism. Caribbean countries get half their GDP from tourism. The top six tourist destination countries are France, Spain, the USA, China, Italy and the UK. Germans spend more per person than any other nation on holiday, followed by Americans, British, French and Japanese.

Factors affecting tourism's growth

Growth in tourism is explained by three sets of factors.

1 Social and economic factors

Since the 1950s people have become wealthier. Incomes are higher and more money is available for luxuries such as tourism. Most families have two working parents whereas in the past it was usually one.

People have more leisure time. Holiday leave time has increased from two weeks per year in the 1950s to between four and six today. Life expectancy has risen so more people are retired. Many have good pensions and can afford several trips a year. They also have more time to travel.

Study tip

You should be able to interpret tables of statistics. Usually, we look for patterns or trends and drawing a graph can be the easiest way to spot these. Sometimes there are few differences in the data. Nevertheless, tiny differences can still be important and may show a trend, and this is what you need to pick out.

2 Improvements in technology

Travel today is quick and easy – motorways, airport expansion and faster jet aircraft have all contributed to this. Flying has become cheaper and booking online is quick and easy. In 2008 the rapid rise in oil prices had an impact on the cost of flights and more people took domestic holidays to save money.

3 Expansion of holiday choice

During the 1950s and 1960s coastal resorts were popular and in the UK the National Parks were opening and offering new opportunities. The 1970s saw a decline in seaside holidays due to competition from cheap package holidays to mainland Europe, especially Spain. Packages are now available to destinations all over the world that offer a huge variety of sights and activities. Ecotourism and unusual destinations such as Alaska are expanding rapidly.

C *Budget airlines have made international travel quicker and cheaper*

◼ Tourist attractions

Many people choose to visit cities to enjoy the culture associated with museums, art galleries, architecture or shops and restaurants. Cities such as London, Rome and Paris have a huge amount to offer tourists of every age. The natural landscape is also a major 'pull' for tourists, particularly mountains such as the Alps in Europe or the beautiful stretches of coastline found in the Mediterranean or the Caribbean.

Activities

1 Study table **A** on page 295.

a Which continent had the greatest tourism business in 2010?

b Why do you think this continent has such a large tourist industry?

c Which continent had the smallest tourism business in 2010?

d Why do you think this continent has not yet developed its tourism as much as other regions?

e Which continent's tourism grew by the largest percentage between 2006 and 2010?

f Which continent's tourism grew the least?

g Is there a relationship between scale of tourism and rate of growth? Explain your answer.

2 Study photos **D**, **E** and **F** opposite.

a Draw a field sketch of one of the photos. Label all the pull factors that might attract people to come to that region of Italy.

b What types of people are most likely to be attracted to each area? Remember to consider the seasons. Some landscapes are more attractive in winter than in summer.

c Italy is a base for holidays all year round. Explain why this is so.

d For the three Italian holiday types shown, assess their tourist potential for members of your family and/or friends. Give your reasons. Who would be most attracted to what and why?

D   *The Italian Alps*

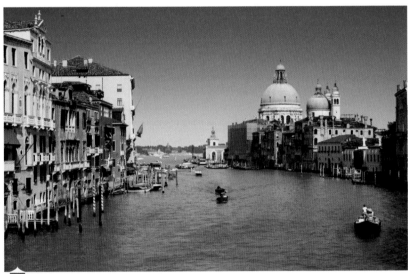
E   *Venice is a popular tourist destination*

F   *Coastal tourism in Vernazza*

Italy

Italy is a country with a great variety of landscapes. Photos **D**, **E** and **F** show the three key types: mountains, cities and coastline. All the places shown have a busy tourist business, making an important contribution to the national economy. Venice is well known for its canals and Renaissance architecture; Florence for its art galleries. Skiing in the Alps and sunbathing on the coast are popular with both Italians and visitors from other countries.

The example of Italy illustrates point 3 above – expansion of holiday choice. People want to visit a greater variety of places and the tourist industry grows and adapts to supply what the market demands.

Study tip

Photos can be labelled directly with arrows to point out the features. There needs to be space around each photo because the labels need to be detailed. Keep what you write clear, straightforward and to the point.

13.2 How important is tourism in different countries?

Tourism is an important part of the economies of many richer countries, especially those in Western Europe and North America. Today, it is increasingly seen by developing countries as one of the best ways to earn foreign income, provide jobs and improve standards of living. Countries want to take advantage of the growing numbers of tourists and the money they have to spend.

In this section you will learn

the economic importance of tourism to countries in contrasting parts of the world

how to compare and contrast tourist regions.

The economic importance of tourism

Tables **A** and **B** show the top 10 countries for tourist receipts (national income from tourism) and most tourist arrivals (number of tourists every year).

- France has had more tourists than any other country for many years. French tourism includes every type of holiday such as city breaks, holiday cottages, camping and skiing.

- The USA earns more than any other country from tourism, and has the second largest number of visitors. Europeans consider a trip to the USA as more special than staying in Europe, so they are likely to stay longer and spend more.

- China is high in both tables **A** and **B**. For many people, distance makes it too expensive a place to visit, but its variety of unusual landscapes and unique culture attracts increasing numbers with both time and money. This trend is likely to continue.

- In the Caribbean almost 50 per cent of visitors come from the nearby USA, with France, Canada and the UK also important sources of business. Expenditure per tourist ranges between $324 per holiday in Belize to $2,117 in the Virgin Islands, which attracts the wealthiest visitors.

Essential jobs are created in all countries, but the contribution that tourism makes to GDP varies greatly between wealthier and poorer countries. Rich countries have a broadly balanced economy, of which tourism is one part. On the other hand, in less well-off countries tourism can be essential. In the Caribbean, for example, several small island countries rely heavily on tourism to provide national income and employment. Around 80 per cent of Barbados's national income comes from tourism.

A *Countries with the largest tourist receipts, 2009*

Country	Annual tourist income ($ billions)
USA	110.1
Spain	61.6
France	55.6
Italy	45.7
China	40.8
Germany	40.0
UK	36.0
Australia	24.7
Turkey	22.0
Austria	21.8

B *Countries with the most tourist arrivals, 2009*

Country	Number of tourists (millions)
France	78.5
USA	57.9
Spain	57.3
China	53.1
Italy	42.7
UK	30.1
Ukraine	25.5
Turkey	25.0
Germany	24.9
Russia	23.7

Dubai

Dubai is one of the United Arab Emirates (UAE). It is located on the Arabian Gulf coast neighbouring Saudi Arabia (map **C**). Because it is easily accessible from Europe, Asia and Africa (120 airlines fly there), tourism in Dubai is growing quickly. Hotel revenue was up by 22 per cent in the first quarter of 2008 compared with the same period the previous year. Around 2.8 million people visited the principality in 2000, 4.9 million in 2003 and 5.4 million in 2004. These numbers are predicted to grow further to 15 million by 2015, which would make Dubai one of the world's top tourist destinations (photo **D**).

The state is famous for its duty-free shopping malls with huge department stores and its markets. Prices are reasonable and there is huge variety. Emirates Airlines, which is based in Dubai, carries millions of long-haul passengers to hundreds of destinations and many stop over in Dubai as part of their trip.

Sightseeing is popular – the markets, the zoo, the dhow-building yards (traditional boats). Watersports, and especially diving, are growing in popularity. Excursions out from the city allow the visitor to see the desert and its wildlife (photo **E**). Bird-watching trips take visitors to the wetland mudflat areas, where there are 400 species.

C   *Location of Dubai*

D   *Dubai waterfront*

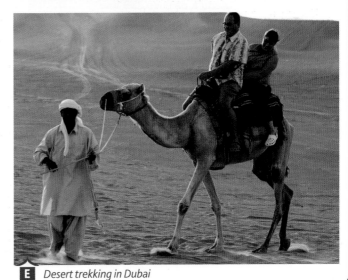

E   *Desert trekking in Dubai*

Benefits of tourism in poorer countries

- Many people are employed to serve tourists such as waiters (photo **F**), souvenir shop assistants and tour guides. In Antigua and Barbuda 30 per cent of the population work in these jobs, but in Jamaica only 8 per cent.

- Tourists spend their holiday money in pounds sterling, US dollars or euros. This foreign exchange is essential to poorer countries. It can be used to buy goods and services from abroad.

- Many governments tax visitors to help pay for the extra services they use such as water supply, drainage, electricity and roads.

- Extra jobs are created indirectly. Hotels buy some produce from local suppliers to feed the visitors.

- Many small businesses have been started up to serve the tourists themselves and supply the services they demand. These include taxis, bars and restaurants, builders and maintenance workers.

Activities

1 Study tables **A** and **B** on page 298.

a Draw a pie chart using the data in table **A**. Calculate the percentage that each country/region is out of the total figure. 100 per cent represents 360 degrees, so multiply each percentage you have calculated by 3.6 to obtain the number of degrees for each sector in your pie chart. Label each sector with the appropriate country/region or add a key to explain your shading. The data in the table is in size order. If you follow this in your chart, starting at the top, it will be easier to read and interpret.

b Which are the top three countries for tourist receipts?

c Which are the top three countries for tourist arrivals?

d Comment on any similarities and differences in your answers to b and c.

e Compare the balance of richer and poorer countries in the two tables.

2 Study photos **D** and **E** on page 299.

a What are the attractions that Dubai has to offer to tourists?

b Conduct some Internet research to discover what is available for tourists outside Dubai and its shopping malls.

c Which groups of people do you think benefit the most from the growth of tourism in Dubai?

d Would you like to go to Dubai? Why?

F *Working as a waiter*

⬤⬤ links

Find out more about Dubai's ambitions at **www.nakheel.com**.

13.3 How do we manage tourism in the UK?

The growth of tourism in the UK

Almost all UK tourism used to be domestic – British people holidaying in the UK. Only the wealthy and privileged were able to go abroad.

Domestic tourism grew quickly in the 1950s and 1960s as the growing UK economy provided higher pay and more time off work. Having an annual holiday became common. UK seaside holidays peaked in the early to mid-1970s, with 40 million visitors annually (graph **A**). After that, Britain's seaside resorts declined as package holidays abroad grew in number and affordability.

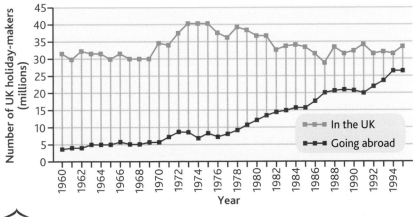

A Numbers of UK residents holidaying in the UK and abroad, 1960–95

B British seaside resorts were popular in the 1960s

Between the world wars, wealthier people began to go abroad. Cheap package holidays with guaranteed hot weather attracted people of all incomes. It was often cheaper to go to a Spanish resort like Benidorm than to holiday in the UK. British weather was seen as too unreliable. Many small coastal hotels were forced to survive by housing the homeless during the 1980s, decreasing their reputation even more. In 2010–11 UK residents made 55.7 million trips abroad.

Did you know ??????

The banking crisis of 2008–09 meant people had less money to spend. People reduced the number of holidays they took while they waited for the economic situation to improve.

The contribution of tourism to the UK economy

The UK economy earns over £114 billion (2008) every year from tourism and leisure. This amount usually grows slightly annually. Around 27.7 million overseas visitors spend over £13 billion of this sum. Restaurants and hotels make up a large proportion of these earnings, at £20 billion and £16 billion respectively. More than 100 new hotels opened in the UK between September 2004 and December 2005, creating more jobs and income. The London Eye is the most visited paying attraction in the UK, with 3.7 million visitors each year. An estimated 1.1 million tourists travelled to London for the Royal Wedding in 2011.

C The Royal Wedding, 2011

The Butler tourist resort life-cycle model

This **life-cycle model** says that any tourist resort starts on a small scale, develops into something more significant, then either goes into decline or makes changes to maintain its attractions (graph **E**). There are six stages.

1 Exploration

Small numbers of visitors are attracted by something particular, e.g. good beaches, attractive landscape, historical or cultural features. Local people have not yet developed many tourist services.

2 Involvement

The local population sees the opportunities and starts to provide accommodation, food, transport, guides and other services for the visitors.

3 Development

Large companies build hotels and leisure complexes and advertise package holidays. Numbers of tourists rise dramatically. Job opportunities for local people grow rapidly, but this brings both advantages and disadvantages.

4 Consolidation

Tourism is now a major part of the local economy, but perhaps at the expense of other types of development. Numbers of visitors are steady making employment more secure. However, some hotels and other facilities are becoming older and unattractive, so the type of customers attracted goes downmarket. Rowdiness becomes a problem.

5 Stagnation

The resort becomes unfashionable and numbers of visitors start to decline. Businesses change hands and often fail.

6 Decline or rejuvenation

Decline: visitors prefer other resorts. Day trippers and weekenders become the main source of income.

Rejuvenation: attempts are made to modernise the resort and attract different people to enjoy new activities.

Blackpool is a good example of a resort reinventing itself. Day trippers and weekenders now bring in most of the income, although websites and brochures make a huge effort to attract people for longer periods.

D *The Mediterranean coastal resort of Kalami on the Greek island of Corfu. In what stage of the Butler model would you place this resort and why?*

E *The Butler model*

Blackpool, a UK coastal tourist resort

Blackpool's growth and stagnation

Located on the Lancashire coast in the north-west of England, Blackpool became a major tourist centre during the 19th century to serve the inhabitants of northern industrial towns. Factory workers could increasingly afford a holiday, travelling by train to the nearby coast.

Blackpool boomed between 1900 and 1950. However, as people's disposable income increased, they preferred to try somewhere different. Soon package holidays abroad created huge competition for Britain's seaside resorts. Blackpool's summer weather can be unreliable, which proved a disadvantage.

F *Factory workers on holiday, 1951*

Responding to the decline

As one of the larger resorts, Blackpool did attract some private investment and local authority grants to upgrade hotels, turn outdoor pools into indoor leisure centres and increase car-parking provision. Many smaller failing hotels were converted into self-catering holiday flats. Blackpool's attractions still made it a little different to other resorts. The famous Blackpool Tower, modelled on the Eiffel Tower in Paris, gives fantastic views up and down the Lancashire coast and inland towards the Pennines. The complex there includes the Tower Ballroom, famous for national ballroom dancing competitions, and the Tower Circus. The town upgraded its zoo and a Sealife Centre was built. The

Blackpool Illuminations – a light show stretching along the Golden Mile (the central section of the sea front) – began in 1879 and has been upgraded several times with advancing technology.

G *Blackpool Tower and the Illuminations*

Blackpool should have been quicker to fight the competition from package holidays. Eventually it lost much of its family holiday business and came to rely on day trippers and stag and hen party business – not popular with residents and bad for the town's image.

The supercasino

One approach taken by Blackpool to get out of recession was to apply to the government to be the home of the UK's first supercasino, a huge leisure and entertainment complex based on those in Las Vegas and Atlantic City in the USA. Blackpool was the favourite applicant on the shortlist. The proposed sea-front site included a conference centre and a wide variety of entertainments. Some 20,000 jobs and £2 billion of investment would have been generated. The town's high 3.6 per cent unemployment rate would have been greatly improved. Nevertheless, not everyone was in favour, but the final decision closed the debate – Blackpool lost the supercasino development to Manchester, coming only third in the vote. The town council was shocked.

Blackpool today

Despite the casino setback millions were spent improving the town as part of the 'Blackpool Masterplan'. Today Blackpool is promoting itself as a shopping and conference centre and as an ideal 'short break' destination. It is popular with day-trippers and for stag and hen parties. In 2008 a new department store (Debenhams) opened as part of a new development in Hounds Hill. In 2010, Blackpool council purchased the famous Winter Gardens and embarked on a number of refurbishment projects.

External factors affecting UK tourism in the early 21st century

Tourism can be limited by political and economic situations. Two key issues have caused difficulties in the early 21st century.

Terrorism

The destruction of the World Trade Center in New York on 11 September 2001 had a huge impact on travel. The USA stepped up its security overnight, as did the UK and the EU. Airport security checks have multiplied and check-in times increased. London is a terrorist target: the Underground bombing of 7 July 2005 is an example. In the aftermath of such events, visitor numbers decline sharply.

Exchange rates and the banking crisis

Currency exchange rates control value for money for tourists on holiday. In 2011 the euro was high against the pound, valued at around 87p (compared with 68p previously), so holidaying in France and other Eurozone countries became more expensive. At the same time, £1 was worth $1.60, making the USA a much more attractive holiday destination. Use the Internet to compare these currencies today to see how things have changed since 2011.

Since 2008, the world has faced economic difficulties. In the UK many people have faced a pay freeze and the rate of unemployment has increased. The factors have led to a reduction in tourism.

Study tip

Note which aspects of the photos you are being asked to compare and contrast and concentrate only on those. Note what each photo shows in each category. Write down all the similarities and then all the differences.

Activities

1 Study graph **A** on page 301.

a In 1960 how many people holidayed within the UK and how many went abroad?

b Which year had the largest gap between the sets of statistics?

c Which year had the smallest gap?

d Describe the trend of holidays taken in the UK.

2 Study graph **E** on page 302. To what extent has Blackpool's development as a tourist resort followed the Butler model? Write at least two paragraphs.

3 Work with a friend to put together some suggestions for making Blackpool attractive to tourists in the future. Use the Internet to give you some ideas. Put together a 'Tourism Plan for Blackpool' using ICT if you wish. Don't forget to justify your plan.

4 Use the internet to find photos that illustrate each stage of the Butler Model. Add labels and annotations to support your choice of photo for each stage.

links

Find out more about Blackpool tourism at **www.visitblackpool.com**.

13.4 What is the importance of National Parks for UK tourism?

National Parks are large areas of mainly rural land. The UK's first was the Peak District of Derbyshire, created in 1951 by an Act of Parliament. National Parks aim to conserve natural and cultural landscapes while allowing access for visitors to enjoy them. The first Scottish Park was designated in 2002. In England, the most recently designated National Parks are the New Forest (2004) and the South Downs (2011).

Many National Parks are uplands such as Snowdonia (photo **B** on page 306) and the Lake District. Several National Parks include stretches of coastline (e.g. Pembrokeshire Coast) and a few are in lowland areas (e.g. The Broads). Land remains privately owned (81 per cent), mostly by farmers, but the Forestry Commission, the National Trust, the Ministry of Defence and the water authorities also own some areas. The National Park Authorities only directly control 1 per cent. Local people make their living from the land and tourism provides much-needed jobs.

In this section you will learn

the contribution of tourism to the UK economy
the importance of National Parks for UK tourism
the conflicts caused by tourism in the Lake District
how to devise management strategies for tourism in the Lake District.

1 Loch Lomond and the Trossachs
2 Lake District
3 Peak District
4 Snowdonia
5 Pembrokeshire Coast
6 Brecon Beacons
7 Exmoor
8 Dartmoor
9 New Forest
10 South Downs
11 The Broads
12 North York Moors
13 Yorkshire Dales
14 Northumberland
15 Cairngorms

- National Park
- Motorway
- Major urban areas

A *The location of National Parks in Britain*

Key terms

National Park: an area where development is limited and planning controlled. The landscape is regarded as unusual and valuable and therefore worth looking after.

Honeypot site: somewhere that attracts a large number of tourists who, due to their numbers, place pressure on the environment and people.

Activities

1 Study map **A**. One of the aims of National Parks is to serve the population with recreation facilities.

a Describe the locations of the National Parks in relation to the major urban areas.

b Based on your answer to **a**, how accessible do you think the National Parks are for most of Britain's population? Make sure you name Parks and cities in your answer.

c Which National Parks are the most accessible? Explain why.

2 Study photo **B**. What types of activities might people undertake in this landscape?

B *Snowdonia National Park*

The Lake District

Attractions and opportunities for tourism

The English Lake District is a glaciated upland area in Cumbria, north-west England. It stretches 64 km from north to south and 53 km east to west. It became a National Park in 1951. Famous for its stunning scenery, abundant wildlife and cultural heritage, it is considered to be England's finest landscape.

The great outdoors

The ribbon lakes and tarns are part of a unique and hugely varied landscape, as well as being a major recreational resource. Lake Windermere specialises in ferry cruises. Most people sail between the main centres of Windermere town (photo **C**) and Ambleside. Small boats are allowed on many lakes. Areas are set aside for windsailing and power-boating so the activities do not clash and quiet areas are left for people seeking peace and quiet. Fishing from the shore or boats is increasing in popularity.

Walking is one of the most popular reasons why people visit the Lake District, whether for a day or longer. Routes vary from short and relatively flat to extremely long and tough. Known as the 'birthplace of mountaineering', even the most experienced climbers find plenty of challenges in scaling back walls of corries and sides of U-shaped valleys (photo **D**). Public access to the fells (open uplands) is unrestricted.

History and culture

Historical and cultural sites also attract tourists. The Lake District has been occupied since the end of the ice age 10,000 years ago and evidence of early settlement remains in the landscape. The land has been farmed for centuries, leaving a distinctive field pattern with drystone walls. Many 19th-century writers and artists, such as John Ruskin, loved the area. The children's author Beatrix Potter lived at Hill Top on the shores of Lake Windermere (map **E**).

C *Windermere town centre*

D *Striding Edge, Helvellyn*

Case study

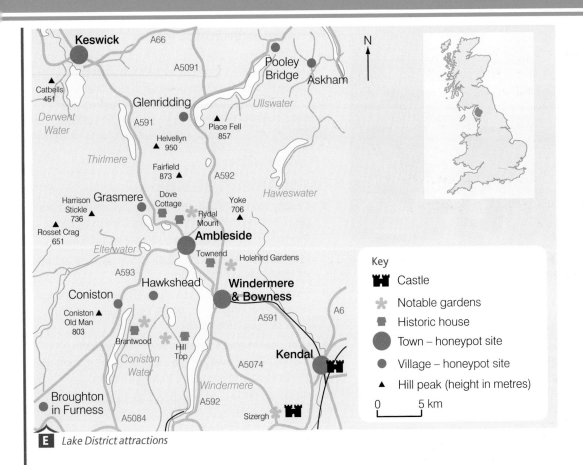

E *Lake District attractions*

Impacts of tourism

There are many times the number of visitors in the Lake District National Park as local population: 12 million tourists (22 million visitor days) to 42,239 residents. The impacts are potentially huge and must be managed as well as possible. There are both negative and positive impacts.

1 Traffic problems

Over 89 per cent of visitors come by car, often just for the day. Many roads, including A roads, are narrow and winding. Buses and large delivery vehicles have to use these to service both locals and tourists. Queues are a common problem, especially towards the end of the day when day trippers are heading home.

Bowness-on-Windermere

Towns like Bowness-on-Windermere were not built originally for the huge volumes of traffic that arrive daily in the summer, especially at weekends. Congestion and parking are serious problems. Bowness has built a new car park at Braithwaite Fold on the edge of town and has extended another, but capacity is still inadequate. In desperation, in the countryside people park on grass verges, causing serious damage.

2 Honeypot sites

The Lake District has both physical and cultural **honeypot sites**. Beauty spots, small shopping centres and historic houses all attract hundreds of visitors daily. Catbells (map **E**) is quite an easy climb, so many people walk up this smaller mountain. It therefore suffers from serious footpath erosion (photo **F**). Honeypot sites need to provide access and facilities while remaining as unspoilt as possible.

F *Footpath erosion in the Lake District*

G *Hill Top, Beatrix Potter's house – a honeypot site in the summer*

3 Pressure on property

Almost 20 per cent of property in the Lake District National Park is either second homes or holiday let accommodation (15 per cent of all housing in 2007). Some local people make a good income from owning and letting such property. The main issues include the following:

- Holiday cottages and flats are not occupied all year.
- Holidaymakers do not always support local businesses, often doing a supermarket shop at home before their trip. On the other hand, the main supermarket in Windermere is often full of visitors buying a great deal of food and drink for their stay.
- Demand for property from outsiders increases property prices in the Lake District. This causes problems for local people who are forced out to find affordable homes on the edge of the region in Kendal or Penrith. This is the most serious tourist problem affecting local communities.

4 Environmental issues

Water sports are not allowed on some of the lakes. However, Windermere, the largest lake, has ferries and allows power-boating, windsurfing and other faster and more damaging activities (photo **H**). The main issue is the wash from faster vehicles eroding the shore. Fuel spills are not uncommon, causing pollution.

Tourism management strategies

In 2007 the Lake District National Park launched its 'Visions for the National Park in 2030'. It aims to maximise economic opportunities in a sustainable way. In 2008 the Cumbria Tourist Board published its new tourism strategy 'Making the Dream a Reality 2008–2018'.

1 Traffic solutions

Planning an efficient road network:

- County strategic roads, often dual carriageways, have been built on the edges of the Lake District to help move traffic in and out as efficiently as possible.
- Distributor roads link the small towns and key tourist villages such as Ambleside.
- Develop transport hubs to allow efficient interchange between parking, buses, boats, cycling and walking (for example, Ambleside).
- Traffic on smaller roads has been slowed down by traffic-calming measures in villages, cattle grids in the countryside and an overall maximum speed limit.
- Heavy lorries should be kept off scenic roads.

Planning public transport:

- Where possible bus lanes operate in towns, although narrow streets limit this.
- A park-and-ride scheme called the 'Honister Rambler' operates from Keswick on the edge of the National park. Ramblers are transported to popular sites where parking is a problem, for example, Catbells.
- The use of low-carbon vehicles, for example, buses, have been encouraged.

H *Tourists queue to take a cruise on Lake Windemere*

2 Honeypot management

Footpaths:

- The 'Upland Path Landscape Restoration Project (2002-2011)' resulted in the repair of 145 paths which involved creating steps, surfacing with local stone and re-planting native plants.

- A severely eroded path at Whiteless Pike, Buttermere has been repaired using a technique called 'stone pitching'. Large stones are dug into the path to create solid, hard-wearing footpaths. It costs £1,000 per metre.

Parking:

- Roadsides have been fenced off so that cars cannot damage verges.

- Car-park surfaces have been reinforced to prevent damage. 'Waffles' are large concrete slabs with holes in them, like an edible waffle. Soil fills the holes and grass grows, giving a hard green surface.

Litter:

- Bins are provided at popular sites and emptied regularly.

- Signs encourage people to be responsible and reduce litter.

3 Property prices

This is the most difficult issue. Management strategies cannot control house prices. Local authorities could build more homes for rent and developers could erect more low-cost homes for sale. Little has yet been achieved.

4 Environmental issues

Speed limits for boats can limit the amount of wash caused. But to prevent erosion, speeds would have to be very low, which clashes with the main pleasure of the sport – going fast! The speed limit on Windermere is 18 kph. Limiting the noisiest and most damaging sports to certain parts of the lake can restrict the amount of damage done.

Tourism conflicts and opportunities

1 Farming

Tourism and farming are often thought to be in conflict, which can be true. Visitors can trample crops and disturb livestock, but signs and education have limited these problems. Tourists have offered hill farmers new opportunities for diversification in difficult economic times. Income can be made from B&B accommodation, holiday cottages converted from farm buildings, camping and caravan sites. Activities such as pony trekking and paintballing can be offered.

2 Employment

The impact of tourism on employment must be positive as so many jobs are created. Many businesses thrive and make a profit. Conversely, seasonality is a problem, as well as low pay. Visitor numbers can be unpredictable.

I *Elterwater village*

Activities

1 Study photo **H**.

a How can overcrowding spoil people's enjoyment of Lake Windermere?

b What environmental problems are affecting Lake Windermere?

c Suggest ways in which the lake could be managed more effectively.

2 Study photo **I**. Elterwater is a small village near Lake Windermere. This pretty settlement is close to a small lake offering flat walking, and the more demanding Great Langdale and Little Langdale walks are close by. The village has few parking spaces. Visitors park in residents' private spaces and right under their windows, making noise an issue. Outside the village, there is limited off-road parking so many cars find spaces on grass verges along the approach road.

How could the National Park Authority:

a improve the quality of life for Elterwater village residents?

b improve the recreational experience of visitors with various interests?

∞links

Find out more about the Lake District at **www.lake-district.gov.uk**.

13.5 Why do so many countries want mass tourism?

Advantages and disadvantages of mass tourism

Mass tourism involves large numbers of tourists coming to one destination (photos **A** and **B**). There is usually a particular purpose and a particular type of location, such as skiing in a mountain resort or sunbathing at a beach location. Many countries and regions want to develop mass tourism because they believe it will bring many advantages (table **C**).

In this section you will learn

the term 'mass tourism'

about Jamaica – an established tropical tourist area that attracts a large number of visitors

some strategies to counter the negative environmental effects of tourism in Jamaica and to ensure its continued success.

A Mass tourism in Barcelona, Spain

Did you know ??????

In the USA the first mass tourist resorts were Atlantic City in New Jersey and Long Island in New York State. In Europe, Ostend developed to serve the citizens of Brussels, Deauville attracted Parisians and Boulogne, people from Normandy.

B The Parthenon in Athens, Greece, is the most visited ancient monument in Europe

Key terms

Mass tourism: tourism on a large scale to one country or region. This is linked to the Development and Consolidation phases of the Butler tourist resort life-cycle model.

C *Advantages and disadvantages of mass tourism*

Advantages	Disadvantages
• Tourism brings jobs. People who previously survived on subsistence agriculture or day labouring gain regular work with a more reliable wage.	• The activity may be seasonal – skiing only happens in winter. Local people may find themselves out of work for the rest of the year.
• New infrastructure must be put in place for tourists – airports, hotels, power supplies, roads and telecommunications. These also benefit the local population.	• The industry is dominated by large travel companies who sell package holidays by brochure or on the internet. • New construction can damage the environment and cause pollution.
• Construction jobs often go to local people, but they are temporary.	• Lower- and middle-income customers are the target market – this type of tourism does not appeal to wealthier groups of people.
• New leisure facilities may be open to local people.	• Few local employees are well paid. The higher level jobs are often taken by people from the companies involved in developing the resort, who are not locals.
• The economy benefits from tourism through taxation, the creation of jobs and spending money in shops, hotels and at attractions.	• Investing companies are usually based in foreign countries. Profits therefore go outside the tourist country and they do not benefit the host country.
	• New building developments need land. Local farmers may be tempted to sell their land, which reduces local food production.
	• Tourists can be narrow-minded and often prefer familiar food, so much is imported rather than produced locally.
	• Culture clashes may occur and tourism can lead to problems with drugs and alcohol. Sex tourism is a problem in some areas.

Tourism in Jamaica

Jamaica is one of the Caribbean's main tourist destinations, with 1.9 million visitors in 2010. After this, competition from other islands began to be something of a problem. Tourism is the country's second biggest earner and 262,000 (2011) Jamaicans work in this sector. Other local businesses also depend on tourism, such as food production for visitors and other hotel suppliers. Jamaica has much to offer the tourist (map **D** and fact file **E** on page 312) including watersports, for which it is famous, wildlife sanctuaries and, increasingly, golf.

Case study

Key
- Main tourist areas
- Hotels outside main tourist areas
- Beach/bathing areas
- Watersports
- Deep-sea fishing
- Plantation house
- Caves
- Botanic garden
- Golf course
- Museum
- Bird sanctuary/ wildlife reserve
- National Park
- Parish boundary
- Airport

N

0   30 km

D *Jamaican tourist attractions*

Community tourism

A recent trend has been the growth in community tourism where visitors stay in local people's homes. Families provide bed and breakfast accommodation and local businesses, such as restaurants and bars, supply their other needs. This style of holiday provides greater interaction between tourists and local people, gives the visitors a clearer idea of local life, supports local businesses and uses fewer resources. Money goes directly to the people rather than to large international businesses.

E *Jamaican tourism fact file, 2010*

Jamaican tourism facts and figures	
Total number of tourist arrivals	1.9 million
Population employed in tourism	22.6%
Contribution to GDP	24%
Passengers arriving by cruiseships	910,000
Rooms available to tourists	31,000
Visitors from USA and UK (% of total)	70% and 10%

∞ links

Find out more about Jamaican tourism at **www.visitjamaica.com**.

Ecotourism

Jamaica needs to maintain its tourist resources into the future and some companies offer ecotourism, which is becoming more popular. This utilises the inland area of the island such as the Blue Mountains as well as parts of the coast, spreading tourists further around the island. Nature reserves are increasing and eco-lodges are being built. Tourist densities are kept low in these areas, which keeps pressure off the environment.

F *Ocho Rios, Jamaica*

Activities

1 Study map **D** on page 311 and fact file **E**.

a Name two main tourist areas in Jamaica.

b Which tourist activities are found in these areas?

c Make two separate lists of the advantages and disadvantages to Jamaica of the holiday industry.

d Research on the internet or in holiday brochures to discover any other advantages or disadvantages you could add to your lists.

e Write a minimum of three paragraphs to discuss whether tourism is beneficial to Jamaica's people and economy. Add a clear conclusion at the end of your discussion.

2 This is a group exercise. At least three members of the class should be in each group. Imagine a new tourist enterprise is being set up in Jamaica, aiming to be as eco-friendly and sustainable as possible. (Read pages 316–317 later in this chapter to understand sustainable tourism better.) You are members of the travel company (you may be from Jamaica or from a country that tourists come from – you choose) and you are preparing your proposals for the government of Jamaica and a local environmental interest group.

a Plan an exciting programme for the clients. Name locations and the activities on offer there.

b What type of accommodation is provided? How is it serviced?

c How would the workforce be recruited?

d Emphasise the advantages of your proposals and how you would aim to overcome any difficulties.

e Compare your plans with those of other groups.

13.6 / What attracts people to extreme environments?

Extreme environments and activities

Extreme environment tourism involves dangerous landscapes often with a difficult climate, and remote places that are sparsely settled or not occupied at all. Increasing numbers of tourists are attracted to extreme environments where they can take part in adventurous activities such as rock climbing, paragliding and white-water rafting.

Extreme environments are spread across the globe and cover a wide variety of locations including mountains, deserts, rainforests, caves and ice-covered terrain (photos **A** to **D**). Adventure activities involve an element of risk and people often choose such a trip for the adrenaline rush. Examples include ice-diving in the White Sea, north Russia, with almost freezing temperatures, and travelling across the Chernobyl Zone of Alienation in Ukraine, the area devastated by nuclear contamination in 1986. In Jamaica such activities include climbing waterfalls and cliff-diving. Adventure tourism is one of the fastest-growing types of tourism in the world.

> ### In this section you will learn
>
> what we mean by 'extreme' tourism
>
> which environments are classified as extreme
>
> what is happening in Antarctica in tourism development and the likely consequences of this
>
> how to assess whether particular remote landscapes should be developed for tourism on any scale.

A *Exploring the icy landscape in Greenland*

B *Setting up a camp under the stars in the desert*

C *Paddling in a dug out canoe in the Amazon*

D *Hiking in the foothills of the Himalayas*

> ### Key terms
>
> **Extreme environments:** locations with difficult environments where tourism has only recently occured due to people wanting to visit somewhere with different physical challenges.

The target market

Adventure tourists look for physical challenge and risks. They are often around 30 years old, unmarried and without children, have high-powered jobs and a good income – these trips are expensive. Groups are small and distances great. However, there are enough wealthy individuals with a taste for something completely different to allow this sector to grow. It will never be large but in some areas it is increasing in significance. Most companies advertise on the internet rather than by brochure.

Little investment is needed to set up such trips. The usual costly expenses of building hotels and roads are irrelevant. Part of the experience is to sleep 'rough' and travel over untouched landscapes. This tourism sector is growing rapidly in Peru, Chile, Argentina, Azerbaijan and Pakistan. Northern Pakistan is one of the most mountainous and difficult landscapes in the world and even its risky political situation as the base of Al Qaeda terrorists adds a thrill for some.

Case study

Antarctica

In the 1950s small-scale tourism started in Antarctica when commercial shipping began to take a few passengers. The first specially designed cruise ship made its first voyage in 1969. Some 9,000 tourists in 1992–93 have now grown to 33,824 (2010–11) (table **E**). This is thousands more than the scientific workers and their support staff who are there temporarily for research purposes.

Tourists from the northern hemisphere usually fly to New Zealand or Argentina, taking their cruise ship onwards for one to two weeks. Smaller boats take them ashore at key locations for short visits, mainly to the peninsula or nearby islands (map **F**).

Landing sites on Antarctica are limited and quickly become honeypot sites. Tourists have the potential to cause environmental and ecological damage, so management is important. Walking, kayaking, skiing, climbing, scuba diving and helicopter/small aircraft flights are some of the activities offered to tourists (chart **H** opposite).

F *The Antarctic Peninsula and nearby islands*

E *Antarctic tourist numbers (2010–11)*

Country of origin	Numbers	Percentage of total
USA	12,629	37.4
Australia	3,220	9.5
UK	2,763	8.1
Canada	2,531	7.5
Germany	2,378	7.0
Japan	936	2.8
Netherlands	889	2.6
Others	8,478	25.1
Total	33,824	100.0

G *Cruise ship in Antarctic waters*

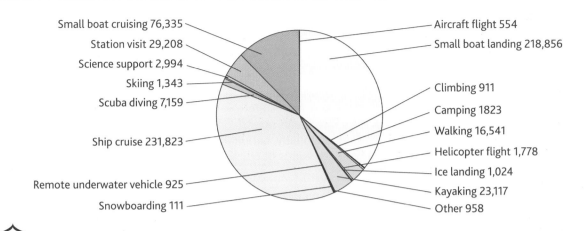

Small boat cruising 76,335
Station visit 29,208
Science support 2,994
Skiing 1,343
Scuba diving 7,159
Ship cruise 231,823
Remote underwater vehicle 925
Snowboarding 111

Aircraft flight 554
Small boat landing 218,856
Climbing 911
Camping 1823
Walking 16,541
Helicopter flight 1,778
Ice landing 1,024
Kayaking 23,117
Other 958

H *Tourist numbers in Antarctica, 2007–08*

Tourists only spend a short time ashore, but their impacts can be considerable. Animals, especially penguins and seals, are disturbed by more than a few people (photo **I**). Not used to humans, they do not like to be touched. If they leave as a result, they may abandon eggs and young.

There have been accidents when ships have struck uncharted rocks or ice floes. The great majority of shipping in Antarctic waters is tourist-based. Oil spills are becoming an increasing hazard for wildlife. Tourist ships must discharge all waste materials well away from the shore of Antarctica.

Coping with tourism in Antarctica

All tour operators are members of IAATO, which directs tourism to be safe and environmentally friendly. Around 100 companies are involved. In line with the Antarctic Treaty, tourism is an acceptable activity in Antarctica – it is the scale that has to be controlled. Visitors are not allowed to visit Sites of Special Scientific Interest (SSSIs) in order to conserve precious wildlife and landscapes. Bird Island on South Georgia is one example.

Although tourist numbers have increased rapidly in Antarctica, protection remains a high priority. A permit must be gained for any activities on the continent. No ship carrying over 500 passengers can land in Antarctica. Nevertheless, there is concern that larger ships will eventually be allowed to land and that the volume of tourists will be beyond sustainable limits.

I *The impact of tourists can be great*

Activity

Use the information about Antarctica to help you make a study of tourism in this extreme environment. Use the Internet to help you investigate the following themes:

a   What are the attractions to tourists?

b   Where do tourists come from? (Here you could use table **E** opposite to make a flow map.)

c   What are the issues associated with tourism?

d   How should tourism be controlled in the future?

links

Find out more about tourism in Antarctica at **www.coolantarctic.com**.

13.7 How can tourism become more sustainable?

Stewardship and conservation

In the Middle Ages a steward was in charge of his master's estate and business. Today, the term **stewardship** is used to mean careful management of the environment on a large scale, regionally, nationally and globally. We all have a responsibility for being stewards of our environment to ensure that it is sustainable.

Conservation is stewardship on a smaller and more manageable scale. People feel much more involved at this level. An individual building can be conserved and protected because of its historical importance. Habitats and landscapes in rural areas can be protected. Careful use of non-renewable resources such as oil is also a form of conservation. Planned use allows them to last as long as possible. Conservation can involve improving energy efficiency and recycling waste.

The aims of ecotourism

Ecotourism is environmentally friendly tourism. It caters for a small but growing niche market of environmentally aware tourists and is the fastest expanding tourism sector.

Ecotourists want to experience the natural environment directly, undertaking activities such as trekking and bird-watching. They want their holiday to have as little impact on the environment as possible. Energy use should be sustainable and no waste should be generated that cannot be dealt with efficiently. Ecotourists prefer small-scale accommodation in lodges that may not even have electricity, rather than large hotels. They eat local food. Local people are their guides as their knowledge and experience is seen to be more valuable. The impact on the environment is low but, because ecotourism is small in scale, the price paid by each tourist is high. The market for such tourism is therefore limited.

In this section you will learn

the concept of sustainable tourism

different types of sustainable tourism and be able to compare them.

Key terms

Stewardship: the personal responsibility of us all for looking after things, in this case the environment. No one should damage the present or future environment.

Conservation: the thoughtful use of resources; managing the landscape in order to protect ecosystems and cultural features.

A *Ecotourism in a Costa Rican rainforest*

Study tip

Ensure you can use an example to explain how ecotourism can contribute to sustainable development.

The Galapagos Islands

The 50 volcanic Galapagos Islands lie 1,000 km off the west coast of South America in the Pacific Ocean. They belong to Ecuador. Here, Charles Darwin formulated his theory of evolution. Around 90 per cent of these islands are designated as National Park or marine reserve. Protection began in the 1930s. The islands are among the most fragile and precious ecosystems in the world, becoming the first Unesco World Heritage Site in 1979. The area is also a biosphere reserve and whale sanctuary.

Today, tourists visit under strict rules. They arrive mainly by small ships that tour the islands and allow people onshore only at specific locations in limited numbers.

The tour boats are owned by locals and take 10 to 16 tourists each, many accompanied by professional guides. Visitors are given accurate information and prevented from causing damage.

Benefits

- Environmental – the Galapagos Conservation Trust receives approximately £25 from each tourist out of the cost of their holiday. This pays for conservation work on the islands.

- Economic – local people act as paid guides and small businesses have been started, for example boat companies providing trips around the islands. Local people run guest houses and provide other services.

Problems

- Honeypot sites – even though tourism is controlled, some sites are over-used and are showing signs of environmental stress.

- Pollution – oil pollution from boats can affect fragile marine ecosystems.

B   *Ecotourism on the Galapagos Islands*

Activities

1 a   Write a definition of ecotourism.

   b   What are the main characteristics of ecotourism?

   c   Do you think ecotourism is a good thing? Why?

2   Choose one of this chapter's case studies – Jamaica or the Galapagos Islands. Write an extract from a travel company brochure to sell this holiday to potential customers. Think of your target market and make sure you use language that would appeal to them. For your chosen tourist destination, find a photo from the internet to illustrate the holiday you are advertising.

3   The Geography and Biology departments at your school want to run a trip to the Galapagos Islands. Your class has been asked to help promote the trip by producing posters and PowerPoint presentations. The trip is to be as environmentally sensitive as possible so you need to stress the principles of ecotourism. Work in pairs or small groups and use the Internet to help you.

Levels of response marking

Levels of response marking is normally used for answers with a mark allocation of four and above. Parts of questions with fewer marks are point marked. With point marked questions there is a mark allocated for each point made. It is possible to allocate a mark to a particular point in the answer where there is a correct and relevant response. For this reason it is possible to put ticks on the correct, relevant information. The question will be worded so that it is clear that a certain number of points have to be made. For example, give *one advantage and one disadvantage of* ……… would be worth two marks. In levels marking, the mark allocated is for the overall quality of the answer *as a whole* and not for specific points within it.

There will be some questions on a Higher Tier paper which have only a maximum of two levels possible. In the vast majority of cases this will mean that the total mark would be four, which gives both levels a range of two marks i.e. level one with 1–2 marks and level two worth 3–4 marks. If six marks are allocated to a question then the split is likely to 1–4 and 5–6 marks. Those questions with the possibility of achieving a level three response will have an allocation of eight marks, with a breakdown of 1–4, 5–6 and 7–8 marks.

There are descriptions for each level as follows:

■ Level 1: Basic

- Knowledge of basic information
- Simple understanding
- Little organisation with few links, little or no detail, uses a limited range of specialist terms
- Reasonable accuracy in spelling, punctuation and grammar
- Text is legible.

■ Level 2: Clear

- Knowledge of accurate information
- Clear understanding
- Organised answers with some links, occasional detail/exemplar, uses a good range of specialist terms where appropriate
- Considerable accuracy in spelling, punctuation and grammar
- Text is legible.

■ Level 3: Detailed

- Knowledge of accurate information appropriately contextualised and/or at correct scale
- Detailed understanding, supported by relevant evidence and exemplars
- Well-organised, demonstrating detailed links and the inter-relationships between factors
- Clear and fluid expression of ideas in a logical form; uses a wide range of specialist terms where appropriate
- Accurate use of spelling, punctuation and grammar.

In a physical geography question testing your knowledge and understanding of the geomorphological formation of a landform, such as a corrie or a wave cut platform, level marking would normally work as follows:

- A level one answer would consist of simple, descriptive statements with either an incomplete or inaccurate sequence in the formation of the landform and with no reference to any processes. Alternatively, there may be some explanation of processes but limited or random understanding of sequence.
- At level two, examiners would expect a complete sequence and at least the names of the erosion or depositional processes involved.

- The detail in a level three answer would come from a full description of these landscape processes.

- On other occasions, the explanation of landforms may only go to level two. If a question goes to level three, then there may be a requirement to include a diagram. The diagram needs to be clear and must add something to what is given in the text.

- If the formation of two landforms are required in a question, then both must be covered if level three is to be given.

- A perfect answer is not usually expected, even for full marks.

You can also gain further marks if the spelling, punctuation and grammar is accurate.

Do not work through all the levels. Write at the highest level possible right at the beginning of your answer. Always try to write linked statements, because this triggers access to level two. No matter how many simple unlinked statements you write, your answer will remain in level one. Linking two or more of these statements, by means of a conjunction or another 'joining' word, means that there has been some development or elaboration of a simple or basic fact or idea. This will get you level two.

If after reading a point the reader wants to say 'so what?', the answer has not been developed and so remains in level one. Consider the answer to a question such as – *What is the advantage of a conservation swap to a country in the Poor World?'* If your answer consists merely of, *'It brings money into the country'*, the reader wants to know more. On the other hand if the answer reads *'It brings money into the country in return for agreeing not to cut down any more rainforest',* there is some clarity to the answer, as a result of developing the simple idea of the poor country receiving money. No marks to be deducted for any incorrect or irrelevant information.

The main feature of a level three response is the depth of detail in the answer. This can often be achieved with the effective use of a case study, even if there is not a requirement for one in the wording of the question. There is, however, one major requirement that has to be satisfied if your answer is to be considered for access to level three. You have to answer *all* parts of the question. On a Higher Tier paper, a question that allows access to level three may have several parts to it, all of which have to be answered. The question is very likely to have two command words. You may be asked to *describe* and *explain*. There may be plurals in the question. It may ask for consideration of *causes, effects,* or *responses* for example, or even *advantages* and/or *disadvantages*. In physical geography questions, they may be asked to consider the effect of physical features on *both* the environment *and* on the lives of people. In all these cases, if only one is considered then the candidate cannot be considered for level three, even if the quality of what has been written is of level three quality. For this reason it is important that you get into the habit of breaking down a question. Get into the habit of highlighting or underlining on the examination paper all the command words and any plurals etc. in order to ensure that all parts are covered.

What's in a Question ?

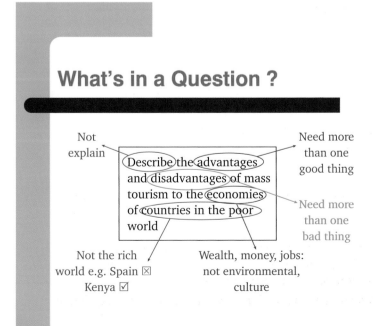

Consider the following questions and the examples of possible candidates' answers.

■ Water on the land

Hard and soft engineering are used to manage flooding.

Choose **either** hard engineering **or** soft engineering and explain why it is a better strategy.   *(8 marks)*

Level 1 (Basic) 1–4 marks

The answer will be made up of simple statements, which are mainly descriptions of one or more flooding strategy. There may be some confusion between hard and soft engineering. The information is not given in a logical order

> Trees are planted. A dam is built. The river is straightened. The area next to the river is not built on.

There are four basic statements without any real development. More would be expected for the top of level one, so this answer could be awarded three marks out of a possible four. Point marking should not take place within a level.

Level 2 (Clear) 5–6 marks

The answer has linked statements, with some attempt to explain why one is a better option. There are clear advantages of one option and/or the disadvantages of alternatives

> Hard engineering controls flooding by building large constructions like dams and reservoirs, raising the banks, straightening a river and planting trees. The building of a dam is a good way of controlling flooding because it stops the water overflowing the banks. It can be used to produce hydroelectric power (HEP) and the reservoir formed behind the dam is a source of water. Its disadvantage is that dams are expensive to build.

This answer is not entirely clear, suggesting that the candidate has not fully understood the difference between hard and soft engineering. There is an attempt to consider both advantages and disadvantages using a linked statement, so satisfies the requirement for level two. There is no attempt to say why one option is better than the other as required by the question, so the answer cannot be considered for level three. The definition of hard engineering is not relevant to the question.

Greater clarity could have been achieved in this answer if some indication had been given of the disadvantage of some form of soft engineering, which would have given some indication that it was felt that hard engineering was preferable to soft engineering. This answer would have scored five out of the possible six marks available at level two.

Level 3 (Detailed) 7–8 marks

The answer contains linked, detailed statements clearly focused on why the selected option is better. The advantages of the option are presented and/or the disadvantages of an alternative are considered.

> It is impossible to completely control flooding so it is better to try to manage the effect of the flooding. This is done by soft rather than hard engineering strategies. There may be benefits from a hard engineering strategy such as building a dam – the production of HEP and providing a reservoir as a source of water – but the disadvantages are much greater. Building a dam is very expensive and sediment can be trapped behind the dam. This can lead to the formation of a large malarial swamp as in Lake Volta in Ghana, or the loss of rich alluvium which has happened in Egypt after the building of the Aswan Dam. Soft engineering is a better option as it works with nature and is less expensive. If trees are planted on steep slopes, more rainwater will be delayed before reaching the river making it less likely to flood. Land use zoning is where there are strict planning controls

on what can be built on the flood plain of a river. The land next to the river is not built on and as the distance from the river increases, so does the value of the land. Important buildings such as factories and schools should be built away from the river. This does restrict the area available for building and is no good as a plan if the area has already been built upon. In these areas there needs to be good preparation or prediction plans which are also examples of soft engineering.

There is no requirement for the use of case studies in this question but their use is an excellent way of achieving the detail required for a level three answer.

Different examples have been used to show the advantages and disadvantages of different hard and soft engineering strategies. There is an advantage in doing this, as it is unlikely that a single example could provide enough factual information to cover all parts of the question. This answer does not achieve a balance between advantages and disadvantages or between the consideration of different strategies but full marks do not demand a perfect answer. The answer indicates clearly what the preferred option is and includes sufficient detailed information so that the full eight marks can be awarded.

▆ Tourism

Choose **either** a National Park **or** a coastal resort in the UK.

Describe **one** or **more** strategies that your chosen area has used to maintain a successful tourist industry.

(8 marks)

Level 1 (Basic) 1–4 marks

The answer will consist of a number of simple statements which will be largely a list of strategies. There may not be a named example.

> The National Park has mended fences and repaired footpaths. New activities have been introduced. People go there because of the beautiful scenery and they are able to go for walks. New motorways have been built so people can get there easily.

or

> People go to a coastal resort because there is a beach and they can go swimming or sunbathe. There are lots of things to do and often there are amusement arcades and lots of shops. Some new fairground attractions are built. There are new hotels built.

In both examples the question has not been fully answered. Part of each answer give reasons why the tourist industry developed in the area rather than describing what is being done to ensure the future success of the industry. Where strategies are referred to, they are given as a list and there has been no attempt to explain how the strategy could impact on the tourist industry's future. The strategies mentioned could apply to anywhere and there are no named examples as required by the question. In both examples there is not enough correct relevant information to reach the top of the level and they would each have gained two marks out of a possible four.

Level 2 (Clear) 5–6 marks

There will be linked statements which show how the strategies may have an effect on ensuring the future success of the tourist trade. Even if there is a named example the strategies are generalised.

> In the Lake District there are farms that have introduced tourist activities and so encourage more people to go there because there are more things to do. Minibuses take people to more remote areas and this reduces traffic congestion which would destroy the peace of the area. Footpath erosion ruins the beauty of the area and so people may no longer want to go, so these footpaths are being repaired.

> In Bournemouth they have built conference places so more people go to the area. New shops have been built so people can go shopping. This means that people who do not want to lie on the beach will also enjoy going to the town. Luxury hotels have been built which will attract people who will not want to stay in cheaper accommodation.

In both these examples there are named examples and while the strategies described are relevant they are not given in enough detail or are insufficiently specific to these places to move to the highest level. There is clarity to these answers, consisting of linked statements that show how the strategies described encourage more tourists to visit and so maintain or strengthen the position of the industry. These answers would both reach the top of level two and so gain a total of six marks out of a possible eight.

Level 3 (Detailed) 7–8 marks

There will be detailed specific strategies and evidence of how the named example has implemented them and what results are expected.

> People may be discouraged from going to the Lake District because of traffic congestion on the small country roads. The Lake District National Park wants to reduce the use of the car by developing the B4 network. B4 means bus, boat, bike and boot and allows people to get around the Coniston and Hawkshead areas. It is hoped that fewer cars will reduce traffic pollution and so more people will want to go to the area. There is a bus–boat–bus service linking Windermere and Coniston which, in turn, links to the many footpaths in the area. There are also cycle racks on the boats and minibuses. A recent survey showed that 57% of the people using the service had cars but chose not to use them. The 'Give the Driver a break' strategy has produced a series of leaflets which encourage visitors to leave their car behind and travel by alternative sources of transport such as steam trains, open topped buses and boats throughout the Lake District.

or

> Newquay in Cornwall is promoting itself as the surf capital of Britain. This has drawn in a lot of young people which has led to problems with drugs and alcohol and has put off many older people going to the resort. The police have attempted to stop teenagers bringing in drugs and alcohol , with some success especially those going on the traditional end of term parties. Police now patrol the airport and the train station and use sniffer dogs in order to stop underage drinkers and make the place safer so that families will feel happy to come back to the town for their holidays. Newquay airport now has scheduled flights to and from ten places in the UK and Europe, so people can now go to the town for a weekend rather than just the traditional week or fortnight and so a different kind of holiday maker will visit.

Both these answers have taken one or two strategies and described them in detail. It is always better to look at fewer examples in detail then try and cover a larger number which will only be achieved with a loss of detail. In both cases the examples are specific to the named area – by reference to named locations in the case of the Lake District and dealing with a specific problem in the case of Newquay. The strategies are described, the reasons for them are explained and there is the required link to the hoped for impact the plans will have on the future of the tourist industry. Both these answers would gain the full eight marks.

Practice questions

These Practice questions are in the style you may encounter in the examination paper, but are not representative of the full range of questions and mark schemes you will find in the actual examination.

These questions have been written based on existing content within the student book; in the examination you will not necessarily be tied to one specific case study.

1 The restless earth

a)   i)   Look at figure C on page 9. Name **two** plates that meet at a destructive plate margin.   *(2 marks)*
         ii) Give **one** reason why the plate margin shown on Figure D on page 10 can be described as destructive.   *(1 mark)*
         iii) Explain why earthquakes occur at conservative plate margins.   *(4 marks)*

b)   Describe **one** way people make a living in an area of fold mountains.   *(4 marks)*

c)   With reference to a named volcanic eruption, explain how the effects can be both positive and negative.   *(6 marks)*

d)   Explain how **the three P's** described on page 30 help to explain the different responses to earthquakes in the rich and poor worlds.   *(8 marks)*

2 Rocks, resources and scenery

a)   Use Figure A on page 34 to explain the difference between an era and a period.   *(2 marks)*

b)   Explain how climate can affect the way that rocks are weathered.   *(4 marks)*

c)   i)   In south east England the chalk rocks form cuestas or escarpments. Use Figure B on page 43 to explain how this landform was formed   *(6 marks)*
         ii) Name **one** way that people use a chalk landscape   *(1 mark)*

d)   Figure A on page 45 describes carboniferous limestone as a hard, well jointed and permeable rock. Explain how these characteristics are important in the formation of features such as limestone pavements, swallow holes and caverns.   *(8 marks)*

e)   Describe how a quarry can be managed to reduce harmful effects on the environment.   *(4 marks)*

3 Challenge of weather and climate

a)   What is the difference between climate and weather?   *(2 marks)*

b)   i)   Study Figures Ca and Cb on page 55. Outline how the pattern of temperatures over the UK varies between January and July.   *(2 marks)*
         ii) Study Figure Cc on page 55. Explain why it is wetter in the west than the east of the UK   *(2 marks)*

c)   Study Figure D on page 58. Explain why the type and duration of the rainfall differ as the warm and cold fronts pass over.   *(4 marks)*

d)   Use Figure K on page 60 to give **one** reason why the weather does not change much when the UK is experiencing anticyclonic conditions.   *(1 mark)*

e)   Describe evidence which supports the view that the UK's weather is becoming more extreme.   *(6 marks)*

f)   Discuss the global and local responses to the threat of climate change.   *(8 marks)*

4   Living world

a)   i)   Draw a labelled diagram of a **named** small scale ecosystem.   *(4 marks)*

ii)   Underline **one** producer named on your ecosystem diagram.   *(1 mark)*

iii)   Outline how a change in one part of the ecosystem can affect the others.   *(2 marks)*

b)   i)   Describe and explain the main characteristics of the soil found in tropical rainforest areas.   *(4 marks)*

ii)   Explain how the vegetation in a tropical rainforest is adapted to its climate.   *(6 marks)*

c)   Use a case study of a hot desert in **either** the rich world **or** the poor world to describe how threats to the area are being managed.   *(8 marks)*

5   Water on the land

a)   i)   Study Figure C on page 101. Give **two** pieces of evidence that the photograph of Grindsbrook Clough was taken near its source.   *(2 marks)*

ii)   Name one way that a river erodes its bed and banks.   *(1 mark)*

iii)   Draw two or more annotated diagrams to show how a waterfall changes over time.   *(4 marks)*

b)   Explain how physical and human factors can affect a river's discharge.   *(8 marks)*

c)   Explain the different responses to the floods in Cockermouth and Bangladesh described on pages 114–116.   *(6 marks)*

d)   Explain the need for the transfer of water within the UK.   *(4 marks)*

6   Ice on the land

a)   Describe the sources and the extent of the ice cover 18,000 years ago as shown on Figure C on page 124.   *(4 marks)*

b)   i)   What is meant by ablation?   *(1 mark)*

ii)   Use Figure D on page 127 to describe the changes in the glacial budget of the South Cascade glacier between 2000 and 2005.   *(2 marks)*

c)   Use Figure G on page 133 to draw a labelled sketch map of a corrie and tarn.   *(4 marks)*

d)   Refer to the case study of the French Alps on pages 135–137. Do the benefits brought by tourism outweigh the social and environmental costs to the area? Explain your decision.   *(8 marks)*

e)   Comment on the effectiveness of the different measures aimed at reducing the impact of avalanches shown on Figure D on page 143.   *(6 marks)*

7   The coastal zone

a)   i)   Describe the difference between a constructive and a destructive wave.   *(4 marks)*

ii)   Give two factors that affect the characteristics of waves.   *(2 marks)*

b)   i)   Study the geology map Figure A on page 152. Why is the south coast straighter than the east coast?   *(1 mark)*

ii)   Explain how the structure of the coast influences the coastal landforms that develop in the Swanage area shown on Figure C on page 153.   *(4 marks)*

c)   Use Figure A on page 158 to support the view that the coastline of East Anglia will be very different from its present form in the future.   *(6 marks)*

d)   Discuss whether hard or soft engineering strategies are the most appropriate for managing the coastline.   *(8 marks)*

8 Population change

a) What is the meaning of the term 'natural increase'? *(1 mark)*

b) i)   Describe the pattern shown on Figure E on page 176. *(4 marks)*

ii) Explain why birth and death rates are declining in many countries in the poor world. *(6 marks)*

c) i)   Since the 1990s China's One Child Policy has been relaxed in some areas for the following groups:

Ethnic minorities   People living in rural areas   Parents with no brothers or sisters

Choose **two** of the above and suggest why these groups are now allowed to have more than one child. *(4 marks)*

ii) Using the case studies described on pages 181–185, comment on the effectiveness of the different population strategies adopted by China and Indonesia as ways of coping with a rapidly increasing population. *(8 marks)*

d) Explain the difference between a refugee and an economic migrant. *(2 marks)*

9 Changing urban environments

a) State the difference between urbanisation and urban growth. *(2 marks)*

b) i)   Explain why there are increasing housing needs in different parts of cities in the UK. You should refer to at least two different parts of a city in your answer. *(8 marks)*

ii) Describe two different approaches to urban regeneration used in inner cities in a country in the rich world. *(4 marks)*

c) Describe the features of the Kibera squatter settlement shown on Figures E and F on pages 208 and 209. *(4 marks)*

d) i)   Name **one** type of toxic waste that is found in many cities in the poor world. *(1 mark)*

ii) Use the information on page 210 to suggest why there is a great problem of waste disposal in many cities in the poor world. *(4 marks)*

e) Name **two** characteristics of sustainable urban living. *(2 marks)*

10 Changing rural environments

a) i)   Use Figure A on page 220 to show how the Bluewater Park described on page 221 illustrates many of the pressures faced by the rural-urban fringes of many cities in the rich world. *(6 marks)*

ii) In what respects does Chalgrove, which is described on page 223, have the characteristics of a village expanding in size? *(4 marks)*

iii) What is meant by commuting? *(1 mark)*

b) Choose **two** of the strategies aimed at sustaining rural living detailed on pages 228–231. For **each** suggest how effective it will be in achieving sustainable rural living. *(4 marks)*

c) Use the case study of East Anglia on page 233 to explain why modern farming has had such an impact on the environment. *(8 marks)*

d) Suggest why the development of organic farming has slowed down in recent years. *(2 marks)*

11 The development gap

a) i) Compare Figures A and B on pages 251 and 252. Why is the five-fold division more appropriate than a simple two-fold one? *(4 marks)*

ii) Explain why HDI is more useful than GNI as a measure of development. *(2 marks)*

b) Use the case studies on pages 265–266 to explain why smaller scale development projects can be more successful in improving a poor country's development than a large scale scheme. *(8 marks)*

c) Using evidence from Bulgaria and Ireland on pages 267–268, explain how physical and human factors cause the great differences in the development of these two countries. *(6 marks)*

d) i) Name **one** way the E.U. has tried to reduce inequalities within Europe. *(1 mark)*

ii) Suggest how well this strategy has achieved its objective. *(4 marks)*

12 Globalisation

a) i) What is the meaning of the term globalisation? *(1 mark)*

ii) Explain how developments in ICT have contributed to globalisation. *(6 marks)*

iii) Describe the impact of globalisation on older established industrial areas. *(4 marks)*

b) i) Describe and explain the trends of the graph shown on Figure A on page 279. *(4 marks)*

ii) Explain the reasons for China's rapid economic development. *(8 marks)*

c) Explain why any attempt at pollution control has to be international if it is to be successful. *(2 marks)*

13 Tourism

a) i) Use the information on **either** Blackpool on page 303 **or** the Lake District on page 306 to show how the area you have chosen is planning to ensure the continuing success of its tourist industry. *(8 marks)*

ii) What are the features of the exploration/development/stagnation phase of the Butler (tourist resort/life-cycle) model? *(1 mark)*

iii) Give one reason why a resort may decline in popularity. *(2 marks)*

b) Explain why the north coast of Jamaica shown in Figure D on page 311 is an example of mass tourism. *(4 marks)*

c) Use the information about the Antarctic given on pages 314–5 to show the extent to which the area can cope with the development of a tourist industry. *(6 marks)*

d) Explain why the Galapagos Islands described on page 317 is an example of ecotourism. *(4 marks)*

Glossary

This is a glossary of key terms that appear in the GCSE Geography A specification. Additional key terms are defined in the text.

A

Ablation: outputs from the glacier budget, such as melting.

Abrasion: a process of erosion involving the wearing away of the valley floor and sides (glaciers) and the shoreline (coastal zones).

Abrasion (*rivers*): happens when larger loads carried by the river hits the bed and banks, causing bits to break off.

Accumulation: inputs to the glacier budget, such as snowfall and avalanches.

Age structure: the proportions of each age group in a population. This links closely to the stage a country has reached in the demographic transition model.

Aid: money, food, training and technology given by richer countries to poorer ones, either to help with an emergency or for long-term development.

Air pollution: putting harmful substances into the atmosphere such as carbon dioxide.

Altitude: height above sea level, usually given in metres.

Anticyclone: an area of high atmospheric pressure.

Aquifer: an underground reservoir of water stored in pores and/or joints in a rock such as chalk.

Arable farming: growing crops.

Arch: a headland that has been partly broken through by the sea to form a thin-roofed arch.

Areas of water deficit: areas where the rain that falls does not provide enough water and there may be shortages.

Areas of water surplus: areas that have more water than is needed – often such areas receive a high rainfall total, but have a relatively small population.

Arête: a knife-edged ridge, often formed between two corries.

Attrition: the knocking together of stones, making them gradually smaller and smoother.

Avalanche: a very fast downhill movement of a mass of snow, ice and rocks.

B

Bar: a spit that has grown across a bay.

Bay: a broad coastal inlet often with a beach.

Beach: a deposit of sand or shingle at the coast, often found at the head of a bay.

Biofuels: the use of living things such as crops like maize to make ethanol (an alcohol-based fuel) or biogas from animal waste. It is the use of crops that has become especially important.

Biological weathering: weathering caused by living things such as tree roots or burrowing animals.

Birth rate (BR): the number of babies born per 1,000 people per year.

Bottom-up aid: aid used to provide basic health care for communities, clean drinking water and money for education.

Brownfield sites: land that has been built on before and is to be cleared and reused. These sites are often in the inner city.

Bulldozing: the pushing of deposited sediment at the snout by a glacier as it advances.

C

Call centres: offices where groups of people answer telephone queries from customers. Employees use a computer to give them information that helps them answer questions.

Carbon credits: a means of trading carbon between organisations or countries in order to meet an overall target.

Carbon footprint: the amount of carbon generated by things people do, including creating a demand for out-of-season food.

Carbonation: weathering of limestone and chalk by acidic rainwater.

Carbon emissions: release of carbon (usually in the form of carbon dioxide) often by burning fossil fuels.

Cash crops: crops grown in order to sell to make a financial profit.

Cave: a hollowed-out feature at the base of an eroding cliff.

Cavern: a large underground cave.

Cement: mortar used in building, made from crushed limestone and shale.

Central business district (CBD): the main shopping and service area in a city. The CBD is usually found in the middle of the city so that it is easily accessible.

Channel: the part of the river valley occupied by the water itself.

Chemical weathering: the process where chemical reactions change or destroy minerals when rock comes into contact with water and/or air.

Cliff: a steep or vertical face of rock often found at the coast.

Climate: the average weather conditions recorded over a period of at least 30 years.

Climate change: long-term changes in the climate, such as cooling leading to an Ice Age or the current trend of global warming.

Commercial farming: a type of farming where crops and/or livestock are sold to make a profit.

Commuter village: a village located in the rural–urban fringe, many of whose inhabitants commute to work in surrounding towns or cities.

Commuting: The daily movement of people travelling between home and work and back again.

Composite volcano: a steep-sided volcano that is made up of a variety of materials, such as lava and ash.

Congestion charging: charging vehicles to enter cities, with the aim of reducing the use of vehicles.

Conservation: the thoughtful use of resources; managing the landscape in order to protect ecosystems and cultural features.

Conservation swaps: agreements made between countries where some debts are written off in exchange for conservation projects being done.

Conservative plate margin: a plate margin where two plates are sliding alongside each other.

Constructive plate margin: a plate margin where two plates are moving apart.

Constructive wave: a powerful wave with a strong swash that surges up a beach.

Consumer: organisms that get their energy by eating other organisms.

Continental plate: a tectonic plate made of low density continental rock that will not sink under another plate.

Corrie: a deep depression on a hillside with a steep back wall, often containing a lake.

Cross profile: a line that represents what it would be like to walk from one side of a valley, across the channel and up the other side.

Crust: the outer layer of the earth.

Curtain: a broad deposit of calcite usually formed when water emerges along a crack in a cavern.

D

Dam: an artificial structure designed to hold back water to create a reservoir.

Death rate (DR): the number of deaths per 1,000 people per year.

Debt: money owed to others, to a bank or to a global organisation such as the World Bank.

Debt repayment: paying back money borrowed to support development to banks or governments.

Decomposers: organisms such as bacteria that break down plant and animal material.

Deforestation: the removal of trees and undergrowth.

De-industrialisation: a process of decline in some types of industry over a long period of time. It results in fewer people being employed in this sector and falling production.

Demographic transition model: a theoretical model that shows changes in population information (birth and death rates and population growth) over a period of time.

Deposition: the dumping (deposition) of sediment that has been transported by a river.

Depression: an area of low atmospheric pressure.

Destructive plate margin: a plate margin where two plates are moving towards each other resulting in one plate sinking beneath the other.

Destructive wave: a wave formed by a local storm that crashes down onto a beach and has a powerful backwash.

Development measure: statistics used to show the level of development, which allows countries to be compared.

Discharge: the volume of water passing a given point in a river at any moment in time.

Disposal of waste: safely getting rid of unwanted items such as solid waste.

Donor country: a country giving aid to another country.

Drainage basin: area from which a river gets its water. The boundary is marked by an imaginary line of highland known as a watershed.

Drumlin: an egg-shaped hill found on the floor of a glacial trough.

Dry valley: a valley formed by a river during a wetter period in the past but now without a river.

E

Earthquake: a sudden and often violent shift in the rocks forming the earth's crust, which is felt at the surface.

Economic: this relates to costs and finances at a variety of levels, from individuals to government.

Economic core: the centre of a country or region economically, where businesses thrive, people have opportunities and are relatively wealthy. A highly developed area.

Economic periphery: the edge of a country or region in terms of economics. It may not physically be the edge, but is a more remote, difficult area where people tend to be poorer and have fewer opportunities. A less well developed area.

Ecosystem: the living and non-living parts of an environment and the interrelationships between them.

Ecotourism: tourism that focuses on protecting the environment and the local way of life. Also known as green tourism.

Emigrant: someone leaving their country of residence to move to another country.

Environmental: this is the impact on our surroundings, including the land, water and air as well as features of the built-up areas.

Environmental degradation: undesirable changes to the natural environment through the removal of natural resources and disruption to natural ecosystems. Human activity is a major cause.

Epicentre: the point at the earth's surface directly above the focus of an earthquake.

Erosion: the sculpting of a landscape, for example by rivers, involving the removal of material.

Escarpment/cuesta: an outcrop of chalk made up of a steep scarp slope and a more gentle dip slope.

European Union (EU): a group of countries across Europe that work towards a single market, i.e. they trade as if they were one country, without any trade barriers.

Exfoliation: flaking of the outer surface of rocks mainly caused by repeated cycles of hot and cold.

Exponential growth: a pattern where the growth rate constantly increases – often shown as a J-curve graph.

Extreme environments: places with particularly difficult environments, such as being very hot or cold. Tourism to these places has only recently occurred due to people wanting to visit somewhere with different physical challenges.

Extreme weather: a weather event such as a flash flood or severe snowstorm that is significantly different from the average.

F

Fair trade: a system whereby agricultural producers in countries at lesser stages of development are paid a decent price for their produce. This helps them to attain a reasonable standard of living.

Flashy: a hydrograph that responds quickly to a period of rain so that it characteristically has a high peak and a short lag time.

Flood or storm hydrograph: a line graph drawn to show the discharge in a river in the aftermath of a period of rain, which is shown as a bar graph.

Floodplain: the flat area next to the river channel, especially in the lower part of the course. This is a natural area for water to spill onto when the river reaches the top of its banks.

Floodplain zoning: controlling what is built on the floodplain so that areas that are at risk of flooding have low-value land uses.

Floods: these occur when a river carries so much water that it cannot be contained by its banks and so it overflows onto surrounding land – its floodplain.

Focus: the point in the earth's crust where an earthquake begins.

Fold mountains: large mountain ranges where rock layers have been crumpled as they have been forced together.

Food chain: a line of linkages between producers and consumers.

Food miles: the distance that food items travel from where they are grown to where they are eaten.

Food web: a diagram that shows all the linkages between producers and consumers in an ecosystem.

Fragile environment: an environment that is easily unbalanced and damaged by natural or human factors.

Freeze–thaw weathering: weathering involving repeated cycles of freezing and thawing.

Function: the purpose of a particular area, for example for residential use, recreation or shopping.

G

Gender structure: the balance between males and females in a population. Small differences can tell us a great deal about a country or city.

Geological timescale: the period of time since life became abundant 542 million years ago, which geologists have divided into eras and periods.

Glacial retreat: melting of the ice causes a glacier to retreat up-valley.

Glacial trough: a wide, steep-sided valley eroded by a glacier.

Glacier: a finger of ice usually extending downhill from an ice cap and occupying a valley.

Glacier budget: the balance between the inputs (accumulation) and the outputs (ablation) of a glacier.

Global warming: an increase in world temperatures as a result of the increase in greenhouse gases (carbon dioxide, methane, CFCs and nitrous oxide) in the atmosphere brought about by the burning of fossil fuels, for example.

Globalisation: the increasing links between different countries throughout the world and the greater interdependence that results from this.

GNI: Gross National Income – the total value of goods and services produced within a country including income received from and payments made to other countries.

GNP: Gross National Product – the total value of all goods and services produced by a nation in a particular year.

Gorge: a narrow steep-sided deep valley.

Greenfield sites: land that has not been built on before, usually in the countryside on the edge of the built-up area.

Gross domestic product (GDP): the total value of goods and services produced by a country divided by its total population. Foreign income is not included.

Ground moraine: glacial material deposited on the valley floor, often forming hummocks.

Groyne: timber or rock structure built out to sea to trap sediment being moved by longshore drift.

H

Habitat: the home to a community of plants and animals.

Hanging valley: a tributary glacial trough perched up on the side of a main valley, often marked by a waterfall.

Hard engineering: building artificial structures such as sea walls aimed at controlling natural processes.

Hazard: an event where people's lives and property are threatened and deaths and/or damage result.

Hazard map: A map that shows areas that are at risk from hazards such as earthquakes, volcanoes, landslides, floods and tsunamis.

HDI: Human Development Index – an index based on three variables: life expectancy at birth; level of education, including both literacy rate and years spent in school; income adjusted for purchasing power (how much it will buy). Maximum HDI = 1. Wealthy countries like Japan have an HDI of over 0.9, whereas poor countries are around half that figure or less. HDI concentrates on people's experience rather than economic measures.

Headland: a point of usually high land jutting out into the sea.

Honeypot site: somewhere that attracts a large number of tourists who, due to their numbers, place pressure on the environment and people.

Hot deserts: deserts have a rainfall of less than 250 mm per year. Hot deserts are generally found between 30°N and 30°S.

Hurricane: a powerful tropical storm with sustained winds of over 120 kph (75 mph). Also known as a tropical cyclone, a cyclone or a typhoon.

Hydraulic action: the power of the volume of water moving in the river.

Hydraulic power: the sheer power of the waves.

Hydroelectric power: the use of flowing water to turn turbines to generate electricity.

I

Igneous rocks: rocks formed from the cooling of molten magma.

Immediate responses: how people react during a disaster and straight afterwards.

Impermeable: rock that does not allow water to pass through it.

Industrialisation: a process usually linked with the development of an economy, where an increasing proportion of people work in industry.

Infant mortality: the number of babies that die under a year of age, per 1,000 live births.

Informal sector: that part of the economy where jobs are created by people to try to get an income (for example taking in washing, mending bicycles) and which are not recognised on official figures.

Inner city: the area around the CBD – usually built before 1918 in the UK.

Insolation: heating of the earth's surface by the sun.

Interdependence: the relationship between two or more countries, usually in terms of trade.

Irrigation: artificial watering of the land.

K

Kyoto Protocol: an international agreement to try and reduce carbon emissions from industrialised countries.

L

Landslip: a type of mass movement common at the coast involving material slipping downhill usually along a curved slip surface.

Land use: the type of buildings or other features that are found in the area, for example terraced housing, banks, industrial estates, roads, parks.

Landfill: digging a large hole in the ground and lining it before filling it with rubbish.

Lateral erosion: sideways erosion, for example in a river channel at the outside bend of a meander.

Lateral moraine: a ridge of sediment running along the edge of a glacier where it meets the valley side.

Latitude: determines the geographic north-south position of a point on the earth. 0° is at the Equator and 90° are at the poles.

Levees: raised banks along the course of a river in its lower course. They are formed naturally but can be artificially increased in height.

Life-cycle model: a theoretical model used to describe the changes that take place as a tourist resort develops.

Life expectancy: the number of years a person is expected to live, usually taken from birth.

Limestone pavement: a bare rocky surface, with blocks (clints) and enlarged joints (grikes).

Literacy rate: the percentage of adults in a country who can read and write sufficiently to function fully in work and society.

Living standards: people's quality of life, mostly measured economically but also socially, culturally and environmentally.

Load: material of any size carried by the river.

Long profile: a line representing the course of the river from its source (relatively high up) to its mouth where it ends, usually in a lake or the sea, and the changes in height along its course.

Long profile (glacier): this shows the changes in height and shape along the length of a glacier, from its source high in the mountains to its snout.

Longshore drift: the transport of sediment along a stretch of coastline caused by waves approaching the beach at an angle.

Long-term aid: aid given over a long period, which aims to promote economic development.

Long-term responses: later reactions that happen in the weeks, months and years after an event.

M

Managed retreat: allowing controlled flooding of low-lying coastal areas or cliff collapse in areas where the value of the land is low.

Marginal land: land that is only just good enough to be worth farming. It may be dry, wet, cool, stony or steep.

Maritime influence: the influence of the sea on climate.

Mass movement: the downhill movement of material under the influence of gravity.

Mass tourism: tourism on a large scale to one country or region. This is linked to the Development and Consolidation phases of the Butler tourist resort life-cycle model.

Meander: a bend or curve in the river channel.

Mechanical weathering: a process where physical forces break down or reduce a rock into smaller fragments.

Medial moraine: a ridge of sediment running down the centre of a glacier formed when two lateral moraines merge.

Mercalli scale: a means of measuring earthquakes by describing and comparing the damage done on a scale of I to XII.

Metamorphic rocks: rocks formed when the chemistry and texture have been changed because of heating and/or pressure.

Migration: the movement of people from one permanent home to another, with the intention of staying at least a year. This move may be within a country (national migration) or between countries (international migration).

Moraine: sediment carried and deposited by ice.

Multiplier effect: where initial investment and jobs lead to a knock-on effect, creating more jobs and providing money to generate services.

N

National Park: an area where development is limited and planning controlled. The landscape is regarded as unusual and valuable and therefore worth looking after.

Natural change: the difference between birth rate and death rate given as a percentage.

Natural hazard: an event over which people have little control, which threatens people's lives and possessions. This is different from a natural event as volcanoes can erupt in unpopulated areas without being a hazard.

Nutrient cycling: the recycling of nutrients between living organisms and the environment.

O

Oceanic plate: a tectonic plate made of dense iron-rich rock that forms the ocean floor.

Ocean trenches: deep sections of the ocean, where an oceanic plate is sinking below a continental plate.

Organic farm: a farm that does not use chemicals in the production of crops or livestock.

Outer city or suburbs: the area on the edge of the city. Many suburbs were built after 1945 and get newer as they reach the edge of the city.

Oxbow lake: a horseshoe or semicircular area that used to be a meander. Oxbow lakes are cut off from a supply of water and so will eventually become dry.

P

Permeable rock: a rock that allows water to pass through it.

Pervious: rock that allows water to pass through it via vertical joints and horizontal bedding planes.

Physical quality of life index (PQLI): the average of three social indicators: literacy rate, life expectancy and infant mortality.

Pillar: a calcite feature stretching from floor to ceiling in a cavern.

Plate: a section of the earth's crust.

Plate margin: the boundary where two plates meet.

Pleistocene period: a geological time period lasting from about 2 million years ago until 10,000 years ago. Sometimes this period is called the Ice Age.

Plucking: a process of glacial erosion where individual rocks are plucked from the valley floor or sides as water freezes them to the glacier.

Porous: rock that allows water to soak into it via spaces between particles.

Precipitation: the transfer of water from the atmosphere to the ground, for example rain and snow.

Prediction: attempts to forecast an event – where and when it will happen – based on current knowledge.

Preparation: organising activities and drills so that people know what to do if an earthquake happens.

Pressure (atmospheric): pressure exerted on the Earth's surface by the mass of the overlying atmosphere.

Primary effects: the immediate effects of an event, for example a volcanic eruption, caused directly by it.

Producers: organisms that get their energy from a primary source such as the sun.

Protection: constructing buildings so that they are safe to live in and will not collapse.

Push–pull factors: push factors are the negative aspects of a place that encourage people to move away. Pull factors are the attractions and opportunities of a place that encourage people to move there.

Pyramidal peak: a sharp-edged mountain peak.

Q

Quality of life: how good a person's life is as measured by such things as quality of housing and environment, access to education, health care, how secure people feel and how happy they are with their lifestyle.

Quarry restoration: restoring or improving the environmental quality of a quarry, either during its operation or afterwards.

R

Recipient country: a country receiving aid from another country.

Recycling: using materials, such as aluminium or glass, time and again.

Regeneration: improving an area.

Relief: the height and slope of the land.

Reservoir: commonly an artificial lake formed behind a dam and used for water supply.

Resurgence: a stream that emerges from underground.

Retail parks: large warehouse-style shops often grouped together on the edge of a town or city, aiming to serve as many people as possible.

Retirement migration: migration to an area for retirement.

Ribbon lake: a long narrow lake in the bottom of a glacial trough.

Richter scale: a scale ranging from 0 to 10 used for measuring earthquakes, based on scientific recordings of the amount of movement.

Rock armour: piles of large boulders dumped at the foot of a cliff to protect it by forcing waves to break and absorbing their energy.

Rock cycle: connections between the three rock types, shown in the form of a diagram.

Rotational slip: slippage of ice along a curved surface.

Rural debt: money borrowed and now owed by farmers to banks or other organisations.

Rural depopulation: people leaving a rural area to live elsewhere, usually in a town or city.

Rural–urban fringe: an area around a town or city where there is a mix of urban and rural land uses.

S

Saltation: the bouncing movement of small stones and grains of sand along the river or sea bed.

Second home: a home bought to stay in only at weekends or for holidays.

Secondary effects: the after-effects that occur as an indirect effect of an event, for example a volcanic eruption, on a longer timescale.

Sea wall: concrete or rock barrier built at the foot of cliffs or at the top of a beach.

Sediment: loose rock debris that has been weathered or eroded before being transported and then deposited.

Sedimentary rocks: most commonly, rocks formed from the building up of sediment on the sea floor.

Segregation: occurs where people of a particular ethnic group choose to live with others from the same ethnic group, separate from other groups.

Selective logging: the cutting down of selected trees, leaving most of the trees intact.

Self-help: sometimes known as assisted self-help (ASH), this is where local authorities help the squatter settlement residents to improve their homes by offering finance in the form of loans or grants and often installing water, sanitation, etc.

Shield volcano: a broad volcano that is mostly made up of lava.

Shock waves: seismic waves generated by an earthquake that pass through the earth's crust.

Shoreline Management Plan (SMP): an integrated coastal management plan for a stretch of coastline in England and Wales.

Short-term aid: aid given to help a disaster situation, for example people who have been made homeless and are starving after a serious flood.

Site and service: occurs where land is divided into individual plots and water, sanitation, electricity and basic track layout are supplied before any building by residents begins.

Slash and burn: a form of subsistence farming in tropical rainforests where some trees are felled and land is cleared by burning before being replanted

Sliding: a type of mass movement involving material moving downhill on a flat surface (a landslide).

Slumping: a type of mass movement involving material moving downhill under its own weight.

Social: refers to people's health, their lifestyle, community, etc.

Soft engineering: a sustainable approach to managing the coast without using artificial structures.

Soft engineering (rivers): this option tries to work with the natural river system and involves avoiding building on areas most likely to flood, warning people of a possible flood and planting trees to increase lag time.

Soil erosion: the removal of the layer of soil above the rock where plants grow.

Solution: the dissolving of rocks and minerals by rainwater. This is a means of transportation as well as an erosion process.

Solution (coastal transportation): the transport of dissolved chemicals.

Spit: a finger of new land made of sand or shingle, jutting out into the sea from the coast.

Spring: water re-emerging from the rock onto the ground surface. Springs often occur as a line of springs (spring line) at the base of a scarp slope.

Squatter settlements: areas of cities (usually on the outskirts) that are built by people from any materials they can find on land that does not belong to them. They have different names in different parts of the world (for example *favela* in Brazil) and are often known as shanty towns.

Stack: an isolated pinnacle of rock sticking out of the sea.

Stalactite: an icicle-like calcite feature hanging down from a cavern roof.

Stalagmite: a stumpy calcite feature formed on a cavern floor.

Stewardship: the personal responsibility for looking after things, in this case the environment. No one should damage the present or future environment.

Straightening meanders: making the river follow a more direct, rather than its natural course, so that it leaves an area more quickly.

Strikes: periods of time when large numbers of employees refuse to work due to disagreements over pay or other grievances.

Subsistence farming: farming to produce food for the farmer and his/her family only.

Suburbanised village: a village with easy access to a large urban area much in demand. Housing estates attached to the village edges aim to fulfil this demand.

Supervolcano: a mega colossal volcano that erupts at least 1,000 km³ of material.

Suspension: small material carried (suspended) within the water.

Sustainability: development that looks after future resources and considers the needs of future generations.

Sustainable: making sure there is enough water in the long term without harming the environment.

Sustainable city: an urban area where residents have a way of life that will last a long time. The environment is not damaged and the economic and social fabric are able to stand the test of time.

Sustainable community: community (offering housing, employment and recreation opportunities) that is broadly in balance with the environment and offers people a good quality of life.

Sustainable development: this allows economic growth to occur, which can continue over a long period of time and will not harm the environment. It benefits people alive today but does not compromise future generations.

Sustainable management: a form of management that makes sure that developments are long lasting and do not harm the environment.

Swallow hole: an enlarged joint into which water falls.

T

Tectonic activity: activity (such as volcanic eruptions and earthquakes) caused by the movement of tectonic plates.

Temperate deciduous forest: forests made up of broad-leaved trees such as oak that drop their leaves in the autumn.

Terminal moraine: a high ridge running across the valley representing the maximum advance of a glacier.

Top-down aid: aid used so that governments can run more efficiently or to build infrastructure such as roads and bridges.

Tor: an isolated outcrop of rock on a hilltop, usually in granite landscapes.

Track: the path or course of a hurricane.

Traction: the rolling along of the largest rocks and boulders along the sea or river bed.

Transmigration: a population policy that aims to move people from densely populated areas to sparsely populated areas and provide them with opportunities to improve the quality of their lives.

Transnational corporations (TNCs): companies that spread their operations around the world to try to reduce costs.

Transportation: the carrying of sediment downstream from the point where it has been eroded to where it is deposited.

Tropical rainforests: the natural vegetation found in the tropics, well suited to the high temperatures and heavy rainfall associated with these latitudes.

Truncated spur: where ice has 'cut off' an interlocking spur and left a very steep cliff.

Tsunami: a special type of wave created where an event, often an earthquake, moves the entire depth of the water above it.

U

Urban sprawl: the spreading of urban areas into the surrounding rural/rural-urban fringe areas.

Urbanisation: the increase in the proportion of people living in cities, resulting in their growth.

V

Vale: in the landscape, a flat plain typically formed on clay.

Vertical erosion: downwards erosion, for example when a river gouges out a deep valley.

Volcano: an opening in the earth's crust through which molten lava, ash and gases are ejected.

W

Water pollution: putting poisonous substances into water courses, such as sewage, industrial effluent and harmful chemicals.

Waterfall: the sudden, and often vertical, drop of a river along its course.

Wave-cut platform: a wide, gently sloping rocky surface at the foot of a cliff.

Weather: the day-to-day conditions of the atmosphere involving, for example, temperature, cloud cover and wind direction.

Weathering: the breakup or decay of rocks in their original place at or close to the earth's surface.

Index

Acknowledgements

The author and publisher would like to thank the following for permission to reproduce material:

Source texts:

P63 Quote from BBC news article 'Is extreme weather due to Climate change?' by Paul Rincon, 23 August 2005. © bbc.co.uk/news; p111 Extract from 'Cost of deluge will be millions' from the Sheffield Star Special Edition. © 2007 by Johnston Press. Reprinted with permission from The Editor of The Sheffield Star, www.thestar.co.uk; p111 Quote from BBC news article ' Why Bangladesh floods are so bad' by Tracey Logan, 27 July, 2004. © bbc.co.uk/news; p183 Extract from BBC news article 'Has China's one-child policy worked?', 20 September 2007. © bbc.co.uk/news; p187 Extract from ' The great betrayal: how the NHS fails the elderly', by Jeremy Laurance. The Independent, 27 March 2006. © 2006 Newspaper Publishing plc. Reprinted by permission of The Independent; p209 extract from BBC News article 'Nairobi slum life: Into Kibera' by Andrew Harding, 4 October 2002. © bbc.co.uk/news; p269 Extract from BBC website 'Q&A: Common Agricultural Policy'. © bbc.co.uk/news; p277 © Toyota Motor Manufacturing (UK) Ltd. Reprinted with permission; p290 Quote from Gareth Thomas, Minister for Trade and Development, taken from 'How the myth of food miles hurts the planet', by Robin McKie & Caroline Davies, The Observer, 23 March 2008. © 2008 by Guardian News & Media Ltd 2008. Reprinted with permission; p293 Quote from Gordon Ramsay, taken from 'Gordon Ramsay's war on out-of-season vegetables', by Caroline Gammell, 9 May 2008. © 2008 by Telegraph Media Group Limited. Reprinted with permission.

Photographs courtesy of:

1.3A Lonely Planet Images/Woods Wheatcroft; 1.3B Christian Ostrosky/Alamy; 1.3C Frans Lanting/Corbis; 1.3E, 1.4C AFP/Getty Images; 1.4E KPA/Zuma/Rex Features; 1.4J George Steinmetz/Science Photo Library; 1.4K USGS; 1.5C istockphoto; 1.6D Craig Greenhill/Newspix/Rex Features; 1.7B AFP/Getty Images; 1.7C Noboru Hashimoto/Sygma/Corbis; 1.7E Claudia Dewald/Getty; 1.7F Pascal Deloche/Getty; 1.7G Charles E. Rotkin/Corbis; 1.8B Aflo/Rex Features; 2.1B (1) Tony Waltham/geophotos; 2.1B (2) Tony Waltham/geophotos; 2.1B (3) Fotolia; 2.3A Tony Waltham/geophotos; 2.3C Simon Ross; 2.4B Tony Howell/tonyhowell.co.uk; 2.4C Simon Lewis/www.westcountryviews.co.uk; 2.5D iStockphoto; 2.6B Tony Waltham/geophotos; 2.7B iStockphoto; 2.8B Dave Dunford; 2.9A West Sussex County Council; 2.9B Bell Ingram Limited; 3.2B Satellite Receiving Station, University of Dundee; 3.2C Satellite Receiving Station, University of Dundee; 3.2H Clifford Rhodes/Alamy; 3.2I Andrew Parker/Alamy; 3.2J, 3.2L Satellite Receiving Station, University of Dundee; 3.3A Roland Gal/Rex Features; 3.3C Apex News & Pictures; 3.3D Simon Ross; 3.4C Arctic-Images/Corbis; 3.6A Sam Toren/Alamy; 3.6B Gerard Fritz/Getty Images; 3.7A NOAA/Science Photo Library; 4.2C Tony Waltham/geophotos; 4.2G geogphotos film/Alamy; 4.2H (1) Tim Gartside USA America/Alamy; 4.2H (2) Photolibrary; 4.2H (3), 4.2H (4) iStockphoto; 4.3A Tony T/Alamy; 4.3B Jon Sparks/Alamy; 4.4B Nigel Dickinson/Still Pictures; 4.4C Reuters/Corbis; 4.5B Rhett Butler; 4.5C Alex Hipkiss/RSPB; 4.6B imagebroker/Alamy; 4.6D Biosphoto/Eichaker Xavier/Still Pictures; 4.6F Getty Images; 5.1A, 5.1C, 5.1C Judith Canavan; 5.2B iStockphoto; 5.2F geogphotos film/Alamy; 5.2G iStockphoto; 5.2I Sue Ogrocki/AP/Press Association Images; 5.3F Tony Waltham/geophotos; 5.3G Ed Maynard/Alamy; 5.5B Anna Gowthorpe/PA Archive/Press Association Images; 5.5C Kirsty Wigglesworth/AP/Press Association Images; 5.5E The Environment Agency; 5.5H AFP/Getty Images; 5.6B Xinhua Press/Corbis; 5.7D The Photolibrary Wales/Alamy; 6.2C U.S. Geological Survey; 6.3A Simon Ross; 6.4A Tony Waltham/geophotos; 6.4H Photolibrary; 6.4I Dr. Marli Miller/Visuals Unlimited/Corbis; 6.5B Photoshot; 6.5D Photolibrary; 6.5E Simon Ross; 6.6A Brian North/Alamy; 6.6B Laurent Cipriani/AP/Press Association Images; 6.6C Ross Woodhall/Cultura/Corbis; 6.7A John Heilprin/AP/Press Association Images; 6.7B Fotolia; 6.7C AFP/Getty Images; 7.1A Gemunu Amarasinghe/AP/Press Association Images; 7.1C Steve Allen Travel Photography/Alamy; 7.2A Jason Hawkes; 7.2B Peter Smith Photography; 7.3A Tony Waltham/geophotos; 7.4B Simon Ross; 7.5B Photolibrary; 7.6A Tony Waltham/geophotos; 7.6B David Lyons/Alamy; 7.6D J Farmar/Skyscan; 7.7B Jason Hawkes; 7.8B iStockphoto; 7.9A Ian West Photographs; 7.10A Robert Harding Picture Library Ltd/Alamy; 7.10B Manor Photography/Alamy; 7.10E Martin Keene/PA Archive/Press Association Images; 7.10G Flight Images LLP/Getty Images; 7.10I Defra Biodiversity team; 7.11A Peter Hutchings, Hampshire & Isle of Wight Wildlife Trust; 7.11D Peter Hutchings, Hampshire & Isle of Wight Wildlife Trust; 8.1B iStockphoto; 8.1C Fotolia; 8.2B Threshing the wheat (colour litho) by Tunnicliffe, Charles Frederick (1901–79) Private Collection/The Stapleton Collection/The Bridgeman Art Library; 8.2C iStockphoto; 8.2D AFP/Getty Images; 8.2F Gerard Fritz/Getty Images; 8.3B iStockphoto; 8.3D Hornbil Images/Alamy; 8.4C Nir Elias/Reuters; 8.4D Gareth Brown/Corbis; 8.5B Mangiwau/Getty Images; 8.6A, 8.6B, 8.6D, 8.7A iStockphoto; 8.7FDavid Pearson/Rex Features; 8.7G Irene Abdou/Alamy; 9.1C (1) Philippe Bourseiller/Getty Images; 9.1C (2) Fabienne Fossez/Alamy; 9.2A a Paul White, Leeds the modern city/Alamy; 9.2A b, 9.2A c, 9.2 A Simon Ross; 9.3A (l) christopher Pillitz/Alamy; 9.3A (r) Getty Images; 9.3C a Judith Canavan; 9.3C b iStockphoto; 9.3C c iStockphoto; 9.3C d Judith Canavan; 9.3E Skyscan/Jefferson Air; 9.3F Urban Splash www.urbansplash.co.uk; 9.3G De Agostini/Photoshot; 9.3H c Fotolia; 9.3H d 2007 Getty Images; 9.3H e Fotolia; 9.3I, 9.3J Judith Canavan; 9.4A a UPPA/Photoshot; 9.4A b Jenny Matthews/Alamy; 9.4A c Mark Edwards/Still Pictures; 9.4B Peter Treanor/Alamy; 9.4C Art Directors & Trip/Helene Rogers; 9.4E Sean Sprague/Still Pictures; 9.4F iStockphoto; 9.5A Getty Images; 9.5B Sipa Press/Rex Features; 9.5C Getty Images; 9.5D Amit Bhargava/Corbis; 9.6A David R. Frazier Photolibrary, Inc./Alamy; 9.6B Titanic Quarter Ltd/Handout/Reuters/Corbis; 9.6C a. iStockphoto; 9.6C b. Paul Thompson Images/Alamy; 9.6C c. iStockphoto; 9.6C d. iStockphoto; 9.6E UIG via Getty Images; 9.6F Robert Brook/Alamy; 9.6G William Robinson/Alamy; 9.6I Jeff Morgan 12/Alamy; 9.6J London 2012; 9.6K Judith Canavan; 10.1C Bluewater; 10.1F Martin Sookias; 10.1G Mykel Nicolaou/Rex Features; 10.2E Gary Brunning/Alamy; 10.3A FLPA/Peter Wilson; 10.3B Tandridge District Council; 10.3C Peter Cragg/Harting Stores; 10.3D Alison Thompson/Alamy; 10.4C geogphotos/Alamy; 10.5A iStockphoto; 10.5C Andrew Olney/Getty Images; 10.6A Bubbles Photolibrary/Alamy; 10.6B Fotolia; 10.7B Art Directors & Trip/Helene Rogers; 10.7C Christophe Smets/Luna/VISUM/Still Pictures; 10.8A National Geographic/Getty Images; 10.8C Mark Edwards/Still Pictures; 10.8D South American Pictures/Tony Morrison; 10.9A Mark Boulton/Alamy; 10.9B Corbis; 10.10A Panos/Stefan Boness; 10.10C Fotolia; 10.11A Friedrich von Hörsten/Alamy; 11.1C Getty Images/John Powell; 11.3A Jerome Delay/AP/Press Association Images; 11.4A Getty Images; 11.4C AFP/Getty Images; 11.5A Alistair Linford/Rex Features; 11.5B Fotolia; 11.5C Rex Features; 11.6B Imagestate Media Partners Limited - Impact Photos/Alamy; 11.7E iStockphoto; 12.1A Sports Illustrated/Getty Images; 12.1C Sports Illustrated/Getty Images; 12.2B Fotolia; 12.2D Rex Features; 12.3E David Wootton/Alamy; 12.4B Amanda Hall/Robert Harding World Imagery/Corbis; 12.4C Scott Stulberg/Getty Images; 12.4E EIGHTFISH/Getty Images; 12.4D PhotoLink/Getty Images; 12.4G AFP/Getty Images; 12.4H Xinhua Press/Corbis; 12.5C Peer Grimm/epa/Corbis; 12.6C Getty Images; 12.7B World Illustrated/Photoshot; 12.7C Getty Images; 12.7E Fotolia; 12.7F 2006 Per-Anders Pettersson/Getty Images; 12.7H iStockphoto; 13.1B iStockphoto; 13.1D iStockphoto; 13.1E iStockphoto; 13.1F iStockphoto; 13.2D iStockphoto; 13.2E Weixin Shen/Alamy; 13.2F Arthur Tilley/Getty Images; 13.3B Evening Standard/Getty Images; 13.3C Chris Ison/PA Archive/Press Association Images; 13.3D Simon Ross; 13.3F Topham Picturepoint; 13.3G Rex Features; 13.4B Eli Pascall-Willis/Getty Images; 13.4C Annie Griffiths Belt/Corbis; 13.4D curved-light/Alamy; 13.4F Jason Friend/Alamy; 13.4G World Pictures/Alamy; 13.4H Peter Titmuss/Alamy; 13.4I Darryl Gill/Alamy; 13.5A Lee Christensen/Getty; 13.5B iStockphoto; 13.5F iStockphoto; 13.6A Nordicphotos/Alamy; 13.6B Frans Lemmens/Alamy; 13.6C Bruce Farnsworth/Alamy; 13.6D iStockphoto; 13.6G iStockphoto; 13.6H Arcticphoto/Alamy; 13.7A Martin Shields/Alamy; 13.7B Craig Lovell/Eagle Visions Photography/Alamy.

Ordnance Survey maps (2.5C, 2.7D, 4.3C, 5.1F, 5.2C, 5.2E, 5.2J, 5.5F, 6.4G, 7.5C, 7.7A. 7.10H, 9.2B, 12.3F) reproduced by permission of Ordnance Survey on behalf of HMSO. © Crown copyright 2012. All rights reserved. Ordnance Survey Licence number 100017284